SAMS
Teach Yourself

Game Programming

in **24** *Hours*

Michael Morrison

SAMS 201 West 103rd St., Indianapolis, Indiana 46290 USA

Sams Teach Yourself Game Programming in 24 Hours

Copyright © 2003 by Sams Publishing

International Standard Book Number: 0-672-32461-x

Library of Congress Catalog Card Number: 2002106906

Printed in the United States of America

First Printing: October 2002

05   04   03   02   4   3   2

Trademarks

Warning and Disclaimer

ASSOCIATE PUBLISHER
Michael Stephens

ACQUISITIONS EDITOR
Carol Ackerman

DEVELOPMENT EDITOR
Mark Renfrow

MANAGING EDITOR
Charlotte Clapp

PROJECT EDITOR
Andy Beaster

COPY EDITOR
Rhonda Tinch-Mize

INDEXER
Kelly Castell

PROOFREADER
Leslie Joseph

TECHNICAL EDITOR
David Franson

TEAM COORDINATOR
Lynne Williams

INTERIOR DESIGNER
Gary Adair

COVER DESIGNER
Aren Howell

PAGE LAYOUT
Michelle Mitchell

GRAPHICS
Tammy Graham
Oliver Jackson

Contents at a Glance

Table of Contents

About the Author

Michael Morrison is a writer, developer, toy inventor, and author of a variety of computer technology books and interactive Web-based courses. In addition to his primary profession as a writer and freelance nerd for hire, Michael is the creative lead at Stalefish Labs, an entertainment company he co-founded with his wife, Masheed. The first commercial debut for Stalefish Labs is a traditional social/trivia game called *Tall Tales: The Game of Myths, Legends, and Creative One-Upmanship* (http://www.talltalesgame.com/). When not glued to his computer, playing hockey, skateboarding, or watching movies with his wife, Michael enjoys hanging out by his koi pond. You can visit Michael on the Web at http://www.michaelmorrison.com/.

About the Technical Editor

David Franson has been a professional in the field of networking, programming, and computer graphics since 1990. In 2000, he resigned his position as Information Systems director of one of the largest entertainment law firms in New York City to pursue a full-time career in game development. Currently, he is authoring *2D Artwork* and *3D Modeling for Game Artist*s, to be published November 2002.

Dedication

To my late friend Randy Weems, who taught me practically everything I know about game programming, and who was brave enough to live by his own rules.

Acknowledgments

Thanks to Mike Stephens, Carol Ackerman, Mark Renfrow, Rhonda Tinch-Mize, David Franson, Andy Beaster, and the rest of the gang at Sams Publishing for making this yet another pleasurable writing experience. A big thanks goes to my literary agent, Chris Van Buren, who keeps me in business. And finally, a tremendous thanks to my wife, Masheed, and my parents, who are my best friends and biggest supporters.

We Want to Hear from You!

As the reader of this book, *you* are our most important critic and commentator. We value your opinion and want to know what we're doing right, what we could do better, what areas you'd like to see us publish in, and any other words of wisdom you're willing to pass our way.

As an associate publisher for Sams, I welcome your comments. You can email or write me directly to let me know what you did or didn't like about this book—as well as what we can do to make our books better.

Please note that I cannot help you with technical problems related to the *topic* of this book. We do have a User Services group, however, where I will forward specific technical questions related to the book.

When you write, please be sure to include this book's title and author as well as your name, email address, and phone number. I will carefully review your comments and share them with the author and editors who worked on the book.

Email: feedback@samspublishing.com

Mail: Michael Stephens
Associate Publisher
Sams Publishing
201 West 103rd Street
Indianapolis, IN 46290 USA

Reader Services

For more information about this book or others from Sams Publishing, visit our Web site at www.samspublishing.com. Type the ISBN (excluding hyphens) or the title of the book in the Search box to find the book you're looking for.

Introduction

Although it's kind of hard to imagine now, there was a time not so long ago when the concept of a video game was a "pie in the sky" idea. Computers were barely seen as useful tools in business, and were viewed as having even less potential for entertainment. Technology has a way of changing the way we think about things, and it wasn't long before early video games captured the minds and quarters of an entire generation. Yes, I am a child of the eighties, and I feel fortunate to have spent part of my childhood in the decade where video games went from a pipe dream to a cultural phenomenon.

Video games are interesting in that they represent the first form of interactive digital entertainment. Perhaps more importantly, video games represent the first truly interactive art form. When you think about it, there aren't many paintings, sculptures, or musical compositions that allow you to interact with them and change them in any way. Video games allowed their creators to share something more with the game player by giving players a chance to put part of themselves into a game, and then see what comes out. In fact, the best games are the ones that allow players to express their own unique style and technique when playing the game, while at the same time being entertained by the game designer's vision of an imaginary world portrayed by the game.

If you think this introduction is setting you up for a book filled with nostalgia and artsy video game talk, think again. Although I appreciate the history of video games, as well as the artistry that goes into their design, I realize that you're interested in creating your own games. The trick is to learn from the past while equipping yourself to create a new future. So, I'll use past video games to explain game construction techniques and give you ideas, but my ultimate goal is to empower you with the game programming knowledge to realize your own vision of the perfect computer game.

I'm sure you already know that computer programming is a challenging, yet rewarding endeavor that gives you the freedom to do some interesting things within the context of a computer. Unfortunately, game programming has often been somewhat of a mysterious discipline within computer programming. Although there are a lot of games, there really aren't all that many game programmers. The reason is primarily because game programming is a uniquely challenging area of software development that requires a mastery of several different disciplines. To create even a simple game, you must understand how to write code to draw bitmapped graphics, carry out sprite animation, play sampled digital sound effects, and process user input from a keyboard, mouse, and/or joystick. If these tasks sound somewhat overwhelming, it's because they are if you aren't properly prepared to tackle them.

This book tackles each game programming discipline one at a time, and in a manner that allows you to build one skill on top of the previous one you just learned. The end result is that you start with a few fundamental game programming skills, and slowly build up a base of knowledge that allows you to tackle increasingly more complex games. The significance of this approach is that it allows you to ease into game programming a step at a time, with a focus on ramping up your skills throughout the book to tackle more challenging projects.

Will this book make you a game programming guru? Not exactly. The idea here is to provide you with a solid foundation in game programming skills that you can use to create interesting games of your own. This book does not cover DirectX, which is Microsoft's advanced game programming library. DirectX is a complex technology used to create commercial games. You should definitely aspire to learn DirectX if you decide to get more serious about game programming, but the purpose of this book is to show you how to create fun games with a minimal amount of pain. DirectX has a significant learning curve, so I decided that it was best left to more advanced game programming books. The good news is that you don't need DirectX to create interesting and highly entertaining games of your own, as you learn throughout this book.

How This Book Is Structured

As the title suggests, this book is organized into 24 lessons that are intended to take about an hour each to digest. Don't worry, there are no penalties if you take more than an hour to finish a given lesson, and no financial rewards if you speed through them faster! The lessons themselves are organized into seven parts, each of which tackles a different facet of game programming:

- Part I, "Getting Started"—In this part, you learn the basics of video game development, and what goes into creating a game. You learn about the fundamentals of Windows programming, and how to create an engine for games. You also find out how to draw basic graphics, including bitmapped images.

- Part II, "Interacting with Game Players"—In this part, you learn how to interact with players through input devices such as the keyboard, mouse, and joysticks. This part of the book also guides you through the development of your first complete game, which is a tile matching memory game called Brainiac.

- Part III, "Animating Games with Sprites"—In this part, you learn the ropes of sprite animation, which is the cornerstone of two-dimensional game programming. You uncover the basics of game animation, and then build classes to support animation in games. You also develop your second complete game in this part of the book, which is a game called Henway that is somewhat of a takeoff on the classic Frogger arcade game.

- Part IV, "Making Noise with Sound and Music"—In this part, you get acquainted with music and sound effects as they apply to games. More specifically, you find out how to create wave sound effects and then play them in games, as well as how to play MIDI music. With a solid foundation in sound under your belt, you move on to create Battle Office, which is your third complete game.

- Part V, "Taking Animation to the Next Level"—In this part, you go beyond the basics of sprite animation to learn some advanced animation techniques that are valuable in action games. You learn how to animate the appearance of sprites, as well as how to create animated backgrounds. You then put this new knowledge to work in another complete game called Meteor Defense, which is roughly similar to the Missile Command arcade game.

- Part VI, "Adding Brains to Your Games"—In this part, you learn the fundamentals of artificial intelligence (AI), and why it is important to games. AI can be a daunting topic, so I focus on some basic AI techniques that are easy to understand and apply in your own games. This part of the book also includes the development of another complete game, Space Out, which is a space shoot-em-up that incorporates virtually everything you've learned throughout the book.

- Part VII, "Spicing Up Your Games"—In this part, you explore some interesting game programming techniques that allow you to add a professional touch to your games. You learn how to create a splash screen, a demo mode, and a high score list that is stored to disk. Along the way, you spice up the Space Out game with each new technique so that it ends up being the most comprehensive game example in the book. This provides you with a good game to use as a starting point for your own game programming projects.

What You'll Need

This book assumes that you have a knowledge and understanding of the C++ programming language. Although the program examples and games you develop throughout the book are Windows programs, you aren't required to have a background in Windows programming. And in truth, I really don't rely on any complex C++ programming constructs, so a basic understanding of C++ is all you need. However, it is important that you understand how to build a C++ program using a development environment on the Windows platform. If you already have a favorite C++ development environment, that's great. If not, you'll probably want to check out Appendix B, "Selecting a Game Development Tool," which describes some of the more popular Windows C++ development tools.

All of the examples in the book are available on the accompanying CD-ROM, along with project files for Visual C++ 7.0 (2002). If you decide to go with a different development tool from Visual C++, you'll need to create a new project for each example and then add the source code files. Your development tool may allow you to import the Visual C++ projects, so take a look before creating new projects by hand. If you have trouble building a project, make sure that you're linking in the appropriate standard libraries because there are a couple of libraries (winmm.lib and msimg32.lib) that you must import in most of the program examples and games.

Beyond some C++ knowledge and a good C++ development tool, all you really need is an open mind and a bit of creativity. They will serve you well as you embark on this journey into the world of game creation. Have fun!

PART I
Getting Started

Hours

HOUR 1

Learning the Basics of Game Creation

If you've ever seen or played Pong, you can certainly appreciate the advancements made over the last 30 years that allow us to now have video games that literally rival movies in audiovisual appeal. If you've ever been curious about how these games work, you've certainly come to the right place. I started my journey into video game development through this same sense of amazement and curiosity that I had the power to create my own little virtual world that lived by its own rules, my rules. Armed with a little programming knowledge and a desire to see where my imagination could take me, I learned the essentials of video game creation. Unfortunately, I had to learn it the hard way by inventing my own solutions and using trial and error to solve even the simplest of problems. Fortunately for you, this painful approach is no longer necessary. This hour introduces you to the fundamentals of game creation.

In this hour, you'll learn

- About the different kinds of video games
- The main things to consider when designing a new game
- Why object-oriented programming (OOP) is important for game development
- What kinds of tools you'll use as a game developer

Getting to Know Video Games

From its early days as a niche entertainment business that was never taken seriously, the video game industry has grown into a very important sector of global business. Video games are now funded in a manner and at a scale comparable to Hollywood movies, and often involve famous actors, actresses, screenwriters, musicians, and other entertainment professionals whom we previously only associated with movies. In fact, the production of a modern video game is in many ways like producing a movie. There are pitches, storyboards, and market tests, and that's just to get a game financed. Once a game rolls into production, there are teams of designers, animators, and programmers—not to mention various other talented individuals and companies who pitch in to help make a finished game. Modern games cost millions of dollars to produce, and can reap enormous rewards for those willing to put up the time and money.

You're probably reading this book because you don't have a few million extra dollars laying around to throw into a video game project. Or maybe you'd just rather spend your pile of cash elsewhere. Either way, you maybe had a faint hope that it's still possible for one person to create a highly entertaining video game with little more than elbow grease. It's not only possible, it's also highly rewarding and quite empowering. However, video games have traditionally represented one of the most complex and mysterious facets of programming, and therefore have likely scared away many a curious would-be game creator. My goal is to demystify the game development process and show you that you don't have to be a millionaire or a genius to have fun creating your own games.

Why Video Games?

If you're an avid game player, you might already know the answer to this question, but it's worth asking anyway: Why are video games so popular? And why are so many people interested in learning how to create their own? I think it has something to do with the allure of creating a little world all your own, where the limits are only your technical skills and your imagination. The goal of this book is to strengthen one while sparking the other.

1

To better understand why so many people gravitate toward video games, consider how popular movies are in modern cultures. Few of us are able to watch a great movie without at some point envisioning ourselves right there taking part in a scene. Video games enable us to step beyond the role of an audience member and become a participant in an interactive story. Essentially, all video games enable you to step into a world and take part in it, even if that world consists solely of an outer space background and a few aliens. When walking through a video game arcade, it's as if each screen is a window into another reality just begging you to come inside and see what's going on.

Enough of the dreamy talk—what do video games mean to the would-be game programmer? From a development perspective, video games are quite interesting in that they require such a wide range of talents. Video games provide us with all the usual technical challenges associated with software development, usually more, along with illustration, animation, sound effects, and music. And that doesn't even touch on the story aspect of games—where entire screenplays are often developed. By developing a video game from start to finish, you'll practically become a modern renaissance person, acquiring some degree of expertise in many disciplines. You'll also successfully merge many divergent interests into a greater medium enjoyable by others. It's for this reason that so many of us are intrigued by the endless possibilities associated with video game design and development.

Types of Video Games

Speaking of creating your own games, you might be wondering why I keep referring to "video games" when the games created in this book are played on a computer. Although I hate to split hairs over terminology, it's worth pointing out that a *video game* is an interactive electronic entertainment medium that uses a video screen as its primary display. In other words, the term video game applies to all games with a screen and a joystick or some other controller. Contrast this with a traditional pinball machine, for example, which can certainly be played but doesn't rely on a video screen for output. Video games can be further classified into three categories: arcade games, console games, and computer games.

Arcade games are video games that are built into hefty cabinets with payment mechanisms that require you to pay in order to play the games. Arcade games represent the birth of video games, and are responsible for separating quite a few 80s American youth from their hard-earned (or hard-begged) quarters. Arcade games often rely on custom hardware components and unique physical controls to separate them from other types of video games. Although arcade games certainly still exist, they are a minor component of the video game market, and aren't the bastion of innovation they once were. Don't get me wrong, there are some really cool new arcade games out there, but you have to look beyond arcade games to get to the really active portion of the video game market.

Console games followed quickly on the coattails of arcade games, and they represent home gaming systems from the classic Pong and Atari 2600 systems to today's Sony Playstation 2 and Microsoft XBox. Console game systems are designed from the ground up as consumer game machines and rival arcade games in terms of game quality. We are currently in the midst of a convergence of digital entertainment technologies that is quite capable of placing console games at the center of the home entertainment equation. In fact, Microsoft already has long range plans for its XBox console game system to become an all-encompassing digital entertainment device. The next few years should be interesting in terms of seeing how console games merge with traditional entertainment equipment.

Computer games were last to the video game show simply because it took longer for personal computers to become technically capable of doing enough interesting things with graphics and sound to make good games possible. Computer games now represent a massive segment of the video game industry and rival console games in terms of popularity and sales. Interestingly enough, most popular games are now available in both console and computer versions, so you have the option of deciding whether to use a computer or a dedicated console gaming system to play games. The XBox console system is somewhat unique among console systems in that it shares a software game development platform with computer games. I'm referring to DirectX, which is Microsoft's game development toolkit that originated on PCs, and now carries over to the XBox.

> Unfortunately, this book doesn't cover game programming using the DirectX game development toolkit. The reason for this is because DirectX is a complex technology with a steep learning curve. Rather than spend half the book on the basics of how DirectX works, I decided to spend the entire book teaching you how games work. If, after reading this book, you decide to move forward and learn DirectX, I highly recommend Clayton Walnum's *Teach Yourself Game Programming with DirectX in 21 Days*.

I want to clarify the different types of video games because there is a great deal of difference in developing each type. For example, arcade games rely on specialized hardware and proprietary development tools that are expensive and difficult to obtain for a startup game programmer. Console games run a close second in terms of presenting a significant barrier to entry for new game programmers. Not only are the tools expensive and difficult to get your hands on, but also they often require a very specialized set of programming skills that are usually learned on the job while working for a game company. Computer games are really the only type of video games that are accessible to the individual from a development perspective. Tools for computer game programming are readily available and are either free or relatively inexpensive. Not only that, but you can leverage existing knowledge in a mainstream programming language such as C++ to develop computer games. This book focuses on the development of computer games using C++, although most of the concepts and techniques also apply to arcade and console games.

Game Design Essentials

Now that you have some perspective on the types of video games and the viability of each from a development view, you're ready to start learning about designing games. Do you have some ideas of games you'd like to create, or are you clueless about where to begin? Regardless of which camp you're in, I'm here to help. Keep in mind that coming up with a good game idea is often the easy part; taking the concept to reality is where the difficulty arises, and where many of us fall short. As long as you take things a step at a time and don't get overwhelmed by the details, you'll do just fine.

The first step in taking a game from the drawing board to the keyboard is to get a solid idea of what you want the game to be. I'm not saying you have to create an itemized list of every scene and every creature and minute interaction. However, it is very important to establish some minimal ground rules about the big picture of what you envision for the final game. Following are the key items you should focus on when putting together the overall concept of your game:

- Basic idea
- Storyline
- Graphics
- Sound
- Controls
- Play modes

The next few sections explore these game design considerations in more detail.

Coming Up with the Basic Idea

The most important design step in creating a game is to determine the basic idea behind the game. Is it a shoot-em-up, a maze game, a role-playing game (RPG), a driving game, a puzzle game, or some combination of these? Or do you have a truly original game idea that doesn't neatly fit into an existing genre? Is the object to rescue good guys, eliminate bad guys, or just explore a strange environment? What time frame is your game set in, and does it even have a time frame? These are just a few of the questions you need to ask yourself when developing the basic idea for a new game. Think about it and write everything down. Whatever comes to mind, write it down because brainstorms come and go and you don't want to forget anything. Forcing yourself to formalize your ideas and get them on paper causes you to think about it more and usually clears up a lot of uncertainties.

If you're having trouble coming up with a basic game idea, think about the influences of some of the more popular games around. Many games are based on movies, some on historical events, and others on sports; some games are so popular that there are movies based on the games (Tomb Raider, Final Fantasy, Resident Evil, and so on). Ultimately, most computer games are models of the world around us, whether fantasy or real, so look no further when dreaming up your game. Movies in particular can provide a lot of good creative settings and storylines for games—just be careful not to "borrow" too much.

Regardless of your inspiration, just remember that your game has to be fun. No matter how fancy the graphics are or how immersive the sound, the overriding design goal of any game is always to maximize fun. Who wouldn't want to spend all day trying to figure out the best way to have fun? That, my friend, is the real allure of game programming. If your game isn't fun to play, no amount of fancy graphics, sound, or celebrity voice-overs will save it. Some of the best games of all time have weak graphics and sound by modern standards, but their fun factor has never diminished.

A good example of a painfully simple game that is surprisingly fun is the classic Atari 2600 Combat game. This game came with most Atari 2600 console systems, so most Atari gamers got a chance to try it out. Combat suffered from the severely limited technology of the time, and its graphics and sound show it. However, the game play of Combat was great, and in my opinion rivals modern games. When you think about it, the one aspect of game development that hasn't changed much over the years is the user input side of the equation. Granted, there are fancier joysticks and some new gadgety features such as force feedback, but at the end of the day it's still just an interface to your hands. This helps to explain why arcade games created in 1982 still can be quite fun even though they are technically inferior to modern games in just about every way. The creators of those games didn't have the luxury of 3D rendered graphics and CD quality sampled sound, so they went to work on the way their games played.

The point I'm trying to make is that you must make fun the priority when designing your game. After you have a basic idea of what your game will be and have decided that you're going to make it fun at all costs, you can then move on to developing a storyline.

Putting Together the Storyline

Aren't storylines just for movies and complicated cinematic games? Absolutely not. Even if your game is a simple action game with a couple of characters fighting it out, developing a storyline helps you to establish the mood and landscape, and also think up creatures to populate the game world. Putting your game in the context of a story also brings the game player closer to your world. Remember the classic Pong game mentioned at the opening of this lesson? Although it succeeded without a good story, it would have been much more interesting if it had been designed with a story in mind. Maybe the ball is an atom bouncing around in a damaged nuclear reactor, and if it goes off the screen the whole thing will melt down. It's up to you and your friend to control the "atomic deflectors" and keep the atom from escaping. Now that I think about it, maybe Pong was better off just being a blip and some lines, but you get the idea.

If you get really serious about a storyline for your game, you might want to consider creating a storyboard. Commonly used to pitch movies, a *storyboard* tells a story scene by scene using rough sketches of each scene. Storyboards are important visual tools because they enable you to visualize a game based on a storyline. Having a storyboard to reference helps ensure that you don't lose sight of the story when you get heavily into development. Figure 1.1 shows a simple storyboard of a popular movie you might recognize. Can you guess what it is?

FIGURE 1.1
Even a stick figure storyboard can convey a recognizable story.

Give up? This is my stick figure interpretation of the movie *Jaws*, which is probably my favorite movie of all time. As you can see in the figure, even my limited artistic abilities and love of stick figures can convey the basics of a story. Of course, a storyboard for a real game or movie would likely consist of more than four frames.

Visualizing the Graphics

My stick figure artistry is the perfect segue into the next major component of game design: graphics. Although games can certainly be fun without fancy graphics, you can significantly improve any game by the graphics you use. It's important to select a level of graphics consistent with your design goals and resources. There was a time when you also had to factor in the graphics capabilities of computers, but these days even relatively low-end computers are quite powerful enough for games of moderate to medium complexity. Even so, you may decide to stick with 256 colors for your games just to make it a little faster should it be played on an older computer. Remember, the more colors used in a game, the longer it takes the computer to manipulate and draw images in the game.

 Some amazing graphics tools are out there that make it possible to create surprisingly cool graphics without necessarily being an artist. On the other hand, if you have a friend with more artistic ability than you, it might be worth it to recruit him to help you out with your game.

Screen resolution is an important consideration for most games. If you've ever noticed your screen flickering and your monitor making a strange noise when you first start a commercial game, you're familiar with different screen resolutions; the game is switching to a resolution different from what you were using. The most common resolution these days for Windows PCs is 800×600, which means that there are 800 *pixels* (colored graphical squares) across the screen and 600 down the screen. If you have a monitor larger than 15 inches, your resolution can be set much higher; mine is currently set at 1280×1024. The significance of resolution is that it directly affects the size of the graphics in games. Most commercial games are designed to run at several different resolutions, but you might not want to hassle with that for your own games. In fact, in this book I opted to stick with a fixed size for the game screen in each example game, which is an approach that works fairly well and simplifies the game graphics.

Another design decision worth considering in regard to graphics is the player's perspective of the game. Will the playfield be 2D, 3D, or some combination of the two? Will the player be able to see his character onscreen or will everything be in first person as if looking through the character's field of vision? These considerations have an enormous impact on the programming complexity of a game and therefore should be decided very early in the design phase.

Developing an Ear for the Sound

Sound is one element of games that might not seem as significant as graphics until you try playing a game without it. Seriously, just turn off the speakers while playing one of your favorite games and notice how it impacts the overall experience. On the other hand, if the game play and graphics alone are enough to make your game appealing, the sound will be the icing on the cake. It's important to use sound everywhere you can; sound

1

effects are a bare minimum, and if you really want to do it right, you'll consider using some sort of music soundtrack.

The first thing to decide regarding sound is the quality of sounds in a game, which can dramatically impact memory requirements and overall game performance. For sound effects, you'll be dealing with sampled sounds in the form of wave (WAV) files. You must select a sampling rate, whether you want mono or stereo sound, and whether the sound uses 8 bits or 16 bits to store each sample. You learn much more about what these sound properties mean in Hour 13, "Getting Acquainted with Digital Sound and Music," but for now just understand that they directly impact both the quality and performance of sounds. For example, CD-quality sound is sampled at 44kHz in 16-bit stereo. CD-quality sound provides the best quality at the expense of a huge storage overhead; a typical music CD holds about 70 minutes and requires more than 600MB of storage space. You will more than likely settle on a lower sound quality in games to minimize storage space and improve performance.

> *Sampling* refers to the process of converting sound waves into a digital format that can be stored and played on a computer. You learn more about how sampling works in Hour 13.

In games, music is often handled differently from sound effects. Although it is possible to record music as a sampled sound, this can take up a lot of space. For this reason, a good alternative to sampled music is *MIDI (Musical Instrument Digital Interface)* music, which is the standard for arranging and playing musical compositions on computers. Unlike sampled music, MIDI music involves specifying the individual musical notes in a piece of music and associating them with virtual musical instruments. Creating a MIDI soundtrack can be difficult if you have no music background, but you might be able to find existing MIDI music to meet your needs. Fortunately, all you really need to know at this stage of a game's design is that you should consider developing programming code that can play a MIDI soundtrack.

Dictating Game Play with the Controls

The controls used to interface with the game player are an extremely important part of a game's design, and they shouldn't be taken lightly. It's important to support as many input devices (mouse, keyboard, joystick, and so on) as possible so that people with a preference for certain devices can use them. Game players use a wide variety of controls, and it's your job to decide which ones you think are worth supporting and how they will be used to control the game. It never hurts to support extra input devices.

At the very least, you can count on supporting the keyboard and mouse. You might as well plan on supporting joysticks in most games too, providing it makes sense to use a joystick in the context of the game. Beyond those three input devices, it's up to you to decide whether it's worth the extra effort to support other devices. Some input devices might not even be applicable to your game; in which case, the decision is easy. Between steering wheels, virtual reality helmets, and touch sensitive gloves, there are plenty of advanced input options if you want to go the distance in supporting input devices. And who knows what other kinds of far-out input devices are on the horizon.

 Game pads work similarly to joysticks, and therefore don't usually require any special design considerations; a game that works with a joystick will likely work with most game pads.

Deciding on the Play Modes

The last consideration to make in regard to the overall design of a game is that of play modes. Will the game be a one-player game, a two-player game, or will it be networked to allow a lot of players? If it supports multiplayer mode, is it competitive play, cooperative play, or some of both? These important decisions can dramatically impact both the fun factor and the technical difficulties of developing the game. For one thing, networking a multiplayer game presents some pretty serious technical hurdles at the programming level. I'm not trying to scare you away from networking; I just want to point out that it's a fairly advanced area of game programming.

To better understand the considerations that can go into determining play modes for a game, allow me to give you a practical example. I once developed a simple combat game called Combat Tanks that was along the lines of the old Atari 2600 Combat game. When designing the game, I initially envisioned two players fighting each other head-to-head. At the time I had no interest in adding networking support, which was very difficult to program at the time, so the players played at the same computer using keys on different sides of the keyboard to control their respective tanks. After some testing, it became apparent that a one-player mode for the game would be fun too. I mistakenly thought it would be easy to design a computer tank that could think and react like a human player. I was seriously naïve about that idea.

I learned pretty quickly that adding intelligence to computer opponents is a tricky business; all the little strategic decisions we make as humans while playing a game are very difficult to program into a mindless computer opponent. So, I figured out a workaround. Rather than have a single intelligent computer opponent, I opted for an army of stupid computer opponents. The resulting game played as a head-to-head tank game in two-player mode, and as a one-against-all shoot-em-up in one-player mode. It still turned out being quite fun as a one-player game, and I didn't have to deal with the complexities of "teaching" the computer tank how to be as crafty as a human.

 Although my tank game is now close to ten years old, it's still kind of fun in a nostalgic kind of way. If you'd like to try it out, you can download it from my Web site at http://www.michaelmorrison.com/compgames.html. I actually co-wrote Combat Tanks with my good friend Randy Weems, who I gladly credit for a great deal of my knowledge of game programming.

Please understand that I'm not advocating taking the easy way out when it comes to determining the play modes of your games, like I did. I'm only trying to make the point that there are many ways to arrive at a desired result. For me, the simplest solution ended up working out great because it allowed me to inject some interesting enemies into the game, such as foot soldiers, bombers, and helicopters. A little creativity can often go a long way toward overcoming technical hurdles.

Object-Oriented Programming and Games

Because you have some experience with C++, you've no doubt heard of object-oriented programming. *Object-oriented programming*, or *OOP*, is a programming technique in which you treat parts of a program as *objects*, as opposed to chunks of programming code. OOP is particularly useful in games because games are actually easier to understand when you break them down into objects. For this reason, programming languages such as C++ are ideal for developing games. The next two sections provide you with an OOP refresher and then put OOP in the context of game development.

Understanding OOP

The idea behind OOP is to make programming more akin to the way people think, as compared to the way computers think. People tend to think in terms of meaningful things (objects). As an example, if you were to describe a hockey game, you might talk about the rink, the players, the nets, and the puck. From a computer's perspective, a computer hockey game is no different from any other program—it's just a bunch of ones and zeros. Programming languages free programmers from having to think in terms of ones and zeros. OOP languages take things a step further by allowing you to think in terms of objects.

Classes of objects are an important part of OOP. A *class* is a category of objects. Another way to say this is that an object is an *instance* of a class. If you were creating a computer hockey game, you might create a single hockey player class; the actual players in the game are instances of this class. Figure 1.2 shows how the hockey player objects are related to the single player class.

The figure reveals how several objects are created from a single class, which serves as a template for the objects. Using a food analogy instead of hockey, you can think of the class as a cookie cutter and the objects as the cookies. Another important feature of classes is that they allow you to create *subclasses*, which add to the properties and features in a class to make it more specific. A subclass *inherits* the properties and features from its *parent class*, and then adds some of its own. In this way, a subclass is similar to a human child in that it inherits traits from its parent, but also has its own new traits.

FIGURE 1.2
Several hockey player objects can be created from a single player class.

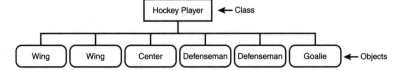

Applying OOP to Games

In order to understand the benefits that OOP offers in terms of game development, it's helpful to think of a game as a type of abstract simulation. If you think about most of the games you've seen or played, it's almost impossible to think of one that doesn't simulate something. All the adventure games and sports games are clearly simulations, and even the most far-out space games are modeling objects that exist in some kind of virtual world. Knowing that games are models of worlds, you can make the connection that most of the things in games (landscapes, creatures, and so on) correspond to things in these worlds. And once you can resolve a game into a collection of "things," you can apply OOP techniques to the design. This is possible because things can easily be translated into objects in an OOP environment.

To better understand what I'm talking about, consider the OOP design of a simple fantasy adventure game. The object representing the world for this game might contain information such as its map and images that represent the visualization of the map, as well as time and weather. All other objects in the game would include positional information that describes where in the world they are located. This positional information could be a simple XY value that pinpoints the object's location on the world map.

1

The object for the main character in the game would include information such as life points and any items picked up during the game (weapons, lanterns, keys, and so on). The game itself would interact with the character object by telling it to move in different directions based on user input. The items carried by the character would also be created as objects. For example, the lantern object would probably keep track of how much fuel is left in the lantern, and whether it is on or off. Interactions with the lantern would simply include turning it on or off; the lantern object would be smart enough to reduce its fuel supply when the lantern is turned on.

Creatures in the game could all be based on a single creature class that describes general characteristics shared by all creatures such as life points, aggression, and how much damage they inflict when fighting. Specific creature objects would then be created and turned loose in the virtual world. The creature objects and the main character object could all be subclassed from the same organism object. Unlike the character object, which is driven by user interactions, the creature objects would be controlled by some type of intelligence programmed into the game. For example, more aggressive creatures might always chase after the main character when they are on the screen together, whereas passive creatures might have a tendency to hide and avoid contact. You could create creature subclasses that enhance the basic creature with unique capabilities such as the ability to fly, swim, or breathe fire. Figure 1.3 shows how the different classes in this hypothetical adventure game might be organized.

FIGURE 1.3
Classes in a hypothetical adventure game are built on one another to establish a virtual world of objects.

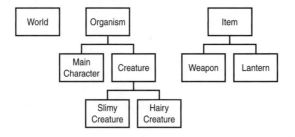

Don't forget that classes are templates for objects, which means that the classes shown in the figure are designed as a blueprint for creating objects in the game. However, it's not until you actually create the objects themselves that they are able to exist in the virtual world and interact with one another. Again, the class is the cookie cutter, and the object is the cookie. So, the development of a game using OOP first involves designing classes for the various "things" in the game, and then creating objects using those classes.

The beauty of the OOP approach to game development is that the game more or less runs itself once everything is in place. In other words, each object is responsible for handling its own business, so the game doesn't have to concern itself too much with what each object is doing; the game is just providing a framework for the objects to exist in. This framework primarily consists of a game screen for the objects to be drawn on, and an update loop that tells the objects some time has passed. For creatures, this update would entail determining the direction to move in and whether they should attack or run. For the main character, an update involves performing an action based on user input. The main point I'm trying to make is that objects are independent entities that basically know how to take care of themselves.

A more practical benefit of OOP design in games has to do with reusing code. Let's say that you've completed your fantasy adventure game we just talked about and would like to create a similar game set in outer space. Instead of starting over from scratch, you could take the objects you developed for the first game and reuse them in the new game. Granted, some changes would be in order, but many of the changes could be made by creating new subclasses, as opposed to rewriting the originals. Code reuse is certainly one of the most dramatic benefits to using an OOP approach to game development.

Exploring the Tools of the Trade

Before embarking on any game development project, it's important to assemble a set of tools that you will use to construct the game. Although there are a variety of different tools that could feasibly factor into the development of a complex game, the most critical tools are as follows:

- Compiler
- Graphics tools
- Sound and music tools

The next few sections take a look at these tools in greater detail.

Compiler

Regardless of what programming language you're using to develop games, you will likely need a compiler to turn the programming code into an executable game application. Because this book focuses on using C++ as the programming language for creating games for Windows, you'll need a C++ compiler that is capable of creating Windows applications. C++ compilers range from high-powered commercial development environments such as Microsoft Visual C++ and Borland C++Builder to free compilers such as DJGPP. Appendix B, "Selecting a Game Development Tool," provides more details on selecting a compiler for game development. The example games presented throughout the book can be compiled using any of these compilers.

1

Graphics Tools

Similar to compilers, graphics tools range from high-end commercial tools to tools that you can download free; you can also use graphics tools built into Windows such as Paint. If you decide to draw your graphics by hand, you will need to scan in the artwork and clean it up in a special tool. Of course, you'll need a scanner to scan in artwork, but those are fortunately very affordable. Even if you don't plan on drawing game graphics by hand, you'll need an image editing program, or paint program, as they are often called. Paint is the standard image editor built into Windows, which is surprisingly useful for creating and editing basic game images. At the other end of the spectrum are tools such as Adobe Photoshop, which are used by graphics professionals to perform extremely powerful special effects on images.

Sound and Music Tools

You learned earlier in the lesson that sound effects used in games are typically sampled, which means that you record them using a microphone or maybe from an audio CD. The sound card on your computer likely already has a line-in port and a microphone port, both of which can be used to sample sounds. You can use the built-in Sound Recorder application in Windows to sample sounds, or you can invest in a fancier commercial tool such as Cool Edit Pro. Either way, the process is very straightforward: just hook up the sound source (microphone, CD player, and so on) and start recording using the sound editing software. You'll need to perform some cleanup on the sound after recording, such as removing extra noises that appear before and after the sound.

In addition to sampled sound effects, you might want to experiment with creating your own MIDI music. To do so, you must use another special tool known as a MIDI authoring tool. This kind of tool is different from a sound editor in that it is designed so that you enter musical compositions similar to what you see on a sheet of written music. You then assign instruments to different notes as if a band was playing the tune. A more intuitive approach to using a MIDI authoring tool is to connect a MIDI music keyboard to your computer and play the music on it. If your sound card has a MIDI port, and most of them do, the music you play will be recorded by the MIDI software and saved. You can then further arrange the music and alter the way it sounds.

Summary

Although you didn't get to wrap your hands around any example code, this lesson served as an important starting point for learning the basics of game development. The goal of this lesson was to help you direct your brain power toward the primary issues involved in designing a game at a conceptual level. You found out about the essential game design concepts required to get started down the path to creating your own games. You also learned about object-oriented programming (OOP), and why it is important for game development. The lesson concluded by introducing you to the different kinds of development tools commonly found in the arsenal of the game programmer.

Hour 2, "A Windows Game Programming Primer," introduces you to Windows programming with a slant toward games. You learn the basics of the Windows API, and what it has to offer for the game developer. More importantly, you develop a skeletal Windows application that will form the basis of games you create throughout the remainder of the book.

Q&A

Q Why is screen resolution such a big deal for games?

A Screen resolution is the physical size of the screen, not in inches, but in pixels. Most screens these days are set at a resolution of 800x600 or greater. You can check your own resolution in Windows by right-clicking on the Desktop and then selecting Properties in the drop-down menu. Click the Settings tab in the Display Properties dialog box, and you'll be able to see your screen resolution in the lower portion of the box. You can experiment with different resolutions by dragging the slider control around. Games you develop later in the book avoid the varying resolution problem by focusing on a specific game screen size.

Q Should I invest in game development tools?

A The answer to this question has a lot to do with how serious you are about developing games and how much money you have to spend. There is no arguing that good development tools can make certain parts of the game development process much easier. However, I would recommend spending some time with free or inexpensive tools initially so that you can gain an appreciation for what the higher end tools have to offer. Having said that, you certainly won't go wrong by investing in a quality development environment with a C++ compiler, such as Microsoft Visual C++. If there is one tool to recommend buying, the compiler would be the one; this is mainly because you can find surprisingly good shareware graphics and sound editors out there. Please see Appendix B for more information about the different compilers and development environments available for Windows game development.

Workshop

1

The Workshop is designed to help you anticipate possible questions, review what you've learned, and begin learning how to put your knowledge into practice. The answers to the quiz can be found in Appendix A, "Quiz Answers."

Quiz

1. What are the different types of video games?

2. What's the main priority to consider when designing a game?

3. What's a storyboard?

4. What's the highest quality sound you can use in a game?

Exercises

1. Play some video games and pay particular attention to how they can be broken down into groups of objects. Also pay attention to how sounds and music are weaved into the flow of the game, and how they are coordinated with interactions between objects.

2. Develop a class hierarchy for a game idea of your own, similar to the one created for the hypothetical fantasy adventure game discussed in this lesson.

Hour 2

A Windows Game Programming Primer

Believe it or not, there was a time not so long ago when the notion of a game other than Solitaire on Windows was considered a joke. I should know because during that same time period I was attempting to get a job as a game programmer who specialized in Windows games. I knew it was only a matter of time before DOS went away and games had to migrate to Windows, but back then no one wanted to think about it. So I found work elsewhere. Now only a few short years later, the concept of developing a computer game for any operating system other than Windows is considered a joke, barring a few Macintosh and Linux games. If you've never written a program specifically for Windows, you're in for somewhat of a surprise because Windows programs are unique in terms of how they are put together. This lesson shows you how to assemble a minimal Windows program, which will get you a step closer toward creating your first Windows game.

In this hour, you'll learn

- How Windows programming differs from traditional programming
- What makes a Windows program tick
- How to develop a minimal Windows program

Windows Programming Essentials

Before you can even think about developing games for Windows, you need to have some knowledge about what it takes to develop a basic Windows program. Windows programming is unlike other kinds of traditional programming, as you'll soon find out. Windows programming begins and ends with the Win32 *API (Application Programming Interface)*, which is the set of data types and functions that are used to create Windows programs. The Win32 API is quite massive, and requires a significant learning curve to get comfortable with its many facets. Fortunately, you only need to use a relatively small portion of the Win32 API to create Windows games.

The Win32 API is built into all compilers that support Windows programming, such as Microsoft Visual C++. By the way, the "32" in Win32 has to do with the fact that the API is a 32-bit API. This is significant because the original Windows API was developed for 16-bit programming. Remember Windows 3.1?

Certain aspects of Win32 programming are common to all Windows programs, regardless of whether you're creating a game or a word processor. These common Windows program features are primarily what you learn about in this lesson. This will provide you with a solid foundation on which to build game specific knowledge and code. If you're getting antsy, just hang in there through this lesson, and I promise you'll get to create some interesting programs soon enough.

In the previous lesson, you learned how object-oriented programming is important for game development. You might be curious as to how OOP impacts Windows programming with Win32. Win32 is a procedural API that relies on object-oriented constructs to represent Window elements such as windows and icons. An example of this is the window object, which represents a rectangular area on the screen. Window objects have data associated with them along with Win32 API functions that are used to manipulate them.

You can think of Win32 programming as a hybrid type of object-oriented programming.

Event-Driven Programming

The most dramatic switch for most people new to Windows programming is the fact that Windows programs are *event-driven*. This is a fancy way of saying that Windows programs respond to their environment, as opposed to the environment taking cues from the program. In the world of events, the flow of your program follows events external to the program such as mouse clicks and key presses. Instead of writing code to scan for a key press, you write code to take some action whenever a key press is delivered to the program. As you get more comfortable with the concept of events, you'll see how just about any change in the environment can trigger an event. You can design your programs to ignore or respond to any events you choose.

The event-driven nature of Windows has a lot to do with the fact that it is a graphical operating system. When you think about it, Windows faces a seriously challenging problem in allowing multiple programs to run at the same time and share screen space, memory, input devices, and virtually every other system resource. The event-driven approach to handling user interactions and system changes is extremely important in making Windows as flexible and powerful as it is. In terms of games, events make it possible to divide tasks according to what has taken place. In other words, a left mouse click, a right mouse click, and a key press on the keyboard are handled as separate events.

Communicating with Messages

In traditional non-graphical programs, a program calls a system function to accomplish a given task. Graphical Windows programs introduce a twist on this scenario by allowing Windows to call a program function. When I say "Windows calls a program function," I mean that Windows sends the program a *message*, which is a notification containing information about an event. Windows sends messages whenever something takes place that a program might want to know about and respond to, such as the user dragging the mouse or resizing the main program window.

Windows programs are also commonly referred to as Windows applications. So, you'll often see me using the terms *program* and *application* interchangeably—just know that they mean the same thing.

Messages are always sent to a specific window, usually the main program window; every Windows program has a main window. Many windows are floating around in a typical Windows session, and all of them are receiving messages at one time or another that inform them of changes going on around them. Each of these windows has a *window procedure*, which is a special function that processes messages for the window. Windows handles the details of routing messages to the appropriate window procedures; your job is to write code in the window procedure for your program that responds to certain messages.

With the probability of many different messages being sent to a window, you might wonder how many of them you need to worry about in a game. And what happens to the messages you ignore? In the average Windows program, including most games, you usually only concern yourself with a handful of messages. You write code to respond to these messages, and you allow a default Windows message handler to take care of messages you ignore; Windows provides default handlers for all messages. By the way, a *handler* is simply a chunk of code that is called in response to a message; its job is to "handle" the event.

Understanding Device Independence

In the golden era of DOS games, it was common for game developers to program games so that they worked directly with the memory on your graphics card. The benefit to this was that it made games extremely fast because the graphics for a game was being processed directly by the graphics card. Although this worked great for DOS games, you don't have quite the same luxury in Windows. Generally speaking, Windows is specifically designed to keep you from interacting directly with hardware such as graphics cards. This design is known as *device independence*, which simply means that Windows programs draw graphics in a manner that is independent of the specific hardware devices that get drawn on. The upside to this approach is that Windows programs work on a wide range of hardware without any special modification. This was impossible in the DOS world.

Device independence in Windows is made possible by the *Graphical Device Interface*, or *GDI*, which is the part of the Win32 API that deals with graphics. The GDI sits between a program and the physical graphics hardware. Under the GDI, graphics are drawn to a virtual output device; it is up to Windows to resolve the virtual device down to a specific hardware device via the system configuration, hardware drivers, and so on. Even though the GDI is designed to keep you at an arm's length from graphics hardware, it is still quite powerful. In fact, all the games developed throughout this book are based solely on the GDI.

Storing Program Information as Resources

Just about every Windows program relies to some extent on *resources*, which are pieces of information related to a program outside of the program code itself. For example, icons are a good example of resources, as are images, sounds, and even menus. You specify all the resources for a Windows program in a special resource script, which is also known as an RC file. The resource script is a text file containing a list of resources that is compiled and linked into the final executable program. Most resources are created and edited with visual resource tools, such as the icon editor integrated into the Visual C++ development environment.

Dealing with Strange Data Types

Perhaps the toughest part of Windows programming is getting comfortable with the strange data types that are a part of every Windows program. One of the most common data types you'll see is called a handle, and it's nothing like a door handle in the real world. A *handle* in Windows is a number that refers to a graphical Windows object such as a window or icon. Handles are important because an object is often moved around in memory by Windows, which means that its memory address is a moving target. A handle gives you a fixed reference to an object independent of the object's physical location in memory. Handles are used throughout the Win32 API when dealing with Windows objects. Don't worry if handles sound a little complicated right now because they'll start making more sense as you see them used in a real Windows program.

In addition to handles, the Win32 API introduces a variety of new and different data types that you might find strange at first. All Win32 data types appear in uppercase, so they are easily identifiable. For example, a fairly simple and commonly used Win32 data type is RECT, which represents a rectangle structure. There is also an HWND data type, which represents a handle to a window. Win32 is chock full of data types, so it's futile to try and cover them all in one place. Instead, you'll learn about new data types as you encounter them throughout the book.

In order for your Windows programs to be able to recognize and use Win32 data types, you must import them into your program's source files. This is accomplished with a single line of code:

```
#include <windows.h>
```

The header file windows.h defines the entire Win32 API, and is essential in every Win32 application. It's generally a good idea to import it first in every relevant source file.

Unconventional Coding Conventions

If you've ever seen the code for a Windows program before, you might have wondered what was going on with the weird variable names. Programmers have long struggled with the problem of writing code that is easy to understand. Windows makes this problem worse by introducing a lot of different data types, which makes it difficult to keep up with which variables are of which type. Legendary Microsoft programmer Charles Simonyi came up with a pretty crafty solution to this problem that is now known as *Hungarian notation*. (Mr. Simonyi is Hungarian.) With Hungarian notation, variable names begin with a lowercase letter or letters that indicate the data type of the variable. For example, integer variable names begin with the letter *i*. Following are some Hungarian notation prefixes commonly used in Windows programming:

- i—integer
- b—Boolean (BOOL)
- sz—string terminated by zero
- p—pointer
- h—handle
- w—unsigned short integer (WORD)
- dw—unsigned long integer (DWORD)
- l—long integer

> BOOL, WORD, and DWORD are commonly used Win32 data types.

Applying Hungarian notation is very simple. For example, an integer count might be named iCount, whereas a handle to an icon might be named hIcon. Similarly, a null-terminated string storing the name of a sports team might be named szTeamName. Keep in mind that Hungarian notation is completely optional, but it really is a good idea. You'll encounter Hungarian notation in all the code in this book, and after a while you'll hopefully begin to appreciate the convenience it offers.

Peeking Inside a Windows Program

Although I could certainly go on and on about the Win32 API, the best way to get you closer to creating a Windows game is to take a look at what actually goes into a Windows program. The next few sections break apart the major aspects of a Windows program, along with the code that makes them tick. It's not terribly important for you to understand every line of code at this point because much of what goes into a generic Windows program is overhead code that you won't bother with again once you dive into game creation. Nevertheless, it's important to at least have a feel for what is required of every Windows program.

Where It All Begins

If you come from the world of traditional C/C++ programming in non-graphical environments, you are no doubt familiar with the main() function. The operating system calls main() when a program is first run, and your program code starts executing inside main(). There is no main() function in a Windows program. However, Windows offers a similar function called WinMain() that serves as the starting point for a Windows program. Unlike main(), WinMain() simply creates and initializes some things and then eases out of the picture. After WinMain() creates a main window for the program, the rest of the program executes by responding to events in the main window procedure. The window procedure is where most of the really interesting things take place in a Windows program.

The Window Class

All windows in a Windows program are created based on a *window class*, which is a template that defines the attributes of a window. Multiple windows can be created from a single window class. For example, there is a standard Win32 window class that defines the attributes of a button, and all buttons in Windows are created from it. If you want to create a new window of your own, you have to register a window class and then create a window from it. In order to create new windows from a window class, the window class must be registered with Windows using the RegisterClassEx() Win32 API function. After a window class has been registered, you can use it to create as many windows as you want.

Window classes are represented by a data structure in the Win32 API called WNDCLASSEX, which defines the attributes of a window. Following is how the WNDCLASSEX structure is defined in the Win32 API:

```
typedef struct _WNDCLASSEX {
    UINT        cbSize;
    UINT        style;
    WNDPROC     lpfnWndProc;
    int         cbClsExtra;
    int         cbWndExtra;
    HINSTANCE   hInstance;
    HICON       hIcon;
    HICON       hIconSm;
```

```
    HCURSOR      hCursor;
    HBRUSH       hbrBackground;
    LPCSTR       lpszMenuName;
    LPCSTR       lpszClassName;
} WNDCLASSEX;
```

This code reveals some of those strange Win32 data types I talked about earlier. It isn't important right now to go through each and every member of this structure. Instead, let's focus on a few of the more interesting members:

- lpfnWndProc—A pointer to the window procedure for the window class
- hIcon—The icon for the window class
- hIconSm—An optional small icon for the window class
- hCursor—The mouse cursor for the window class
- hbrBackground—The background brush for the window class

These members hopefully make some sense because they are related to fairly obvious parts of a window. The first member, lpfnWndProc, is probably the trickiest because it is a pointer to the window procedure for the window class; you find out what this procedure looks like in a moment. The hIcon and hIconSm members are used to set the icons for the window class, and they correspond to the program icons you see when a program is running in Windows. hCursor is used to set a special mouse cursor (pointer) for the window class if you decide you want something other than the standard arrow cursor. And finally, hbrBackground is used to set the background for the window class, which is the color that fills the background of the inside of the window. Most windows use white as a background color, but you're free to set it to any color you want.

Again, it's not imperative that you feel totally comfortable with the window class structure at this point. The goal right now is just to get acclimated with Win32 programming to a degree in which we can assemble a complete program. Later in the lesson, you put the window class structure to use in creating a minimal Windows program.

Creating a Window

A critical part of any Windows program, including games, is the creation of the main program window. Creating a window involves using a window class, which you learned about in the previous section. Although window classes define general characteristics for a window, other attributes of a window must be defined when a window is created. These attributes are provided as arguments to the CreateWindow() function, which is the Win32 API function used to create windows. Following is an example of creating a window using the CreateWindow() function:

```
hwnd = CreateWindow(szAppName,
  "My Game",
  WS_OVERLAPPEDWINDOW,
  CW_USEDEFAULT,
  CW_USEDEFAULT,
  CW_USEDEFAULT,
  CW_USEDEFAULT,
  NULL,
  NULL,
  hInstance,
  NULL);
```

It's not terribly important to understand every line of this code, but it is possible to focus on a few interesting aspects of the window creation. First of all, the name of the window class is specified as the first argument, szAppName. The second argument is the window title, "My Game", which is displayed in the title bar of the window when the program is run. The WS_OVERLAPPEDWINDOW style is a standard Win32 style that identifies a traditional window that can be resized. The four CW_USEDEFAULT styles indicate the initial XY position of the window on the screen, as well as the window's width and height; you can use specific numbers for these settings, but CW_USEDEFAULT tells Windows to use a reasonable default value. The remaining parameters aren't terribly important right now, so we won't bother with them at the moment.

Keep in mind that I'm not expecting you to immediately absorb all this information; the main goal here is to start getting familiar with the general structure of the CreateWindow() function and its arguments. Notice that CreateWindow() returns a window handle to the newly created window. It's also worth pointing out that I could've used numeric values when specifying the window's X position, Y position, width, and height. For example, the previous code could have used hard-coded values such as 0, 0, 640, and 480. In fact, it is often helpful for games to use a fixed window size, which is why you'll eventually be plugging in real numbers for the width and height of your game windows.

Handling Messages

Earlier in the lesson, you learned that Windows communicates with your program by sending it messages. Let's take a closer look at messages to see how they work. A message has three pieces of information associated with it:

- A window
- A message identifier
- Message parameters

The window associated with a message is the window to which the message is being sent. The *message identifier* is a number that specifies the message being sent. The

Win32 API defines numeric constants that represent each message. For example, WM_CREATE, WM_PAINT, and WM_MOUSEMOVE are all numeric constants defined in the Win32 API that identify messages associated with window creation, window painting, and mouse movement, respectively.

The message parameters consist of two pieces of information that are entirely specific to the message being sent. These 32-bit values are called wParam and lParam, and their meaning is completely determined by the message being handled. For example, the wParam parameter for the WM_SIZE message contains information about the type of sizing performed on the window, whereas the lParam parameter contains the new width and height of the window's inside area, which is also known as the window's *client area*. The width and height are packed into the low and high words of the 32-bit lParam value, which is a common approach that Win32 uses to shove two pieces of information into a single location. If low words and high words sound intimidating, don't worry because I show you exactly how to extract useful information from lParam later in the book when you need it.

When a message is delivered to a program by Windows, it is processed in the WndProc() function. Although WndProc() is responsible for handling messages for a given window class, your program must still take on the task of routing messages to the appropriate window procedures. This is taken care of by a *message loop*, which must be placed in the heart of the WinMain() function:

```
while (GetMessage(&msg, NULL, 0, 0)) {
  TranslateMessage(&msg);
  DispatchMessage(&msg);
}
```

This code essentially processes all messages at the application level and routes them to the appropriate window procedures. Code in each different window procedure is then responsible for taking action based on the messages they receive. If window procedures sound mysterious at this stage, read on to learn how they work.

The Window Procedure

Every window in a Windows program has an associated *window procedure*, which is a special function that is capable of being called by Windows. Windows calls a window procedure to deliver messages to a given window. You can think of a window procedure as a message processing function. In object-oriented terms, a window procedure is the behavioral part of a window object, whereas Windows maintains the data part of the object. Figure 2.1 shows how a window procedure fits into the object-oriented concept of a window.

FIGURE 2.1

In object-oriented terms, a window is an object whose behavior is determined by a window procedure and whose data is managed by Windows.

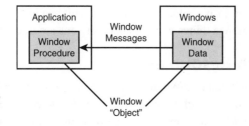

2

Window procedures are actually associated with window classes, which means that multiple windows created from a single class share the same window procedure. This is logical because the behavior of a given class of windows should be the same. A window procedure is defined in the Win32 API like this:

```
LRESULT CALLBACK WndProc(HWND hwnd, UINT iMsg, WPARAM wParam, LPARAM lParam);
```

Don't sweat it if this prototype looks a little intimidating. You are only concerned right now with the meaning of the arguments, which should be somewhat familiar from the previous explanation of messages:

- hwnd—Handle of the window to which the message is being sent
- iMsg—Message identifier
- wParam—Primary message parameter
- lParam—Secondary message parameter

Practically every WndProc() function contains a large switch statement that is responsible for separating the messages being handled. Following is an example of a WndProc() function with a very common piece of code that handles the WM_DESTROY message, which is passed to a window whenever it is being destroyed:

```
LRESULT CALLBACK WndProc(HWND hwnd, UINT iMsg, WPARAM wParam, LPARAM lParam) {
  switch (iMsg) {
    case WM_DESTROY :
      PostQuitMessage(0);
      return 0;
  }
  return DefWindowProc(hwnd, iMsg, wParam, lParam);
}
```

Notice that the switch statement operates on the iMsg argument, and in this case only looks for the WM_DESTROY message. The PostQuitMessage() function call causes the application to quit because the main window is being destroyed. This code gets called when you click the X in the upper right corner of a window. Notice in this code how any messages not handled in the switch statement are passed through to the DefWindowProc() function. This is a strict requirement of all window procedures because `DefWindowProc()` is responsible for the default handling of messages. If you left this code out, some strange things would happen in your program.

Working with Resources

You might not realize it, but as a Windows user you are already very familiar with an important part of Windows programming: resources. *Resources* are special data items associated with a Windows program that typically define portions of a program's user interface. Unlike data such as variables used in program code, resources are stored in a program's executable file and loaded only as needed. Following are some of the standard resources supported by Windows:

- Bitmap
- Cursor
- Dialog box
- Icon
- Menu

In addition to these standard resources, Windows also supports *user-defined resources*, which are custom resources that you write special code to handle. User-defined resources are very important in game programming because they allow you to include sound effects and music with a program as resources.

Resources are defined in a program using a *resource script*, which is a text file with a .RC extension. You use a resource compiler to compile a resource script into a binary resource file with a .RES extension. This binary resource file is then linked with an application's object code to create a complete executable application. The process of compiling and linking resources to an application's .EXE file is usually a standard part of a Windows compiler's overall build process; in other words, you shouldn't have to worry about manually compiling resource scripts. Following is an example of a simple resource script that defines an icon and a cursor:

```
IDI_MINE ICON   "Mine.ico"
IDC_MINE CURSOR "Mine.cur"
```

You might initially be a little confused by the fact that resources are compiled into a binary form, especially considering that resources don't have any C/C++ code directly associated with them. The compilation process for resources is actually quite different from the process for C/C++ code. A special resource compiler is required to compile resources, but its main job is to assemble all the resources defined in a resource script into a single binary file. A compiled binary resource file is also very different from an object file of compiled C/C++ code. You can think of a compiled resource file as a group of resources combined into binary form. Even though compiled resource files aren't directly related to object files, they are merged together at the link stage of application development to create an executable application file (.EXE).

Perhaps the most commonly used resource is the icon, which forms a vital part of the user interface for Windows applications. If you don't specifically set a custom icon for an application, the default Windows icon is used. Fortunately, it's very simple to set a custom icon for an application. In fact, it only involves two steps:

1. Define the icon in the application's resource script.
2. Load the icon when you define and register the application's window class in the `WinMain()` function.

The first step is accomplished by adding a single line to the resource script for your application:

```
IDI_MINE ICON "Mine.ico"
```

This code uses the `ICON` resource statement to define an icon named `IDI_MINE` that is stored in the file `Mine.ico`. When the resource script is compiled, the icon will be referenced from the `Mine.ico` file and compiled into the binary resource file. The size of the icon can be either 32×32 or 16×16, depending on how you are going to use it; the default icon size for an application is 32×32. In the next section of the lesson, you learn how to define both a small (16×16) and a large (32×32) icon for the Skeleton program example.

The second step to setting a custom icon involves loading the icon and assigning it to the `hIcon` field of the `WNDCLASSEX` structure used to define a window class. You do this by calling the `LoadIcon()` Win32 API function and passing in the name of the icon:

```
wndclass.hIcon = LoadIcon(hInstance, "Mine.ico");
```

The `hInstance` parameter to `LoadIcon()` is passed into the `WinMain()` function by Windows, and is a handle to the application instance. This handle references the executable file from which the icon resource is to be loaded.

Building the Skeleton Example Program

At this point, you've seen the major portions of a Windows program isolated into individual parts. Understandably, it's difficult to get a feel for a complete Windows program when viewing it in small chunks of code. For this reason, it's very important to see how a complete Windows program comes together. This section shows you a complete, yet minimal, Windows program called Skeleton that will form the basis for games to come throughout the book. Following are the files that go into the Skeleton program example:

- Skeleton.h—Header file for the application
- Skeleton.cpp—Source code file for the application
- Resource.h—Header file for the resource IDs
- Skeleton.rc—Resource file for the application

The next couple of sections explore the program code and the related resources that go into the Skeleton application. All of this code is available on the accompanying CD-ROM, along with Microsoft Visual C++ project files.

Writing the Program Code

The Skeleton.h header file is surprisingly simple, and does nothing but import a couple of headers for use by Skeleton.cpp. Listing 2.1 contains the code for this file.

LISTING 2.1   The Skeleton.h Header File Simply Imports a Couple of Header Files

```
1: #pragma once
2:
3: //----------------------------------------------------------------
4: // Include Files
5: //----------------------------------------------------------------
6: #include <windows.h>
7: #include "Resource.h"
```

In case you aren't familiar with it, line 1 shows how to use the #pragma once compiler directive to keep the Skeleton.h header from being accidentally referenced more than once. This gets to be more of an issue in larger programs in which there are a lot of dependencies between different source files, but it's a good idea to get in the habit of using the directive. Lines 6 and 7 contain the important code, which is the inclusion of the standard windows.h header file and the Resource.h resource identifier header file, which you learn about in a moment.

The bulk of the code for the Skeleton program is in the Skeleton.cpp source code file, which is shown in Listing 2.2.

LISTING 2.2   The Skeleton.cpp Source Code File Builds on the Code You Saw Throughout This Lesson to Create a Complete Windows Program

```
1: //----------------------------------------------------------------
2: // Include Files
3: //----------------------------------------------------------------
4: #include "Skeleton.h"
5:
```

LISTING 2.2   Continued

```
 6: //-----------------------------------------------------------
 7: // Global Function Declarations
 8: //-----------------------------------------------------------
 9: LRESULT CALLBACK  WndProc(HWND hWindow, UINT msg, WPARAM wParam,
10:   LPARAM lParam);
11:
12: //-----------------------------------------------------------
13: // Global Functions
14: //-----------------------------------------------------------
15: int WINAPI WinMain(HINSTANCE hInstance, HINSTANCE hPrevInstance,
16:   PSTR szCmdLine, int iCmdShow)
17: {
18:   static TCHAR   szAppName[] = TEXT("Skeleton");
19:   WNDCLASSEX     wndclass;
20:   HWND           hWindow;
21:   MSG            msg;
22:
23:   // Create the window class for the main window
24:   wndclass.cbSize        = sizeof(wndclass);
25:   wndclass.style         = CS_HREDRAW | CS_VREDRAW;
26:   wndclass.lpfnWndProc   = WndProc;
27:   wndclass.cbClsExtra    = 0;
28:   wndclass.cbWndExtra    = 0;
29:   wndclass.hInstance     = hInstance;
30:   wndclass.hIcon         = LoadIcon(hInstance,
31:     MAKEINTRESOURCE(IDI_SKELETON));
32:   wndclass.hIconSm       = LoadIcon(hInstance,
33:     MAKEINTRESOURCE(IDI_SKELETON_SM));
34:   wndclass.hCursor       = LoadCursor(NULL, IDC_ARROW);
35:   wndclass.hbrBackground = (HBRUSH)(COLOR_WINDOW + 1);
36:   wndclass.lpszMenuName  = NULL;
37:   wndclass.lpszClassName = szAppName;
38:
39:   // Register the window class
40:   if (!RegisterClassEx(&wndclass))
41:     return 0;
42:
43:   // Create the window
44:   hWindow = CreateWindow(szAppName, szAppName, WS_OVERLAPPEDWINDOW,
45:     CW_USEDEFAULT, CW_USEDEFAULT, CW_USEDEFAULT, CW_USEDEFAULT, NULL,
46:     NULL, hInstance, NULL);
47:
48:   // Show and update the window
49:   ShowWindow(hWindow, iCmdShow);
50:   UpdateWindow(hWindow);
51:
52:   // Enter the main message loop
53:   while (GetMessage(&msg, NULL, 0, 0))
54:   {
55:     // Process the message
```

2

LISTING 2.2   Continued

```
56:        TranslateMessage(&msg);
57:        DispatchMessage(&msg);
58:      }
59:    return (int)msg.wParam;
60: }
61:
62: LRESULT CALLBACK WndProc(HWND hWindow, UINT msg, WPARAM wParam,
63:    LPARAM lParam)
64: {
65:    HDC          hDC;
66:    PAINTSTRUCT ps;
67:    RECT         rect;
68:
69:    switch (msg)
70:    {
71:      case WM_PAINT:
72:        // Draw some text centered in the client area of the main window
73:        hDC = BeginPaint(hWindow, &ps);
74:        GetClientRect(hWindow, &rect);
75:        DrawText(hDC, TEXT("This is a skeleton application!"), -1, &rect,
76:          DT_SINGLELINE | DT_CENTER | DT_VCENTER);
77:        EndPaint(hWindow, &ps);
78:        return 0;
79:
80:      case WM_DESTROY:
81:        // Exit the application
82:        PostQuitMessage(0);
83:        return 0;
84:    }
85:    return DefWindowProc(hWindow, msg, wParam, lParam);
86: }
```

This is admittedly a lot of code to throw at you at once, but I wanted you to see the Skeleton.cpp source code file in its entirety so that there would be no mysteries regarding what goes into a Windows program. Fortunately, the game engine that you build in the next lesson helps to hide a great deal of this code so that you never have to worry with it again. But for now we must push on and learn how it works!

Line 4 of the code imports the Skeleton.h header file, which is important because it in turn imports windows.h and Resource.h. Line 9 is a forward declaration of the WndProc() function, which is necessary because the function must be referenced in WinMain() before its code appears. Speaking of WinMain(), its job is to create the main window class (lines 24–37), register the window class (lines 40 and 41), create the main window (lines 44–46), show the main window (lines 49 and 50), and then get the application message loop going (lines 53–58). This certainly looks like a lot of interesting code, but it's actually quite boring once you see a few Windows programs; this code is largely duplicated verbatim in every Windows program. Fortunately, you'll be hiding this code in the game engine in the next lesson.

Getting back to WinMain(), you might be curious why the string for the program name is placed inside the apparent function call, TEXT() (line 18). TEXT() is actually a macro, not a function, and its job is to convert text into a form that can be used on a wide range of Windows systems. I won't get into all the details, but let's just say that it's a good idea to work with text using the TEXT() macro so that your program won't act strange on computers that are set up with a version of Windows designed for another language, such as Japanese.

Another important thing to notice in WinMain() is how both large and small icons are set for the program (lines 30–33). This is more important than you might realize because Windows XP typically displays the small 16x16 icon for programs even though the large 32x32 size was more prevalent in older versions of Windows.

The remainder of the code in the Skeleton.cpp source code file is the WndProc() function, which handles only two messages: WM_PAINT and WM_DESTROY. The WM_PAINT message is sent whenever a program needs to paint the client area (inside) of its window. In this case, a sentence of text is being drawn in the center of the client area to indicate that this is a skeleton application (lines 73–77). You learn all about painting both text and graphics in Hour 4, "Drawing Basic Graphics," so I'll skip explaining this code in more detail at this point.

Assembling the Resources

The Skeleton program only uses two resources: the large and small application icons. Before listing these icons in a resource script, it's important to assign them unique numeric identifiers, which are also known as *resource IDs*. This is accomplished in the Resource.h header file, which is shown in Listing 2.3.

LISTING 2.3 The Resource.h Header File Contains Resource IDs for the Skeleton Program Example

```
1: //------------------------------------------------------------
2: // Icons                  Range : 1000 - 1999
3: //------------------------------------------------------------
4: #define IDI_SKELETON      1000
5: #define IDI_SKELETON_SM   1001
```

As you can see, it only takes two lines (4 and 5) to define identifiers for the icon resources. Pulling the resources into the Skeleton application simply involves listing them in the application's resource script, as shown in Listing 2.4.

LISTING 2.4   The Skeleton.rc Resource Script Contains the Resources for the Skeleton Program Example

```
 1: //----------------------------------------------------------
 2: // Include Files
 3: //----------------------------------------------------------
 4: #include "Resource.h"
 5:
 6: //----------------------------------------------------------
 7: // Icons
 8: //----------------------------------------------------------
 9: IDI_SKELETON        ICON        "Skeleton.ico"
10: IDI_SKELETON_SM     ICON        "Skeleton_sm.ico"
```

Notice that the Skeleton.rc resource script first includes the Resource.h header file (line 4), and it then specifies the two icon resources by referencing their IDs (identifiers) and their physical locations (filenames). As long as you associate the Skeleton.rc file with the project file for your program in the development environment (compiler) that you're using, it will be automatically compiled and linked in with the application. As an example, I used Visual C++ to create the examples in this book, and after I added Skeleton.rc to the Skeleton project, I didn't have to worry about compiling or linking it.

Testing the Finished Product

I wish I could tell you that the Skeleton program example is full of excitement and intrigue when you run it for the first time, but unfortunately this just isn't the case. Seeing as how it is a minimal Windows application, there isn't a whole lot you can do with it. However, when you consider that the program "inherits" a lot of functionality from Windows because you can minimize it, maximize it, resize it, drag it around with the mouse, and so on, you start to realize that the Win32 API is quite powerful in its own way. Figure 2.2 shows the finished Skeleton application in action.

I warned you: There isn't much to look at here. Fortunately, you now have enough basic Windows programming skills to start doing some fun things.

FIGURE 2.2

The Skeleton program is a good example of a minimal Windows program, and not much else.

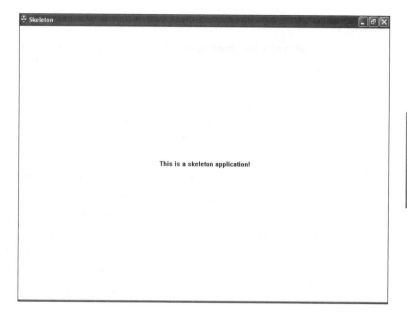

This is a skeleton application!

2

Summary

If there was one lesson that I dreaded writing in this book, it was this one. This is because I didn't relish the idea of departing from the emphasis on creating games for a whole lesson to teach Windows programming. Not only that, but I worried incessantly over how to explain enough of a complex topic in a single lesson without scaring you away from the remainder of the book. Now that it's behind both of us, let me say that from here on you'll find the book smooth sailing. Even the most complex game code in the book pales in comparison to being slapped with Windows code when you've never faced it before. So, please take this lesson for what it is: a necessary speed bump on the way to becoming a Windows game developer.

Hour 3, "Creating an Engine for Games," picks up where this lesson leaves off by freeing you from the messy Windows code that lies beneath every Windows program. More specifically, you learn how to develop a game engine that allows you to focus only on the game specific parts of your game programs, as opposed to the overhead code that is only there to satisfy Windows. The game engine also lays the groundwork for integrating advanced game features throughout the remainder of the book.

Q&A

Q **What really happens when "Windows sends a program a message"?**

A When Windows sends a program a message, what really happens is that Windows calls the `WndProc()` function in the program, which is then responsible for performing an action based upon the message. Within the `WndProc()` function, there is a `switch` statement that looks at one of the function arguments to see what kind of message was sent from Windows. There are also a couple of arguments that contain data specific to the message.

Q **Why is it necessary for a main program window to have a window class?**

A Window classes are very important in Windows programming because they describe the general characteristics of a window. It is necessary to create a window class for a main program window because the window must be of a type that is uniquely identifiable to Windows. In other words, you can think of all the windows that are floating around in Windows as belonging to different window classes, whereas the main window of your Windows program belongs to its own unique class. In some ways, you can think of a window class as a license to create a certain kind of window.

Workshop

The Workshop is designed to help you anticipate possible questions, review what you've learned, and begin learning how to put your knowledge into practice. The answers to the quiz can be found in Appendix A, "Quiz Answers."

Quiz

1. What's a handle?

2. What problem does Hungarian notation attempt to solve?

3. What standard Win32 function is akin to the `main()` function in traditional C/C++ programs?

4. What header file is required as an import into all Windows programs?

Exercises

1. Use Hungarian notation to come up with variable names for the following variables: an integer that stores the score of a game, a string that stores the name of a color, and a Boolean that keeps track of whether a player in a game is alive.

2. Change the text displayed in the `WM_PAINT` message handler in the Skeleton application, and then rebuild and run the program to see the different results.

HOUR 3

Creating an Engine for Games

A game is a specialized type of program, but it is still just a program written in a programming language. This means that you can create a game just as you would any other Windows program, such as the Skeleton application you saw in Hour 2, "A Windows Game Programming Primer." However, certain game-specific tasks must be carried out in all games. Therefore, it would be quite helpful to organize the code in your games so that the game-specific code is isolated from the general Windows application code. In isolating this code, it might also be useful to build in some cool features that apply solely to games. The idea I'm suggesting is that of a *game engine*, which is a grouping of program code that performs tasks common to games. This lesson guides you through the design and development of a game engine that you'll build on throughout the remainder of the book.

In this hour, you'll learn:

- The importance of a game engine in game development
- How to design and develop a basic game engine for Windows game programming
- How to create an example program that demonstrates the power of the game engine

What Is a Game Engine?

Think about a few different games you like, and try to think of them in terms of how they might be designed under the hood. More importantly, see if you can figure out any common design elements that would apply to all the games. For example, do all the games have a background, a title screen, and background music? If so, it's possible that they are designed around the concept of a game engine. Game engines are particularly useful in situations in which you plan on creating more than one game, and you don't want to have to reinvent the wheel each time around. The idea is that you figure out what common functionality all games use, and you write it once and stick it in the game engine.

Another significant benefit of a game engine for Windows games is that it allows you to hide the messy details of Windows-specific code that doesn't necessarily have anything to do with a game. For example, most of the code you saw in the previous lesson has nothing to do with a game, but it's required of every Windows application. Rather than have you cut and paste this generic code to create a new game, I prefer hiding it in a game engine where you never have to fool with it again. You have an understanding of how it works, and you know it's there, but by not having to look at it you're free to focus on the more important and fun parts of your game code.

In case you're wondering, there's nothing magical or mysterious about a game engine. A game engine represents an organization of the code for a game so that general application tasks are separated from game-specific tasks. The benefit to the game developer is that you can add features to a game engine that you will be able to reuse in all of your future games. Additionally, using a game engine allows you to simplify the code for your games and focus your attention on the game code that matters most. Once you get accustomed to using a game engine, you'll wonder how games could be created any other way. In reality, most commercial game developers do have their own custom game engines that they've developed over years of learning what common features most games require.

Pondering the Role of a Game Engine

It is the responsibility of a game engine to handle the chores of setting up a game, making sure that it runs properly, and then shutting it down. Although it is true that these tasks are required of any program, certain aspects of initializing, running, and cleaning up after games are truly unique to games. Therefore, it is important for a game engine to address the unique needs of games and help make the process of building games around the engine as simple and straightforward as possible. With a well-designed game engine, you'll find that creating a game requires a lot less code than if you had not relied on a game engine. The idea is to develop certain core game routines once, stick them in the game engine, and then never bother with them again.

Breaking a Game Down into Events

You learned in the previous lesson that every Windows program can be broken down into events, which are things that take place while a program is running, such as mouse clicks and window resizes. Just as Windows programs have events that they must handle, games have their own unique set of events that must be taken into consideration during development. The initialization process of a game can be considered an event, and its responsibility is to load graphics and sounds for the game, clear the playing field, zero out the score, and so on. Similarly, user input carries over to games as well, meaning that mouse clicks and key presses are events that games certainly must concern themselves with. Additionally, keep in mind that in Windows it's possible for a game to be minimized or otherwise placed into the background, which means that you'll probably want to pause the game. This activation and reactivation process can be represented by a couple of events.

Although many other events could certainly factor into a game engine, the following are some of the core events applicable to just about any game:

- Initialization
- Start
- End
- Activation
- Deactivation
- Paint
- Cycle

3

The initialization event occurs when a game is first launched, and gives a game a chance to perform critical initial setup tasks, including creating the game engine itself. The start and end events correspond to the start and end of a game, and provide a good place to perform initialization and cleanup tasks associated with a specific game session. The activation and deactivation events come into play when a game is minimized or sent to the background, and then later restored. The paint event is sent when a game needs to draw itself, and is similar to the Windows WM_PAINT message. Finally, the cycle event allows a game to perform a single game cycle, which is very important, as you learn next.

Establishing the Timing for Games

If you've never taken a look at a game from a programming perspective, it might surprise you to learn how all the movement and animation in a game is orchestrated. You will learn all of the details of animated graphics in Hour 9, "A Crash Course in Game Animation," but for now I want to touch on the importance of game timing as it applies to animation and other facets of games. Every game except extremely simple card games relies on some sort of timing mechanism to allow the game to break down its execution into frames, or cycles. A *cycle* of a game is one slice of time, which usually corresponds to a snapshot of the game's graphics and data. If you think of a game as a movie playing on a VCR or DVD player, pressing pause allows you to view a single cycle. Stepping forward one frame in the video is like moving to the next cycle of the game. At any given cycle, a game takes care of updating its graphics, as well as performing any other calculations and processing related to how characters and objects are moving and interacting with each other.

A good way to get a grasp on the importance of game cycles is to take a practical game as an example. The classic Asteroids game was mentioned in the opener for this lesson, so let's use it as an example to demonstrate game cycles. When Asteroids first starts, the ship is created, along with a few asteroids. Each of these objects has an initial position and velocity. If Asteroids had no timing or game cycles, the game would be forever frozen in its initial state, as if you had pressed a permanent pause button when the game started. We know this isn't the case, however, because Asteroids starts out with the asteroids floating around the screen. If you could slow down Asteroids and view it a cycle at a time, you would notice that in each cycle the asteroids are only moved slightly. This is because there happen to be quite a few cycles taking place in a given period of time, which gives the effect of smooth motion. Figure 3.1 shows a few hypothetical cycles of Asteroids and how the asteroids move ever so slightly, along with the ship rotating counterclockwise.

FIGURE 3.1

A few cycles of a hypothetical Asteroids game reveals how the objects in the game change slightly with each cycle.

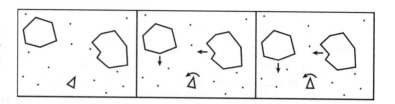

Figure 3.1 reveals how each cycle of the Asteroids game reflects a small change in the state of the objects in the game. Therefore, the role of a game cycle is to update the status of all the objects in the game, and then reflect these changes by updating the graphics shown on the screen. Judging by how fast things are visibly changing in most games, can you guess how often game cycles take place? Even the most sluggish of games include no less than 12 cycles per second, which is incidentally the minimum rate required to trick your eyes into thinking that they are seeing movement instead of a series of changing images. As a comparison, televisions display 30 different images (cycles) per second, whereas motion pictures rely on 24 images per second. You learn much more about the significance of different rates of animation in Hour 9. For now, it's important to understand that just about every game is highly dependent on periodic cycles.

A single screen of graphics in a game is known as a *frame*. Because a new screen of graphics is drawn during each game cycle, the speed of games is often measured in *frames per second*, or *fps*. Because the discussion in this lesson is centered on cycles, as opposed to frames, I refer to game speeds in *cycles per second*. However, cycles per second and frames per second are really the same measurement.

The more cycles a game can run through in a given amount of time, the smoother the game appears to run. As an extreme example, compare the "smoothness" of a slideshow to a motion picture. The slideshow abruptly moves from one still image to another with no transition or sense of smooth movement, whereas a motion picture shows fluid motion as if you were experiencing it in real time. Similarly, a game with only a few cycles per second will appear choppy, whereas a higher number of cycles per second will result in a much smoother game. A larger number of cycles per second also gives you more flexibility in speeding up or slowing down a game to arrive at a perfect speed.

Knowing that more cycles result in smoother graphics and better flexibility, you might think that you could crank up the cycles per second really high. As with most things in life, there is a trade-off when it comes to game cycles and game efficiency. The problem lies in the fact that the amount of processing taking place in a game in each cycle is often considerable, which means that to perform numerous cycles per second, your computer's processor and graphics card have to be able to keep up. Even with the blazingly fast computers prevalent these days, there are practical limitations as to how fast most computers can perform game processing. In reality, most games will fall in the range of 15 to 20 cycles per second, with a maximum speed approaching that of a motion picture at 30 cycles per second. Except for some rare situations, the minimum speed you should shoot for is 12 cycles per second.

Now that you understand how the timing of a game is expressed in terms of cycles, you can probably see why a cycle is a type of game event. It works like this: When a game first starts, you initialize the game engine with the game speed, in cycles per second. Let's say that you go with 12 cycles per second. The game engine is then responsible for setting up and managing a timer that fires a cycle event 12 times each second. The game code receives these cycle messages and handles them by updating the objects in the game and redrawing the game screen. You can think of a cycle event as a snooze alarm that keeps going off over and over; except in this case it's going off 12 times a second. Your game clearly isn't getting much sleep!

Speaking of sleep, another role of a game engine is to put a game to sleep whenever it is no longer the active window. In practical terms, putting a game to sleep simply means that the game engine stops sending cycle messages. Because no cycle messages are being sent, the game is effectively paused.

Developing a Game Engine

You now understand enough about what a game engine needs to accomplish that you can start assembling your own. In this section, you create the game engine that will be used to create all the games throughout the remainder of the book. Not only that, but also you'll be refining and adding cool new features to the game engine as you develop those games. By the end of the book, you'll have a powerful game engine ready to be deployed in your own game projects.

The Game Event Functions

The first place to start in creating a game engine is to create handler functions that correspond to the game events mentioned earlier in the lesson. Following are these functions, which should make some sense to you because they correspond directly to the game events:

```
BOOL GameInitialize(HINSTANCE hInstance);
void GameStart(HWND hWindow);
void GameEnd();
void GameActivate(HWND hWindow);
void GameDeactivate(HWND hWindow);
void GamePaint(HDC hDC);
void GameCycle();
```

The first function, GameInitialize(), is probably the only one that needs special explanation simply because of the argument that gets sent into it. I'm referring to the hInstance argument, which is of type HINSTANCE. This is a Win32 data type that refers to an application instance. An *application instance* is basically a program that has been loaded into memory and that is running in Windows. If you've ever used Alt+Tab to switch between running applications in Windows, you're familiar with different application instances. The HINSTANCE data type is a handle to an application instance, and it is very important because it allows a program to access its resources since they are stored with the application in memory.

The GameEngine Class

The game event handler functions are actually separated from the game engine itself, even though there is a close tie between them. This is necessary because it is organizationally better to place the game engine in its own C++ class. This class is called GameEngine and is shown in Listing 3.1.

> If you were trying to adhere strictly to object-oriented design principles, you would place the game event handler functions in the GameEngine class as virtual methods to be overridden. However, although that would represent good OOP design, it would also make it a little messier to assemble a game because you would have to derive your own custom game engine class from GameEngine in every game. By using functions for the event handlers, you simplify the coding of games at the expense of breaking an OOP design rule. Such are the trade-offs of game programming.

LISTING 3.1 The GameEngine Class Definition Reveals How the Game Engine Is Designed

```
1: class GameEngine
2: {
3: protected:
4:   // Member Variables
5:   static GameEngine*  m_pGameEngine;
6:   HINSTANCE           m_hInstance;
```

LISTING 3.1   Continued

```
 7:    HWND               m_hWindow;
 8:    TCHAR              m_szWindowClass[32];
 9:    TCHAR              m_szTitle[32];
10:    WORD               m_wIcon, m_wSmallIcon;
11:    int                m_iWidth, m_iHeight;
12:    int                m_iFrameDelay;
13:    BOOL               m_bSleep;
14:
15: public:
16:    // Constructor(s)/Destructor
17:          GameEngine(HINSTANCE hInstance, LPTSTR szWindowClass,
18:            LPTSTR szTitle, WORD wIcon, WORD wSmallIcon, int iWidth = 640,
19:            int iHeight = 480);
20:    virtual ~GameEngine();
21:
22:    // General Methods
23:    static GameEngine*  GetEngine() { return m_pGameEngine; };
24:    BOOL                Initialize(int iCmdShow);
25:    LRESULT             HandleEvent(HWND hWindow, UINT msg, WPARAM wParam,
26:                          LPARAM lParam);
27:
28:    // Accessor Methods
29:    HINSTANCE GetInstance() { return m_hInstance; };
30:    HWND      GetWindow() { return m_hWindow; };
31:    void      SetWindow(HWND hWindow) { m_hWindow = hWindow; };
32:    LPTSTR    GetTitle() { return m_szTitle; };
33:    WORD      GetIcon() { return m_wIcon; };
34:    WORD      GetSmallIcon() { return m_wSmallIcon; };
35:    int       GetWidth() { return m_iWidth; };
36:    int       GetHeight() { return m_iHeight; };
37:    int       GetFrameDelay() { return m_iFrameDelay; };
38:    void      SetFrameRate(int iFrameRate) { m_iFrameDelay = 1000 /
39:                iFrameRate; };
40:    BOOL      GetSleep() { return m_bSleep; };
41:    void      SetSleep(BOOL bSleep) { m_bSleep = bSleep; };
42: };
```

The GameEngine class definition reveals a subtle variable naming convention that wasn't mentioned in the previous lesson. This naming convention involves naming member variables of a class with an initial m_ to indicate that they are class members. Additionally, global variables are named with a leading underscore (_), but no m. This convention is useful because it helps you to immediately distinguish between local variables, member variables, and global variables in a program. The member variables for the GameEngine class all take advantage of this naming convention, which is evident in lines 5 through 13.

The GameEngine class defines a static pointer to itself, m_pGameEngine, which is used for outside access by a game program (line 5). The application instance and main window handles of the game program are stored away in the game engine using the m_hInstance and m_hWindow member variables (lines 6 and 7). The name of the window class and the title of the main game window are stored in the m_szWindowClass and m_szTitle member variables (lines 8 and 9). The numeric IDs of the two program icons for the game are stored in the m_wIcon and m_wSmallIcon members (line 10). The width and height of the game screen are stored in the m_iWidth and m_iHeight members (line 11). It's important to note that this width and height corresponds to the size of the game screen, or play area, not the size of the overall program window, which is larger to accommodate borders, a title bar, menus, and so on. The m_iFrameDelay member variable in line 12 indicates the amount of time between game cycles, in milliseconds. And finally, m_bSleep is a Boolean member variable that indicates whether the game is sleeping (paused).

The GameEngine constructor and destructor are defined after the member variables, as you might expect. The constructor is very important because it accepts arguments that dramatically impact the game being created. More specifically, the GameEngine() constructor accepts an instance handle, window classname, title, icon ID, small icon ID, and width and height (lines 17–19). Notice that the iWidth and iHeight arguments default to values of 640 and 480, respectively, which is a reasonable minimum size for game screens. The ~GameEngine() destructor doesn't do anything, but it's worth defining it in case you need to add some cleanup code to it later (line 20).

I mentioned that the GameEngine class maintains a static pointer to itself. This pointer is accessed from outside the engine using the static GetEngine() method, which is defined in line 23. The Initialize() method is another important general method in the GameEngine class, and its job is to initialize the game program once the engine is created (line 24). The HandleEvent() method is responsible for handling standard Windows events within the game engine, and is a good example of how the game engine hides the details of generic Windows code from game code (lines 25 and 26).

The remaining methods in the GameEngine class are *accessor methods* used to access member variables; these methods are all used to get and set member variables. The one accessor method to pay special attention to is SetFrameRate(), which sets the frame rate, or number of cycles per second, of the game engine (lines 38 and 39). Because the actual member variable that controls the number of game cycles per second is m_iFrameDelay, which is measured in milliseconds, it's necessary to perform a quick calculation to convert the frame rate in SetFrameRate() to milliseconds.

The source code for the GameEngine class provides implementations for the methods described in the header that you just saw, as well as the standard WinMain() and

3

WndProc() functions that tie into the game engine. The GameEngine source code also initializes the static game engine pointer, like this:

```
GameEngine *GameEngine::m_pGameEngine = NULL;
```

Listing 3.2 contains the source code for the game engine's WinMain() function.

LISTING 3.2   The WinMain() Function in the Game Engine Makes Calls to Game Engine Functions and Methods, and Provides a Neat Way of Separating Standard Windows Program Code from Game Code

```
 1: int WINAPI WinMain(HINSTANCE hInstance, HINSTANCE hPrevInstance,
 2:   PSTR szCmdLine, int iCmdShow)
 3: {
 4:   MSG         msg;
 5:   static int  iTickTrigger = 0;
 6:   int         iTickCount;
 7:
 8:   if (GameInitialize(hInstance))
 9:   {
10:     // Initialize the game engine
11:     if (!GameEngine::GetEngine()->Initialize(iCmdShow))
12:       return FALSE;
13:
14:     // Enter the main message loop
15:     while (TRUE)
16:     {
17:       if (PeekMessage(&msg, NULL, 0, 0, PM_REMOVE))
18:       {
19:         // Process the message
20:         if (msg.message == WM_QUIT)
21:           break;
22:         TranslateMessage(&msg);
23:         DispatchMessage(&msg);
24:       }
25:       else
26:       {
27:         // Make sure the game engine isn't sleeping
28:         if (!GameEngine::GetEngine()->GetSleep())
29:         {
30:           // Check the tick count to see if a game cycle has elapsed
31:           iTickCount = GetTickCount();
32:           if (iTickCount > iTickTrigger)
33:           {
34:             iTickTrigger = iTickCount +
35:               GameEngine::GetEngine()->GetFrameDelay();
36:             GameCycle();
37:           }
38:         }
```

LISTING 3.2   Continued

```
39:        }
40:      }
41:      return (int)msg.wParam;
42:    }
43:
44:    // End the game
45:    GameEnd();
46:
47:    return TRUE;
48: }
```

Although this WinMain() function is similar to the one you saw in the previous lesson, there is an important difference. The difference has to do with the fact that this WinMain() function establishes a game loop that takes care of generating game cycle events at a specified interval. The smallest unit of time measurement in a Windows program is called a *tick*, which is equivalent to one millisecond, and is useful in performing accurate timing tasks. In this case, WinMain() counts ticks in order to determine when it should notify the game that a new cycle is in order. The iTickTrigger and iTickCount variables are used to establish the game cycle timing in WinMain() (lines 5 and 6).

The first function called in WinMain() is GameInitialize(), which gives the game a chance to be initialized. Remember that GameInitialize() is a game event function that is provided as part of the game-specific code for the game, and therefore isn't a direct part of the game engine. A method that is part of the game engine is Initialize(), which is called to get the game engine itself initialized in line 11. From there WinMain() enters the main message loop for the game program, part of which is identical to the main message loop you saw in the previous lesson (lines 17—24). The else part of the main message loop is where things get interesting. This part of the loop first checks to make sure that the game isn't sleeping (line 28), and then it uses the frame delay for the game engine to count ticks and determine when to call the GameCycle() function to trigger a game cycle event (line 36). WinMain() finishes up by calling GameEnd() to give the game program a chance to wrap up the game and clean up after itself (line 45).

The other standard Windows function included in the game engine is WndProc(), which is surprisingly simple now that the HandleEvent() method of the GameEngine class is responsible for processing Windows messages:

```
LRESULT CALLBACK WndProc(HWND hWindow, UINT msg, WPARAM wParam, LPARAM lParam)
{
  // Route all Windows messages to the game engine
  return GameEngine::GetEngine()->HandleEvent(hWindow, msg, wParam, lParam);
}
```

All WndProc() really does is pass along all messages to HandleEvent(), which might at first seem like a waste of time. However, the idea is to allow a method of the GameEngine class to handle the messages so that they can be processed in a manner that is consistent with the game engine.

Speaking of the GameEngine class, now that you have a feel for the support functions in the game engine, we can move right along and examine specific code in the GameEngine class. Listing 3.3 contains the source code for the GameEngine() constructor and destructor.

LISTING 3.3   The GameEngine::GameEngine() Constructor Takes Care of Initializing Game Engine Member Variables, Whereas the Destructor is Left Empty for Possible Future Use

```
 1: GameEngine::GameEngine(HINSTANCE hInstance, LPTSTR szWindowClass,
 2:   LPTSTR szTitle, WORD wIcon, WORD wSmallIcon, int iWidth, int iHeight)
 3: {
 4:   // Set the member variables for the game engine
 5:   m_pGameEngine = this;
 6:   m_hInstance = hInstance;
 7:   m_hWindow = NULL;
 8:   if (lstrlen(szWindowClass) > 0)
 9:     lstrcpy(m_szWindowClass, szWindowClass);
10:   if (lstrlen(szTitle) > 0)
11:     lstrcpy(m_szTitle, szTitle);
12:   m_wIcon = wIcon;
13:   m_wSmallIcon = wSmallIcon;
14:   m_iWidth = iWidth;
15:   m_iHeight = iHeight;
16:   m_iFrameDelay = 50;   // 20 FPS default
17:   m_bSleep = TRUE;
18: }
19:
20: GameEngine::~GameEngine()
21: {
22: }
```

The GameEngine() constructor is relatively straightforward in that it sets all the member variables for the game engine. The only member variable whose setting might seem a little strange at first is m_iFrameDelay, which is set to a default frame delay of 50 milliseconds (line 16). You can determine the number of frames (cycles) per second for the game by dividing 1,000 by the frame delay, which in this case results in 20 frames per second. This is a reasonable default for most games, although specific testing might reveal that it needs to be tweaked up or down.

The Initialize() method in the GameEngine class is used to initialize the game engine. More specifically, the Initialize() method now performs a great deal of the messy Windows setup tasks such as creating a window class for the main game window and then creating a window from the class. Listing 3.4 shows the code for the Initialize() method.

LISTING 3.4   The GameEngine::Initialize() Method Handles Some of the Dirty Work That Usually Takes Place in WinMain()

```
 1: BOOL GameEngine::Initialize(int iCmdShow)
 2: {
 3:   WNDCLASSEX    wndclass;
 4:
 5:   // Create the window class for the main window
 6:   wndclass.cbSize         = sizeof(wndclass);
 7:   wndclass.style          = CS_HREDRAW | CS_VREDRAW;
 8:   wndclass.lpfnWndProc    = WndProc;
 9:   wndclass.cbClsExtra     = 0;
10:   wndclass.cbWndExtra     = 0;
11:   wndclass.hInstance      = m_hInstance;
12:   wndclass.hIcon          = LoadIcon(m_hInstance,
13:     MAKEINTRESOURCE(GetIcon()));
14:   wndclass.hIconSm        = LoadIcon(m_hInstance,
15:     MAKEINTRESOURCE(GetSmallIcon()));
16:   wndclass.hCursor        = LoadCursor(NULL, IDC_ARROW);
17:   wndclass.hbrBackground  = (HBRUSH)(COLOR_WINDOW + 1);
18:   wndclass.lpszMenuName   = NULL;
19:   wndclass.lpszClassName  = m_szWindowClass;
20:
21:   // Register the window class
22:   if (!RegisterClassEx(&wndclass))
23:     return FALSE;
24:
25:   // Calculate the window size and position based upon the game size
26:   int iWindowWidth = m_iWidth + GetSystemMetrics(SM_CXFIXEDFRAME) * 2,
27:       iWindowHeight = m_iHeight + GetSystemMetrics(SM_CYFIXEDFRAME) * 2 +
28:         GetSystemMetrics(SM_CYCAPTION);
29:   if (wndclass.lpszMenuName != NULL)
30:     iWindowHeight += GetSystemMetrics(SM_CYMENU);
31:   int iXWindowPos = (GetSystemMetrics(SM_CXSCREEN) - iWindowWidth) / 2,
32:       iYWindowPos = (GetSystemMetrics(SM_CYSCREEN) - iWindowHeight) / 2;
33:
34:   // Create the window
35:   m_hWindow = CreateWindow(m_szWindowClass, m_szTitle, WS_POPUPWINDOW |
36:     WS_CAPTION | WS_MINIMIZEBOX, iXWindowPos, iYWindowPos, iWindowWidth,
37:     iWindowHeight, NULL, NULL, m_hInstance, NULL);
38:   if (!m_hWindow)
39:     return FALSE;
```

3

LISTING 3.4   Continued

```
40:
41:    // Show and update the window
42:    ShowWindow(m_hWindow, iCmdShow);
43:    UpdateWindow(m_hWindow);
44:
45:    return TRUE;
46: }
```

This code should look at least vaguely familiar from the Skeleton program example in the previous lesson because it is carried over straight from that program. However, in Skeleton this code appeared in the WinMain() function, whereas here it has been incorporated into the game engine's Initialize() method. The primary change in the code is the determination of the window size, which is calculated based on the size of the client area of the window. The GetSystemMetrics() Win32 function is called to get various standard Window sizes such as the width and height of the window frame (lines 26 and 27), as well as the menu height (line 30). The position of the game window is then calculated so that the game is centered on the screen (lines 31 and 32).

The creation of the main game window in the Initialize() method is slightly different from what you saw in the previous lesson. The styles used to describe the window here are WS_POPUPWINDOW, WS_CAPTION, and WS_MINIMIZEBOX, which results in a different window from the Skeleton program (lines 35 and 36). In this case, the window is not resizable, and it can't be maximized; however, it does have a menu, and it can be minimized.

The Initialize() method is a perfect example of how generic Windows program code has been moved into the game engine. Another example of this approach is the HandleEvent() method, which is shown in Listing 3.5.

LISTING 3.5   The GameEngine::HandleEvent() Method Receives and Handles Messages That Are Normally Handled in WndProc()

```
 1: LRESULT GameEngine::HandleEvent(HWND hWindow, UINT msg, WPARAM wParam,
 2:    LPARAM lParam)
 3: {
 4:    // Route Windows messages to game engine member functions
 5:    switch (msg)
 6:    {
 7:      case WM_CREATE:
 8:        // Set the game window and start the game
 9:        SetWindow(hWindow);
10:        GameStart(hWindow);
11:        return 0;
12:
```

LISTING 3.5 Continued

```
13:      case WM_ACTIVATE:
14:      // Activate/deactivate the game and update the Sleep status
15:      if (wParam != WA_INACTIVE)
16:      {
17:        GameActivate(hWindow);
18:        SetSleep(FALSE);
19:      }
20:      else
21:      {
22:        GameDeactivate(hWindow);
23:        SetSleep(TRUE);
24:      }
25:      return 0;
26:
27:      case WM_PAINT:
28:        HDC         hDC;
29:        PAINTSTRUCT ps;
30:        hDC = BeginPaint(hWindow, &ps);
31:
32:        // Paint the game
33:        GamePaint(hDC);
34:
35:        EndPaint(hWindow, &ps);
36:        return 0;
37:
38:      case WM_DESTROY:
39:        // End the game and exit the application
40:        GameEnd();
41:        PostQuitMessage(0);
42:        return 0;
43:    }
44:    return DefWindowProc(hWindow, msg, wParam, lParam);
45: }
```

The HandleEvent() method looks surprisingly similar to the WndProc() method in the Skeleton program in that it contains a switch statement that picks out Windows messages and responds to them individually. However, the HandleEvent() method goes a few steps further than WndProc() by handling a couple more messages, and also making calls to game engine functions that are specific to each different game. First, the WM_CREATE message is handled, which is sent whenever the main game window is first created (line 7). The handler code for this message sets the window handle in the game engine (line 9), and then calls the GameStart() game event function to get the game initialized (line 10).

The WM_ACTIVATE message is a new one that you haven't really seen, and its job is to inform the game whenever its window is activated or deactivated (line 13). The wParam message parameter is used to determine whether the game window is being activated or deactivated (line 15). If the game window is being activated, the `GameActivate()` function is called and the game is awoken (lines 17 and 18). Similarly, if the game window is being deactivated, the `GameDeactivate()` function is called and the game is put to sleep (lines 22 and 23).

The remaining messages in the `HandleEvent()` method are pretty straightforward in that they primarily call game functions. The `WM_PAINT` message handler calls the standard Win32 `BeginPaint()` function (line 30) followed by the `GamePaint()` function (line 33). The `EndPaint()` function is then called to finish up the painting process (line 35); you learn a great deal more about `BeginPaint()` and `EndPaint()` in the next hour. Finally, the `WM_DESTROY` handler calls the `GameEnd()` function and then terminates the whole program (lines 40 and 41).

You've now seen all the code for the game engine, which successfully combines generic Windows code from the Skeleton example with new code that provides a solid framework for games. Let's now take a look at a new and improved Skeleton program that takes advantage of the game engine.

Building the Game Skeleton Example Program

The Skeleton program from the previous lesson demonstrated the basics of Windows programming, and it represents a minimal Windows program. The game engine you created in this lesson includes much of the code found in the Skeleton program, which allows you to create games without having to repeat any of that code again. In this section, you use the game engine to create a new program example called Game Skeleton that is somewhat of a revamped Skeleton program. However, you'll quickly realize that the Game Skeleton program is much easier to follow and understand because the game engine hides most of the mess associated with Windows programs.

You'll be glad to know that the Game Skeleton program isn't just a remake of the Skeleton program with the game engine thrown in. Because the game engine includes support for establishing a game loop complete with timed game cycles, it only makes sense to take advantage of that feature. So, the Game Skeleton program demonstrates the power of game cycles and how they make it possible to get interesting graphical effects with little effort. More specifically, you find out how to rapidly draw skeleton icons at random locations on the game screen and see firsthand how the speed of the game loop impacts the performance of a game.

Writing the Program Code

The Game Skeleton program example is divided into two source files: the Skeleton.h header file and the Skeleton.cpp source code file. Listing 3.6 contains the code for the Skeleton.h header file, which is relatively simple. Keep in mind that all of the code for the Game Skeleton example program is available on the accompanying CD-ROM.

LISTING 3.6 The Skeleton.h Header File Simply Imports a Few Header Files and Declares the Important Global Game Engine Pointer

```
 1: #pragma once
 2:
 3: //------------------------------------------------------------
 4: // Include Files
 5: //------------------------------------------------------------
 6: #include <windows.h>
 7: #include "Resource.h"
 8: #include "GameEngine.h"
 9:
10: //------------------------------------------------------------
11: // Global Variables
12: //------------------------------------------------------------
13: GameEngine* _pGame;
```

This header file includes the familiar windows.h, as well as Resource.h and GameEngine.h. After importing these header files, a global game engine pointer, pGame, is defined. This pointer is very important because it will provide the Game Skeleton program access to the game engine.

The Game Skeleton program is fleshed out in the Skeleton.cpp source code file, which is shown in Listing 3.7

LISTING 3.7 The Skeleton.cpp Source Code File Reveals How Straightforward the Program Code for a Minimal Windows Program Becomes When a Game Engine Is Used

```
 1: //------------------------------------------------------------
 2: // Include Files
 3: //------------------------------------------------------------
 4: #include "Skeleton.h"
 5:
 6: //------------------------------------------------------------
 7: // Game Engine Functions
 8: //------------------------------------------------------------
 9: BOOL GameInitialize(HINSTANCE hInstance)
10: {
```

3

LISTING 3.6   Continued

```
11:    // Create the game engine
12:    _pGame = new GameEngine(hInstance, TEXT("Game Skeleton"),
13:      TEXT("Game Skeleton"), IDI_SKELETON, IDI_SKELETON_SM);
14:    if (_pGame == NULL)
15:      return FALSE;
16:
17:    // Set the frame rate
18:    _pGame->SetFrameRate(15);
19:
20:    return TRUE;
21: }
22:
23: void GameStart(HWND hWindow)
24: {
25:    // Seed the random number generator
26:    srand(GetTickCount());
27: }
28:
29: void GameEnd()
30: {
31:    // Cleanup the game engine
32:    delete _pGame;
33: }
34:
35: void GameActivate(HWND hWindow)
36: {
37:    HDC    hDC;
38:    RECT   rect;
39:
40:    // Draw activation text on the game screen
41:    GetClientRect(hWindow, &rect);
42:    hDC = GetDC(hWindow);
43:    DrawText(hDC, TEXT("Activated!"), -1, &rect,
44:      DT_SINGLELINE | DT_CENTER | DT_VCENTER);
45:    ReleaseDC(hWindow, hDC);
46: }
47:
48: void GameDeactivate(HWND hWindow)
49: {
50:    HDC    hDC;
51:    RECT   rect;
52:
53:    // Draw deactivation text on the game screen
54:    GetClientRect(hWindow, &rect);
55:    hDC = GetDC(hWindow);
56:    DrawText(hDC, TEXT("Deactivated!"), -1, &rect,
57:      DT_SINGLELINE | DT_CENTER | DT_VCENTER);
58:    ReleaseDC(hWindow, hDC);
59: }
60:
```

LISTING 3.6 Continued

```
61: void GamePaint(HDC hDC)
62: {
63: }
64:
65: void GameCycle()
66: {
67:    HDC    hDC;
68:    HWND   hWindow = _pGame->GetWindow();
69:
70:    // Draw the skeleton icon at random positions on the game screen
71:    hDC = GetDC(hWindow);
72:    DrawIcon(hDC, rand() % _pGame->GetWidth(), rand() % _pGame->GetHeight(),
73:      (HICON)(WORD)GetClassLong(hWindow, GCL_HICON));
74:    ReleaseDC(hWindow, hDC);
75: }
```

3

The really interesting thing about the code for the Game Skeleton program is how the only functions present in the code are the game event functions described in GameEngine.h. The first of these functions is GameInitialize(), whose responsibility is to get the program started off on the right foot. More specifically, the GameInitialize() function creates a GameEngine object and assigns it to the _pGame global variable (lines 12–15). The GameInitialize() function then sets the frame rate for the game to 15 frames per second, which is a little slower than the default setting of 20 frames per second (line 18). This change is primarily to demonstrate how you will often change the default frame rate for games depending on their specific needs.

The GameStart() function is next, and its job is to initialize game data and start a game. In the case of the Game Skeleton program, there really isn't any game data, so the only code in GameStart() is code to seed a random number generator. I mentioned earlier that the Game Skeleton program draws skeleton icons at random positions on the screen. In order to successfully generate random numbers for these positions, you have to seed the random number generator. This is accomplished with a call to the standard C library function, srand() (line 26).

Similar to the GameStart() function, the GameEnd() function is designed to clean up game data once a game is over. In this case the GameEnd() function is only required to cleanup the game engine (lines 29–33).

The GameActivate() and GameDeactivate() functions are very similar to each other in the Game Skeleton program. Both are here just to demonstrate how you can respond to game activations and deactivations, and they do so by drawing text on the game screen. For example, the GameActivate() function obtains the client rectangle for the game window (line 41), and then uses it as the basis for drawing a line of text centered on the game screen (lines 43 and 44). I realize that some of this graphics code probably looks a little strange, but don't worry too much about it because the next lesson gives you the whole scoop on how to draw graphics in Windows. Speaking of strange graphics code, the GamePaint() function is responsible for painting the game screen, but in this case all the painting takes place in the GameCycle() function, so GamePaint() does nothing.

The GameCycle() function is the last function in the Game Skeleton program, and without a doubt the most interesting. The job of this function is to draw a skeleton icon at a random location on the game screen. This might not seem like a big deal, but keep in mind that you set the frame rate to 15 frames per second, which means that the GameCycle() function is getting called 15 times every second; that means 15 icons get drawn in random locations every second! The first step in the GameCycle() function is to obtain a window handle for the main game window (line 68); this window handle is important because it allows you to draw on the game screen. The drawing actually takes place on lines 72 and 73 when the Win32 DrawIcon() function is called to draw the skeleton icon. The standard rand() function is called to determine a random location on the game screen, and the icon is extracted from the game window class using the Win32 GetClassLong() function.

Although I admittedly threw you a few curves with the graphics code in the Game Skeleton program, you've got to admit that it's considerably easier to follow than the original Skeleton program. This is the benefit of relying on the game engine to take care of a lot of the dirty work associated with Windows game programming.

Testing the Finished Product

You'll be glad to know that the Game Skeleton program is much more fun to tinker with than the Skeleton program—thanks to the game engine. When you run Game Skeleton, you are presented with a game screen that rapidly fills up with skeleton icons, as shown in Figure 3.2.

It doesn't take too long for the Game Skeleton screen to fill up with skeleton icons, as shown in Figure 3.3. This has a lot to do with the fact that you have the game set up so that it runs through 15 game cycles per second. You could dramatically slow down or speed up the icons being drawn by altering the frame rate of the game in the GameInitialize() function.

Another interesting point to make about the Game Skeleton program is how it isn't smart enough to repaint the skeleton icons. In other words, if you minimize the program or activate another window in front of it, the game screen will get cleared. This happens because the GamePaint() function doesn't have any code to redraw the skeleton icons in response to the game screen needing a repaint.

FIGURE 3.2

The Game Skeleton program example demonstrates how the game engine makes it possible to focus solely on the game-specific aspects of a Windows program.

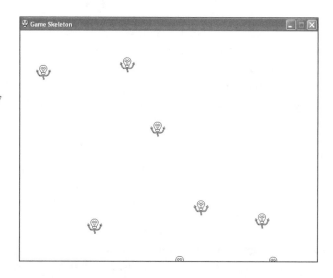

FIGURE 3.3

The timing aspect of the game engine causes the Game Skeleton program to fill up quite quickly with randomly placed skeleton icons.

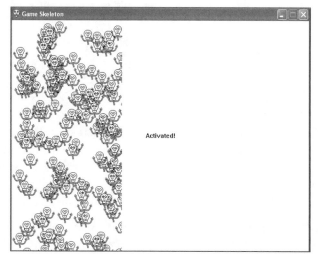

The repaint problem in the Game Skeleton program is addressed in Hour 4, "Drawing Basic Graphics," when you explore Windows graphics in more detail.

Summary

This hour took an important leap forward in your game development path by guiding you through the design and development of a basic game engine for Windows games. You learned about the importance of a game engine, as well as what code goes into creating a fully functioning game engine. Although features certainly need to be added to the game engine to make it more powerful, the elements are in place for creating Windows games with much less effort than if you didn't create the engine. It's okay if you don't fully appreciate the role of the game engine in making your life easier as a game programmer. But trust me; you will eventually come to appreciate the game engine for how it simplifies game development and allows you to focus on the most important facets of game design.

Hour 4 finally explains the mysteries behind the graphics code that you've seen in both the Skeleton and Game Skeleton program examples. You learn some of the fundamental graphics techniques that will carry you forward throughout the rest of the book. You also get to create a pretty neat example program that demonstrates your new graphics knowledge.

Q&A

Q Why doesn't the game engine code include implementations of the game event functions?

A The game event functions are deliberately left unimplemented in the game engine because it is up to each game program to provide implementations for them. This is how the game engine allows games to perform game-specific tasks in a structured manner. Put another way, your job in developing games via the game engine is to flesh out the game event functions with your own game code.

Q Why is the main game window created in the game engine not resizable?

A The main game window is not resizable so that the game code can be dramatically simplified. You will typically create game graphics that target a particular resolution, or game screen size; in which case, all the code in the game revolves around this size. If the user can change the game screen size at will, it becomes very difficult to scale the graphics appropriately. Granted, this is less of a problem in some games in which the playfield is somewhat open-ended (Asteroids, for example), but in other games it can be a real problem because the playfield might be a very specific shape and size (Pac-Man, for example). The game engine allows you to set the game screen to any size you want, but it doesn't allow the user to change that size.

Workshop

The Workshop is designed to help you anticipate possible questions, review what you've learned, and begin learning how to put your knowledge into practice. The answers to the quiz can be found in Appendix A, "Quiz Answers."

Quiz

1. What is a game cycle?

2. What is the minimum speed you should shoot for with games, and why?

3. What does it mean to "put a game to sleep?"

Exercises

1. Try out different sizes for the game screen to see how it impacts the Game Skeleton example program. Remember, the width and height of the game screen are set as the last two arguments to the GameEngine() constructor.

2. Experiment with different frame rates for the Game Skeleton program to see how they impact the speed at which the skeleton icons are drawn.

3

HOUR 4

Learning to Draw Basic Graphics

A computer game consists of many different pieces, all of which must come together to form a unique entertainment experience for the player. By far the most important piece of any game is the graphics. Graphics are used to represent the characters and creatures in a game, as well as background worlds and other interesting objects that factor into the overall game design. Granted, games have certainly done well because of factors outside of graphics, such as game play and sound quality, but those games are very rare. Besides, nowadays game players expect to see high-quality graphics just as we all expect to see high-quality visual effects in Hollywood movies. So, it's important to develop a solid understanding of graphics programming and how to use graphics wisely in your games.

In this hour, you'll learn:

- The basics of drawing graphics using the Windows Graphics Device Interface

- What a device context is, and why it's important to GDI graphics

- How to paint text and primitive graphics in Windows
- How to create a sample program that demonstrates GDI graphics in the context of the game engine

Graphics Essentials

Before jumping into the details of how graphics work in Windows and how they are applied to games, it's important to establish some ground rules and gain an understanding of how computer graphics work in general. More specifically, you need to have a solid grasp on what a graphics coordinate system is, as well as how color is represented in computer graphics. The next couple of sections provide you with this knowledge, which you'll put to practical use a little later in the hour.

The Graphics Coordinate System

All graphical computing systems use some sort of *graphics coordinate system* to specify how points are arranged in a window or on the screen. Graphics coordinate systems typically spell out the *origin* (0,0) of the system, as well as the axes and directions of increasing value for each of the axes. If you're not a big math person, this simply means that a coordinate system describes how to pinpoint any location on the screen as an XY value. The traditional mathematical coordinate system familiar to most of us is shown in Figure 4.1.

FIGURE 4.1

The traditional XY coordinate system is commonly used in math.

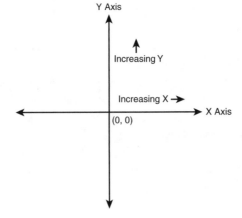

Windows graphics relies on a similar coordinate system to specify how and where drawing operations take place. Because all drawing in Windows takes place within the confines of a window, the Windows coordinate system is applied relative to a particular window. The Windows coordinate system has an origin that is located in the upper-left corner of the window, with positive X values increasing to the right and positive Y values increasing down. All values in the Windows coordinate system are positive integers. Figure 4.2 shows how this coordinate system looks.

FIGURE 4.2

The Windows XY coordinate system is similar to the traditional coordinate system except that it applies to the client area of windows.

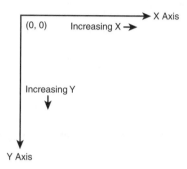

If the Windows graphics coordinate system sounds a little complicated, just think of it in terms of a classic game of Battleship. In Battleship, you try to sink enemy ships by firing torpedoes at specific locations on a grid. Battleship uses its own coordinate system to allow you to specify locations on the grid where ships might be located. Similarly, when you draw graphics in Windows you specify locations in the client area of a window, which is really just a grid of little squares called *pixels*.

The Basics of Color

A topic that impacts almost every area of game graphics is color. Fortunately, most computer systems take a similar approach to representing color. The main function of color in a computer system is to accurately reflect the physical nature of color within the confines of a computer. This physical nature isn't hard to figure out; anyone who has experienced the joy of Play-Doh can tell you that colors react in different ways when they are combined with each other. Like Play-Doh, a computer color system needs to be able to mix colors with accurate, predictable results.

Color computer monitors provide possibly the most useful insight into how software systems implement color. A color monitor has three electron guns: red, green, and blue. The output from these three guns converges on each pixel on the screen, exciting phosphors to produce the appropriate color. The combined intensities of each gun determine the resulting pixel color. This convergence of different colors from the monitor guns is very similar to the convergence of different colored Play-Doh.

Technically speaking, the result of combining colors on a monitor is different from that of combining similarly colored Play-Doh. The reason for this is that color combinations on a monitor are *additive*, meaning that mixed colors are added together to become white; Play-Doh color combinations are *subtractive*, meaning that mixed colors are subtracted from each other to become black. The additive or subtractive nature of a color combination is dependent on the physical properties of the particular medium involved.

The Windows color system is very similar to the physical system used by color monitors; it forms unique colors by using varying intensities of the colors red, green, and blue. Therefore, Windows colors are represented by the combination of the numeric intensities of the primary colors (red, green, and blue). This color system is known as *RGB (Red Green Blue)* and is standard across most graphical computer systems.

Table 4.1 shows the numeric values for the red, green, and blue components of some basic colors. Notice that the intensities of each color component range from 0 to 255 in value.

TABLE 4.1 Numeric RGB Color Component Values for Commonly Used Colors

Color	Red	Green	Blue
White	255	255	255
Black	0	0	0
Light Gray	192	192	192
Dark Gray	128	128	128
Red	255	0	0
Green	0	255	0
Blue	0	0	255
Yellow	255	255	0
Purple	255	0	255

The Win32 API defines a structure named COLORREF that combines the red, green, and blue components of an RGB color into a single value. The COLORREF structure is important because it is used throughout the Win32 API to represent RGB colors. To create a color as a COLORREF structure, you use the RGB() macro, which accepts red, green, and blue color components as arguments. Here is an example of creating a solid green color using RGB():

```
COLORREF green = RGB(0, 255, 0);
```

The color created in this line of code is green because the green component (the middle argument) is specified as 255, whereas the red and blue components are specified as 0. Changing the values of these three arguments alters the mix of the color—with lower numbers resulting in darker colors and higher numbers resulting in brighter colors.

Examining Graphics in Windows

In order to seamlessly support a wide range of graphical output devices, Windows handles the painting of graphics a little differently from you might expect. Instead of allowing you to draw directly to the screen, a layer called the *Graphics Device Interface*, or *GDI*, is used to separate drawing operations from physical graphics devices such as monitors and printers. You learned about the GDI to some extent in Hour 2, "A Windows Game Programming Primer," but now it's time to dig in and see how it actually works.

The role of the GDI is to provide a programmatic interface for painting graphics in a generic manner. GDI operations work in concert with Windows graphics drivers to communicate with physical graphics devices. Figure 4.3 shows the architecture of GDI.

FIGURE 4.3
The GDI in Windows provides a layer between graphics operations at the application (game) level and physical graphics devices.

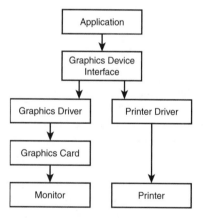

4

Keep in mind that although I use the term "generic" to describe GDI graphics, the Win32 API provides a broad range of GDI graphics operations. In fact, the remainder of this hour is devoted to showing you some of the interesting things you can do with GDI graphics.

Working with Device Contexts

The key component in GDI graphics is the graphics context, or *device context*, which acts as a gateway to a physical graphics device. You can think of a device context as a generic drawing surface to which graphics are painted. In other words, a device context is like a piece of paper that you can draw on, except once you've drawn on it the resulting image can be displayed on a variety of different devices. Device contexts are very important in Windows programming because they make it possible to have device-independent graphics.

A device context is really just a way to allow you to draw in a generic manner, without worrying about where the drawing is physically taking place. Device contexts are necessary so that the same graphics routines can be used regardless of whether you are drawing to the screen, to memory, or to a printer. Granted, in game programming you'll always be drawing to the screen, but that doesn't mean you can just ignore the GDI. You have to go through a device context in order to draw graphics using the GDI, so you might as well get comfortable with them. The important thing to remember is that all the drawing you do in Windows is actually done to a device context. It is then up to Windows to make sure that the drawing on the device context gets properly displayed on the screen.

You normally obtain a device context by calling the Win32 `BeginPaint()` function. If you recall from earlier hours, `BeginPaint()` is paired with `EndPaint()` to form a graphics drawing pair, like this:

```
PAINTSTRUCT ps;
HDC hDC = BeginPaint(hWindow, &ps);
*** GDI drawing operations go here ***
EndPaint(hWindow, &ps);
```

The `BeginPaint()` function requires a window handle and a `PAINTSTRUCT` structure. The `PAINTSTRUCT` structure is filled with information pertaining to the device context, and is rarely used. The `BeginPaint()` function returns a handle to a device context, which is all you need to start drawing graphics using the GDI. The `EndPaint()` function is then responsible for releasing the device context once you're finished with it.

It's also possible to paint outside of the `BeginPaint()`/`EndPaint()` function pairing, in which case you have to obtain a device context in a slightly different manner. This is done using the `GetDC()` function, which only requires a window handle to obtain a device context. You must match the `GetDC()` function with the `ReleaseDC()` function to release the device context when you're finished using it. Following is an example of how these two functions are used together:

```
hDC = GetDC(hWindow);
*** GDI drawing operations go here ***
ReleaseDC(hWindow, hDC);
```

In addition to device contexts, the GDI also supports the following common graphics components that you'll find useful in developing game graphics:

- Pens
- Brushes
- Palettes
- Bitmaps

The next few sections look at these graphics components in more detail, and help you to understand how they fit into the GDI, as well as game graphics.

Writing with Pens

Pens in the GDI are analogous to ink pens in the real world; they are used to draw lines and curves. Pens can be created with varying widths and in different colors. There are two kinds of pens: cosmetic and geometric. A *cosmetic pen* draws lines of fixed width and lines that need to be drawn quickly. A *geometric pen* draws scaleable lines, lines that are wider than a single pixel, and lines with unique styles. Given that cosmetic pens offer the speediest approach to drawing, they are the pen type most commonly used in game programming.

Painting with Brushes

Brushes in GDI are analogous to paint brushes in the real world; they are used to paint the interior of polygons, ellipses, and paths. Although you might commonly think of a paint brush as using a solid color, GDI brushes can also be defined based on a bitmap pattern, which means that they paint in a pattern instead of as a solid. Brushes and pens go hand in hand when drawing graphics using the GDI. For example, if you were to draw a circle, a pen would be used to draw the outline of the circle, whereas a brush would be used to paint its interior.

4

Drawing Images with Bitmaps

A *bitmap* is a graphical image stored as an array of pixels. If you've ever used a digital camera or seen pictures on a Web site, you are already familiar with bitmaps. Bitmaps are rectangular, so the number of pixels in a bitmap is the width of the bitmap multiplied by its height. Bitmaps can contain multiple colors and are often based on a specific palette, or set of colors. Bitmaps are, without a doubt, the most important graphics component in game programming because they provide the most flexibility in terms of using high-quality artwork. Unfortunately, bitmaps are a little more complex to use at the programming level, which is why you don't go into details with them until the next hour.

Managing Color with Palettes

A *palette* is a set of colors used by the GDI when rendering a bitmap. As an example, many images (bitmaps) are stored as 256-color images, which means that they use colors from a palette of 256 colors. Depending on the specific settings of your screen in Windows, the GDI might have to map the color palette for a bitmap to the color palette used by the screen. Most of the complexities of palette management are handled automatically by Windows. However, you do have to concern yourself somewhat with the palette used by bitmaps. Hour 5, "Drawing Graphical Images," shows you how to work with palettes as they relate to bitmaps.

Painting Windows

As you might remember from previous hours, the Win32 API includes a special message that is delivered to a Window whenever it needs to be painted. This message is called WM_PAINT, and it serves as one of the main ways in which graphics are drawn to a window. A window might need to be repainted when the window is first created, when the window is uncovered from behind other windows, or a variety of other reasons. The bottom line is that you must handle the WM_PAINT message in order to paint the inside (client area) of a window.

When I refer to painting or drawing to a window, I'm really referring to the *client area* of a window. This is the rectangular part of a window inside the window's border that doesn't include the window frame, caption, menu, system menu, or scrollbars. Figure 4.4 reveals how the coordinates of the client area begin in the upper-left corner of the window and increase down and to the right, as you learned earlier in the hour. This coordinate system is very important because most GDI graphics operations are based on them.

FIGURE 4.4

Most graphics in a Windows program are drawn to the client area of a window, which uses the Windows graphics coordinate system.

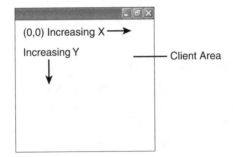

As you might recall, the handling of messages takes place in the WndProc() function for a window. However, we were smart enough to make things simpler with the game engine you created in the previous hour. More specifically, a WndProc() function is hidden in the game engine that handles the WM_PAINT message and calls the GamePaint() function. However, the call to the GamePaint() function is sandwiched between calls to the Win32

BeginPaint() and EndPaint() functions. This allows you to place graphics code in the GamePaint() function of your game without having to worry about obtaining a device context. Following is the WM_PAINT message handler in the WndProc() function, which shows how the GamePaint() function is called:

```
case WM_PAINT:
  HDC          hDC;
  PAINTSTRUCT ps;
  hDC = BeginPaint(hWindow, &ps);

  // Paint the game
  GamePaint(hDC);

  EndPaint(hWindow, &ps);
  return 0;
```

The device context obtained from BeginPaint() is passed into the GamePaint() function to delegate the specifics of drawing graphics to each individual game. Following is an example of a simple GamePaint() function:

```
void GamePaint(HDC hDC)
{
  *** GDI drawing operations go here ***
}
```

GDI painting operations are performed on a device context, or DC, which is passed into the function via the hDC argument. Following is an example of drawing a line in the GamePaint() function:

```
void GamePaint(HDC hDC)
{
  MoveToEx(hDC, 0, 0, NULL);
  LineTo(hDC, 50, 50);
}
```

This code shows how to draw a line using GDI functions. You learn more about how these functions work in a moment, but first let's take a look at how to draw text.

Painting Text

In Windows, text is treated no differently from graphics, which means that text is painted using GDI functions. The primary GDI function used to paint text is TextOut(), which looks like this:

```
BOOL TextOut(HDC hDC, int x, int y, LPCTSTR szString, int iLength);
```

Following are the meanings of the different arguments to the TextOut() function:

- hDC—Device context handle
- x—X coordinate of text position
- y—Y coordinate of text position
- szString—The string to be painted
- iLength—Length of the string to be painted

The first argument to TextOut() is a handle to a device context, which is provided by the BeginPaint() function. All GDI functions require a handle to a device context, so you should get comfortable with seeing it in graphics code. The x and y arguments specify the position of the upper-left corner of the first string character relative to the client area (Figure 4.5), whereas the last two arguments are a pointer to a string and the length of the string, in characters.

FIGURE 4.5

Text is drawn at the upper-left corner of the first character with respect to the client area of a window.

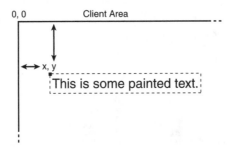

Following is an example of how to use the TextOut() function to draw a simple string of text:

```
void GamePaint(HDC hDC)
{
  TextOut(hDC, 10, 10, TEXT("Michael Morrison"), 16);
}
```

Another text-related function that you might consider using is DrawText(), which allows you to draw text within a rectangle, as opposed to drawing it at a specified point. As an example, you can use DrawText() to center a line of text on the screen by specifying the entire client window as the rectangle in which to draw the text. Following is an example of using the DrawText() function in place of TextOut():

```
void GamePaint(HDC hDC)
{
  RECT rect;
  GetClientRect(hWindow, &rect);
  DrawText(hDC, TEXT("Michael Morrison"), -1, &rect,
    DT_SINGLELINE | DT_CENTER | DT_VCENTER);
}
```

In this example, the text is drawn centered both horizontally and vertically in the entire client area of the window. Notice that the length of the text string isn't necessary; this is because -1 is provided as the length, which means that the length should be automatically determined because the string is null-terminated. The flags in the last argument of DrawText() are used to determine how the text is drawn, which in this case causes the text to be centered both horizontally and vertically.

Painting Primitive Graphics

Graphics primitives form a fundamental part of GDI, and consist of lines, rectangles, circles, polygons, ovals, and arcs. You can create pretty impressive graphics by using these primitives in conjunction with each other. Following are the major graphics primitives you can paint with GDI functions:

- Lines
- Rectangles
- Ellipses
- Polygons

The next few sections demonstrate how to draw each of these graphics primitives, along with how to use pens and brushes to add color to them.

Lines

Lines are the simplest of the graphics primitives and are therefore the easiest to draw. Lines are painted using the MoveToEx() and LineTo() functions, which set the current position and draw a line connecting the current position to a specified end point, respectively. The idea is that you use MoveToEx() to mark the position of a point, and then use LineTo() to draw a line from that point to another point. You can continue to draw lines connecting points by calling LineTo() again. Following are what these functions look like:

```
BOOL MoveToEx(HDC hDC, int x, int y, LPPOINT pt);
BOOL LineTo(HDC hDC, int x, int y);
```

An XY coordinate in Windows is referred to as a *point*, and is often represented by the Win32 POINT structure. The POINT structure is used throughout Windows to represent coordinates for a variety of different operations. The POINT structure consists solely of two long integer fields, x and y.

Both functions accept a handle to a device context and an X and Y value for the point of the line. The MoveToEx() function also allows you to provide an argument to store the previous point. In other words, you can pass a pointer to a point as the last argument of MoveToEx() if you're interested in finding out the last point used for drawing. Following is an example of using MoveToEx() and LineTo() to draw a couple of lines:

```
void GamePaint(HDC hDC)
{
  MoveToEx(hDC, 10, 40, NULL);
  LineTo(hDC, 44, 10);
  LineTo(hDC, 78, 40);
}
```

In this code, the drawing position is first set by calling MoveToEx() and providing the XY position of a point. Notice that the final argument is passed as NULL, which indicates that you aren't interested in finding out the previous point. The LineTo() function is then called twice, which results in two connected lines being drawn.

Rectangles

Rectangles represent another type of graphics primitive that are very easy to draw. The Rectangle() function enables you to draw a rectangle by specifying the upper-left corner and the lower-right corner of the rectangle. Following is the prototype for the Rectangle() function, which helps to reveal its usage:

```
BOOL Rectangle(HDC hDC, int xLeft, int yTop, int xRight, int yBottom);
```

The Rectangle() function is straightforward in that you pass it rectangular dimensions of the bounding rectangle for the rectangle to be painted. Following is an example of how to draw a couple of rectangles:

```
void GamePaint(HDC hDC)
{
  Rectangle(hDC, 16, 36, 72, 70);
  Rectangle(hDC, 34, 50, 54, 70);
}
```

There isn't really anything remarkable about this code; it simply draws two rectangles of differing sizes and positions. Don't forget that the last two arguments to the Rectangle() function are the X and Y positions of the lower-right corner of the rectangle, not the width and height of the rectangle.

Ellipses

Although they are curved, ellipses are drawn in a manner very similar to rectangles. An ellipse is simply a closed curve, and therefore can be specified by a bounding rectangle.

The circular explosions in the classic Missile Command game are a very good example of a filled ellipse. Ellipses are painted using the `Ellipse()` function, which looks like this:

```
BOOL Ellipse(HDC hDC, int xLeft, int yTop, int xRight, int yBottom);
```

The `Ellipse()` function accepts the rectangular dimensions of the bounding rectangle for the ellipse to be painted. Following is an example of drawing an ellipse using the `Ellipse()` function:

```
void GamePaint(HDC hDC)
{
  Ellipse(hDC, 40, 55, 48, 65);
}
```

Not surprisingly, this code draws an ellipse based on four values that specify a bounding rectangle for the ellipse.

> Arcs, chords, and pies can also be drawn using Win32 GDI functions very similar to the `Ellipse()` function.

Polygons

The trickiest of graphics primitives is the polygon, which is a closed shape consisting of multiple line segments. The asteroid shapes in the popular Asteroids game are a great example of polygons. Polygons are painted using the `Polygon()` function, which follows:

```
BOOL Polygon(HDC hDC, CONST POINT* pt, int iCount);
```

As you can see, the `Polygon()` function is a little more complex than the other graphics primitives functions in that it takes an array of points and the number of points as arguments. A polygon is painted by connecting each of the points in the array with lines. Following is an example of how to draw a polygon shape using the `Polygon()` function:

```
void GamePaint(HDC hDC)
{
  POINT points[3];
  points[0] = { 5, 10 };
  points[1] = { 25, 30 };
  points[2] = { 15, 20 };
  Polygon(hDC, points, 3);
}
```

The key to this code is the creation of the array of points, `points`, which contains three `POINT` structures. These three `POINT` structures are initialized with XY pairs, and the whole array is then passed into the `Polygon()` function, along with the total number of points in the array. That's all that is required to draw a polygon shape consisting of multiple line segments.

Working with Pens and Brushes

It's one thing to simply draw graphics primitives in their default mundane black and white style. It's quite another to control the line and fill colors of the primitives to get more interesting results. This is accomplished by using pens and brushes, which are standard GDI objects used in drawing graphics primitives. Whether you realize it or not, you're already using pens and brushes when you draw graphics primitives. It's just that the default pen is black, and the default brush is the same color as the window background.

Creating Pens

If you want to change the outline of a graphics primitive, you need to change the pen used to draw it. This typically involves creating a new pen, which is accomplished with the `CreatePen()` function:

```
HPEN CreatePen(int iPenStyle, int iWidth, COLORREF crColor);
```

The first argument is the style of the pen, which can be one of the following values: `PS_SOLID`, `PS_DASH`, `PS_DOT`, `PS_DASHDOT`, `PS_DASHDOTDOT`, or `PS_NULL`. All but the last value specify different kinds of lines drawn with the pen, such as solid, dashed, dotted, or a combination of dashed and dotted. The last value, `PS_NULL`, indicates that no outline is to be drawn; in other words, the pen doesn't draw. The second argument to `CreatePen()` is the width of the pen, in logical units, which typically correspond to pixels when drawing to the screen. The final argument is the color of the pen, which is specified as a `COLORREF` value. To help make things clear, following is an example of how to create a solid blue pen that is one-pixel wide:

```
HPEN hBluePen = CreatePen(PS_SOLID, 1, RGB(0, 0, 255));
```

Keep in mind that simply creating a pen isn't enough to begin drawing with it. In a moment you learn how to select a pen into a device context and begin drawing with it. However, let's first learn how to create brushes.

Creating Brushes

Although several different kinds of brushes are supported in the GDI, I'd like to focus on solid brushes, which allow you to fill in graphics shapes with a solid color. You create a solid brush using the Win32 `CreateSolidBrush()` function, which simply accepts a `COLORREF` structure. Following is an example of creating a purple brush:

```
HBRUSH hPurpleBrush = CreateSolidBrush(RGB(255, 0, 255));
```

Notice in this code that a value of 255 is used to set the red and blue components of the color, which is how you are achieving purple in the final mixed color. Now that you have a handle to a brush, you're ready to select it into a device context and begin painting with it.

Selecting Pens and Brushes

In order to use a pen or brush you've created, you must select it into a device context using the Win32 SelectObject() function. This function is used to select graphics objects into a device context, and applies to both pens and brushes. Following is an example of selecting a pen into a device context:

```
HPEN hPen = SelectObject(hDC, hBluePen);
```

In this example, the hBluePen you just created is selected into the device context. Also notice that the previously selected pen is returned from SelectObject() and stored in hPen. This is important because you will typically want to restore GDI settings to their original state when you're finished painting. In other words, you want to remember the original pen so that you can set it back when you're finished. Following is an example of restoring the original pen using SelectObject():

```
SelectObject(hDC, hPen);
```

Notice that it is no longer important to remember the return value of SelectObject() because you are restoring the original pen.

One more important task related to creating pens is that of deleting graphics objects that you create. This is accomplished with the DeleteObject()function, which applies to both pens and brushes. It is important to delete any graphics objects that you create after you've stopped using them and they are no longer selected into a device context. Following is an example of cleaning up the blue pen:

```
DeleteObject(hBluePen);
```

Selecting and deleting brushes is very similar to selecting and deleting pens. Following is a more complete example to illustrate:

```
HBRUSH hBrush = SelectObject(hDC, hPurpleBrush);
// *** Do some drawing here! ***
SelectObject(hDC, hBrush);
DeleteObject(hPurpleBrush);
```

In this example, the purple brush from the previous section is selected into the device context, some drawing is performed, and the old brush is restored. The purple brush is then deleted to clean up everything.

4

Building the Trippy Example Program

At this point, you've seen bits and pieces of GDI graphics code, and you've learned how to carry out basic drawing operations with a variety of different graphics shapes. You've also learned how to tweak the appearance of those shapes by creating and using different pens and brushes. You're now ready to put what you've learned into a complete example program that demonstrates how to draw graphics in the context of a game. Okay, you're not really creating a game in this hour, but you are using the game engine to draw some pretty neat graphics. The example program I'm referring to is called Trippy, and its name comes from the fact that it displays a psychedelic series of rectangles in different sizes and colors.

The idea behind the Trippy program is to draw a random rectangle in each cycle of the game engine. Although the rectangles are drawn outside of the GamePaint() function in response to a game cycle, it is still important to demonstrate how to draw within GamePaint() so that the drawing isn't lost when the window is minimized or hidden. For this reason, Trippy draws a grid of lines in GamePaint() to demonstrate how graphics drawn in this function are retained even if the window must be repainted. The actual rectangles are drawn in GameCycle(), which means that they are lost if the window is repainted. Let's take a look at how the code actually works for this example program.

Writing the Program Code

The fun begins in the Trippy program example with the header file, Trippy.h, which is shown in Listing 4.1. All of the code for the Trippy program is available on the accompanying CD-ROM.

LISTING 4.1   The Trippy.h Header File Imports a Few Header Files and Declares the Global Game Engine Pointer, as Well as the Previous Rectangle That Was Drawn

```
 1: #pragma once
 2:
 3: //------------------------------------------------------------
 4: // Include Files
 5: //------------------------------------------------------------
 6: #include <windows.h>
 7: #include "Resource.h"
 8: #include "GameEngine.h"
 9:
10: //------------------------------------------------------------
11: // Global Variables
12: //------------------------------------------------------------
13: GameEngine* _pGame;
14: RECT        _rcRectangle;
```

This code isn't too mysterious. In fact, the only real difference between this header and the one you saw for the Game Engine example in the previous hour is the declaration of the _rcRectangle global variable (line 14). This rectangle stores the previously drawn rectangle, which allows you to alter its position randomly for the next rectangle. The end result is that the rectangles tend to randomly drift around the screen, as opposed to popping up in random locations all over the place.

Moving right along, remember that we're now taking advantage of the game engine to simplify a great deal of the work in putting together programs. In fact, all that is really required of the Trippy program is to provide implementations of the core game functions. Listing 4.2 contains the code for the first of these functions, GameInitialize().

LISTING 4.2 The GameInitialize() Function Creates the Game Engine and Sets the Frame Rate to 15 Cycles Per Second

```
 1: BOOL GameInitialize(HINSTANCE hInstance)
 2: {
 3:   // Create the game engine
 4:   _pGame = new GameEngine(hInstance, TEXT("Trippy"),
 5:     TEXT("Trippy"), IDI_TRIPPY, IDI_TRIPPY_SM);
 6:   if (_pGame == NULL)
 7:     return FALSE;
 8:
 9:   // Set the frame rate
10:   _pGame->SetFrameRate(15);
11:
12:   return TRUE;
13: }
```

The GameInitialize() function is responsible for creating the game engine (lines 4 and 5) and setting the frame rate for it (line 10). In this case, the frame rate is set at 15 cycles per second (frames per second), which is plenty to demonstrate the psychedelic nature of the rectangles.

Following up on GameInitialize() is GameStart(), which actually gets things going. Listing 4.3 shows the code for the GamStart() function.

LISTING 4.3 The GameStart() Function Seeds the Random Number Generator and Establishes an Initial Rectangle

```
 1: void GameStart(HWND hWindow)
 2: {
 3:   // Seed the random number generator
 4:   srand(GetTickCount());
 5:
```

LISTING 4.3 Continued

```
 6:   // Set the position and size of the initial rectangle
 7:   _rcRectangle.left = _pGame->GetWidth() * 2 / 5;
 8:   _rcRectangle.top = _pGame->GetHeight() * 2 / 5;
 9:   _rcRectangle.right = _rcRectangle.left + _pGame->GetWidth() / 5;
10:   _rcRectangle.bottom = _rcRectangle.top + _pGame->GetHeight() / 5;
11: }
```

Any program that makes use of random numbers is responsible for seeding the built-in random number generator. This is accomplished in line 4 with the call to srand(). You'll see this line of code in virtually all the program examples throughout the book because most of them involve the use of random numbers; random numbers often play heavily into the development of games. The remainder of the GameStart() function is responsible for setting the position and size of the initial rectangle to be drawn (lines 7–10). This rectangle is sized proportionally to the client area of the main program window, and positioned centered within the client area.

I mentioned earlier that part of the Trippy program was to demonstrate the difference between drawing graphics in the GamePaint() function, as opposed to drawing them in GameCycle(). Listing 4.4 shows the code for GamePaint(), which in this case is responsible for drawing a bunch of grid lines as a background for the rectangles.

LISTING 4.4 The GamePaint() Function Draws a Grid of Lines to Fill the Entire Client Area

```
 1: void GamePaint(HDC hDC)
 2: {
 3:   // Draw grid lines as a background for the rectangles
 4:   const int iGridLines = 50;
 5:   for (int i = 1; i <= iGridLines; i++)
 6:   {
 7:     // Draw a horizontal grid line
 8:     MoveToEx(hDC, _pGame->GetWidth() * i / iGridLines , 0, NULL);
 9:     LineTo(hDC, _pGame->GetWidth() * i / iGridLines, _pGame->GetHeight());
10:
11:     // Draw a vertical grid line
12:     MoveToEx(hDC, 0, _pGame->GetHeight() * i / iGridLines, NULL);
13:     LineTo(hDC, _pGame->GetWidth(), _pGame->GetHeight() * i / iGridLines);
14:   }
15: }
```

The line drawing functions you learned about in this hour, MoveToEx() and LineTo(), are both used to draw a series of horizontal (lines 8 and 9) and vertical (lines 12 and 13) grid lines in the client area. Because these lines are being drawn in GamePaint(), they are not lost when the window is repainted. You can easily alter the number of grid lines by changing the value of the iGridLines variable (line 4).

The GameCycle() function is where the actual rectangles are drawn, as shown in Listing 4.5.

LISTING 4.5   The GameCycle() Function Randomly Alters the Position of the Rectangle, and Then Draws It in a Random Color

```
 1: void GameCycle()
 2: {
 3:    HDC          hDC;
 4:    HWND         hWindow = _pGame->GetWindow();
 5:    HBRUSH       hBrush;
 6:
 7:    // Randomly alter the position and size of the rectangle
 8:    int iInflation = (rand() % 21) - 10;
 9:    InflateRect(&_rcRectangle, iInflation, iInflation);
10:    OffsetRect(&_rcRectangle, (rand() % 19) - 9, (rand() % 19) - 9);
11:
12:    // Draw the new rectangle in a random color
13:    hBrush = CreateSolidBrush(RGB(rand() % 256, rand() % 256, rand() % 256));
14:    hDC = GetDC(hWindow);
15:    FillRect(hDC, &_rcRectangle, hBrush);
16:    ReleaseDC(hWindow, hDC);
17:    DeleteObject(hBrush);
18: }
```

4

The GameCycle() function is interesting in that it does a few things you haven't seen before. First of all, it uses two new Win32 functions, InflateRect() and OffsetRect(), to randomly alter the size and position of the previous rectangle. A random inflation value is first calculated, which is in the range of -10 to 10 (line 8). This value is then used as the basis for shrinking or growing the rectangle using the InflateRect() function (line 9). The rectangle is then offset by a random amount between -9 and 9 using the OffsetRect() function (line 10).

With the new rectangle size and position figured out, the GameCycle() function moves on to determine a new fill color for it. This is accomplished by randomly selecting a color for a new solid brush (line 13). If you recall, earlier I mentioned that you had to select a graphics object into a device context in order to use it. In this case, however, it's possible to use a different rectangle function that allows you to directly provide the brush to be used. I'm referring to FillRect(), which accepts a handle to a device context, a rectangle, and a brush (line 15). After filling the rectangle with the solid brush, the device context is released (line 16) and the brush is deleted (line 17).

Testing the Finished Product

Now that you've worked through the code for the Trippy program example, I suspect that you're ready to see it in action. Figure 4.6 shows the program running in all of its psychedelic splendor.

FIGURE 4.6
The Trippy program example uses rapidly drawn rectangles to achieve a psychedelic effect.

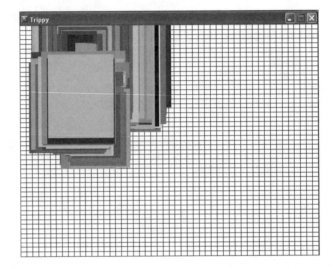

If you recall from the code, the Trippy program is smart enough to redraw the grid lines in the background if the window is minimized or resized, but it doesn't take into account redrawing the rectangles. You can test this out by covering part of the window with another window, and then revealing the window again. The portion of rectangles not covered will be erased because of the repaint, but the part of the window that was visible will remain untouched. This redraw problem is not too difficult to fix. In fact, you solve the problem in Hour 5 when you build a slideshow program example using bitmap images.

Summary

This hour laid the groundwork for the game graphics that you develop and use throughout the remainder of the book. I know; you're no doubt getting antsy because you've yet to touch on anything terribly game-specific. However, keep in mind that game programming, especially in Windows, involves a variety of different programming disciplines that must come together before a complete game can be built. Even so, hopefully you're feeling a significant sense of accomplishment now that you know how to draw graphics with a little animated pizzazz using the GDI.

Hour 5 continues along in the exploration of GDI graphics programming by uncovering the most important game development concept: graphical images. You find out about bitmap images, how they work, and how to load and display them in a Windows program. You also put your image handling skills to work by creating a slideshow that you can use to display storyboards for your games, or maybe just pictures from your last vacation.

Q&A

Q Why are color components specified in the range 0 to 255?

A This has to do with the fact that Windows assumes that you are okay with using 8 bits to represent each color component. Allowing 8 bits for each component results in 256 possible shades of that component (0–255). 8 bits was chosen because 24-bit color is largely considered enough to display extremely high-quality color in graphical images. By combining three 8-bit color components, you arrive at 24-bit graphics. Of course, you might be familiar with the fact that many computers now take advantage of 32-bit color. 32-bit color adds an extra 8-bit channel to a standard 24-bit color to represent the transparency of the resulting pixel. In other words, a 32-bit color consists of three 8-bit color components, as well as an 8-bit value that indicates how transparent (or opaque) the image pixel is.

Q Why is it necessary to delete graphics objects after creating them when drawing graphics?

A Deleting graphics objects is very important because Windows doesn't inherently know when you are finished using them, and therefore they have a tendency to sit around wasting memory. In fact, undeleted graphics objects represent one of the common *memory leaks* in Windows programs, which are objects created by a program that are no longer used but still take up memory. Memory leaks are a very bad thing, and should be avoided at all costs. If you stay disciplined about cleaning up after yourself, you shouldn't have too much trouble with graphics objects being inadvertently left in memory.

Workshop

The Workshop is designed to help you anticipate possible questions, review what you've learned, and begin learning how to put your knowledge into practice. The answers to the quiz can be found in Appendix A, "Quiz Answers."

Quiz

1. How is the Windows graphics coordinate system laid out?

2. What three colors form the components of a color in Windows?

3. If you use the GetDC() function to obtain a device context for drawing graphics, what function must you call to release the device context?

4. When you use the TextOut() function to draw text, what is the drawing position based on?

Exercises

1. Create a pen in a color of your choosing, and then use it in the GamePaint() function of the Trippy program to draw grid lines in that color.

2. Modify the random color values used for the brush in the GameCycle() method of the Trippy program to see how different combinations work. For example, change the red component so that it is fixed at either 0 or 255, and then shorten the range of the green or blue component.

Hour 5

Drawing Graphical Images

We've all heard that a picture is worth a thousand words, and when it comes to computer games, they might be worth even more than that. Or to translate into nerd talk, a 640x480 image is worth 307,200 pixels. Okay, maybe nerd talk is something I should avoid. The point is that pictures (images) are extremely important in computer games because they provide the only means of incorporating artwork into the games. Sure, it's nice to be able to draw lines, rectangles, and ellipses using GDI functions, but it would take a great deal of effort to draw a menacing creature out of graphics primitives. For that reason, we use graphical images as a means of visualizing graphical parts of games. This hour is all about showing you how to load and display graphical images.

In this hour, you'll learn:

- The fundamentals of bitmap images and why they are important in game programming
- About the inner workings of bitmap images

- How to develop an all-purpose bitmap class for use in games
- How to use the bitmap class to represent slide images in a slideshow program

The Basics of Bitmap Images

Images in windows games are represented by *bitmaps*, which are rectangular graphics objects containing rows and columns of little squares called *pixels*. The name bitmap comes from the fact that the rows and columns determine how to map the pixels to the screen; the pixels themselves are composed of bits. Each pixel in a bitmap is a solid color. In fact, the only information associated with a pixel is its color. So, you can think of a bitmap as a rectangular arrangement of little colored squares. If you're old enough to remember the popular Lite Brite toy, you definitely have an understanding of how a bitmap works. Lite Brite, which is still manufactured today by Hasbro, allows you to plug colored pegs into a black plastic grid to draw pictures.

Two types of bitmaps are supported in Windows: *device-dependent bitmaps* and *device-independent bitmaps*. Device-dependent bitmaps are stored in a manner determined by a specific device, whereas device-independent bitmaps are stored in such a way that they can be displayed on any device. All the bitmaps you work with in this book are device-independent bitmaps, which are sometimes referred to as *DIBs*. Just keep in mind that when I refer to "bitmaps" from here on, I'm really referring to DIBs.

You are probably familiar with bitmaps from the popular .BMP file type that is used throughout Windows. BMP is the standard image format used in Windows, and is also the format you'll be using to work with bitmaps throughout this book. Although GIF and JPEG have certainly surpassed BMP as image formats for use on the Web, BMP is still used a great deal by Windows users. Not only that, but the BMP image format is considerably simpler and easier to work with at a programming level than GIF and JPEG. You can use the standard Paint program built into Windows to create and edit BMP files, or use Microsoft Photo Editor, which offers more features for working with photographic images.

Although there is only one bitmap image format, not all bitmap images are created equal. First of all, the bitmap image format allows you to create bitmaps with varying numbers of colors. More specifically, you can create 8-bit bitmaps that use 256 (palletized) colors or 24-bit bitmaps that use more than 16 million colors. You can also create bitmaps that use a technique known as *compression* to help reduce the size of the bitmap file. To help keep the code simple, the bitmaps you use throughout the book are limited to 8-bit uncompressed bitmaps. This is very important to remember because other types of bitmaps won't work with the bitmap code you develop in this hour.

Regardless of how you create a bitmap, it ultimately ends up as a file with a .BMP file extension. To use such a bitmap in a Windows program, you have two options:

- Read the bitmap directly from the file
- Store the bitmap as a resource and read it from memory

In the first option, the Windows program opens the bitmap file from disk and reads in the image data. It then uses the bitmap image data to create a GDI bitmap graphics object that can be drawn to a device context. The second option involves storing a bitmap as a resource within the executable program, which means that you don't have to include the bitmap file with the program once it is compiled. The advantage to this option is that you are able to distribute your game as a single program file. Fortunately, the bitmap class you create later in this hour supports both approaches to using bitmaps.

Peeking Inside a Bitmap

In order to use bitmaps in your games, you must have a basic understanding of how they are put together. More specifically, you need to have knowledge of the inner structure of a bitmap because you must write code that reads this structure and extracts information about the bitmap. This is necessary so that you can create a bitmap object that can be drawn. You'll be glad to know that bitmaps aren't too terribly complicated, as is evident in Figure 5.1.

FIGURE 5.1

The structure of a bitmap consists of three parts: a header, color table, and image data.

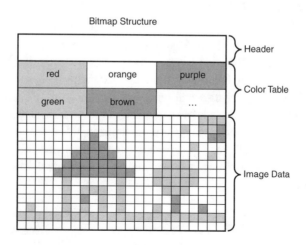

The figure reveals that every bitmap consists of three basic parts:

- Header
- Color table
- Image data

The header contains information pertaining to the overall makeup of the bitmap, such as its width, height, number of bits per pixel (8 or 24), and so on. The color table contains the palette for the bitmap, which is the list of colors used throughout the image. The color table is extremely important for 8-bit bitmaps because it describes up to 256 colors used by pixels in the image. 24-bit bitmaps don't need a color table because their colors are sufficiently described by the pixels themselves. The image data is where the actual pixels of the bitmap are stored. For example, if a bitmap is 10x12, it is 10 pixels across and 12 pixels down for a total of 120 pixels. If it is an 8-bit image, each pixel requires 8 bits (1 byte) to describe its color. So, the image data for this bitmap would consist of 120 bytes. To determine the color of each pixel, you would look up the byte value in the color table to see what color the pixel is.

Of course, all this color table and image data stuff takes place automatically once you load an image and start using it with GDI functions. In other words, you only have to worry yourself with the inner workings of bitmaps when you first load the bitmap from a file or resource. Once loaded, you use a handle to a bitmap to draw it to a device context in much the same way as you drew graphics primitives to a device context in Hour 4, "Learning to Draw Basic Graphics."

Developing a Bitmap Class

Although I could provide you with a handful of bitmap functions and set you on your way, bitmaps provide a perfect opportunity to take advantage of object-oriented programming. More specifically, you can create a class that includes all the code required to load and draw bitmaps, and then use the class to create bitmap objects that are much easier to use than if you had created several functions. Knowing this, the next couple of sections are devoted to the design and development of a bitmap class that you will use throughout the book in just about every example program from here on. Although the bitmap class is admittedly a little tricky in places, once created it is unbelievably easy to use. So, the idea is to create the class once with the knowledge that it will make your life incredibly easier in coming hours.

How It Will Work

The idea behind the `Bitmap` class is to provide a means of loading bitmaps from a file or resource, as well as drawing bitmaps to a device context. By incorporating these capabilities into a class, you'll be able to create `Bitmap` objects in your games that are very easy to use and that hide the messy aspects of working with bitmaps. The `Bitmap` class has the following requirements:

- Loads a bitmap from a file
- Loads a bitmap from a resource
- Creates a blank bitmap
- Draws a bitmap to a device context
- Obtains the width and height of a bitmap

The first two requirements are fairly obvious from the earlier discussion. The third requirement isn't terribly important just yet, but you might find yourself wanting to create a blank bitmap for some reason, so why not have that capability? Besides, later in Hour 10, "Making Things Move with Sprites," you'll see how bitmaps are important for solving a flicker problem associated with animation; the solution requires blank bitmaps. The final requirement isn't terribly important, but you might encounter a situation in which it's necessary to determine the width and height of a bitmap. The information is readily available when you load a bitmap, so you might as well make it accessible from the `Bitmap` class.

Putting the Code Together

The code for the `Bitmap` class is admittedly complex in places, so I'm not suggesting that you expect to understand every nuance of it immediately. In fact, my goal isn't really to make you a bitmap expert, which is practically a requirement in order to fully understand the `Bitmap` class. Even so, I don't like the idea of accepting code at face value without any explanation, so I'd like for you to have a general understanding of what is going on in the `Bitmap` class. If I gloss over a section of code, just understand that the goal here is to get you using bitmaps in as little time as possible so that you can quickly move on to placing them in games.

The Class Definition

Win32 defines several data structures that pertain to bitmaps, so you'll see several different ones throughout the `Bitmap` class code. One of these structures is `BITMAPINFOHEADER`, which is a structure that stores the header information associated with a bitmap. When you read a bitmap from a file or resource, you will store its header in a

BITMAPINFOHEADER structure. Another important bitmap-related structure is RGBQUAD, which is used to store the four 8-bit components of a 32-bit color. Even though you're working with 8-bit images, it's still necessary to use the RGBQUAD structure for loading bitmaps.

Speaking of 8-bit images, you know that an 8-bit bitmap requires up to 256 colors. The following code is for a custom structure named BITMAPINFO_256 that stores the header and a color table for a bitmap with 256 colors:

```
struct BITMAPINFO_256
{
  BITMAPINFOHEADER  bmiHeader;
  RGBQUAD           bmiColors[256];
};
```

This structure will come in quite handy in a moment when you begin loading bitmaps. Before we get into that, however, let's take a look at the Bitmap class definition, which is shown in Listing 5.1.

LISTING 5.1   The Bitmap Class Definition Includes the Member Variables and Methods Used to Manage Bitmaps

```
 1: class Bitmap
 2: {
 3: protected:
 4:   // Member Variables
 5:   HBITMAP m_hBitmap;
 6:   int     m_iWidth, m_iHeight;
 7:
 8:   // Helper Methods
 9:   void Free();
10:
11: public:
12:   // Constructor(s)/Destructor
13:   Bitmap();
14:   Bitmap(HDC hDC, LPTSTR szFileName);
15:   Bitmap(HDC hDC, UINT uiResID, HINSTANCE hInstance);
16:   Bitmap(HDC hDC, int iWidth, int iHeight, COLORREF crColor =
17:     RGB(0, 0, 0));
18:   virtual ~Bitmap();
19:
20:   // General Methods
21:   BOOL Create(HDC hDC, LPTSTR szFileName);
22:   BOOL Create(HDC hDC, UINT uiResID, HINSTANCE hInstance);
23:   BOOL Create(HDC hDC, int iWidth, int iHeight, COLORREF crColor);
24:   void Draw(HDC hDC, int x, int y);
25:   int  GetWidth() { return m_iWidth; };
26:   int  GetHeight() { return m_iHeight; };
27: };
```

This listing reveals the overall makeup of the Bitmap class, including its member variables, constructors, destructor, and methods. The m_hBitmap member variable is used to store a handle to the bitmap, which is extremely important for drawing the bitmap to a device context using the GDI (line 5). The m_iWidth and m_iHeight member variables store the width and height of the bitmap, respectively (line 6).

The Constructors and Destructor

Notice in Listing 5.1 that there are three constructors in the Bitmap class in addition to the default constructor, each of which corresponds to one of the different approaches to creating bitmaps (lines 14–16)). Each Bitmap() constructor has a corresponding Create() method that is used to handle the work of loading the bitmap data and creating it as a GDI object (lines 20–22). The Free()method is a helper method used within the Bitmap class to free up the memory associated with the bitmap (line 9). The Draw() method shouldn't be too surprising because it provides a means of drawing the bitmap to a device context (line 23). And finally, the GetWidth() and GetHeight() methods are simply used to obtain the width and height of the bitmap, respectively (lines 25 and 26).

The CD-Rom for this book contains the code for all the Bitmap() constructors, as well as the destructor and the Free() method.

The Bitmap() constructors are all very simple in that they call a corresponding Create() function to carry out the specifics of creating a bitmap based on a file, a resource, or a solid color. The default constructor doesn't do much of anything other than initialize member variables; the idea behind this constructor is that you will eventually call the Create() method directly to load the Bitmap object with data. The destructor calls the Free() method to release the memory associated with the bitmap and clear the bitmap handle.

The Free() method first checks to see if the bitmap handle, m_hBitmap, is valid—in which case, it deletes the GDI bitmap object and clears out the handle. This is all that's required to free the memory associated with the bitmap.

Three Ways to Create a Bitmap

There are three Create() methods in the Bitmap class that are fairly long, but you can access them from the CD-ROM. The first Create() method is responsible for loading a bitmap from a file.

The method starts out by calling Free() to make sure that any previous bitmap data is cleaned up; this would apply if the same Bitmap object was being reused for a different bitmap. The file is then opened, and the resulting file handle is checked to make sure that the open proceeded without a hitch. The file header for the bitmap is then read from the

5

file, and some checks are made to ensure that it was read without any problems. The file header contains information about the bitmap file itself, whereas the info header contains information about the bitmap. The info header is read next, and another error check is performed.

With the headers properly read from the file, the Create() method is ready to get down to the real business of reading the bitmap data. The color table for the bitmap is read and followed by the image data. It is worth pointing out the usage of the CreateDIBSection() Win32 function, which is used to obtain a handle to a GDI bitmap object from raw bitmap data. This function ultimately makes it possible to read a bitmap and prepare it for use with the GDI. The last step in the Create() method is to free the bitmap memory if an error occurred while reading its data.

The second Create() method supported by the Bitmap class is used to load a bitmap from a resource.

This method follows roughly the same pattern as the first Create() method—except in this case, the bitmap information is retrieved from a resource in memory, as opposed to being read from a file. The first step is to find the bitmap resource, load the resource into memory, and then lock the resource so that you can access its raw data. You don't have to worry about the color table in this case because it is already included in the bitmap information. The width and height of the bitmap are stored next, and the image data is copied and used as the basis for obtaining a bitmap handle using CreateDIBSection(). Finally, the method concludes by performing some clean up in case an error occurred.

The last of the Create() methods is the one that creates a blank bitmap in a solid color.

This method is considerably different from the other two Create() methods because it has the luxury of not having to involve itself with any existing bitmap data. Instead, it uses a Win32 function called CreateCompatibleBitmap() to create an entirely new bitmap based on the supplied device context. Because the width and height are provided as arguments to the method, they are easy to store. Most of the work in the method has to do with filling the bitmap with a solid color. A compatible device context is first created to hold the bitmap for drawing, and then a solid brush in the specified color is created. The bitmap is then selected into the device context and filled with the solid brush. The graphics objects are then cleaned up to finish the job of this Create() method .

Drawing the Bitmap

The three Create() methods are by far the toughest parts of the Bitmap class, so the Draw() method will be a welcome relief.

The Draw() method is actually similar to the third Create() method because it involves drawing a bitmap. However, in this case the bitmap is being drawn to an outside device context, as opposed to you drawing on the bitmap itself. The Draw() method accepts a device context and an XY coordinate as arguments. This reveals how simple it is to use the method to draw a bitmap. The first step in drawing the bitmap is ensuring that the bitmap handle is valid. If the handle checks out okay, a compatible device context is created to temporarily store the bitmap, and the bitmap is selected into the device context. This is an important step because drawing images always takes place from one device context to another.

The bitmap is actually drawn using the Win32 BitBlt() function, which draws an image from a source device context to a specified location on a destination device context. Drawing a bitmap image is sometimes referred to as *blitting*, which is where the name BitBlt() comes from; you are blitting the image bits when you draw the image. The Draw() method finishes up by cleaning up the temporary device context.

The x and y arguments to the Bitmap::Draw() method are specified relative to the device context the bitmap is being drawn on, and they indicate the upper left corner of the bitmap image.

You now have a complete, fully working Bitmap class that is ready to be used in games to load and draw bitmap images. Let's move on and take a look at a program example that puts the Bitmap class through its paces.

Building the Slideshow Example Program

Because you haven't learned about how to process user input such as key strokes and mouse clicks, it still isn't quite possible to create a game yet. However, the remainder of the hour guides you through the creation of a surprisingly practical example program that happens to serve as a great demonstration of the Bitmap class. I'm referring to the Slideshow program, which uses a series of bitmap images to present a slideshow. The Slideshow program takes advantage of the timing mechanism built into the game engine to provide a delay between moving to each successive image in a slideshow. The Bitmap class proves to be quite useful as a means of loading and drawing bitmaps from both files and resources.

Before looking at the code for the Slideshow program, let's quickly go over what it is supposed to accomplish:

5

- Create several bitmaps from files
- Create several bitmaps from resources
- Create a blank bitmap in a solid color
- Draw the bitmaps one at a time as part of a slideshow
- Time the presentation of the slides in the slideshow appropriately

These requirements for the Slideshow program make it pretty clear what is supposed to happen. The only thing worth mentioning is that you wouldn't normally mix the two approaches of loading bitmaps from files and resources. Generally speaking, it makes sense to commit to one approach or the other. In the case of a slideshow, it probably makes more sense to load bitmaps from files because you might want to change the images without recompiling the program. However, in this case it's important to demonstrate the different uses of the Bitmap class.

Writing the Program Code

The header for the Slideshow program example is the best place to start in terms of getting acquainted with how it works. Check out Listing 5.2 to get a feel for what the header is all about. Don't forget that you can access all of the code for the Slideshow program on the accompanying CD-ROM.

LISTING 5.2   The Slideshow.h Header File Imports a Few Header Files and Declares Several Global Variables

```
 1: #pragma once
 2:
 3: //----------------------------------------------------------------
 4: // Include Files
 5: //----------------------------------------------------------------
 6: #include <windows.h>
 7: #include "Resource.h"
 8: #include "GameEngine.h"
 9: #include "Bitmap.h"
10:
11: //----------------------------------------------------------------
12: // Global Variables
13: //----------------------------------------------------------------
14: HINSTANCE    _hInstance;
15: GameEngine*  _pGame;
16: const int    _iNUMSLIDES = 7;
17: Bitmap*      _pSlides[_iNUMSLIDES];
18: int          _iCurSlide;
```

Other than declaring a few global variables, there aren't really any surprises here. The _hInstance variable is necessary to store because a program instance handle is necessary in order to load bitmaps as resources (line 14). An *instance* is simply a program loaded into memory; all the programs you have open and running in Windows are considered instances. An *instance handle* is a reference to an instance, which allows you to interact with the instance and do things such as load resources that are stored in the executable program file. Because you're going to be loading bitmaps as resources, it's important to store away an instance handle for the Slideshow program.

The _pGame global variable is used to store a pointer to the game engine, which should be familiar to you by now (line 15). The remaining member variables relate specifically to the slideshow functionality. The global constant _iNUMSLIDES is used to set the number of slides in the slideshow, and should be changed if you modify the number of slides in the slideshow (line 16). The _pSlides variable is perhaps the most important because it stores away pointers to the Bitmap objects (line 17); these objects correspond to the slides in the slideshow. Finally, the _iCurSlide variable represents the array index of the current slide, which is the slide currently being displayed (line 18). This variable is important because it keeps track of where the slideshow is in the slide sequence.

The global variables in the Slideshow header file are somewhat revealing, but you obviously have to look at the code for the game functions to really get a feel for what's going on. Listing 5.3 contains the code for the GameInitialize() function, which is the first of the Slideshow game functions.

LISTING 5.3   The GameInitialize() Function Creates the Game Engine, Sets the Frame Rate to One Cycle Per Second, and Stores Away the Instance Handle for the Program

5

```
 1: BOOL GameInitialize(HINSTANCE hInstance)
 2: {
 3:   // Create the game engine
 4:   _pGame = new GameEngine(hInstance, TEXT("Slideshow"),
 5:     TEXT("Slideshow"), IDI_SLIDESHOW, IDI_SLIDESHOW_SM);
 6:   if (_pGame == NULL)
 7:     return FALSE;
 8:
 9:   // Set the frame rate
10:   _pGame->SetFrameRate(1);
11:
12:   // Store the instance handle
13:   _hInstance = hInstance;
14:
15:   return TRUE;
16: }
```

The GameInitialize() function is pretty basic in terms of doing things you've gotten accustomed to seeing in a program that makes use of the game engine. Notice, however, that the frame rate for the game engine is set to 1, which means that there is only one game cycle per second (line 10). This is important because it helps to establish the timing of the slideshow. The problem is that one second is still too short a period to flip between slides, so we'll have to trick the game engine into displaying each slide a little longer; you tackle this problem in a moment. The only other task carried out in GameInitialize() is storing away the instance handle, which is very important for loading bitmaps from resources (line 13).

Although GameInitialize() creates and initializes the game engine, it's the GameStart() function that really gets the Slideshow program on track. Its counterpart is GameEnd(), which cleans up the bitmaps created in GameStart(). The code for both functions is shown in Listing 5.4.

LISTING 5.4   The GameStart() and GameEnd() Functions Take Care of Initializing and Cleaning Up the Slide Bitmaps

```
 1: void GameStart(HWND hWindow)
 2: {
 3:   // Create and load the slide bitmaps
 4:   HDC hDC = GetDC(hWindow);
 5:   _pSlides[0] = new Bitmap(hDC, TEXT("Image1.bmp"));
 6:   _pSlides[1] = new Bitmap(hDC, TEXT("Image2.bmp"));
 7:   _pSlides[2] = new Bitmap(hDC, TEXT("Image3.bmp"));
 8:   _pSlides[3] = new Bitmap(hDC, IDB_IMAGE4, _hInstance);
 9:   _pSlides[4] = new Bitmap(hDC, IDB_IMAGE5, _hInstance);
10:   _pSlides[5] = new Bitmap(hDC, IDB_IMAGE6, _hInstance);
11:   _pSlides[6] = new Bitmap(hDC, 640, 480, RGB(128, 128, 64));
12:
13:   // Set the first slide
14:   _iCurSlide = 0;
15: }
16:
17: void GameEnd()
18: {
19:   // Cleanup the slide bitmaps
20:   for (int i = 0; i < _iNUMSLIDES; i++)
21:     delete _pSlides[i];
22:
23:   // Cleanup the game engine
24:   delete _pGame;
25: }
```

The GameStart() function takes on the responsibility of creating the slide bitmaps. It first obtains a device context, which is necessary to create any bitmaps (line 4). It then loads several bitmaps from files (lines 5–7), as well as loading a few bitmaps as resources (lines 8–10). The final bitmap is a solid color blank bitmap that is created using the third Bitmap() constructor (line 11). After creating the bitmaps, the GameStart() function sets the current slide to the first bitmap (line 14).

The GameEnd() function simply cleans up the slide bitmaps by stepping through the array and deleting them one at a time (lines 20 and 21). This is an important part of the Slideshow program because you definitely want to clean up after yourself.

The current slide is drawn to the game screen in the Slideshow program thanks to the GamePaint()function, which is shown in Listing 5.5.

LISTING 5.5   The GamePaint() Function Simply Draws the Current Slide Bitmap

```
1: void GamePaint(HDC hDC)
2: {
3:   // Draw the current slide bitmap
4:   _pSlides[_iCurSlide]->Draw(hDC, 0, 0);
5: }
```

The GamePaint() function is probably simpler than you might have expected. Here, you're really getting to see how helpful the Bitmap class is because it allows you to draw a bitmap image with a very simple call to the Draw() method (line 4) of the Bitmap object. The _iCurSlide global variable is used to make sure that the appropriate slide is drawn.

The GameCycle() function is responsible for moving to the next slide after imposing a small delay, as shown in Listing 5.6.

LISTING 5.6   The GameCycle() Function Steps Through the Slides After Waiting a Few Seconds

```
1: void GameCycle()
2: {
3:   static int iDelay = 0;
4:
5:   // Establish a 3-second delay before moving to the next slide
6:   if (++iDelay > 3)
7:   {
8:     // Restore the delay counter
9:     iDelay = 0;
10:
```

5

LISTING 5.6   Continued

```
11:        // Move to the next slide
12:        if (++_iCurSlide == _iNUMSLIDES)
13:          _iCurSlide = 0;
14:
15:        // Force a repaint to draw the next slide
16:        InvalidateRect(_pGame->GetWindow(), NULL, FALSE);
17:    }
18: }
```

Because the game engine is limited to a minimum frame rate of one second, it's necessary to slow down the slideshow further by imposing a delay in the GameCycle() function. Three seconds is a reasonable delay for viewing each slide, so the GameCycle()
function uses a static variable, iDelay, to delay each slide for three seconds before moving to the next (line 3). In order to move to the next slide, the iCurSlide variable is
incremented (line 12); if it is incremented past the last slide, the slideshow cycles back to
the first slide (line 13).

Just because you increment the current slide variable doesn't mean that the slideshow
updates to show the new slide bitmap. Keep in mind that the current slide bitmap is
drawn in the GamePaint() function, which is called whenever the client area of the
Slideshow window needs to be repainted. The trick is to force a repaint of the window,
which is possible using the Win32 InvalidateRect()function. The GameCycle() function calls InvalidateRect() to force a repaint and display the new slide bitmap (line
16). The second argument to InvalidateRect() indicates that the entire client area is to
be repainted, whereas the last argument indicates that it isn't necessary to erase the client
area before repainting.

Assembling the Resources

You've now seen the vast majority of the code for the Slideshow program example,
which hopefully wasn't too overwhelming seeing as how the Bitmap class removed a
great deal of the work required to display images. The only remaining code to address
involves the bitmap resources used in the program. To demonstrate how to use bitmaps as
resources, I decided to go ahead and include all the slide bitmaps as resources, even
though the program only loads three of them as resources. Listing 5.7 contains the code
for the Resource.h header file, which defines unique resource IDs for the bitmaps.

LISTING 5.7   The Resource.h Header File Contains Resource IDs for the Icons and Bitmap Images in the Slideshow Program Example

```
 1: //-------------------------------------------------------------
 2: // Icons                    Range : 1000 - 1999
 3: //-------------------------------------------------------------
 4: #define IDI_SLIDESHOW        1000
 5: #define IDI_SLIDESHOW_SM     1001
 6:
 7: //-------------------------------------------------------------
 8: // Bitmaps                  Range : 2000 - 2999
 9: //-------------------------------------------------------------
10: #define IDB_IMAGE1           2000
11: #define IDB_IMAGE2           2001
12: #define IDB_IMAGE3           2002
13: #define IDB_IMAGE4           2003
14: #define IDB_IMAGE5           2004
15: #define IDB_IMAGE6           2005
```

This code reveals how resources are typically organized according to type. It also shows how the numbers used to distinguish between resources are specified as ranges for each resource type. This is primarily an organizational issue, but it does help to keep things straight. The bitmap resource IDs are created in lines 10–15, and are pretty straightforward. Notice that there is no ID for the seventh bitmap, the solid color bitmap, because it is a blank bitmap that doesn't derive from a resource.

The bitmap resource IDs come into play in the Slideshow.rc resource script, which is shown in Listing 5.8.

5

LISTING 5.8   The Slideshow.rc Resource Script Contains the Resources for the Slideshow Program Example, Including the Bitmap Resources

```
 1: //-------------------------------------------------------------
 2: // Include Files
 3: //-------------------------------------------------------------
 4: #include "Resource.h"
 5:
 6: //-------------------------------------------------------------
 7: // Icons
 8: //-------------------------------------------------------------
 9: IDI_SLIDESHOW        ICON        "Slideshow.ico"
10: IDI_SLIDESHOW_SM     ICON        "Slideshow_sm.ico"
11:
12: //-------------------------------------------------------------
13: // Bitmaps
14: //-------------------------------------------------------------
15: IDB_IMAGE1           BITMAP      "Image1.bmp"
```

LISTING 5.8   Continued

```
16: IDB_IMAGE2          BITMAP          "Image2.bmp"
17: IDB_IMAGE3          BITMAP          "Image3.bmp"
18: IDB_IMAGE4          BITMAP          "Image4.bmp"
19: IDB_IMAGE5          BITMAP          "Image5.bmp"
20: IDB_IMAGE6          BITMAP          "Image6.bmp"
```

This resource script reveals how bitmap resources are included using the BITMAP resource type. Including bitmaps in a resource script is similar to including icons, and involves specifying the resource ID, resource type, and image file for each bitmap (lines 15–20). By including bitmaps in the resource script, you are alleviating the need to include separate bitmap image files with the completed program.

Testing the Finished Product

The Slideshow program example is definitely the most practical program you've seen thus far. You can use the program to display any kind of slideshow of images that you want, provided that you store the images as 8-bit (256 color) bitmaps with no compression. To demonstrate the practicality of the program, I decided to put together a slideshow of photos from a recent trip I took to Arizona. Figure 5.2 shows a photo of a jackrabbit, which happens to be the opening slide in the slideshow.

You'll notice that every three seconds the slide will change, eventually leading to the end of the slideshow, after which it wraps around and begins with the first image again. Figure 5.3 shows another slide in the slideshow to demonstrate how the slides are changed.

Whether or not you decide to place your family album of digital photographs into a Slideshow program of your own, you've hopefully gained an appreciation of bitmaps and how to work with them at the programming level. You also now have the Bitmap class, which you will be using heavily throughout the remainder of the book.

FIGURE 5.2

The Slideshow program example demonstrates how to display bitmap images, and also serves as a good way to relive a vacation.

FIGURE 5.3

Each successive slide in the Slideshow program is separated by a three second delay.

5

Summary

This hour tackled one of the most important topics of game development by introducing you to bitmap images, as well as how they are loaded and displayed in a Windows program. You first analyzed the inner structure of a bitmap, which was necessary in order to gain an understanding of what it takes to write code that can load a bitmap from a file or resource. You then used this knowledge to assemble a bitmap class that handles the messy details of creating bitmaps based on files, resources, or solid colors. The hour concluded by demonstrating how to use the bitmap class in a practical example program.

This hour concludes the first part of the book, which laid the groundwork for game programming in Windows. The next part of the book addresses the all-important topic of interacting with game players. You find out how to receive and process user input from a keyboard, mouse, and joystick, as well as creating your first complete game.

Q&A

Q **Why isn't the `Bitmap` class in this hour more flexible in supporting other image types?**

A There are two reasons for the Bitmap class being limited in its support for image types. The first reason has to do with coding simplicity—it takes considerably more complex code to handle multiple image types. Because the goal of this book is to get you creating games with minimal distractions, keeping the `Bitmap` class as simple as possible is extremely important. The second reason has to do with performance—using an image format with fewer colors results in faster games. This is because less colors results in less information being transferred when an image is drawn to a device context, which means speedier draws. Performance is a critical factor in virtually all games, so sacrificing zillions of colors in favor of a smoother and quicker game is usually worth the trade-off.

Q **What's the purpose of the third `Create()` method in the `Bitmap` class?**

A The third `Create()` method in the `Bitmap` class is used to create a blank bitmap in a solid color, which might not seem very useful at first. However, later on in the book, you'll find out how bitmaps don't always originate with bitmap files or resources. Besides, you might want to create a bitmap as a background for a game that gets customized specifically for the game. For example, consider a space background with several planets. You might create a solid black bitmap and then draw the planets on top of it.

Workshop

The Workshop is designed to help you anticipate possible questions, review what you've learned, and begin learning how to put your knowledge into practice. The answers to the quiz can be found in Appendix A, "Quiz Answers."

Quiz

1. Why would you want to store bitmaps as resources in an executable program, as opposed to using them straight from files?

2. What is the purpose of the color table in a bitmap?

3. What kind of bitmap is supported by the `Bitmap` class created in this hour?

Exercises

1. Modify the Slideshow program example so that it uses your own bitmap images as slides. Make sure to change the number of slides in the program to accommodate how many you're using. Also, if you choose to use a different size for your images, simply change the size of the game screen to match when you create the game engine.

2. Alter the frame rate of the Slideshow program example to see how it impacts the speed of the slide images being drawn. You should notice the program reach a maximum speed, after which it doesn't really make any difference how fast you set the rate. In other words, there are limits as to how fast of a frame rate you can get.

5

PART II

Interacting with Game Players

Hours

HOUR 6

Controlling Games with the Keyboard and Mouse

All the graphics in the world wouldn't save a game if you couldn't interact with it. There's a name for a game with no user interaction—it's called a screensaver! User interaction can come from several different places, but you can generally break it down into a short list of user input devices: the keyboard, the mouse, and joysticks. The keyboard and mouse are by far the two most standard user input devices on computers, and are just about guaranteed to be supported on all personal computers. Joysticks are also quite common, but aren't nearly as commonplace as keyboards and mice. So, you should consider the keyboard and mouse the two most important game input devices, with joysticks following behind in third place. This hour focuses on interacting with the user via the keyboard and mouse, whereas Hour 7, "Improving Input with Joysticks," tackles joysticks.

In this hour, you'll learn:

- Why user input is so important in games
- How each of the major types of input devices impact games
- How to efficiently detect and respond to keyboard input
- How to handle mouse input
- How to create a program with an animated graphical object that you can control with the keyboard and mouse

Gaming and User Input

User input is the means by which the user interacts with a game. Considering the fact that user input encompasses the entire communications between a player and a game, you would think that designing an intuitive, efficient interface for user input would be at the top of the list of key game design elements. However, that isn't always the case. With all the hype these days surrounding real-time, texture-mapped 3D graphics engines and positional 3D audio in games, effective user input support is often overlooked. In fact, user input is perhaps the most overlooked aspect of game design, which is truly a tragedy. It's a tragedy because user input support in a game directly impacts the playability of the game; and when the user input isn't effective, the play suffers.

You see, I'm from the old school of game players, and I still remember paying homage to the gods of gaming with my hard earned allowance in arcades, well before there was an option of playing anything other than Pong at home (see the opener for Hour 1, "The Basics of Game Creation"). In return for my quarter offerings, the game gods usually provided me with incredibly fun games that usually had to survive on their playability alone. Because the hardware at that time simply couldn't provide a very high level of graphic and sound intensity, game developers were forced to make up for it with game play. Of course, they didn't consider their focus on playability as making up for anything; with the limited graphics and sound capabilities at the time, they didn't have an option.

Let me give you a quick example of what I'm talking about in regard to playability and user input. One of my all-time favorite games is Ring King, which is a boxing game for the Nintendo Entertainment System (NES). Ring King is definitely considered "old" by current gaming standards—possibly even ancient. Compared to current games, it has weak graphics, animation, and sound. However, I still play the game simply because it plays so well. And that playability is largely based on how the game handles user input; it allows for very subtle timing when you punch and dodge, which goes a long way in a boxing game! Since then, I've tried to find a modern replacement for Ring King, but I've had no luck. When I get beyond the fancy graphics and sound, I start missing the responsiveness of the controls in my old favorite. I'm still looking, though.

Lest you think I'm being overly critical of current games, plenty of recent games have incredible user input support, along with awesome graphics and sound. However, an equal number of recent games have killer graphics and sound, but little substance when it comes to playability and user input. These types of games might be visually stunning and fun to listen to, but they rarely have any lasting appeal beyond the initial "Wow!"

Now, let me step down from the soapbox and get to the real point, which is that you should carefully plan the user input for your games just like you carefully plan the graphics, sound, and game logic. This doesn't mean only deciding between supporting a keyboard or a mouse for the user interface. It means putting some real thought into making the user interface as intuitive as possible. You want the controls for the game to feel as natural as possible to the player.

Taking a Look at User Input Devices

Input devices are the physical hardware that allows a user to interact with a game. Input devices all perform the same function: converting information provided by the user into a form understandable by the computer. Input devices form the link between the user and your game. Even though you can't directly control the input device hardware, you can certainly control how it is interpreted in your game. As I mentioned earlier, there are three primary types of user input devices:

- The keyboard
- The mouse
- Joysticks

> In case you're wondering, trackballs are functionally very similar to mice and are often treated just like mice from a software perspective. In fact, the Win32 API doesn't discern between trackballs and mice, so the mouse support in your games indirectly supports trackballs as well.

6

The next few sections get you acquainted with these devices and their relationship to game user input.

The Keyboard

The keyboard has been the computer input device of choice since its inception. Although mice, joysticks, flight sticks, and many other user input devices have brought extended input capabilities to the game player, none is as established as the keyboard. At the bare minimum, you can always count on a game player having a keyboard.

The keyboard is a surprisingly useful input device for a wide range of games. The sheer amount of keys alone gives the keyboard appeal for games that require a wide variety of user input. Even more useful in the keyboard is the natural feel of pressing keys for games requiring quick firing and movement. This usefulness is evident in the amount of arcade games that still use buttons, even when powerful digital joysticks are readily available. Keys (or buttons) simply are easier to use in many games, including those with many input combinations.

When assessing the potential use of the keyboard in a game, try to think in terms of the most intuitive user interface possible. For example, any game involving the player moving an object around would benefit from using the arrow keys. A good example is the classic 3D shooter Doom, which makes creative use of a keyboard-specific feature that greatly enhances the playability of the game. The left and right arrow keys, when used alone, rotate the player left and right in the game world. However, when the Shift key is held down, the same left and right arrow keys cause the player to *strafe*, meaning that the player moves sideways without changing direction. This seemingly small enhancement to the keyboard controls goes a long way when playing the game.

When you're deciding on specific keys to use for keyboard controls in your game, consider the potential limitations on players using other platforms or hardware configurations. For example, I primarily use a Windows XP PC equipped with a Microsoft Natural keyboard. If you aren't familiar with these keyboards, they are split down the middle for ergonomic reasons. If you don't use one of these keyboards, it might not occur to you that key combinations near the center of the keyboard will be separated a few inches for people like me. So, remember that if you use the G and H keys (or other middle keys) in your game, and it plays well for you, it might not work out so well for players with different keyboards.

The most common keys used in games are the arrow keys. If you're writing an action game, you might also have keys for firing and selecting between weapons. When you're deciding on the keys to use, keep in mind things like the creative usage of the Shift key in Doom. If you can limit the number of primary game control keys by making use of a secondary key such as Shift, you've made the game controls that much easier to use.

The Mouse

Although the keyboard is firmly in place as the most necessary of user input devices, the graphical nature of modern computers establishes the mouse, or a similar pointing device, as a standard input device as well. The mouse, however, doesn't share the wide range of input applications to games that the keyboard has. This stems from its primary usage as a point-and-click device; if you haven't noticed, a lot of games don't follow the point-and-click paradigm.

In regard to gaming, the usefulness of the mouse is dependent totally on the type of game and, therefore, the type of user interaction dictated by the game. However, as quickly as some people write off the mouse as being a useless interface in some games, others praise the fine control it provides. Again, a good example is Doom. Personally, I think the keyboard is much more responsive than the mouse, and the keyboard enables me to get around faster and with more control. But I have friends who feel lost playing the game without a mouse.

Clearly, this is a situation in which the game designers saw a way to provide support for both the keyboard and mouse. With the exception of the most extreme cases, this should be your goal as well. Different game players like different things, and the safest solution is to hedge your bets and support all input devices whenever possible. By following this simple rule, you can develop games that can be appreciated and enjoyed by a broader group of game players.

Joysticks

Although not quite as standard as keyboards and mice, joysticks nonetheless represent a very common component of modern computer systems. Joysticks are in many ways a throwback to video games of old—many of which relied heavily on joysticks for controlling characters, spaceships, and other game objects. Joysticks come in both digital and analog form, although the difference between the two isn't terribly important from a programming perspective. The primary thing to consider when assessing the role of joysticks in games is whether it makes sense to play the game with a joystick. In other words, does the movement in the game lend itself to being carried out with a vertical stick (or flat game pad), as opposed to using keyboard keys or a mouse? Of course, it's not a bad idea to support multiple input devices—in which case you might opt to include joystick support just to be flexible.

6

Most game pads count as joysticks because they provide a similar functionality in terms of providing a multidirectional control for movement, as well as several buttons. From a programming perspective, Windows doesn't distinguish between joysticks and game pads, which is a good thing for you.

It's worth mentioning that some games out there seem to be expressly designed for being played with joysticks. For one, the extremely popular game Halo on the XBox console system uses a unique feature that would be difficult to replicate with a keyboard or mouse. Halo allows you to press the joystick inward to activate a rifle scope on your gun. So, if you see some bad guys off in the distance, you can push in on the joystick to zoom with the scope and pick them off one by one. The scope/zoom feature in Halo is an excellent example of an ingenious game feature made possible by a specific type of input device. Of course, the XBox controller had to include a joystick with the push feature in order for Halo to work, so Microsoft deserves some credit on the hardware side of things.

Assessing Keyboard Input for Games

You know that messages are used heavily throughout the Win32 API to deliver notifications regarding things such as window creation, window destruction, window activation, window deactivation, and so on. You may be glad to find out that this same messaging system is used to deliver notifications regarding key presses on the keyboard. More specifically, the Win32 API defines messages called WM_KEYDOWN and WM_KEYUP that inform you whenever a key has been pressed or released, respectively. These two messages are quite easy to handle in a Windows program, and I'd love to show you how to use them, but there's a problem. The problem is that the standard Windows messaging system is painfully slow when it comes to delivering keyboard messages. Because games rely heavily on responsive controls, it simply isn't acceptable to work with the Windows keyboard messages.

The bottom line is that none of your games can support keyboards. Okay, I'm kidding. The truth is that there is always a workaround in game programming, and the slow keyboard messaging problem presents a perfect opportunity for a workaround. If you recall, the timing for the Game Engine was established back in Hour 3, "Creating an Engine for Games," in the WinMain() function. If you recall, the WinMain() function included a program loop that repeated over and over, processing messages for the program. When the function wasn't processing messages, it spent its time running through cycles of the game engine. In other words, the game engine takes advantage of *idle time* in the main program loop to carry out its game-related tasks. This idle time is what you can use to your advantage when processing key presses and releases on the keyboard.

> The concept of "idle time" with respect to the WinMain() function is a little misleading. When you consider that games don't typically process very many messages from Windows, the vast majority of the time spent by a game program is idle time, or time not responding to standard Windows messages. This time can therefore be put to use running the game engine, which is what I mean when I talk about running through the game cycles during idle time.

The idea behind this juiced up approach to keyboard event handling is that instead of sitting around waiting for Windows to eventually send you a keyboard message, you constantly check the keyboard to see if any of the keys you're interested in have been pressed. If so, the game instantly springs into motion and efficiently responds to the key press. If no key is pressed, the game engine hums along with no interruptions. The strategy here is to basically take keyboard processing into your own hands and bypass the standard Windows approach, which ultimately results in much more responsive keyboard controls for your games. You learn how to implement this speedy keyboard handler in code a little later in the hour. For now, let's take a look at how to respond to mouse events.

Tracking the Mouse

When you move the mouse, a series of events is set off that is very similar to those set off by the keyboard. In fact, the Win32 API includes a series of mouse messages that are used to convey mouse events, similar to how keyboard messages convey keyboard events. You learned in the previous section that the Win32 keyboard messages aren't up to the task of providing efficient input for games. Fortunately, the same cannot be said of the mouse messages. It turns out that the built-in Win32 approach to handling mouse events via messages works out just fine for games. Following are the mouse messages used to notify Windows programs of mouse events:

- WM_MOUSEMOVE—Any mouse movement
- WM_LBUTTONDOWN—Left mouse button pressed
- WM_LBUTTONUP—Left mouse button released
- WM_RBUTTONDOWN—Right mouse button pressed
- WM_RBUTTONUP—Right mouse button released

6

- WM_MBUTTONDOWN—Middle mouse button pressed
- WM_MBUTTONUP—Middle mouse button released

The first mouse message, WM_MOUSEMOVE, lets you know whenever the mouse has been moved. The remaining messages relay mouse button clicks for the left, right, and middle buttons, respectively. Keep in mind that a mouse button click consists of a button press followed by a button release; you can implement a mouse dragging feature by keeping track of when a mouse button is pressed and released, and watching for mouse movement in between.

Regardless of whether you're interested in mouse movement or a mouse button click, the important factor regarding the mouse is where the mouse cursor is located. Fortunately, the mouse cursor position is provided with all the previously mentioned mouse messages. It's packed into the lParam argument that gets sent to the GameEngine::HandleEvent() method. Following is the prototype for this method, just in case you forgot:

```
LRESULT GameEngine::HandleEvent(HWND hWindow, UINT msg, WPARAM wParam,
  LPARAM lParam);
```

If you recall, the wParam and lParam arguments are sent along with every Windows message, and contain message-specific information. In the case of the mouse messages, lParam contains the XY position of the mouse cursor packed into its low and high words. Following is an example of a code snippet that extracts the mouse position from the lParam argument in a WM_MOUSEMOVE message handler:

```
case WM_MOUSEMOVE:
  WORD x = LOWORD(lParam);
  WORD y = HIWORD(lParam);
  return 0;
```

The wParam argument for the mouse messages includes information about the mouse button states, as well as some keyboard information. More specifically, wParam lets you know if any of the three mouse buttons are down, as well as whether the Shift or Control keys on the keyboard are being pressed. In case you don't see it, the wParam argument—used in conjunction with WM_MOUSEMOVE—provides you with enough information to implement your own Doom strafing feature! Following are the constants used with the mouse messages to interpret the value of the wParam argument:

- MK_LBUTTON—Left mouse button is down
- MK_RBUTTON—Right mouse button is down
- MK_MBUTTON—Middle mouse button is down
- MK_SHIFT—Shift key is down
- MK_CONTROL—Control key is down

You can check for any of these mouse constants to see if a button or key is being pressed during the mouse move. The constants are actually *flags*, which means that they can be combined together in the wParam argument. To check for the presence of an individual flag, you must use the bitwise AND operator (&) to see if the flag is present. Following is an example of checking wParam to see if the right mouse button is down:

```
if (wParam & MK_RBUTTON)
  // Yep, the right mouse button is down!
```

This code shows how to use the bitwise AND operator (&) to check for individual flags. This is a technique you use in Hour 7 to check the state of a joystick.

Revamping the Game Engine for Input

Because we've already built a game engine for use in carrying out the various tasks associated with game management, it only makes sense to incorporate user input handling into the game engine. Granted, a certain aspect of handling user input is game specific, and therefore must be handled in the code for each individual game. However, there are some general aspects of keyboard and mouse handling that you can incorporate into the game engine to simplify the work required of specific game code.

If you recall, the idea behind the game engine is to provide a certain degree of game functionality in a self-contained class, and then delegate game specific tasks to a series of functions that each game is responsible for providing. For example, the GamePaint() function must be provided in a game to draw the game screen. Although the game engine doesn't technically provide code for the GamePaint() function, it does make sure that it gets called whenever the game window needs to be painted; it's up to each game to provide the actual code for GamePaint(), which makes sense because every game draws itself differently. Similar functions need to be added to the game engine to provide games with a means of handling user input.

The next couple of sections guide you through modifications to the game engine to add support for keyboard and mouse input handling.

Adding Keyboard Support

Earlier this hour, you found out that the standard Windows approach to keyboard handling with messages simply isn't good enough for games. A much better way to handle keyboard input is to repeatedly check the state of the keyboard for specific key presses, and then react accordingly. Using this strategy, much of the burden of keyboard input handling is passed on to the game code, which means that the game engine is primarily responsible only for calling a keyboard handler function to give the game a chance to respond to key presses. Following is what this function looks like:

```
void HandleKeys();
```

The HandleKeys() function must be provided as part of the game code, and therefore isn't included in the game engine. If you don't want your game to support keyboard input, you can just leave the HandleKeys() function blank. Of course, the game engine must make sure that the HandleKeys() function gets called rapidly enough to give your games a responsive feel. This is accomplished in the WinMain() function within the game engine code. Following is the change made to this function:

```
if (iTickCount > iTickTrigger)
{
  iTickTrigger = iTickCount +
    GameEngine::GetEngine()->GetFrameDelay();
  HandleKeys();
  GameCycle();
}
```

The only change to the WinMain() code is the new call to the HandleKeys() function. Notice that this call occurs just before the GameCycle() function, which means that a game gets a chance to respond to keyboard input before every game cycle. Don't forget; the specifics of handling keyboard input are carried out in each specific game when you create your own HandleKeys() function. You find out how to do this later in the hour.

Adding Mouse Support

Although keyboard input in games is admittedly non-standard in terms of deviating from how things are typically handled in Windows programming, mouse input is handled the old-fashioned way—with messages. It's not that mouse messages are more efficient than keyboard messages; it's just harder to notice sluggish mouse input. In other words, mouse messages appear to be fast enough to allow you to create a responsive mouse interface, whereas keyboard messages do not.

In order to support mouse input, games must support the following three functions, which are called by the game engine to pass along mouse events:

```
void MouseButtonDown(int x, int y, BOOL bLeft);
void MouseButtonUp(int x, int y, BOOL bLeft);
void MouseMove(int x, int y);
```

In order to connect mouse messages with these mouse handler functions, the game engine must look for the appropriate mouse messages and respond accordingly. The following code includes the new portion of the GameEngine::HandleEvent() method that is responsible for handling mouse messages delivered to the main game window.

```
case LBUTTONDOWN:
  // Handle left mouse button press
  MouseButtonDown(LOWORD(lParam), HIWORD(lParam), TRUE);
  return 0;

case WM_LBUTTONUP:
  // Handle left mouse button release
  MouseButtonUp(LOWORD(lParam), HIWORD(lParam), TRUE);
  return 0;

case WM_RBUTTONDOWN:
  // Handle right mouse button press
  MouseButtonDown(LOWORD(lParam), HIWORD(lParam), FALSE);
  return 0;

case WM_RBUTTONUP:
  // Handle right mouse button release
  MouseButtonUp(LOWORD(lParam), HIWORD(lParam), FALSE);
  return 0;

case WM_MOUSEMOVE:
  // Handle mouse movement
  MouseMove(LOWORD(lParam), HIWORD(lParam));
  return 0;
```

This code handles the following mouse messages: WM_LBUTTONDOWN, WM_LBUTTONUP, WM_RBUTTONDOWN, WM_RBUTTONUP, and WM_MOUSEMOVE. Each piece of message handler code simply calls one of the mouse functions with the appropriate arguments. The first and second arguments to all the mouse functions include the X and Y position of the mouse cursor at the moment the message was delivered. The last argument to the mouse button functions is a Boolean value that identifies whether the left (TRUE) or right (FALSE) mouse button is involved in the event.

As you can hopefully tell from the code, the idea behind the mouse functions is to allow games to simply provide MouseButtonDown(), MouseButtonUp(), and MouseMove() functions, as opposed to getting involved with message handling. So, to support the mouse in your games, all you have to do is provide code for these three functions.

Sprucing Up the Bitmap Class

You've now made the necessary changes to the game engine to prepare it for keyboard and mouse input. However, there is another minor change you need to make that doesn't technically have anything to do with input. I'm referring to bitmap *transparency*, which allows bitmaps to not always appear as square graphical objects. Don't get me wrong; bitmaps definitely are square graphical objects, but they don't necessarily have to be drawn that way. The idea behind transparency is that you can identify a color as the

6

transparent color, which is then used to indicate parts of a bitmap that are transparent. When the bitmap is drawn, pixels of the transparent color aren't drawn, and the background shows through.

> Why is there a discussion of bitmap transparency in an hour focused on keyboard and mouse input? The answer has to do with the fact that I want you to view the game engine as a work in progress that is constantly evolving and picking up new features. In this case, the program example at the end of this hour benefits greatly from bitmap transparency, so it only makes sense to add the feature here. You'll continue to make small improvements to the game engine throughout the book even if they don't tie in directly to the topic at hand. The end result will be a game engine with a lot of slick little features that will make your games all the more fun.

From a graphics creation perspective, you create bitmaps with transparency by selecting a color that isn't used in your graphics, such as "hot purple," which is also known as magenta. You then use magenta to fill areas of your bitmaps that need to appear transparent. It's then up to the revamped game engine to make sure that these transparent regions don't get drawn with the rest of the bitmap. You obviously don't want magenta borders around your images!

The trick to making bitmap transparency work in the game engine is to expand the existing `Bitmap::Draw()` method so that it supports transparency. This is accomplished by adding two new arguments:

- `bTrans`—a Boolean value that indicates whether the bitmap should be drawn with transparency
- `crTransColor`—the transparent color of the bitmap

It's important to try and make changes to the game engine that don't cause problems with programs that we've already written. So, rather than add these two arguments to the `Draw()` method and require them of all bitmaps, it's much better to add them and provide default values:

```
void Draw(HDC hDC, int x, int y, BOOL bTrans = FALSE,
  COLORREF crTransColor = RGB(255, 0, 255));
```

If you notice, the default value of `bTrans` is `FALSE`, which means that if you leave off the argument, transparency isn't used. This works great for existing code because it doesn't change the way the `Draw()` method already worked. In case you're curious, the default color specified in `crTransColor` (`RGB(255, 0, 255)`) is magenta, so if you stick with that color as your transparent color, you won't have to specify a transparent color in the `Draw()` method.

The only significant changes to the `Draw()` method involve checking the transparency argument, and then drawing the bitmap with transparency using the Win32 `TransparentBlt()` function if the argument is `TRUE`. Otherwise, it's business as usual with the `BitBlt()` function being used to draw bitmaps without transparency.

> Although the `TransparentBlt()` function is part of the Win32 API, it isn't as widely supported as the traditional `BitBlt()` function. More specifically, the function isn't supported in versions of Windows prior to Windows 98, such as Windows 95.

The `TransparentBlt()` function is part of the Win32 API, but it requires the inclusion of a special library called msimg32.lib in order for your games to compile properly. This is a standard library that should be included with your compiler, but you'll need to make sure that it is linked in with any programs that use the `TransparentBlt()` function. If you aren't familiar with altering linker settings for your compiler, just take a look at the compiler documentation and find out how to add additional libraries to a project; it typically involves simply entering the name of the library, msimg32.lib in this case, in a project settings window. Or, if you happen to be using Microsoft Visual Studio, you can follow these steps:

1. Open the project in Visual Studio (Visual C++).
2. Right-click on the project's folder in Solution Explorer, and click Properties in the pop-up menu.
3. Click the Linker folder in the left pane of the Properties window, and then click Input.
4. Click next to Additional Dependencies in the right pane, and type **msimg32.lib**.
5. Click the OK button to accept the changes to the project.

After completing these steps, you can safely compile a program and know that the msimg32.lib library is being successfully linked into the executable program file.

> The source code for the examples in the book is located on the accompanying CD-ROM, and includes Visual C++ project files with the appropriate linker settings already made.

6

Building the UFO Program Example

In order to really get a feel for how keyboard and mouse input works in games, it's helpful to work through a complete example. The remainder of this hour focuses on a program example called UFO. Although this program isn't technically a game, it's by far the closest thing you've seen to a game yet. It involves a flying saucer that you control with the keyboard and mouse. You're able to fly the flying saucer around a bitmap background image. Perhaps most important is the fact that the UFO program demonstrates how good of a feel you can create for game controls. More specifically, the arrow keys on the keyboard are surprisingly responsive in the UFO program.

Although you haven't really learned about animation yet, the UFO program example makes use of animation to allow you to fly the flying saucer. Fortunately, the program is simple enough that you can get by without knowing the specifics about animation. All you really need to know is that you can alter the position of a bitmap image to simulate movement on the screen. This occurs thanks to the game engine, which redraws the bitmap every game cycle. So, by altering the position of an image and redrawing it repeatedly, you create the effect of movement. The UFO program example reveals how this task is accomplished, as well as how the keyboard and mouse fit into the picture.

 You learn the details of how animation works in Hour 9, "A Crash Course in Game Animation."

Writing the Program Code

The header file for the UFO program example lays the groundwork for the meat of the program, which carries out the details of the flying saucer animation and user input. Listing 6.1 contains the code for the UFO.h header file, which declares global variables used to control the flying saucer.

LISTING 6.1 The UFO.h Header File Declares Global Variables Used to Keep Track of the Flying Saucer

```
1: #pragma once
2:
3: //----------------------------------------------------------------
4: // Include Files
5: //----------------------------------------------------------------
6: #include <windows.h>
7: #include "Resource.h"
8: #include "GameEngine.h"
9: #include "Bitmap.h"
```

LISTING 6.1   Continued

```
10:
11: //------------------------------------------------
12: // Global Variables
13: //------------------------------------------------
14: HINSTANCE    _hInstance;
15: GameEngine*  _pGame;
16: const int    _iMAXSPEED = 8;
17: Bitmap*      _pBackground;
18: Bitmap*      _pSaucer;
19: int          _iSaucerX, _iSaucerY;
20: int          _iSpeedX, _iSpeedY;
```

The first thing of interest in this code is the _iMAXSPEED constant, which establishes the maximum speed of the flying saucer (line 16). The speed of the flying saucer is how many pixels it can travel in a given direction in each game cycle. So, the value of the _iMAXSPEED constant means that the flying saucer can never travel more than 8 pixels in the horizontal or vertical direction in a game cycle.

The _pBackground and _pSaucer global variables store the two bitmaps used in the program, which correspond to a night sky background image and the flying saucer image (lines 17 and 18). The remaining variables pertain to the flying saucer, and include its XY position (line 19) and XY speed (line 20). The XY position of the flying saucer is specified relative to the game screen. The XY speed, on the other hand, simply tells the program how many pixels the flying saucer should be moved per game cycle; negative values for the speed variables indicate that the flying saucer is moving in the opposite direction.

With the global variables in place, we can move on to the game functions. The first game function to consider is GameInitialize(), which creates the game engine and establishes the frame rate. The frame rate for the program is set to 30 frames per second. This is a relatively high frame rate for games, but it results in much smoother motion for the flying saucer, as you soon find out.

Next on the game function agenda is the GameStart() function, which creates and loads the flying saucer bitmaps, as well as sets the initial flying saucer position and speed (Listing 6.2).

6

LISTING 6.2   The GameStart() Function Performs Startup Tasks for the UFO Program Example

```
1: void GameStart(HWND hWindow)
2: {
3:    // Create and load the background and saucer bitmaps
```

LISTING 6.2   Continued

```
 4:    HDC hDC = GetDC(hWindow);
 5:    _pBackground = new Bitmap(hDC, IDB_BACKGROUND, _hInstance);
 6:    _pSaucer = new Bitmap(hDC, IDB_SAUCER, _hInstance);
 7:
 8:    // Set the initial saucer position and speed
 9:    _iSaucerX = 250 - (_pSaucer->GetWidth() / 2);
10:    _iSaucerY = 200 - (_pSaucer->GetHeight() / 2);
11:    _iSpeedX = 0;
12:    _iSpeedY = 0;
13: }
```

The GameStart() function is used to initialize data pertaining to the program such as the bitmaps and other global variables. The flying saucer position is initially set to the middle of the game screen (lines 9 and 10), and then the speed of the saucer is set to 0 so that it isn't moving (lines 11 and 12).

You might think that a program with an animated flying saucer cruising over a background image would require a complex GamePaint() function. However, Listing 6.3 shows how this simply isn't the case.

LISTING 6.3   The GamePaint() Function Draws the Background and Flying Saucer Bitmaps

```
1: void GamePaint(HDC hDC)
2: {
3:    // Draw the background and saucer bitmaps
4:    _pBackground->Draw(hDC, 0, 0);
5:    _pSaucer->Draw(hDC, _iSaucerX, _iSaucerY, TRUE);
6: }
```

As the code reveals, the GamePaint() function for the UFO program is painfully simple. Aside from the standard code that you're now getting accustomed to seeing in the GamePaint() function, all the function does is draw the background and flying saucer bitmaps. The background bitmap is drawn at the origin (0, 0) of the game screen (line 4), whereas the flying saucer is drawn at its current position (line 5). Notice that TRUE is passed as the last argument to the Draw() method when drawing the flying saucer, which indicates that the saucer is to be drawn with transparency using the default transparent color.

The GameCycle() function is a little more interesting than the others you've seen because it is actually responsible for updating the position of the flying saucer based on its speed. Listing 6.4 shows how this is accomplished in the code for the GameCycle() function.

LISTING 6.4   The `GameCycle()` Function Updates the Saucer Position and Then Repaints the Game Screen

```
1: void GameCycle()
2: {
3:    // Update the saucer position
4:    _iSaucerX = min(500 - _pSaucer->GetWidth(), max(0, _iSaucerX + _iSpeedX));
5:    _iSaucerY = min(320, max(0, _iSaucerY + _iSpeedY));
6:
7:    // Force a repaint to redraw the saucer
8:    InvalidateRect(_pGame->GetWindow(), NULL, FALSE);
9: }
```

The `GameCycle()` function updates the position of the flying saucer by adding its speed to its position. If the speed is negative, the saucer will move to the left and/or up, whereas positive speed values move the saucer right and/or down. The seemingly tricky code for setting the position must also take into account the boundaries of the game screen so that the flying saucer can't be flown off into oblivion. Granted, the concept of flying off the screen might sound interesting, but it turns out being quite confusing! Another option would be to wrap the saucer around to the other side of the screen if it goes over the boundary, which is how games like Asteroids solved this problem, but I opted for the simpler solution of just stopping it at the edges. After updating the position of the flying saucer, the `GameCycle()` function forces a repaint of the game screen to reflect the new saucer position (line 8).

The flying saucer is now being drawn and updated properly, but you still don't have a way to change its speed so that it can fly. This is accomplished first by handling keyboard input in the `HandleKeys()` function, which is shown in Listing 6.5.

LISTING 6.5   The `HandleKeys()` Function Checks the Status of the Arrow Keys, Which Are Used to Control the Flying Saucer

```
1: void HandleKeys()
2: {
3:    // Change the speed of the saucer in response to arrow key presses
4:    if (GetAsyncKeyState(VK_LEFT) < 0)
5:      _iSpeedX = max(-_iMAXSPEED, --_iSpeedX);
6:    else if (GetAsyncKeyState(VK_RIGHT) < 0)
7:      _iSpeedX = min(_iMAXSPEED, ++_iSpeedX);
8:    if (GetAsyncKeyState(VK_UP) < 0)
9:      _iSpeedY = max(-_iMAXSPEED, --_iSpeedY);
10:   else if (GetAsyncKeyState(VK_DOWN) < 0)
11:     _iSpeedY = min(_iMAXSPEED, ++_iSpeedY);
12: }
```

6

The HandleKeys() function uses the Win32 GetAsyncKeyState() function to check the status of the arrow keys (VK_LEFT, VK_RIGHT, VK_UP, and VK_DOWN) and see if any of them are being pressed. If so, the speed of the flying saucer is adjusted appropriately. Notice that the newly calculated speed is always checked against the _iMAXSPEED global constant to make sure that a speed limit is enforced. Even flying saucers are required to stay within the speed limit!

> The GetAsyncKeyState() function is part of the Win32 API, and provides a means of obtaining the state of any key on the keyboard at any time. You specify which key you're looking for by using its *virtual key code*; Windows defines virtual key codes for all the keys on a standard keyboard. Common key codes for games include VK_LEFT, VK_RIGHT, VK_UP, VK_DOWN, VK_CONTROL, VK_SHIFT, and VK_RETURN.

If you thought handling keyboard input in the UFO program was easy, wait until you see how the mouse is handled. To make things a little more interesting, both mouse buttons are used in this program. The left mouse button sets the flying saucer position to the current mouse cursor position, whereas the right mouse button sets the speed of the flying saucer to 0. So, you can use the mouse to quickly get control of the flying saucer; just right-click to stop it and then left-click to position it wherever you want. Listing 6.6 shows the code for the MouseButtonDown() function, which makes this mouse magic possible.

LISTING 6.6   The MouseButtonDown() Function Uses the Left and Right Mouse Buttons to Move the Flying Saucer to the Current Mouse Position and Stop the Flying Saucer, Respectively

```
 1: void MouseButtonDown(int x, int y, BOOL bLeft)
 2: {
 3:   if (bLeft)
 4:   {
 5:     // Set the saucer position to the mouse position
 6:     _iSaucerX = x - (_pSaucer->GetWidth() / 2);
 7:     _iSaucerY = y - (_pSaucer->GetHeight() / 2);
 8:   }
 9:   else
10:   {
11:     // Stop the saucer
12:     _iSpeedX = 0;
13:     _iSpeedY = 0;
14:   }
15: }
```

The first step in this code is to check and see which one of the mouse buttons was pressed—left or right (line 3). I know, most PC mice these days have three buttons, but I wanted to keep the game engine relatively simple, so I just focused on the two most important buttons. If the left mouse button was pressed, the function calculates the position of the flying saucer so that it is centered on the current mouse cursor position (lines 6 and 7). If the right button was pressed, the speed of the flying saucer is set to 0 (lines 12 and 13) .

If you determine that supporting two mouse buttons is simply too much of a weakness for the game engine, feel free to modify it on your own. It primarily involves changing the third argument of the MouseButtonDown() function so that it can convey more than two values—one for each of the three mouse buttons.

Testing the Finished Product

The UFO program example is the closest thing you've seen to a game thus far, and is quite interesting in terms of allowing you to fly around an animated graphical object. Hopefully, you'll be pleasantly surprised by the responsiveness of the program's keyboard controls. Figure 6.1 shows the UFO program in action as the flying saucer does a flyby of some desert cacti.

FIGURE 6.1

The UFO program example demonstrates how to control an animated graphical object with the keyboard and mouse.

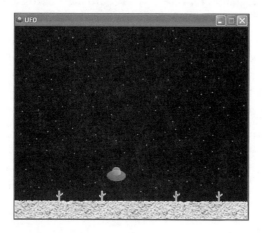

6

If you guide the flying saucer to the edge of the game screen, it will stop, which is to be expected given the program code you just worked through. There are a variety of different ways to tweak this program and make it more intriguing, such as wrapping the flying saucer from one side of the screen to the other, which is why I hope you spend some time tinkering with the code. You'll find some ideas for modifying the program in the Exercises for the lesson, which are coming up.

Summary

The ability to effectively communicate with the people that play your games is a critical factor of game design and development. In one direction a game communicates by displaying graphics and playing sounds and music, but in the other direction the user responds by interacting with a physical input device of some sort. It's very important for game developers to master the fine art of responding to user input through a variety of different user input devices. The keyboard and mouse are the two fundamental user input devices that you can count on virtually all people having. This hour showed you how to handle and respond to keyboard and mouse input in an efficient manner specifically suited to games.

Beyond the keyboard and mouse, it's up to your resources and the specific needs of each game to determine whether you should support additional input devices. Hour 7 tackles the subject of joystick input, which is the next most important input device for games.

Q&A

Q Are there any games that wouldn't require keyboard support?

A Sure. Any game that requires extensive point-and-click style input, such as a card game, would probably be fine without any keyboard support. In fact, you create a memory game in Hour 8, "Example Game: Brainiac," that is perfectly suited for mouse input alone. However, if you can figure out a way to add keyboard controls to mouse-centric games, by all means go for it.

Q Is it possible to mix keyboard and mouse controls?

A Of course! This actually hits on an interesting point not directly covered in this hour: Many games work great by combining mouse and keyboard controls together. A good example is the strafing feature in Doom, which also works with the mouse; it is activated by holding down the Shift key while moving the mouse left or right.

Workshop

The Workshop is designed to help you anticipate possible questions, review what you've learned, and begin learning how to put your knowledge into practice. The answers to the quiz can be found in Appendix A, "Quiz Answers."

Quiz

1. If you had to choose between supporting the keyboard or the mouse, which would you choose?

2. What do you have to do differently in a game to support trackballs?

3. Why is it important to extract information from the `lParam` argument when responding to a mouse message?

Exercises

1. Experiment with different values for the `_iMAXSPEED` global variable in the UFO program example to see how it affects the flying saucer's speed.

2. Modify the UFO program example so that you can click and drag the mouse to move the flying saucer around.

3. Modify the UFO program example so that the flying saucer wraps off the screen and appears on the other side when it reaches a side edge.

6

Hour 7

Improving Input with Joysticks

From its inception, the joystick has been used chiefly as an input device for game systems. Admittedly, its name alone limits its usage to the entertainment industry, as I doubt too many accountants would purchase a "joystick" for crunching numbers in a spreadsheet. At any rate, joysticks and game pads both play an important role in modern video games of all kinds, including computer games. For this reason, it's important for you to have an understanding of how to interpret and respond to joystick input in your own games. This hour introduces you to joysticks and what makes them tick, along with providing you with the knowledge and source code to handle joystick input in games.

In this hour, you'll learn:

- The basics of responding to joystick input in games
- How to properly calibrate a joystick in Windows XP
- How to add joystick support to the game engine

- How to use the new and improved game engine to create interesting programs that respond to a joystick

Joystick Basics

The concept of a joystick is straightforward, although you might be surprised by how loosely a joystick is defined in terms of Windows programming. In Windows, a *joystick* is a physical input device that allows variable movement along different axes with multiple pushbuttons. That's the geeky description of a joystick. What it means is that a joystick is an input device that can move in several different directions. Notice that I said *several* directions, not just two. Although a traditional joystick is thought of in terms of two axes (X and Y), a joystick in Windows can actually go up to six axes. Fortunately, we aren't going to worry about more than two joystick axes in this hour, which helps simplify things considerably.

The six possible joystick axes supported by Windows can be arranged in many different ways. A traditional joystick has two axes that correspond to moving the joystick handle side to side (one axis) and forward and back (another axis). A third axis of movement can be added by allowing the joystick handle to be pushed and pulled vertically. A fourth axis can be the twisting of the joystick handle. The fifth and sixth axes apply to more advanced input devices, and are typically used for keeping track of moving the entire joystick in space, like an input glove.

Because a traditional joystick has only two axes of motion, you can think of the joystick in much the same way as you think of the mouse. Although a mouse can be moved in any direction, its movement is limited to a single plane. In other words, you can always resolve mouse movement into an XY value. Joysticks are similar in this manner because you can identify their movement according to how far the handle is being pushed along each axis. If side to side movement is along the x axis and forward and back movement is along the y axis, a joystick can be tracked in a manner similar to the mouse by using an XY value.

Also similar to the mouse are the buttons on a joystick. Just as mice are capable of supporting multiple buttons (typically three), joysticks are also capable of having several buttons. In fact, joysticks are much more flexible than mice in terms of how many buttons they can have; joysticks in Windows are allowed to have up to 32 buttons. I personally wouldn't want to try and figure out how to use a joystick with that many buttons, but the option is there if someone wants to make a joystick for super humans. A more realistic number for joystick buttons is six, which is still a lot to keep track of for the average game player. Similar to mouse button presses and keyboard key presses, handling joystick button presses is relatively straightforward, as you learn a little later in the hour.

Calibrating Joysticks

Before getting into the details of how to handle joystick input from a programming perspective, it's worth addressing an important issue related to joysticks: calibration. *Calibration* is the process of fine-tuning the settings for a joystick so that the handle is properly centered. Joystick calibration is kind of like having your car aligned; when a joystick isn't properly calibrated, it has a tendency to pull to one side. Fortunately, joystick calibration is easy to perform, and is readily available from the Windows Control Panel. To access joystick settings, just follow these steps in Windows XP:

1. Click the Start button, and select Control Panel.

2. Click Printers and Other Hardware.

3. Click Game Controllers.

4. Select the joystick (game controller) to calibrate, and then click the Properties button.

Even if you aren't using Windows XP, you'll still find some kind of joystick or controller icon in the Control Panel for calibrating and testing your game controllers. The specifics of calibrating your joystick might be a little different from the steps I've listed, but the general idea is the same.

After following these steps, you'll be presented with a window that is specific to your particular joystick. In my case, I'm using a Microsoft SideWinder game pad, so the window I see is shown in Figure 7.1.

To calibrate my joystick (game pad), I just click the Calibrate button. This starts the Device Calibration Wizard, which is shown in Figure 7.2.

Click the Next button to get started calibrating the joystick (see Figure 7.3).

The first step in calibrating a joystick is to leave the handle centered and press a button, as shown in Figure 7.3. In the case of a game pad, you simply don't touch the *control pad* (D-Pad) and then press a button. You are then prompted to calibrate the axes of the joystick by moving the handle or control pad in all of its directions, followed by pressing another button (see Figure 7.4).

7

FIGURE 7.1

The Properties window for your joystick should provide a means of calibrating the joystick.

FIGURE 7.2

The Device Calibration Wizard provides a means of calibrating joysticks in Windows XP.

FIGURE 7.3

Calibrating a joystick first involves pressing a button on the joystick without touching the joystick handle (or control pad for game pads).

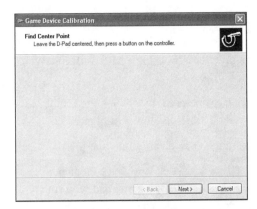

FIGURE 7.4

The Device Calibration Wizard determines the range of each joystick axis by asking you to move the handle or control pad in each direction.

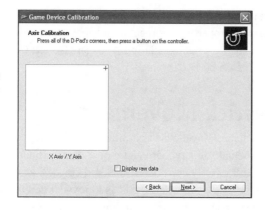

The final step is to leave the handle (control pad) alone once more and press a button. After performing these steps, you can click the Finish button to wrap up the calibration process. Although the steps to calibrating a joystick or game pad might seem kind of pointless, the idea is that your computer is analyzing the range of movement along each axis and properly determining the center point of each. Once the center point and maximum extents are determined, the joystick can then be accurately centered. Again, it's very much like aligning a car so that it steers straight when you aren't touching the steering wheel.

I encourage you to calibrate your joystick any time it starts acting strange because it is possible for a joystick to lose calibration over a period of time as it begins to wear mechanically. Your joystick's Properties window usually provides a test option for testing the joystick after you've calibrated it; this helps to make sure that the calibration worked properly. Figure 7.5 shows an example of a test window for the Microsoft SideWinder game pad.

FIGURE 7.5

The test window for the Microsoft SideWinder game pad allows you to test out the control pad as well as the game pad's buttons.

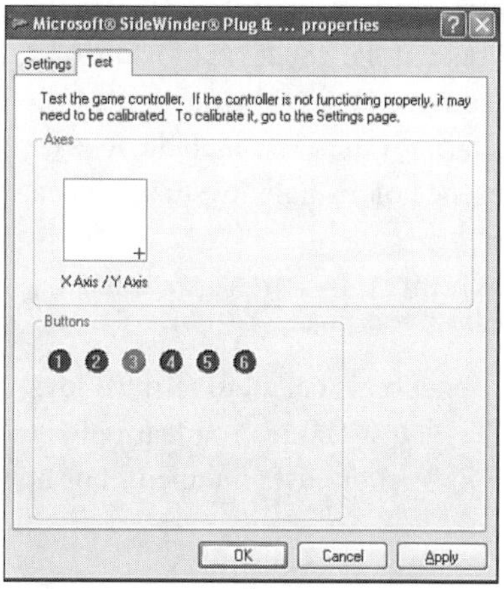

7

The test window for a joystick or game pad is great because it quickly allows you to see if the device is working properly. If you get no response when testing a device, you know that something is wrong with the installation. You can also use the test window to see if a joystick or game pad is properly calibrated.

Tracking Joystick Movements

As you might have guessed, joysticks are a little more complicated to deal with than other input devices such as the keyboard and mouse. This primarily has to do with the fact that joysticks aren't exactly considered standard devices, as well as the fact that there is a fair amount of variance when it comes to joystick features. The added complexity doesn't have so much to do with handling specific joystick events as it does with determining if a joystick is connected and available for use. You also have to concern yourself with the concept of *capturing* a joystick, which gives your program exclusive control over the joystick.

The first step in handling joystick input is checking to see if a joystick driver is installed and available on the computer system. Without the proper hardware driver in place, a physical joystick device is no good. Fortunately, Windows includes built-in drivers for most popular joysticks. However, it's good to perform the check anyway. This is made possible by a call to a Win32 API function called joyGetNumDevs(). The joyGetNumDevs() function tells you how many joysticks are capable of being used on the computer system. Following is an example of how you might call the joyGetNumDevs() function to determine the number of joysticks available for use on the system:

```
UINT uiNumJoysticks = joyGetNumDevs();
```

You now know how many joysticks can be used on the system, but that doesn't tell you much about how many joysticks are actually present. To see if a real joystick is actually plugged in and ready to use, you call the joyGetPos() function, which provides a lot of information about a joystick. You must pass this function an ID that identifies the joystick you're interested in; standard joystick IDs include JOYSTICKID1, JOYSTICKID2, and so on. So, to check for the presence of a single joystick, you can use code like this:

```
JOYINFO jiInfo;
if (joyGetPos(JOYSTICKID1, &jiInfo) != JOYERR_UNPLUGGED)
  // the joystick is plugged in and ready to go!
```

In this code, the joyGetPos() function is called to retrieve joystick information for a single joystick in the form of a JOYINFO structure. You learn how to use the JOYINFO structure to analyze the state of the joystick in just a moment. For now, you're simply providing it because the joyGetPos() function requires it. All you're looking for in this code is the return value of joyGetPos(), which indicates whether the joystick is plugged in and responding to user input. If the function doesn't return JOYERR_UNPLUGGED, you're in good shape.

When working with joysticks in the Win32 API, you always reference a joystick using a unique ID. This ID must be one of the built-in joystick IDs (JOYSTICKID1, JOYSTICKID2, and so on). In the case of the previous sample code, the JOYSTICKID1 ID checked out okay, so it's the ID you must use to continue interacting with the same joystick.

The joyGetPos() function is the function you call to check the status of the joystick, which is how you determine if the user has interacted with your game via the joystick. The status of the joystick is stored in the JOYINFO structure, which is defined as follows:

```
typedef struct {
  UINT wXpos;
  UINT wYpos;
  UINT wZpos;
  UINT wButtons;
} JOYINFO;
```

You'll notice that the JOYINFO structure is designed to accommodate joysticks with up to three axes of movement: x, y, and z. The first three members of the structure (wXpos, wYpos, and wZpos) indicate the position of the joystick with respect to each of these axes. The final member, wButtons, indicates the state of the joystick buttons. The wButtons member supports up to four buttons, as indicated by the following constants: JOY_BUTTON1, JOY_BUTTON2, JOY_BUTTON3, and JOY_BUTTON4.

> Earlier, I mentioned that Windows supports up to six axes and 32 buttons on joysticks, but the JOYINFO structure is obviously more limited than that. The reason for this disparity is because the full range of joystick features are only available through the DirectX game API, which is significantly more complex to use than the built-in Win32 joystick support. If you're planning on supporting a gyroscopic nuclear-powered virtual reality game helmet in your games that takes advantage of all the axes and buttons possible, you definitely need to get to work learning DirectX. Otherwise, I think you'll find the Win32 approach to joystick handling to be sufficient.

7

In order to examine a JOYINFO structure to see what's happened to a joystick, you must first obtain the joystick state using the joyGetPos() function, which is the same function you used to see if a joystick was plugged in. Following is a code example that examines a JOYINFO structure to see if the first joystick button is being pressed:

```
JOYINFO jiInfo;
if (joyGetPos(JOYSTICKID1, &jiInfo) == JOYERR_NOERROR)
  if (jiInfo.wButtons & JOY_BUTTON1)
    // Button 1 was pressed!
```

This code calls the joyGetPos()function to fill a JOYINFO structure with information about the current joystick state. If the return value of the function is JOYERR_NOERROR, there was no problem retrieving the information and we can continue. The bitwise AND operator (&) is then used with the wButtons member of the JOYINFO structure and the JOY_BUTTON1 constant to see if button 1 on the joystick is being pressed. You can use the same approach to look at other joystick buttons.

You're probably wondering why I've avoided talking about the other members of the JOYINFO structure, and how they are used to determine the position of the joystick handle. The reason for this has to do with the fact that you need to understand the range of values possible for these members before you can make sense of them. More specifically, you need to find out the minimum and maximum values for each axis of movement that you're interested in checking. For example, if you want to see if the joystick has been moved left, you first need to find out the range of values for the x axis of the joystick. You can then use this range to see how far left the joystick handle is being pushed, if at all.

You can determine the ranges of joystick axes by calling the Win32 joyGetDevCaps()function. This function fills a JOYCAPS structure with more information about a joystick than you'll probably ever want to know. For that reason, I won't go into all the details of the JOYCAPS structure. Instead, I'd like to focus on how to use it to determine the range of the two primary axes, x and y. Following is a code snippet that determines the center point of the x and y axis, which reveals the ranges of each:

```
JOYCAPS jcCaps;
joyGetDevCaps(JOYSTICKID1, &jcCaps, sizeof(JOYCAPS));
DWORD dwXCenter = ((DWORD)jcCaps.wXmin + jcCaps.wXmax) / 2;
DWORD dwYCenter = ((DWORD)jcCaps.wYmin + jcCaps.wYmax) / 2;
```

The minimum and maximum values for the x axis are wXmin and wXmax, whereas the y axis is bound by wYmin and wYmax. Adding these pairs of numbers and dividing by 2 gives you the center point of each axis, which is the point at which the joystick handle is at rest. With these values in hand, you can now determine a certain value that must be tripped in order to consider the joystick handle as having been moved in a given direction. This simplifies joystick movements into standard directions such as up, down, left, right, and so on. If you want to provide for very fine joystick control in your game, you might consider taking advantage of the full range of movement along each axis.

Revamping the Game Engine for Joysticks

The discussion of joysticks has been leading to a task that you probably knew was coming: another enhancement to the game engine. The idea is to continue beefing up the game engine with features so that the unique code for each game remains as minimal as possible. Knowing this, it's important to place as much joystick handling code in the game engine as possible. Before showing you the code, however, it's important to clarify a compile-time issue related to the Win32 joystick functions and data structures.

Accessing Win32 Multimedia Features

Although joystick support is now a standard part of Win32, this wasn't always the case. Once a multimedia subsystem was added separately to the Win32 API—of which joystick support is a part. For this reason, the joystick functions and data structures are not defined in the standard windows.h header file, and instead are located in the mmsystem.h header file, which is provided as part of the Win32 API. Following is an example of how you include this file in your code:

```
#include <mmsystem.h>
```

Okay, there's nothing tricky there. However, just importing the header file isn't enough because the executable code for the joystick support is located in a separate library that you must link into your games. This library is called winmm.lib, and it is included with all Windows compilers. Before you attempt to compile a Windows program that takes advantage of joystick features of the Win32 API, make sure that you change the link settings for the program so that the winmm.lib library file is linked into the final executable. Refer to the documentation for your specific compiler for how this is done, or follow these steps if you're using Microsoft Visual Studio:

1. Open the project in Visual Studio (Visual C++).
2. Right-click on the project's folder in Solution Explorer, and click Properties in the pop-up menu.
3. Click the Linker folder in the left pane of the Properties window, and then click Input.
4. Click next to Additional Dependencies in the right pane, and type a space followed by `winmm.lib`. You should already have the msimg32.lib library entered here, which is why it is necessary to type a space before entering winmm.lib.
5. Click the OK button to accept the changes to the project.

7

After completing these steps, you can safely compile a program and know that the winmm.lib library is being successfully linked into the executable program file.

 The source code for the examples in the book includes Visual Studio project files with the appropriate linker settings already made.

Developing the Joystick Code

As you now know, games interact with the game engine primarily through a series of functions that are called by the game engine at certain times throughout a game. In order to add joystick support to the game engine, it's important to add a new function that is going to receive joystick notifications. This function is called HandleJoystick(), and its prototype follows:

```
void HandleJoystick(JOYSTATE jsJoystickState);
```

The HandleJoystick() function accepts as its only argument a custom data type called JOYSTATE. The JOYSTATE data type is a custom type used to convey the state of a joystick at any given time. Listing 7.1 contains the code for the JOYSTATE data type.

LISTING 7.1   The JOYSTATE Data Type Includes Constant Flags That Describe the State of the Joystick

```
1: typedef WORD     JOYSTATE;
2: const JOYSTATE   JOY_NONE  = 0x0000L,
3:                  JOY_LEFT  = 0x0001L,
4:                  JOY_RIGHT = 0x0002L,
5:                  JOY_UP    = 0x0004L,
6:                  JOY_DOWN  = 0x0008L,
7:                  JOY_FIRE1 = 0x0010L,
8:                  JOY_FIRE2 = 0x0020L;
```

The JOYSTATE data type is a WORD value capable of containing one or more constant flags that indicate the state of various aspects of a joystick. For example, if the joystick handle is currently in the left position, the JOY_LEFT flag will appear in a JOYSTATE value. Multiple flags can be combined in the JOY_STATE data type, which makes sense when you consider that a joystick could simultaneously be in several of the states listed in the code.

You learned earlier that a joystick is identified by a unique ID, which is basically a number. You also learned that a joystick movement can be simplified into a simple direction by analyzing the range of motion for the joystick handle. This is accomplished by establishing a *trip rectangle* for the joystick, which is an area that determines how far the joystick handle must move in order for it to count as a directional event (up, down, left, right, or a combination). The purpose of the trip rectangle is to only cause joystick movement events to be generated if the handle moves so far, as shown in Figure 7.6.

FIGURE 7.6

A trip rectangle for the joystick helps to ensure that a joystick movement event is only generated if the joystick handle moves a certain minimum distance.

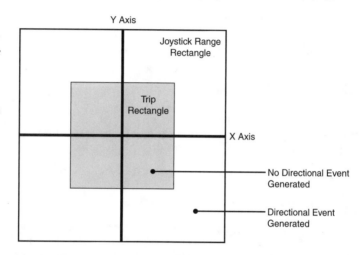

You now know that the game engine needs to keep track of two pieces of information in order to support a joystick: the joystick's ID and a trip rectangle for interpreting joystick movement. Following are the two member variables added to the game engine that account for this information:

```
UINT m_uiJoystickID;
RECT m_rcJoystickTrip;
```

In addition to these member variables, the game engine also requires some support methods for managing joystick input. More specifically, it needs to properly initialize the Win32 joystick input system, which involves making sure that a joystick is connected and retrieving its ID, as well as calculating the trip rectangle. You also need methods to capture and release the joystick, which you learn about in a moment. And finally, you need a method to check the state of the joystick and convert numeric joystick movements into more meaningful directions. Following are the methods added to the game engine that accomplish all of these tasks:

```
BOOL InitJoystick();
void CaptureJoystick();
void ReleaseJoystick();
void CheckJoystick();
```

7

The InitJoystick() method must be called by a game in order to initialize the joystick, retrieve its ID, and determine the trip rectangle. Its code is shown in Listing 7.2.

LISTING 7.2 The GameEngine::InitJoystick() Method Checks to Make Sure That a Joystick Is Present, and Then Initializes It

```
 1: BOOL GameEngine::InitJoystick()
 2: {
 3:   // Make sure joystick driver is present
 4:   UINT uiNumJoysticks;
 5:   if ((uiNumJoysticks = joyGetNumDevs()) == 0)
 6:     return FALSE;
 7:
 8:   // Make sure the joystick is attached
 9:   JOYINFO jiInfo;
10:   if (joyGetPos(JOYSTICKID1, &jiInfo) != JOYERR_UNPLUGGED)
11:     m_uiJoystickID = JOYSTICKID1;
12:   else
13:     return FALSE;
14:
15:   // Calculate the trip values
16:   JOYCAPS jcCaps;
17:   joyGetDevCaps(m_uiJoystickID, &jcCaps, sizeof(JOYCAPS));
18:   DWORD dwXCenter = ((DWORD)jcCaps.wXmin + jcCaps.wXmax) / 2;
19:   DWORD dwYCenter = ((DWORD)jcCaps.wYmin + jcCaps.wYmax) / 2;
20:   m_rcJoystickTrip.left = (jcCaps.wXmin + (WORD)dwXCenter) / 2;
21:   m_rcJoystickTrip.right = (jcCaps.wXmax + (WORD)dwXCenter) / 2;
22:   m_rcJoystickTrip.top = (jcCaps.wYmin + (WORD)dwYCenter) / 2;
23:   m_rcJoystickTrip.bottom = (jcCaps.wYmax + (WORD)dwYCenter) / 2;
24:
25:   return TRUE;
26: }
```

The code in this method should look reasonably familiar from the discussion earlier where you found out how to interact with joysticks. The joystick driver is first queried to make sure that it exists (lines 4–6). A test is then performed to make sure that the joystick is plugged in and ready to go (line 10)—after which, the ID of the joystick is stored in the m_uiJoystickID member variable (line 11). The trip rectangle is then calculated as a rectangle half the size of the joystick bounds in each direction (lines 16–23). This size is somewhat arbitrary, so you could feasibly tweak it if you wanted, meaning that the user has to push the joystick handle half of its total possible distance in a given direction in order for it to register as a directional move.

Listing 7.3 contains the code for the CaptureJoystick() and ReleaseJoystick() methods, which are quite important. In order for a program to receive joystick input, it must first *capture* the joystick, which means that the joystick is only going to communicate with that program. When a program is deactivated, it's important to *release* the joystick so that it is no longer captured; this allows another program to capture the joystick if necessary.

LISTING 7.3 The GameEngine::CaptureJoystick() and GameEngine::ReleaseJoystick() Methods Are Responsible for Capturing and Releasing the Joystick, Respectively

```
 1: void GameEngine::CaptureJoystick()
 2: {
 3:   // Capture the joystick
 4:   if (m_uiJoystickID == JOYSTICKID1)
 5:     joySetCapture(m_hWindow, m_uiJoystickID, NULL, TRUE);
 6: }
 7:
 8: void GameEngine::ReleaseJoystick()
 9: {
10:   // Release the joystick
11:   if (m_uiJoystickID == JOYSTICKID1)
12:     joyReleaseCapture(m_uiJoystickID);
13: }
```

Capturing and releasing a joystick is as simple as calling the joySetCapture() and joyReleaseCapture() Win32 functions, as shown in lines 5 and 12. Keep in mind that it's up to a program to call these two methods at the appropriate time (upon activation and deactivation) in order for joystick input to work properly.

Listing 7.4 contains the last of the new game engine joystick methods, CheckJoystick(), which is the method that is repeatedly called by a program to analyze the current joystick state and see if anything interesting has happened.

LISTING 7.4 The GameEngine::CheckJoystick() Method Checks the State of the Joystick and Passes It Along to the HandleJoystick() Function

```
 1: void GameEngine::CheckJoystick()
 2: {
 3:   if (m_uiJoystickID == JOYSTICKID1)
 4:   {
 5:     JOYINFO jiInfo;
 6:     JOYSTATE jsJoystickState = 0;
 7:     if (joyGetPos(m_uiJoystickID, &jiInfo) == JOYERR_NOERROR)
 8:     {
 9:       // Check horizontal movement
10:       if (jiInfo.wXpos < (WORD)m_rcJoystickTrip.left)
```

7

LISTING 7.4   Continued

```
11:             jsJoystickState |= JOY_LEFT;
12:         else if (jiInfo.wXpos > (WORD)m_rcJoystickTrip.right)
13:             jsJoystickState |= JOY_RIGHT;
14:
15:         // Check vertical movement
16:         if (jiInfo.wYpos < (WORD)m_rcJoystickTrip.top)
17:             jsJoystickState |= JOY_UP;
18:         else if (jiInfo.wYpos > (WORD)m_rcJoystickTrip.bottom)
19:             jsJoystickState |= JOY_DOWN;
20:
21:         // Check buttons
22:         if(jiInfo.wButtons & JOY_BUTTON1)
23:             jsJoystickState |= JOY_FIRE1;
24:         if(jiInfo.wButtons & JOY_BUTTON2)
25:             jsJoystickState |= JOY_FIRE2;
26:     }
27:
28:     // Allow the game to handle the joystick
29:     HandleJoystick(jsJoystickState);
30:   }
31: }
```

The CheckJoystick() method looks kind of complicated, but it's really not too bad. Understand that the idea behind this method is to quickly look at the state of the joystick, determine if enough movement has occurred to qualify as a directional movement (based on the trip rectangle), and then pass the results along to the HandleJoystick() function for game-specific joystick processing.

The standard JOYINFO structure is used to retrieve the joystick state via the joyGetPos() function (line 7). Different members of this structure are then compared against the trip rectangle to see if the joystick movement qualifies as a directional movement. If so, the appropriate directional flag is set on a JOYSTATE variable that is eventually passed to the HandleJoystick() function. The joystick buttons are also checked, and appropriate flags are set for those as well. The bottom line is that the HandleJoystick() function gets called with information that is easily analyzed by game-specific code to determine how to react to the joystick.

Building the UFO 2 Program Example

Hour 6, "Controlling Games with the Keyboard and Mouse," guided you through the design and development of an interesting little program that allowed you to control a flying saucer using the keyboard and mouse. The remainder of this hour focuses on adding joystick support to the UFO program example to create a new version of the program called UFO 2. In addition to providing joystick support, you also enhance the program a little by adding a thrust image to the flying saucer and a hyperspace feature. "Thrusting" in this case simply involves drawing a flying saucer with a flame shooting out of the bottom, whereas going into hyperspace involves repositioning the saucer at a random location on the game screen.

Writing the Program Code

The code for the UFO 2 program starts with the UFO.h header file, which includes a couple of changes from its previous version:

```
Bitmap*     _pSaucer[2];
BOOL        _bSaucerFlame;
```

The first change to this code from the previous version of the program is the modification of the _pSaucer global variable to being an array of two bitmaps, as opposed to one. This is necessary because the thrust bitmap has now been added to show the flying saucer with a flame shooting out. The other change to the code involves the addition of the _bSaucerFlame variable, which keeps track of whether the saucer is to be displayed with a flame.

The GameInitialize() function is the first game function to revisit for the UFO 2 program. The only change to this code from the previous version is the addition of the call to the game engine's InitJoystick() method, which is necessary to get the joystick primed and ready for action:

```
pGame->InitJoystick();
```

The GameStart() function also has changed a little, as shown in Listing 7.5.

LISTING 7.5 The GameStart() Function Initializes the Background and Flying Saucer Bitmaps

```
 1: void GameStart(HWND hWindow)
 2: {
 3:    // Seed the random number generator
 4:    srand(GetTickCount());
 5:
 6:    // Create and load the background and saucer bitmaps
 7:    HDC hDC = GetDC(hWindow);
 8:    _pBackground = new Bitmap(hDC, IDB_BACKGROUND, _hInstance);
 9:    _pSaucer[0] = new Bitmap(hDC, IDB_SAUCER, _hInstance);
10:    _pSaucer[1] = new Bitmap(hDC, IDB_SAUCERFLAME, _hInstance);
11:
12:    // Set the initial saucer position and speed
13:    _iSaucerX = 250 - (_pSaucer[0]->GetWidth() / 2);
14:    _iSaucerY = 200 - (_pSaucer[0]->GetHeight() / 2);
```

7

LISTING 7.5   Continued

```
15:    _iSpeedX = 0;
16:    _iSpeedY = 0;
17: }
```

Because the hyperspace feature of UFO 2 requires the calculation of a random location on the screen, it's necessary to seed the random number generator (line 4). This function also loads the new flaming saucer image (line 10).

Earlier, I mentioned that it's important for any program that supports joysticks to properly capture and release the joystick in response to the main program window being activated and deactivated. In the case of UFO 2, this takes place in the GameActivate() and GameDeactivate() functions, which are shown in Listing 7.6.

LISTING 7.6   The GameActivate()and GameDeactivate() Function Captures and Releases the Joystick in Response to the Main Program Window Being Activated and Deactivated

```
1: void GameActivate(HWND hWindow)
2: {
3:    // Capture the joystick
4:    _pGame->CaptureJoystick();
5: }
6:
7: void GameDeactivate(HWND hWindow)
8: {
9:    // Release the joystick
10:    _pGame->ReleaseJoystick();
11: }
```

The GameActivate() function simply calls the CaptureJoystick() method of the game engine to capture the joystick (line 4). Similarly, the joystick is released in GameDeactivate() with a quick call to the ReleaseJoystick() method.

If you're curious as to how the thrusting flying saucer is drawn, well wonder no more! The GamePaint() function handles drawing the appropriate flying saucer depending on the value of the _bSaucerFlame global variable, as shown in Listing 7.7.

LISTING 7.7   The GamePaint() Function Draws the Background and Flying Saucer Bitmaps, Making Sure to Determine Which Flying Saucer Bitmap to Draw

```
1: void GamePaint(HWND hWindow)
2: {
3:    // Draw the background and saucer bitmaps
```

LISTING 7.7   Continued

```
4:    _pBackground->Draw(hDC, 0, 0);
5:    _pSaucer[_bSaucerFlame ? 1:0]->Draw(hDC, _iSaucerX, _iSaucerY, TRUE);
6: }
```

As the listing reveals, the _bSaucerFlame variable directly determines which flying saucer is drawn (line 5). Of course, you're probably still curious as to how this variable gets modified in the first place; that's where the joystick enters the picture.

If you recall from earlier, a program that uses our super slick game engine to process joystick input must provide its own HandleJoystick() function to perform its own processing of joystick input. In this case, the HandleJoystick() function is responsible for altering the speed of the flying saucer in response to directional joystick movements, as well as controlling the thrust and hyperspace features of the flying saucer when the two joystick buttons are pressed. Listing 7.8 shows how the HandleJoystick() function carries out these tasks.

LISTING 7.8   The HandleJoystick() Function Takes Care of Processing Joystick Input and Altering the Flying Saucer Appropriately

```
 1: void HandleJoystick(JOYSTATE jsJoystickState)
 2: {
 3:    // Check horizontal movement
 4:    if (jsJoystickState & JOY_LEFT)
 5:      _iSpeedX = max(-_iMAXSPEED, _iSpeedX - 2);
 6:    else if (jsJoystickState & JOY_RIGHT)
 7:      _iSpeedX = min(_iMAXSPEED, _iSpeedX + 2);
 8:
 9:    // Check vertical movement
10:    if (jsJoystickState & JOY_UP)
11:      _iSpeedY = max(-_iMAXSPEED, _iSpeedY - 2);
12:    else if (jsJoystickState & JOY_DOWN)
13:      _iSpeedY = min(_iMAXSPEED, _iSpeedY + 2);
14:
15:    // Check primary joystick button
16:    _bSaucerFlame = (jsJoystickState & JOY_FIRE1);
17:
18:    // Check secondary joystick button
19:    if (jsJoystickState & JOY_FIRE2)
20:    {
21:      // Force the flying saucer into hyperspace
22:      _iSaucerX = rand() % (500 - _pSaucer[0]->GetWidth());
23:      _iSaucerY = rand() % 320;
24:    }
25: }
```

7

Seeing as how the HandleJoystick() function is essentially your only real communication link to the joystick in the UFO 2 program, it's really quite simple. The first block of code in the function checks to see if a horizontal movement has occurred—in which case, the X component of the flying saucer's speed if modified (lines 4–7). Similarly, the second block of code performs the same processing on vertical joystick movement (lines 10–13). The _bSaucerFlame global variable is then set using the state of the first joystick button (line 16). And finally, the hyperspace feature is carried out in response to the second joystick button being pressed (lines 19–24) .

Testing the Finished Product

If you haven't done so already, I encourage you to plug in your joystick and take the UFO 2 program for a test spin. You'll hopefully find that the joystick controls for the program have a surprisingly good feel considering that the joystick handling code in the program is relatively simple. Try pressing the two primary buttons on the joystick to get a feel for the thrust and hyperspace features of the program. Figure 7.7 shows the flying saucer as it appears with the flaming thrust beneath it.

FIGURE 7.7

The flying saucer in the UFO 2 program example shows off its new thrusting abilities.

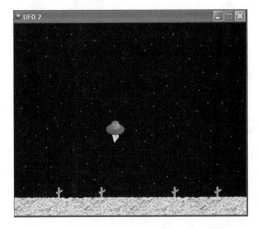

If the flying saucer immediately starts moving without you touching the joystick, it's a pretty good sign that your joystick needs to be calibrated. Please revisit the earlier section "Calibrating Joysticks," to find out how to calibrate your joystick and eliminate this problem.

Granted, you might have a valid concern as to why the flying saucer visually thrusts but doesn't seem to have any additional lift when you press the thrust button. This is something I challenge you to solve as an exercise at the end of the hour. You might also have noticed that hyperspace is quite sensitive. In fact, the hyperspace feature reveals how fast the game engine's joystick processing actually is.

Summary

Although joysticks don't quite share the widespread acceptance on PCs that keyboards and mice do, they are the quintessential user input device for games. There aren't too many serious gamers out there who don't have a joystick. However, you don't have to be serious about games to enjoy the benefits of playing games with a joystick. For this reason and more, it's a good idea to try and support joysticks in games that make sense to use a joystick as input. This hour gave you the nuts and bolts of Windows joystick handling, and even showed you how to build it into the ever evolving game engine. You also saw how easy it is to add joystick support to an existing program.

Mark your calendar because Hour 8, "Example Game: Brainiac," represents a significant milestone in your game programming career—you develop your first complete game. In other words, I've now deemed you knowledgeable enough about game development to turn you loose on a complete game project. Okay, I don't exactly turn you loose, but you work through the design and development of a complete game, nonetheless.

Q&A

Q What's a trip rectangle, and why is it really necessary?

A A trip rectangle is a rectangle that provides a means of simplifying and improving joystick input so that a joystick isn't too sensitive. More specifically, a trip rectangle is calculated to be proportionally smaller than the rectangle that represents the range of motion for a traditional XY joystick. In terms of simplicity, a trip rectangle makes it possible to consider joystick input in terms of a direction (left, right, up, down), as opposed to an XY coordinate value. A trip rectangle is also valuable because it prevents a joystick from feeling overly sensitive, where every time you touch it movement is interpreted. A trip rectangle basically establishes a minimum threshold of movement that the joystick handle must pass beyond before a joystick movement event is generated.

7

Q Why doesn't the code in this hour support more than one joystick?

A The joystick code developed throughout this hour supports only one joystick purely for the sake of simplicity. The code added to the game engine would be somewhat more complex if it were to support multiple joysticks, so I opted to keep it simple and focus on supporting a single joystick. In order to support multiple joysticks, you would primarily need to manage the multiple IDs associated with the joysticks, which isn't terribly difficult. In other words, you should have enough knowledge to add support for multiple joysticks to the game engine.

Workshop

The Workshop is designed to help you anticipate possible questions, review what you've learned, and begin learning how to put your knowledge into practice. The answers to the quiz can be found in Appendix A, "Quiz Answers."

Quiz

1. How many axes is a joystick allowed to have in Windows?
2. Why is it important to calibrate joysticks?
3. What's the purpose of the Win32 `joyGetDevCaps()` function?

Exercises

1. Modify the UFO 2 program so that the thrust button not only causes the flying saucer to appear with thrust, but also so that it acts like it has thrust. In other words, alter its vertical speed in response to the thrust button so that the saucer actually thrusts upward. It might be a good idea to make the thrust button have more of an impact on the saucer's lift than simply pressing up on the joystick; the second exercise will make this feature more important.

2. Experiment with adding gravity to the UFO 2 program by slightly changing the flying saucer's vertical speed in the `GameCycle()` function.

HOUR 8

Example Game: Brainiac

What good is a game book without any games? I have to admit to feeling kind of bad for spending seven lessons getting you primed for game programming. I'd loved to have hit you with a complete game in the first lesson, but you'd probably ended up wanting to hit me. The reality is that it's taken seven lessons to give you enough knowledge for you to create a complete game, which is the purpose of this lesson. In this lesson, you create a tile game called Brainiac that is similar to the classic Concentration memory game in which you match pairs of hidden tiles. Okay, so the game isn't quite a 3D shoot-em-up, but it is a complete game that you can show off to your buddies. In fact, you can plug in your own tile images to customize the game with pictures of your friends and family.

In this hour, you'll learn

- How to dream up the concept for a new game
- How to take a game concept and turn it into a game design
- How to use the game engine and a game design to build a working game from scratch
- That testing a game is the best part of the game development process

How Does the Game Play?

The idea behind the Brainiac game that you design and develop in this hour is to present a grid of paired tiles. More specifically, a 4x4 grid contains sixteen tiles, so eight pairs of tiles are randomly placed on the grid. Each of the pairs of tiles has a unique image that you use to match up the pairs during the game. The unique image on the tiles is hidden when you start the game, and is only revealed as you click tiles and attempt to match them. So, when tiles are unmatched, you see a common tile image that makes the different tiles indistinguishable. It's sort of like having a bunch of playing cards laid out face down. Figure 8.1 shows the grid of tiles in the Brainiac game and how they might be arranged for matching in pairs.

FIGURE 8.1

The Brainiac game consists of a 4x4 grid of randomly arranged tiles that are matched in pairs.

1	8	7	3
2	6	1	2
5	8	4	7
4	6	3	5

The game proceeds by allowing you to pick one tile, and then another. If the two tiles match, they are left visible and you move on to try and find two more matching tiles. If they don't match, they are flipped back over to remain hidden again. Your job is to remember the positions of the tiles as you turn them over so that you can match them up. The game keeps track of how many attempts it takes to finish matching all the tiles and reports the total to you when you finish. This total is essentially your score for the game, and is a good incentive to play more and work on your memory skills.

In case you haven't thought about it, the Brainiac game is a perfect game for mouse input. The most intuitive way to play this kind of game is by pointing and clicking the tiles with the mouse, so in this lesson the only user interface you'll build in to the game is mouse input. It wouldn't be a terrible idea to add keyboard and possibly even joystick support as an enhancement, but I didn't want to add unnecessary code at this point. Keep in mind that both the keyboard and joystick would have to use an additional graphical component in order to work. For example, you would have to come up with some kind of selection or highlight graphic to indicate which tile is currently selected. The mouse doesn't require such a component because you already have the mouse cursor to use as the basis for selecting tiles.

8

I realize that this probably isn't the most fanciful game you might have envisioned as your first complete game, but it is pretty neat when you consider that it does present a challenge and allow you to play and win. Additionally, the Brainiac game is a fun little game for incorporating your own images into the tiles and personalizing it.

Designing the Game

The Brainiac game probably sounds reasonably simple from the perspective of a player, but you'll find that it still requires some effort from a programming perspective. Games generally are not simply programs to write, and Brainiac represents probably the simplest game you'll ever develop. Even so, if you take your time and think through the design of your games, you'll be much farther ahead of the curve when you sit down to hack out the code.

As with most games, the key to designing the Brainiac game is to figure out how to accurately store the state of the game at any given moment. In other words, how will you reflect what's going on in the game in variables? Because the game is arranged as a 4x4 grid of tiles, it makes sense that the first thing you'll need is a two-dimensional array of bitmaps that identifies the tile image to be displayed for each tile. Of course, the bitmap images alone don't say anything about whether a match has been made. So, you also need another two-dimensional array that keeps track of whether a tile has been matched. Together, these two arrays have most of the knowledge required to indicate the state of the game at any given moment.

The other missing pieces to the Brainiac puzzle primarily involve the tile matching process. More specifically, you need to keep up with the two tiles that the user has currently selected so that you can display them properly, as well as perform a match test on them. If the tiles match, you just update their status in the tile state array so that they remain turned over; if not, you make sure that they get returned to their hidden state. Most of the logic in the Brainiac game takes place in the mouse handling code because mouse clicks are the primary means in which the user selects tiles and attempts to make matches.

The two remaining pieces of information critical to the design of the game are the number of matches and number of tries. The number of matches is extremely important because it determines when the game is over; because there are eight pairs of tiles, eight matches constitutes winning the game. The number of tries has more to do with keeping up with how well you did—it's sort of a scorekeeping piece of information.

To recap, the design of the Brainiac game has led us to the following pieces of information that must be managed by the game:

- A two-dimensional array (4×4) of tile bitmaps
- A two-dimensional array (4×4) of tile states
- The tiles selected by the user as a potential match
- The number of matches
- The number of tries

With this information in mind, you're now ready to move on and put the code together for the Brainiac game.

Building the Game

In previous hours, you've seen how the game engine that you've built thus far has made it possible to create interesting programs with a relatively small amount of code. You're now going to see the true value of the game engine as you assemble the code for the Brainiac game. The next couple of sections explore the code development for the Brainiac game, which is surprisingly straightforward considering that you're creating a fully functioning game. The complete source code for the Brainiac game, not to mention all of the examples throughout the book, is located on the accompanying CD-ROM.

Writing the Game Code

The code for the Brainiac game begins with the Brainiac.h header file, which is shown in Listing 8.1.

LISTING 8.1 The Brainiac.h Header File Declares Global Variables That Are Used to Manage the Game

```
 1: #pragma once
 2:
 3: //------------------------------------------------------------
 4: // Include Files
 5: //------------------------------------------------------------
 6: #include <windows.h>
 7: #include "Resource.h"
 8: #include "GameEngine.h"
 9: #include "Bitmap.h"
10:
11: //------------------------------------------------------------
12: // Global Variables
13: //------------------------------------------------------------
14: HINSTANCE    _hInstance;
15: GameEngine*  _pGame;
16: Bitmap*      _pTiles[9];
```

LISTING 8.1   Continued

```
17: BOOL        _bTileStates[4][4];
18: int         _iTiles[4][4];
19: POINT       _ptTile1, _ptTile2;
20: int         _iMatches, _iTries;
```

This code is where the design work you carried out earlier in this hour directly plays out. More specifically, the pieces of information that were mentioned as critical components of the game are now realized as global variables. The _pTiles variable stores away the tile images (line 16). You might be wondering why the array contains nine bitmaps when there are only eight different tile images for matching. The reason is because there is an extra tile image to represent the backs of the tiles when they are hidden.

> You might have noticed in the code that a data type called POINT is being used for the tile selections. This is a standard Win32 data type that stores two pieces of information: an X value and a Y value. The POINT data structure is quite handy and can be used in any situation in which you need to store a point, coordinate, or other numeric data consisting of two integer parts. The X and Y values in the structure are named x and y.

The tile states are stored in a two-dimensional array of Boolean values named _bTileStates (line 17). The idea behind this variable is that a value of TRUE for a tile indicates that it has already been matched, whereas FALSE means that it is still hidden and unmatched. The bitmap associated with each tile is stored in the _iTiles array (line 18), which might seem strange because it doesn't actually reference Bitmap objects. This is because you already have the Bitmap objects available in the _pTiles array, so all the _iTiles array has to do is reference each tile bitmap as an index into the _pTiles array.

The two tile selections are stored in the _ptTile1 and _ptTile2 variables (line 19). These variables are important because they keep track of the user's tile selections, and are therefore used to determine when a successful match takes place. The last two variables, _iMatches and _iTries, are used to keep track of the number of matches made and the number of match attempts, respectively (line 20). The _iMatches variable will be used a little later in the code to determine if the game is over.

The GameInitialize() function for the Braniac game is similar to what you've seen in previous examples. In fact, the only change to this function from earlier examples is that the frame rate is set to 1. This means that the GameCycle() function is only called once per second, which is painfully slow for most games. However, the frame rate theoretically could be zero for Brainiac because there is nothing to update on a regular basis. This is because you know when game updates are necessary—when the user clicks a tile. Therefore, because it's not a big deal having a high frame rate, you might as well minimize its effect on the game.

The GameStart() and GameEnd() functions are responsible for initializing and cleaning up the game data, as shown in Listing 8.2.

LISTING 8.2 The GameStart() Function Creates and Loads the Tile Bitmaps, as well as Initializes Game State Member Variables, Whereas the GameEnd() Function Cleans Up the Bitmaps

```
 1: void GameStart(HWND hWindow)
 2: {
 3:   // Seed the random number generator
 4:   srand(GetTickCount());
 5:
 6:   // Create and load the tile bitmaps
 7:   HDC hDC = GetDC(hWindow);
 8:   _pTiles[0] = new Bitmap(hDC, IDB_TILEBLANK, _hInstance);
 9:   _pTiles[1] = new Bitmap(hDC, IDB_TILE1, _hInstance);
10:   _pTiles[2] = new Bitmap(hDC, IDB_TILE2, _hInstance);
11:   _pTiles[3] = new Bitmap(hDC, IDB_TILE3, _hInstance);
12:   _pTiles[4] = new Bitmap(hDC, IDB_TILE4, _hInstance);
13:   _pTiles[5] = new Bitmap(hDC, IDB_TILE5, _hInstance);
14:   _pTiles[6] = new Bitmap(hDC, IDB_TILE6, _hInstance);
15:   _pTiles[7] = new Bitmap(hDC, IDB_TILE7, _hInstance);
16:   _pTiles[8] = new Bitmap(hDC, IDB_TILE8, _hInstance);
17:
18:   // Clear the tile states and images
19:   for (int i = 0; i < 4; i++)
20:     for (int j = 0; j < 4; j++)
21:     {
22:       _bTileStates[i][j] = FALSE;
23:       _iTiles[i][j] = 0;
24:     }
25:
26:   // Initialize the tile images randomly
27:   for (int i = 0; i < 2; i++)
28:     for (int j = 1; j < 9; j++)
29:     {
30:       int x = rand() % 4;
31:       int y = rand() % 4;
32:       while (_iTiles[x][y] != 0)
33:       {
34:         x = rand() % 4;
35:         y = rand() % 4;
```

LISTING 8.2 Continued

```
36:      }
37:      _iTiles[x][y] = j;
38:    }
39:
40:    // Initialize the tile selections and match/try count
41:    _ptTile1.x = _ptTile1.y = -1;
42:    _ptTile2.x = _ptTile2.y = -1;
43:    _iMatches = _iTries = 0;
44: }
45:
46: void GameEnd()
47: {
48:    // Cleanup the tile bitmaps
49:    for (int i = 0; i < 9; i++)
50:      delete _pTiles[i];
51:
52:    // Cleanup the game engine
53:    delete _pGame;
54: }
```

If you happen to get a "multiple initialization" compiler error while compiling the Braniac program, you can easily fix it by removing the int variable declaration in line 27 of the code. This error stems from the fact that some compilers don't fully support the standard C++ approach of declaring loop initializer variables local to the loop. So, the int variable i is mistakenly interpreted as being declared twice. Just remove int from line 27 and everything will work fine.

The GameStart() function contains a fair amount of code because all the variables in the game must be carefully initialized for the game to play properly. The function begins by seeding the random number generator (line 4), which is necessary because you'll be randomly placing tiles in a moment. The tile bitmaps are then loaded into the _pTiles array (lines 8–16). From there, the real work of initializing the game data begins to take place.

Because a value of FALSE indicates that a tile has not yet been matched, it's necessary to initialize each element in the _bTileStates array to FALSE (line 22). Similarly, the elements in the _iTiles array are initialized to 0 (line 23), but for a different reason. When the tiles are randomly placed in the _iTiles array in a moment, it's important to have the elements initialized to 0 so that you can tell which tile spaces are available for tile placement. The actual tile placement occurs in lines 27–38, and definitely isn't as complicated as it looks. What's happening is that a tile space is randomly selected and tested to see if it has been filled with a tile (line 32). If so, the code continues to select random tiles until an empty one is found. When an empty space is found, the tile is set (line 37).

The last few steps in the GameStart() function involve setting the _ptTile1 and _ptTile2 variables to -1 (lines 41 and 42). Because these variables are POINT structures, each of them contains an X and Y value. So, you're actually initializing two pieces of information for each of the tile selection variables. The value of -1 comes into play because it's a good way to indicate that a selection hasn't been made. In other words, you can tell that the user hasn't made the first tile selection by simply looking at the values of _ptTile1.x and _ptTile1.y and seeing if they are set to -1. The _iMatches and _iTries variables are simply initialized to 0, which makes sense given their purpose (line 43).

The GameEnd() is responsible for cleaning up the tile bitmaps (lines 49 and 50), as well as the game engine (line 53).

The Braniac game screen is painted in the GamePaint() function, which is shown in Listing 8.3.

LISTING 8.3   The GamePaint() Function Draws the Tiles for the Game According to the Tile States Stored in the Game State Member Variables

```
 1: void GamePaint(HDC hDC)
 2: {
 3:   // Draw the tiles
 4:   int iTileWidth = _pTiles[0]->GetWidth();
 5:   int iTileHeight = _pTiles[0]->GetHeight();
 6:   for (int i = 0; i < 4; i++)
 7:     for (int j = 0; j < 4; j++)
 8:       if (_bTileStates[i][j] || ((i == _ptTile1.x) && (j == _ptTile1.y)) ||
 9:         ((i == _ptTile2.x) && (j == _ptTile2.y)))
10:         _pTiles[_iTiles[i][j]]->Draw(hDC, i * iTileWidth, j * iTileHeight,
11:           TRUE);
12:       else
13:         _pTiles[0]->Draw(hDC, i * iTileWidth, j * iTileHeight, TRUE);
14: }
```

The job of the GamePaint() function is to draw the 4x4 grid of tile bitmaps on the game screen. This is primarily accomplished by examining each tile state and either drawing its associated tile image if it is already matched (lines 10 and 11) or drawing a generic tile image if it isn't matched (line 13). One interesting thing to note in this code is that you have to look beyond the tile state when drawing the tiles because it's important to draw the two selected tiles properly even though they might not be a match. This test is performed in lines 8 and 9 where the tile selection values are taken into account along with the tile state.

Although `GamePaint()` is important in providing the visuals for the Brainiac game, the bulk of the game logic is in the `MouseButtonDown()` function, which is shown in Listing 8.4.

LISTING 8.4 The `MouseButtonDown()` Function Carries Out the Majority of the Game Logic for the Brainiac Game

```
 1: void MouseButtonDown(int x, int y, BOOL bLeft)
 2: {
 3:    // Determine which tile was clicked
 4:    int iTileX = x / _pTiles[0]->GetWidth();
 5:    int iTileY = y / _pTiles[0]->GetHeight();
 6:
 7:    // Make sure the tile hasn't already been matched
 8:    if (!_bTileStates[iTileX][iTileY])
 9:    {
10:      // See if this is the first tile selected
11:      if (_ptTile1.x == -1)
12:      {
13:        // Set the first tile selection
14:        _ptTile1.x = iTileX;
15:        _ptTile1.y = iTileY;
16:      }
17:      else if ((iTileX != _ptTile1.x) || (iTileY != _ptTile1.y))
18:      {
19:        if (_ptTile2.x == -1)
20:        {
21:          // Increase the number of tries
22:          _iTries++;
23:
24:          // Set the second tile selection
25:          _ptTile2.x = iTileX;
26:          _ptTile2.y = iTileY;
27:
28:          // See if it's a match
29:          if (_iTiles[_ptTile1.x][_ptTile1.y] ==
30:            _iTiles[_ptTile2.x][_ptTile2.y])
31:          {
32:            // Set the tile state to indicate the match
33:            _bTileStates[_ptTile1.x][_ptTile1.y] = TRUE;
34:            _bTileStates[_ptTile2.x][_ptTile2.y] = TRUE;
35:
36:            // Clear the tile selections
37:            _ptTile1.x = _ptTile1.y = _ptTile2.x = _ptTile2.y = -1;
38:
39:            // Update the match count and check for winner
40:            if (++_iMatches == 8)
41:            {
42:              TCHAR szText[64];
```

LISTING 8.4   Continued

```
43:                   wsprintf(szText, "You won in %d tries.", _iTries);
44:                   MessageBox(_pGame->GetWindow(), szText, TEXT("Brainiac"),
45:                     MB_OK);
46:                 }
47:               }
48:             }
49:       else
50:         {
51:           // Clear the tile selections
52:           _ptTile1.x = _ptTile1.y = _ptTile2.x = _ptTile2.y = -1;
53:         }
54:       }
55:
56:       // Force a repaint to update the tile
57:       InvalidateRect(_pGame->GetWindow(), NULL, FALSE);
58:     }
59: }
```

The first step in the MouseButtonDown() function is to determine which tile was clicked. This determination takes place in lines 4 and 5, and involves using the mouse cursor position provided in the x and y arguments passed into the function. When you know which tile was clicked, you can quickly check and see if it has already been matched (line 8); if so, there is no reason to do anything else because it doesn't make sense to play a tile that has already been matched. Assuming that the tile hasn't already been matched, the next test is to see if this is the first tile selected (line 11); if so, all you have to do is store the tile position in _ptTile1. If not, you have to move on and make sure that it isn't the first tile being reselected, which wouldn't make much sense (line 17). If you pass that test, you have to check and see if this is indeed the second tile selection (line 19); if so, it's time to go to work and see if there is a match. If this isn't the second tile selection, you know it must be the third click in an unsuccessful match, which means that the tile selections need to be cleared so that the selection process can be repeated (lines 47–51).

Getting back to the second tile selection, when you know that the user has just selected the second tile, you can safely increment the number of tries (line 22), as well as store away the tile selection (lines 25 and 26). You can then check for a match by comparing the two tile selections to each other (line 29). If there is a match, the tile states are modified for each tile (lines 32 and 33), and the tile selections are cleared (line 36). The match count is then incremented and checked to see if the game is over (line 39). If the game is over, a window is displayed that notifies you of winning, as well as displays how many tries it took (lines 41–43).

The last step in the MouseButtonDown() function is to force a repaint of the game screen with a call to InvalidateRect() (line 56). This line is extremely important because it results in the user's action (the tile selection with a mouse click) being visually carried out on the screen.

Tweaking Your Compiler for the Brainiac Program

The Brainiac program example, and all the remaining programs in the book for that matter, rely on two standard libraries that aren't automatically linked into a Win32 program. These libraries are called winmm.lib and msimg32.lib, and they are included with all Windows compilers. Before you attempt to compile any of the remaining programs in the book, including Brainiac, make sure that you change the link settings for the program so that the winmm.lib and msimg32.lib library files are linked into the final executable. Refer to the documentation for your specific compiler for how this is done, or follow these steps if you're using Microsoft Visual Studio:

1. Open the project in Visual Studio (Visual C++).

2. Right-click on the project's folder in Solution Explorer, and click Properties in the pop-up menu.

3. Click the Linker folder in the left pane of the Properties window, and then click Input.

4. Click next to Additional Dependencies in the right pane, and type **winmm.lib** followed by a space followed by **msimg32.lib**.

5. Click the OK button to accept the changes to the project.

After completing these steps, you can safely compile a program and know that the winmm.lib and msimg32.lib libraries are being successfully linked into the executable program file.

Testing the Game

The most rewarding part of the game development process is seeing the end result of all your toiling over game code. In fact, one of the most exciting aspects of game programming is how you can experiment with tweaking the code and seeing how it impacts the game play. There admittedly isn't a whole lot to be tweaked on the Brainiac game, but it's nonetheless a neat game to try out now that the code is complete. Figure 8.2 shows the game upon initially starting out, which shows all the tiles hidden and ready for you to attempt a match.

When you click to select a tile, its image is revealed, as shown in Figure 8.3.

FIGURE 8.2

The Brainiac game begins with all the tiles hidden, waiting for you to make the first tile selection.

FIGURE 8.3

Clicking a tile reveals its underlying image, which lets you know what you're attempting to match.

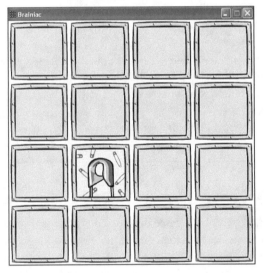

After making your first move, the next step is to try and make a match by selecting another tile. Of course, on the first round of the game, this is essentially a shot in the dark. When you fail to make a match, you have to click once more to return the tiles to their hidden state and attempt another match. This gives you time to memorize the locations of the tiles you attempted to match. Making a match simply involves selecting the same two tiles, as shown in Figure 8.4.

You might be wondering why I selected tools as the basis for the graphics in the Brainiac game. The answer is that I've probably been watching too many home fix-it shows on television lately, so I just had tools on my mind. You could easily change the graphics to just about any theme you want: animals, cartoon characters, family members, you name it.

8

FIGURE 8.4

Matching tiles involves selecting two tiles with the same bitmap image.

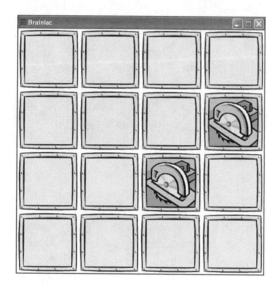

If you're one of those people who can recall the name of every classmate in your kindergarten class, you'll probably find the Brainiac game easy to master. Otherwise, you might just end up clicking aimlessly until you luck out on a few matches. Either way, the game will eventually end, and you'll be able to judge how well you've done by the number of tries it took to match all the tiles. Figure 8.5 shows the window that is displayed upon completing the game.

If you're the obsessive, competitive type, you will no doubt spend hours trying to get the number of tries down to a ridiculously low number. Or you might decide that Brainiac is nothing more than a light diversion on your path toward creating new and more interesting games. Either way, it's a good example of how to pull together a variety of different skills toward the creation of a complete game.

FIGURE 8.5

Upon completing a game of Brainiac, you are presented with a window that lets you know how many tries it took.

Summary

Up until this hour, you focused on individual aspects of game development ranging from drawing basic graphics to handling user input. This hour represents a first attempt at incorporating everything you've learned thus far into the development of a complete game that you can play and share with your friends. The Brainiac game is by most standards a simple game without too many frills, but it does demonstrate what it takes to put together a working game from start to finish. Perhaps more importantly, you got to experience first-hand what it's like to start with an idea, move forward with a design, and then realize that design in actual code. You'll be repeating this process several more times throughout the book as you construct more powerful and exciting games, so this experience will serve you well.

This hour wraps up this part of the book. The next part of the book tackles animation, which is a subject you've learned a little about, but you're still missing a formal introduction. The next part of the book is quite interesting because it presents you with the skills to start building action games complete with animated graphical objects.

Q&A

Q Because the frame rate isn't important for the Brainiac game, why can't it be set to 0?

A This is one of those questions that is best answered by trying out the suggestion. If you try to pass 0 into the SetFrameRate() member function of the game engine,

you'll get a "Divide By Zero" exception because the frame rate is divided into 1,000 (milliseconds) in order to calculate the delay for each game cycle in the game engine's timing loop. So, passing 0 isn't an option unless you modify the game engine so that it reacts differently if 0 is specified as the frame rate. Although this is certainly an option, having a frame rate of one doesn't really hurt anything, and it keeps you from having to add conditional code for a 0 frame rate.

Q What is the purpose of setting the tile selection variables to -1?

A A -1 setting for the tile selection variables indicates that they haven't been set to a specific tile. This is a clue to you that a tile selection hasn't been made; otherwise the tile selection variable would have a value in the range of 0 to 3. (The array contains four elements.) The game code can therefore quickly tell where the user is at in terms of selecting tiles by looking for a value of -1, which indicates that a selection has not yet been made.

Workshop

The Workshop is designed to help you anticipate possible questions, review what you've learned, and begin learning how to put your knowledge into practice. The answers to the quiz can be found in Appendix A, "Quiz Answers."

Quiz

1. Why doesn't the Braniac game support the keyboard or joystick?
2. Why can't the Braniac game keep track of its state with a single 4×4 array?
3. Why is it necessary to keep up with the number of matches in the Braniac game?

Exercises

1. Replace the tile images in the Braniac game with some images of your own. Feel free to modify the existing tile images if you want to make sure that you get the tile size right, or you can resize the entire game screen if you want to go with different sized tiles.

2. You've probably noticed that the Braniac game doesn't provide a means of starting a new game without closing the program and restarting it. You also might have noticed that the game doesn't distinguish between left and right mouse button clicks. Modify the game so that the game is played via the left mouse button, while the right mouse button is used to start a new game.

PART III
Animating Games with Sprites

Hours

HOUR 9

A Crash Course in Game Animation

The heart of graphics in almost all games is animation. Without animation, there would be no movement, and without movement, we'd all be stuck playing board games and card games. This hour presents the fundamental concepts surrounding animation in games and, more specifically, sprite animation. As you'll soon learn, practically every game with animation employs some type of animation engine, typically involving sprites. Although this hour is primarily a theoretical discussion of animation, it is a necessary stepping stone in your path to adding advanced animation features to your games.

In this hour, you'll learn:

- The basics of animation and how it works in games
- The difference between 2D and 3D animation
- The different types of 2D animation, and when to use each one in games

What Is Animation?

Before getting into animation as it relates to games, it's important to understand the basics of what animation is and how it works. Let's begin by asking this fundamental question: What is animation? Put simply, *animation* is the illusion of movement. Am I saying that every animation you've ever seen is really just an illusion? That's exactly right! And probably the most surprising animated illusion is one that captured attentions long before computers—the television. When you watch television, you see a lot of things moving around. But what you perceive as movement is really just a trick being played on your eyes.

Animation and Frame Rate

In the case of television, the illusion of movement is created by displaying a rapid succession of images with slight changes in their appearance. The human eye perceives these changes as movement because of its low visual acuity, which means that your eyes are fairly easy to trick into believing the illusion of animation. More specifically, the human eye can be tricked into perceiving animated movement with as low as 12 frames of movement per second. It should come as no surprise that this animation speed is the minimum target speed for most computer games. Animation speed is measured in *frames per second* (fps), which you've encountered a few times throughout the book already.

Although 12fps is technically enough to fool your eyes into seeing animation, animations at speeds this low often end up looking somewhat jerky. Therefore, most professional animations use a higher frame rate. Television, for example, uses 30fps. When you go to the movies, you see motion pictures at about 24fps. It's pretty apparent that these frame rates are more than enough to captivate your attention and successfully create the illusion of movement.

Unlike television and motion pictures, computer games are much more limited when it comes to frame rate. Higher frame rates in games correspond to much higher processor overhead, so game developers are left to balance the frame rate against the system speed and resources. That is why some games provide different resolution and graphics quality options. By using a lower resolution and simpler graphics, a game can increase its frame rate and generate smoother animations. Of course, the trade-off is a lower resolution and simpler graphics.

When programming animation in Windows games, you typically have the ability to manipulate the frame rate a reasonable amount. The most obvious limitation on frame rate is the speed at which the computer can generate and display the animation frames. Actually, the same limitation must be dealt with by game developers, regardless of the programming language or platform. When determining the frame rate for a game, you usually have some give and take in establishing a low enough frame rate to yield a smooth animation, while not bogging down the processor and slowing the system down. But don't worry too much about this right now. For now, just keep in mind that when programming animation for games, you are acting as a magician creating the illusion of movement.

Making the Move to Computer Animation

Most of the techniques used in computer animation have been borrowed or based on traditional animation techniques developed for animated films. The classic approach to handling traditional animation is to draw a background image separately from the animated objects that will be moving in the foreground. The animated objects are then drawn on clear celluloid sheets so that they can be overlaid on the background and moved independently. This type of animation is referred to as *cel animation*. Cel animation enables artists to save a great deal of time by only drawing the specific objects that change shape or position from one frame to the next. This explains why so many animated movies have detailed backgrounds with relatively simple animated characters. Computer game sprites, which you learn about a little later in the hour, directly correspond to traditional cel animated objects.

As computer power improved in the last two decades, traditional animators saw the potential for automating many of their hands-on techniques. Computers enabled them to scan in drawings and overlay them with transparency, for example. This is a similar approach to cel animation, but with one big difference: The computer imposes no limitations on the number of overlaid images. Cel animation is limited because only so many cel sheets can be overlaid. The technique of overlaying objects with transparency is a fundamental form of computer game animation, as you soon find out.

 Modern animated movies have officially proven that computer animation is for more than just games. Popular movies such as *Toy Story*, *A Bug's Life*, and *Monsters Inc.* are great examples of how traditional animated movies are now being created solely on computers. An even more advanced example of computer animation in movies is the *Final Fantasy* movie, which uses computer animation to simulate live action graphics.

Although computers have certainly improved upon traditional animation techniques, the animation potential available to the game programmer is far more flexible than traditional techniques. As a programmer, you have access to each individual pixel of each bitmap image, and you can manipulate each of them to your heart's desire.

2D Versus 3D Animation

There are two fundamental types of animation that you might consider using when creating games: 2D and 3D. *2D animation* involves objects moving or being manipulated within two dimensions. Objects in a 2D animation can still have a 3D look to them—they just can't physically move in three dimensions. Many 2D animation techniques simulate 3D animation by altering the look of objects, but they aren't truly 3D. As an example, an animation of a car driving off into the distance would involve the car getting smaller as it gets farther away. However, this isn't necessarily a 3D animation because you can achieve the 3D effect by making the car image get smaller as it moves away. Although the end result is three-dimensional, the car is very much a 2D object.

Unlike 2D animation, *3D animation* involves placing and manipulating objects in a three-dimensional virtual world. A 3D object is defined by a model rather than an image because an image is inherently two-dimensional. A 3D model specifies the shape of an object by a series of points in 3D space. In other words, a 3D model is a mathematical representation of a physical object. For this reason, 3D graphics and animation can get extremely complicated because it often relies on heavy-duty mathematical processing.

In reality, many games make use of a mixture of 2D and 3D graphics and animation. For example, the original Doom game uses 3D graphics for the building interiors. However, the monsters in the game are 2D graphics objects. The monsters have a 3D appearance, but they are represented by flat images on the screen. This mixture of 2D and 3D graphics works great in Doom because the 2D monsters look realistic when blending into 3D surroundings. Of course, things have evolved since the original Doom game. Quake and other more modern 3D first-person shooters (FPS) now use 3D objects throughout the game.

The remainder of this hour, and the book in general, focuses on 2D animation because it is the more straightforward and efficient technique of the two. The good news is that you can still do some pretty powerful things with 2D animation.

Types of 2D Animation

Although the focus of this hour is ultimately on sprite animation, it is important to understand the primary types of animation used in game programming. Actually, a lot of different types of animation exist, all of which are useful in different instances. However, for the purposes of implementing animation in games, I've broken animation down into two basic types: frame-based and cast-based animation. Technically speaking, there is also a third animation type known as *palette animation* that involves animating the colors in a graphic object, but I think of it as more of a graphics effect rather than a fundamental type of animation.

Frame-Based Animation

The most simple animation technique is *frame-based animation*, which finds a lot of usage in non-gaming animations. Frame-based animation involves simulating movement by displaying a sequence of pre-generated, static frame images. A movie is a perfect example of frame-based animation; each frame of the film is a frame of animation, and when the frames are shown in rapid succession, they create the illusion of movement.

Frame-based animation has no concept of a graphical object distinguishable from the background; everything appearing in a frame is part of that frame as a whole. The result is that each frame image contains all the information necessary for that frame in a static form. This is an important point because it distinguishes frame-based animation from cast-based animation, which you learn about in the next section. Figure 9.1 shows a few frames in a frame-based animation.

FIGURE 9.1

In frame-based animation, the entire frame changes to achieve the effect of animation.

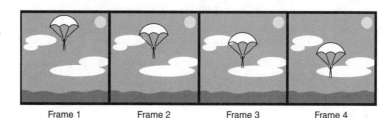

Frame 1   Frame 2   Frame 3   Frame 4

The figure shows how a paratrooper is drawn directly onto each frame of animation, so there is no separation between the paratrooper object and the sky background. This means that the paratrooper cannot be moved independently of the background. The illusion of movement is achieved by redrawing each frame with the paratrooper in a slightly different position. This type of animation is of limited use in games because games typically require the ability to move objects around independently of the background.

Cast-Based Animation

A more powerful animation technique employed by many games is *cast-based animation*, which is also known as *sprite animation*. Cast-based animation involves graphical objects that move independently of a background. At this point, you might be a little confused by the usage of the term graphical object when referring to parts of an animation. In this case, a graphical object is something that logically can be thought of as a separate entity from the background of an animation image. For example, in the animation of a space shoot-em-up game, the aliens are separate graphical objects that are logically independent of the starfield background.

You might be wondering where the term cast-based animation comes from. It comes from the fact that sprites can be thought of as cast members moving around on a stage. This analogy of relating computer animation to theatrical performance is very useful. By thinking of sprites as cast members and the background as a stage, you can take the next logical step and think of an animation as a theatrical performance. In fact, this isn't far from the mark because the goal of theatrical performances is to entertain the audience by telling a story through the interaction of the cast members. Likewise, cast-based animations use the interaction of sprites to entertain the user, while often telling a story.

Each graphical object in a cast-based animation is referred to as a *sprite*, and can have a position that varies over time. In other words, sprites have a velocity associated with them that determines how their position changes over time. Almost every video game uses sprites to some degree. For example, every object in the classic Asteroids game is a sprite that moves independently of the background. Another good example of a rudimentary sprite is the flying saucer from the UFO program example you've seen earlier in the book. Figure 9.2 shows an example of how cast-based animation simplifies the paratrooper example you saw in the previous section.

FIGURE 9.2

In cast-based animation, a graphical object can move independently of the background to achieve the effect of animation.

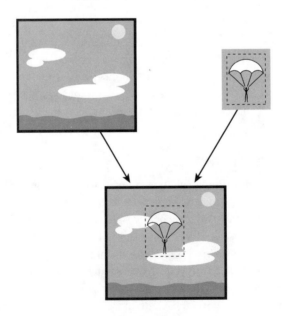

In this example, the paratrooper is now a sprite that can move independently of the background sky image. So, instead of having to draw every frame manually with the paratrooper in a slightly different position, you can just move the paratrooper image around on top of the background. This is the same approach you'll be using to inject animation into games throughout the remainder of the book.

Even though the fundamental principle behind sprite animation is the positional movement of a graphical object, there is no reason you can't incorporate frame-based animation into a sprite. Incorporating frame-based animation into a sprite enables you to change the image of the sprite as well as alter its position. This hybrid type of animation is actually what you will create later in the book as you add sprite support to the game engine.

I mentioned in the frame-based animation discussion that television is a good example of frame-based animation. But can you think of something on television that is created in a manner similar to cast-based animation (other than animated movies and cartoons)? Have you ever wondered how weather people magically appear in front of a computer-generated map showing the weather? The news station uses a technique known as *blue-screening* or *green-screening*, which enables them to overlay the weatherperson on top of the weather map in real time. It works like this: The person stands in front of a solid colored backdrop (blue or green), which serves as a transparent background. The image of the weatherperson is overlaid onto the weather map; the trick is that the colored background is filtered out when the image is overlaid so that it is effectively transparent. In this way, the weatherperson is acting exactly like a sprite!

Seeing Through Objects with Transparency

The weatherperson example brings up a very important point regarding sprites: transparency. Because bitmapped images are rectangular by nature, a problem arises when sprite images aren't rectangular in shape. In sprites that aren't rectangular in shape, which is the majority of sprites, the pixels surrounding the sprite image are unused. In a graphics system without transparency, these unused pixels are drawn just like any others. The end result is sprites that have visible rectangular borders around them, which completely destroys the effectiveness of having sprites overlaid on a background image.

What's the solution? Well, one solution is to make all of your sprites rectangular. Because this solution isn't very practical, a more realistic solution is *transparency*, which allows you to define a certain color in an image as unused, or transparent. When pixels of this color are encountered by drawing routines, they are simply skipped, leaving the original background intact. Transparent colors in images act exactly like the weatherperson's colored screen in the example earlier.

Fortunately, you've already learned how easy it is to support transparency when drawing bitmap images. In fact, you modified the Bitmap class to support transparency in Hour 6, "Controlling Games with the Keyboard and Mouse."

Adding Depth with Z-Order

In many instances, you will want some sprites to appear on top of others. For example, in a war game you might have planes flying over a battlefield dropping bombs on everything in sight. If a plane sprite happens to fly over a tank sprite, you obviously want the plane to appear above the tank and, therefore, hide the tank as it passes over. You handle this problem by assigning each sprite a screen depth, which is also referred to as *Z-order*.

Z-order is the relative depth of sprites on the screen. The depth of sprites is called Z-order because it works sort of like another dimension-like a z axis. You can think of sprites moving around on the screen in the xy axis. Similarly, the z axis can be thought of as another axis projected into the screen that determines how the sprites overlap each other. To put it another way, Z-order determines a sprite's depth within the screen. By making use of a z axis, you might think that Z-ordered sprites are 3D. The truth is that Z-ordered sprites can't be considered 3D because the z axis is a hypothetical axis that is only used to determine how sprite objects hide each other.

Just to make sure that you get a clear picture of how Z-order works, let's go back for a moment to the good old days of traditional animation. You learned earlier that traditional animators, such as those at Disney, used celluloid sheets to draw animated objects. They drew on celluloid sheets because the sheets could be overlaid on a background image and moved independently; cel animation is an early version of sprite animation. Each cel sheet corresponds to a unique Z-order value, determined by where in the pile of sheets the sheet is located. If a sprite near the top of the pile happens to be in the same location on the cel sheet as any lower sprites, it conceals them. The location of each sprite in the stack of cel sheets is its Z-order, which determines its visibility precedence. The same thing applies to sprites in cast-based animations, except that the Z-order is determined by the order in which the sprites are drawn, rather than the cel sheet location.

Detecting Collisions Between Objects

No discussion of animation as it applies to games would be complete without covering collision detection. *Collision detection* is the method of determining whether sprites have collided with each other. Although collision detection doesn't directly play a role in creating the illusion of movement, it is tightly linked to sprite animation and extremely crucial in games.

Collision detection is used to determine when sprites physically interact with each other. In an Asteroids game, for example, if the ship sprite collides with an asteroid sprite, the ship is destroyed. Collision detection is the mechanism employed to find out whether the ship collided with the asteroid. This might not sound like a big deal; just compare their positions and see whether they overlap, right? Correct, but consider how many comparisons must take place when a lot of sprites are moving around; each sprite must be compared to every other sprite in the system. It's not hard to see how the overhead of effective collision detection can become difficult to manage.

Not surprisingly, there are many approaches to handling collision detection. The simplest approach is to compare the bounding rectangles of each sprite with the bounding rectangles of all the other sprites. This method is efficient, but if you have objects that are not rectangular, a certain degree of error occurs when the objects brush by each other. This is because the corners might overlap and indicate a collision when really only the transparent areas are overlapping. The less rectangular the shape of the sprites, the more error typically occurs. Figure 9.3 shows how simple *rectangle collision* works.

FIGURE 9.3

Collision detection using rectangle collision simply involves checking to see if the bounding rectangles of two objects overlap.

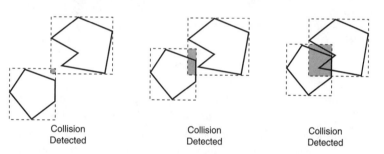

Collision
Detected

Collision
Detected

Collision
Detected

In the figure, the areas determining the collision detection are shaded. You can see how simple rectangle collision detection isn't very accurate, unless you're dealing with sprites that are rectangular in shape. An improvement upon this technique is to shrink the collision rectangles a little, which reduces the corner error. This method improves things a little, but it has the potential of causing error in the reverse direction by allowing sprites to overlap in some cases without signaling a collision. Figure 9.4 shows how shrinking the collision rectangles can improve the error on simple rectangle collision detection. *Shrunken rectangle collision* is just as efficient as simple rectangle collision because all you are doing is comparing rectangles for intersection.

The most accurate collision detection technique is to detect collision based on the sprite image data, which involves actually checking to see whether transparent parts of the sprite or the sprite images themselves are overlapping. In this case, you get a collision only if the actual sprite images are overlapping. This is the ideal technique for detecting collisions because it is exact and allows objects of any shape to move by each other without error. Figure 9.5 shows collision detection using the sprite image data.

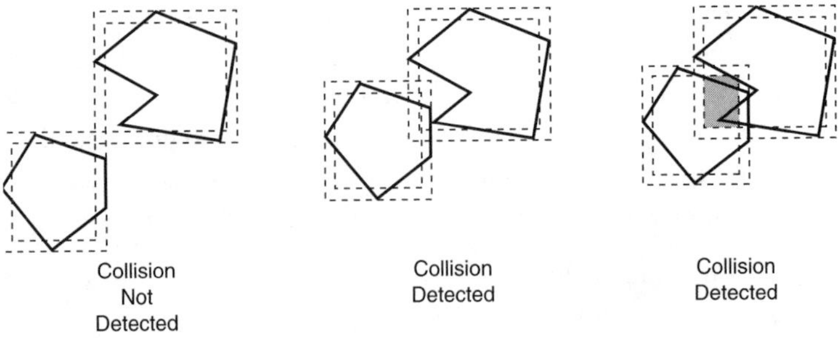

FIGURE 9.4

Collision detection using shrunken rectangle collision involves checking to see if shrunken versions of the bounding rectangles of two objects overlap.

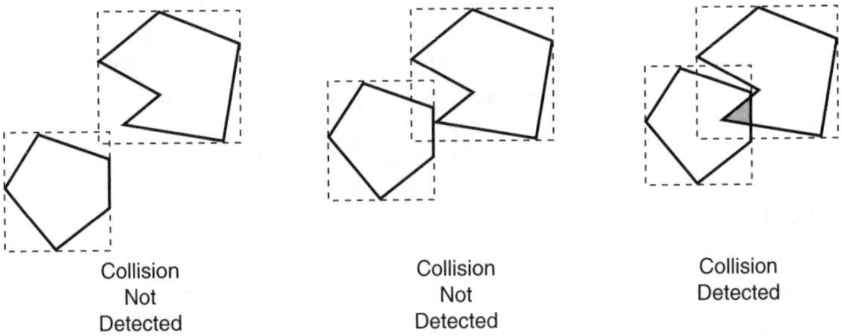

Collision Not Detected

Collision Detected

Collision Detected

FIGURE 9.5

Collision detection using image data collision involves checking the specific pixels of the images for two objects to see if they overlap.

Collision Not Detected

Collision Not Detected

Collision Detected

Unfortunately, the technique shown in Figure 9.5 requires far more processing overhead than rectangle collision detection and is often a major bottleneck in game performance. Furthermore, developing the code to carry out *image data collision detection* can get very messy. Considering these facts, it's safe to say that you won't be worrying about image data collision detection in this book. It might be an avenue worth considering on your own at some point if you are willing to dig into the programming complexities involved in pulling it off.

Applying Animation in Games

Now that you have a basic understanding of the basic types of animation, you're probably wondering which is best for games. I've already alluded to the fact that cast-based animation is more efficient and often gives you more control over game graphics, but the truth is that most games use a combination of the two animation techniques. Each technique offers its own unique benefits, so combining the techniques gives you capabilities that would be hard to get by using one of them alone.

A good example of how games often require the use of more than one animation technique is an animation of a person walking. You obviously need to be able to alter the position of the person so that he appears to be moving across a landscape. This requires cast-based animation because you need to move the person independently of the background on which he appears. However, if we let it go at this, the person would appear to just be sliding across the screen because he isn't making any movements that simulate walking. To effectively simulate walking, the person needs to move his arms and legs like a real person does when walking. This requires frame-based animation because you need to show a series of frames of the leg and arm movements. The end result is an object that can both move and change its appearance, which is where the two animation techniques come together.

This technique of combining cast-based and frame-based animation is very common in 2D games, and will form the basis of the sprite enhancements you make to the game engine in the next two hours.

Summary

This hour introduced you to animation and how it applies to games. As you now know, animation is what makes many forms of modern entertainment work, including movies, television, and video games. Two primary types of animation are used in the development of computer games, and this hour explored how they work and when you would want to use them. If you're a little frustrated that you didn't get to fire up your compiler in this hour, please understand that animation can be a complex topic, so I felt it necessary to lay some conceptual groundwork before diving into a bunch of code. The next two hours provide you with more than enough code to meet your appetite for game programming knowledge as you add support for sprites to the game engine.

Hour 10, "Making Things Move with Sprites," leads you through the development of a sprite class that supports sprite animation in the context of the game engine. I think you'll find the sprite class to be both powerful and intriguing at the same time. Perhaps more importantly, it opens the door for the creation of some exciting games.

Q&A

Q What exactly is Z-order, and do I really need it?

A Z-order is the depth of a sprite relative to other sprites; sprites with higher Z-order values appear to be on top of sprites with lower Z-order values. You only need Z-order when two or more sprites overlap each other, which is in most games.

Q Why bother with the different types of collision detection?

A The different types of collision detection (rectangle, shrunken rectangle, and image data) provide different trade-offs in regard to performance and accuracy. Rectangle and shrunken rectangle collision detection provide a very high-performance solution, but with moderate to poor accuracy. Image data collision detection is perfect when it comes to accuracy, but it can bring your game to its knees in the performance department.

Workshop

The Workshop is designed to help you anticipate possible questions, review what you've learned, and begin learning how to put your knowledge into practice. The answers to the quiz can be found in Appendix A, "Quiz Answers."

Quiz

1. What is animation, and how does it work?
2. What's the difference between 2D and 3D animation?
3. What are the two main techniques used for 2D animation?

Exercises

1. Watch some cartoons and think about how each type of animation is being used.
2. Go see a movie and marvel at how well the illusion of movement works. I can't help it; I'm into entertainment!

HOUR 10

Making Things Move with Sprites

The previous hour mentioned that sprite animation is the predominant form of animation used in two-dimensional games. This hour moves from theory to practicality by showing you how to design and build an all-purpose sprite class that will allow you to incorporate sprite animation into any program. You will end up reusing the Sprite class developed in this hour in every program example and game throughout the remainder of the book, so it's safe to say that it represents one of the most significant programming milestones in the book. Fortunately, the Sprite class is not very complex, and it serves as a great example of how sprite animation doesn't have to be complex. In fact, once you create the Sprite class, sprite animation becomes extremely straightforward to use.

In this hour, you'll learn:

- How sprites are used in games
- How to design a sprite class
- What it takes to develop a sprite class
- How to use sprite animation in the context of a real program

Evaluating the Role of Sprites in Games

Sprites are incredibly important in virtually all two-dimensional games because they provide a simple, yet effective means of conveying movement while also allowing objects to interact with one another. By modeling the objects in a game as sprites, you can create some surprisingly interesting games in which the objects interact with each other in different ways. The simplest example of a sprite used in a game is Pong, which involves a total of three sprites: the ball and the two paddles (vertical bars) along each side of the screen. All these objects must be modeled as sprites because they all move and interact with each other. The ball floats around on its own and bounces off the paddles, which are controlled by each of the two players.

As games get more complex, the role of sprites changes slightly, but their importance only increases. For example, a tank battle game would obviously use sprites to model the tanks and bullets that they shoot at each other. However, you could also use sprites to represent stationary objects such as walls and buildings. Even though the stationary objects don't move, they benefit from being modeled as sprites because you can detect a collision between them and a tank and limit the tank's movement accordingly. Similarly, if a bullet strikes a building, you would want to kill it or make it ricochet off the building at an angle; modeling the building as a sprite allows you to detect the bullet collision and respond accordingly.

It's important to point out that sprites are closely linked with bitmap images. Although it's certainly possible to create a sprite that is drawn out of graphics primitives, sprites are typically based on bitmap images. So, in the example of the tank game, each type of sprite corresponds to a bitmap image that is used to draw the sprite on the screen. The sprite's job is to keep track of the position, velocity, Z-order (depth), and visibility of a tank, whereas the bitmap keeps track of what the tank actually looks like. From a programming perspective, the `Bitmap` class is responsible for the appearance of a tank, whereas the `Sprite` class is responsible for how the tank moves and behaves with other objects.

Speaking of the `Sprite` class, there is no such existing class for us to borrow and use. Apparently, sprites represent a unique enough programming challenge that few standard programming libraries, such as Win32, support them directly. For this reason, you'll have to create your own `Sprite` class. The remainder of this hour focuses on the design, development, and testing of this class.

Designing an All-Purpose Sprite

As you know by now, the primary purpose of a sprite is to model a graphical object in a game that is capable of moving over time. It takes several pieces of information to manage such an object. The following list reveals the specific properties of a sprite that must be accounted for in the `Sprite` class:

- Position
- Velocity
- Z-order
- Bounding rectangle
- Bounds action
- Hidden/visible

The most important property of a sprite is its position on the game screen, followed by its velocity. The idea is that the velocity of a sprite will be used in each cycle of the game to change the sprite's position. So, if a sprite has an X velocity of 1 and a Y velocity of -2, it will move 1 pixel to the right and 2 pixels down the game screen in every game cycle. Obviously, setting higher values for the velocity of a sprite makes it move faster.

Although it's logical to think of a sprite's position in terms of a single coordinate, typically the upper left corner of the sprite, it's actually more useful from a programming perspective to keep track of a rectangular position for the sprite. In other words, the position of a sprite is a rectangle that basically outlines the sprite as it appears on the game screen. This allows you to factor in the width and height of a sprite when you work with its position.

In addition to position and velocity, it is also helpful to assign a Z-order to every sprite in a game. If you recall from the previous hour, Z-order is the depth of a sprite with respect to the screen. If two sprites are sharing the same space on the screen, the sprite with the higher Z-order will appear to be on top of the other sprite. The neat thing about Z-order is that it isn't as difficult to develop as you might think. When you think about it, sprites are naturally drawn on top of each other if you draw them in the proper order. So, establishing the Z-order for a system of sprites is all about ordering the drawing of the sprites so that sprites with a higher Z-order are drawn last. You don't actually learn how to write code to handle Z-order until Hour 11, "Managing a World of Sprites," but you're going to go ahead and build Z-order into the `Sprite` class in this hour so that it will be ready.

A less obvious sprite property that is very useful is a *bounding rectangle*, which is a rectangle that determines the area in which a sprite can travel. Generally speaking, the bounding rectangle would be assumed to be the entire game screen, but there are situations in which you might want to limit the movement of a sprite to a smaller area. For example, maybe you've created a bee sprite that you want to see buzzing around a flower. You could easily accomplish this by setting the bounding rectangle for the bee to

10

be a rectangle that encompasses the flower. Taking the bounding rectangle concept a step further, you can also establish *bounds actions*, which determine how a sprite acts when it encounters a boundary. More specifically, in a billiards game you would probably want the balls to bounce when they hit the pool table boundary. On the other hand, in an Asteroids type game you would probably want the asteroids to wrap around the edges of the game screen boundary. There are four primary bounds actions worth considering for any given sprite: Stop, Wrap, Bounce, and Die. You'll learn about these bounds actions in more detail in a moment, but for now just understand that they determine what happens to a sprite when it encounters a boundary such as the edge of the game screen.

The last sprite property worth considering in the design of a sprite class is the sprite's visibility. Although you could certainly delete a sprite from memory in order to hide it from view, there are situations in which it is better to simply hide a sprite rather than deleting it. As an example, you might want to create a game along the lines of the traditional carnival Whack-A-Mole game in which plastic moles pop-up out of holes and you smash them with a mallet. In this type of game, you would only need to hide the mole sprites after they are hit (clicked with the mouse), as opposed to deleting them from memory and recreating them over and over. For this reason, it is helpful to have a property that determines whether a sprite is hidden.

Although you've learned about several different sprite properties, my goal isn't to explore every property a sprite might ever need; it's just a starting point. In fact, you'll be adding to the `Sprite` class over the course of the book, so you can think of this as version one of your sprite design. In fact, you will hopefully add to the `Sprite` class and make your own enhancements after you finish the book.

Creating the `Sprite` Class

The `Sprite` class is designed to model a single sprite that uses the familiar `Bitmap` class to represent its appearance. Listing 10.1 contains the code for the `Sprite` class definition, which shows the overall design of the `Sprite` class, including its member variables and methods.

LISTING 10.1 The `Sprite` Class Definition Shows How the Design of a Game Sprite Is Realized in Code

```
1: class Sprite
2: {
3: protected:
4:    // Member Variables
5:    Bitmap*      m_pBitmap;
6:    RECT         m_rcPosition;
```

LISTING 10.1   Continued

```
 7:   POINT          m_ptVelocity;
 8:   int            m_iZOrder;
 9:   RECT           m_rcBounds;
10:   BOUNDSACTION   m_baBoundsAction;
11:   BOOL           m_bHidden;
12:
13: public:
14:   // Constructor(s)/Destructor
15:   Sprite(Bitmap* pBitmap);
16:   Sprite(Bitmap* pBitmap, RECT& rcBounds,
17:     BOUNDSACTION baBoundsAction = BA_STOP);
18:   Sprite(Bitmap* pBitmap, POINT ptPosition, POINT ptVelocity, int iZOrder,
19:     RECT& rcBounds, BOUNDSACTION baBoundsAction = BA_STOP);
20:   virtual ~Sprite();
21:
22:   // General Methods
23:   virtual void  Update();
24:   void          Draw(HDC hDC);
25:   BOOL          IsPointInside(int x, int y);
26:
27:   // Accessor Methods
28:   RECT&   GetPosition()             { return m_rcPosition; };
29:   void    SetPosition(int x, int y);
30:   void    SetPosition(POINT ptPosition);
31:   void    SetPosition(RECT& rcPosition)
32:     { CopyRect(&m_rcPosition, &rcPosition); };
33:   void    OffsetPosition(int x, int y);
34:   POINT   GetVelocity()             { return m_ptVelocity; };
35:   void    SetVelocity(int x, int y);
36:   void    SetVelocity(POINT ptVelocity);
37:   BOOL    GetZOrder()               { return m_iZOrder; };
38:   void    SetZOrder(int iZOrder)    { m_iZOrder = iZOrder; };
39:   void    SetBounds(RECT& rcBounds) { CopyRect(&m_rcBounds, &rcBounds); };
40:   void    SetBoundsAction(BOUNDSACTION ba) { m_baBoundsAction = ba; };
41:   BOOL    IsHidden()                { return m_bHidden; };
42:   void    SetHidden(BOOL bHidden)   { m_bHidden = bHidden; };
43:   int     GetWidth()                { return m_pBitmap->GetWidth(); };
44:   int     GetHeight()               { return m_pBitmap->GetHeight(); };
45: };
```

You might notice that the member variables for the Sprite class (lines 5–11) correspond one-to-one with the sprite properties you learned about in the previous section. The only real surprise in these variables is the use of the BOUNDSACTION data type (line 10), which is a custom data type that you learn about in a moment. This data type is used to describe the bounds action for the sprite.

The Sprite class offers several constructors that require differing amounts of information in order to create a sprite (lines 15–19), as well as a destructor that you can use to clean up after the sprite (line 20). There are three general methods in the Sprite class that are extremely important when it comes to using the Sprite class. The first of these is Update(), which updates the sprite by applying its velocity to its position and carrying out any appropriate reactions to the sprite movement (line 23). Next, the Draw() method is responsible for drawing the sprite at its current position using the bitmap that was specified in one of the Sprite() constructors (line 24). Finally, the IsPointInside() method is used to see if a point is located within the sprite's position rectangle (line 25). This method basically performs a *hit test*, which is useful if you want to determine if the sprite has been clicked with the mouse.

The remaining methods in the Sprite class are accessor methods that get and set various properties of the sprite. Some of these methods come in multiple versions to make it more convenient to interact with sprites. For example, the SetPosition() methods allow you to set the position of a sprite using individual X and Y values, a point, or a rectangle (lines 29–32). You might notice that most of the accessor methods include their code directly in the class definition, whereas a few of those do not. The accessor methods whose code isn't directly included next to the method definition are defined as *inline methods*, and their code appears in the Sprite.h header file below the Sprite class definition.

Earlier, I mentioned that a custom data type called BOUNDSACTION was used as the data type for the m_baBoundsAction member variable. This custom data type is defined in the Sprite.h header file as the following:

```
typedef WORD          BOUNDSACTION;
const BOUNDSACTION  BA_STOP   = 0,
                    BA_WRAP   = 1,
                    BA_BOUNCE = 2,
                    BA_DIE    = 3;
```

If you recall, the bounds actions described in the BOUNDSACTION data type correspond directly to those that were mentioned in the previous section when I first explained bounds actions and how they work. The idea here is that you use one of these constants to tell a sprite how it is to react when it runs into a boundary. If you're creating an Asteroids game, you'd want to use the BA_WRAP constant for the asteroids. On the other hand, a game like Breakout would rely on the BA_BOUNCE constant to allow the ball to bounce off the edges of the game screen. Regardless of which bounds action you choose for a sprite, it is entirely dependent on the bounding rectangle you set for the sprite. This rectangle can be as large as the game screen or as small as the sprite itself, although it wouldn't make much sense to bound a sprite with a rectangle the same size of the sprite.

Creating and Destroying the Sprite

You're probably ready to learn some more about how the Sprite class is actually put together. Listing 10.2 contains the code for the three Sprite() constructors, as well as the Sprite() destructor.

LISTING 10.2 The Sprite::Sprite() Constructors and Destructor Are Used to Create and Clean up After Sprites

```
 1: Sprite::Sprite(Bitmap* pBitmap)
 2: {
 3:   // Initialize the member variables
 4:   m_pBitmap = pBitmap;
 5:   SetRect(&m_rcPosition, 0, 0, pBitmap->GetWidth(), pBitmap->GetHeight());
 6:   m_ptVelocity.x = m_ptVelocity.y = 0;
 7:   m_iZOrder = 0;
 8:   SetRect(&m_rcBounds, 0, 0, 640, 480);
 9:   m_baBoundsAction = BA_STOP;
10:   m_bHidden = FALSE;
11: }
12:
13: Sprite::Sprite(Bitmap* pBitmap, RECT& rcBounds, BOUNDSACTION baBoundsAction)
14: {
15:   // Calculate a random position
16:   int iXPos = rand() % (rcBounds.right - rcBounds.left);
17:   int iYPos = rand() % (rcBounds.bottom - rcBounds.top);
18:
19:   // Initialize the member variables
20:   m_pBitmap = pBitmap;
21:   SetRect(&m_rcPosition, iXPos, iYPos, iXPos + pBitmap->GetWidth(),
22:     iYPos + pBitmap->GetHeight());
23:   m_ptVelocity.x = m_ptVelocity.y = 0;
24:   m_iZOrder = 0;
25:   CopyRect(&m_rcBounds, &rcBounds);
26:   m_baBoundsAction = baBoundsAction;
27:   m_bHidden = FALSE;
28: }
29:
30: Sprite::Sprite(Bitmap* pBitmap, POINT ptPosition, POINT ptVelocity,
31:     int iZOrder, RECT& rcBounds, BOUNDSACTION baBoundsAction)
32: {
33:   // Initialize the member variables
34:   m_pBitmap = pBitmap;
35:   SetRect(&m_rcPosition, ptPosition.x, ptPosition.y, pBitmap->GetWidth(),
36:     pBitmap->GetHeight());
37:   m_ptVelocity = ptPosition;
38:   m_iZOrder = iZOrder;
39:   CopyRect(&m_rcBounds, &rcBounds);
40:   m_baBoundsAction = baBoundsAction;
```

10

LISTING **10.2**   Continued

```
41:   m_bHidden = FALSE;
42: }
43:
44: Sprite::~Sprite()
45: {
46: }
```

The first `Sprite()` constructor accepts a single argument, a pointer to a Bitmap object, and uses default values for the remainder of the sprite properties (lines 1–11). Although this constructor can work if you're in a hurry to create a sprite, you'll probably want to use a more detailed constructor to have more control over the sprite. The second `Sprite()` constructor adds a bounding rectangle and bounds action to the `Bitmap` pointer, and uses them to help further define the sprite (lines 13–28). The interesting thing about this constructor is that it randomly positions the sprite within the bounding rectangle (lines 16, 17, 21, and 22). The third constructor is the most useful because it gives you the most control over creating a new sprite (lines 30–42). The `Sprite()` destructor doesn't do anything, but it's there to provide a means of adding cleanup code later should you need it (lines 44–46) .

Updating the Sprite

There are only two methods in the Sprite class that you haven't seen the code for yet: `Update()` and `Draw()`. It turns out that these are the two most important methods in the class. Listing 10.3 contains the code for the `Update()` method, which is responsible for updating the sprite.

LISTING **10.3**   The `Sprite::Update()` Method Updates a Sprite by Changing Its Position Based on Its Velocity and Taking Action in Response to the Movement

```
 1: void Sprite::Update()
 2: {
 3:   // Update the position
 4:   POINT ptNewPosition, ptSpriteSize, ptBoundsSize;
 5:   ptNewPosition.x = m_rcPosition.left + m_ptVelocity.x;
 6:   ptNewPosition.y = m_rcPosition.top + m_ptVelocity.y;
 7:   ptSpriteSize.x = m_rcPosition.right - m_rcPosition.left;
 8:   ptSpriteSize.y = m_rcPosition.bottom - m_rcPosition.top;
 9:   ptBoundsSize.x = m_rcBounds.right - m_rcBounds.left;
10:   ptBoundsSize.y = m_rcBounds.bottom - m_rcBounds.top;
11:
12:   // Check the bounds
13:   // Wrap?
14:   if (m_baBoundsAction == BA_WRAP)
15:   {
```

LISTING 10.3 Continued

```
16:     if ((ptNewPosition.x + ptSpriteSize.x) < m_rcBounds.left)
17:       ptNewPosition.x = m_rcBounds.right;
18:     else if (ptNewPosition.x > m_rcBounds.right)
19:        ptNewPosition.x = m_rcBounds.left - ptSpriteSize.x;
20:     if ((ptNewPosition.y + ptSpriteSize.y) < m_rcBounds.top)
21:       ptNewPosition.y = m_rcBounds.bottom;
22:     else if (ptNewPosition.y > m_rcBounds.bottom)
23:       ptNewPosition.y = m_rcBounds.top - ptSpriteSize.y;
24:   }
25:   // Bounce?
26:   else if (m_baBoundsAction == BA_BOUNCE)
27:   {
28:     BOOL bBounce = FALSE;
29:     POINT ptNewVelocity = m_ptVelocity;
30:     if (ptNewPosition.x < m_rcBounds.left)
31:     {
32:       bBounce = TRUE;
33:       ptNewPosition.x = m_rcBounds.left;
34:       ptNewVelocity.x = -ptNewVelocity.x;
35:     }
36:     else if ((ptNewPosition.x + ptSpriteSize.x) > m_rcBounds.right)
37:     {
38:       bBounce = TRUE;
39:       ptNewPosition.x = m_rcBounds.right - ptSpriteSize.x;
40:       ptNewVelocity.x = -ptNewVelocity.x;
41:     }
42:     if (ptNewPosition.y < m_rcBounds.top)
43:     {
44:       bBounce = TRUE;
45:       ptNewPosition.y = m_rcBounds.top;
46:       ptNewVelocity.y = -ptNewVelocity.y;
47:     }
48:     else if ((ptNewPosition.y + ptSpriteSize.y) > m_rcBounds.bottom)
49:     {
50:       bBounce = TRUE;
51:       ptNewPosition.y = m_rcBounds.bottom - ptSpriteSize.y;
52:       ptNewVelocity.y = -ptNewVelocity.y;
53:     }
54:     if (bBounce)
55:       SetVelocity(ptNewVelocity);
56:   }
57:   // Stop (default)
58:   else
59:   {
60:     if (ptNewPosition.x  < m_rcBounds.left ||
61:       ptNewPosition.x > (m_rcBounds.right - ptSpriteSize.x))
62:     {
63:       ptNewPosition.x = max(m_rcBounds.left, min(ptNewPosition.x,
64:         m_rcBounds.right - ptSpriteSize.x));
65:       SetVelocity(0, 0);
66:     }
```

10

LISTING 10.3   Continued

```
67:      if (ptNewPosition.y  < m_rcBounds.top ||
68:          ptNewPosition.y > (m_rcBounds.bottom - ptSpriteSize.y))
69:      {
70:          ptNewPosition.y = max(m_rcBounds.top, min(ptNewPosition.y,
71:            m_rcBounds.bottom - ptSpriteSize.y));
72:          SetVelocity(0, 0);
73:      }
74:    }
75:    SetPosition(ptNewPosition);
76: }
```

This method is probably considerably longer than you expected it to be, but on closer inspection you'll realize that it is doing several important things. The primary purpose of the Update() method is to use the velocity of the sprite to alter its position, which has the effect of moving the sprite. However, simply changing the position of the sprite isn't good enough because you have to take into consideration what happens if the sprite runs into a boundary. If you recall, every sprite has a bounding rectangle that determines the area in which the sprite can move. A sprite also has a bounds action that determines what happens to the sprite when it runs into a boundary. The Update() method has to check for a boundary and then take the appropriate response based on the sprite's bounds action.

The Update() method begins by making some temporary calculations involving the new position, the size of the sprite, and the size of the boundary (lines 4–10). The rest of the method handles each kind of bounds action, beginning with BA_WRAP. To handle the BA_WRAP bounds action, the sprite is simply moved to the opposite side of the bounding rectangle (lines 14–24), which gives the effect of the sprite wrapping off one side and on to the other. The BA_BOUNCE action has to look a little closer at which boundary the sprite is crossing because it must correctly reverse the sprite's velocity in order to yield a bouncing effect (lines 26–56). The final bounds action handled in the Update() method is BA_STOP, which is actually unnamed in this case because it is the default bounds action. This bounds action ensures that the sprite doesn't cross over the boundary, while setting the sprite's velocity to zero (lines 59–74).

Throughout all the bounds action handling code, the new sprite position is calculated and stored in a temporary variable of type POINT, ptNewPosition. At the end of the Update() method, this variable is used to actually set the new position of the sprite (line 75).

If you're the overly observant type, you might recall that earlier in the hour the Sprite class was designed to support an additional bounds action, BA_DIE, which causes the sprite to be destroyed when it encounters a boundary. Although this bounds action is technically available for the Sprite class to use, it isn't possible to support the action without some additional code in the game engine to manage a system of sprites. You don't develop a sprite manager for the game engine until the next hour, so you won't address the BA_DIE bounds action until then. Fortunately, there is plenty of fun to be had with the three other bounds actions, as you'll soon see.

Drawing the Sprite

The remaining method in the Sprite class is the Draw() method, which is shown in Listing 10.4.

LISTING 10.4   The Sprite::Draw() Method Draws a Sprite by Using the Sprite's Bitmap and Current Position

```
1: void Sprite::Draw(HDC hDC)
2: {
3:   // Draw the sprite if it isn't hidden
4:   if (m_pBitmap != NULL && !m_bHidden)
5:     m_pBitmap->Draw(hDC, m_rcPosition.left, m_rcPosition.top, TRUE);
6: }
```

If the Update() method surprised you by having too much code, hopefully the Draw() method surprises you by having so little. Because the Bitmap class includes its own Draw() method, there isn't much for the Sprite::Draw() method to do. It first checks to make sure that the Bitmap pointer is okay, along with making sure that the sprite isn't hidden (line 4). If all is well, the Draw() method calls on the Bitmap class with the m_rcPosition member variable used to convey the sprite's position for drawing the bitmap (line 5). The last argument to the Bitmap::Draw() method is a Boolean that determines whether the sprite's bitmap should be drawn with transparency, which in this case is TRUE. So, all sprites are assumed to use transparency.

Building the Fore Program Example

Although the Sprite class is certainly an engineering marvel, only so much gratification can be gained from staring at its code. For this reason, it's important to put together a demonstration program to put the Sprite class through its paces. Because I've been

10

obsessed lately with improving my golf game, I thought a golf program example might be fitting as a means of demonstrating how to create and use sprites. If you've ever had to yell "Fore!" you understand that it is a phrase used to inform someone that you've shanked a golf ball in his general direction. The Fore program example uses a woodsy backdrop and several sprite golf balls to get your feet wet with sprite animation.

The idea behind the Fore program is to create several sprite golf balls and let them zing around the game screen. Because it's not terribly important to factor in real-world physics, I opted to use the golf balls to demonstrate the three bounds actions supported by the Sprite class: Wrap, Bounce, and Stop. So, the program creates three golf balls with each of these bounds actions and then turns them loose on the game screen to see how they react. To make things a little more interesting, you can use the mouse to grab and drag any of the balls around the screen. Let's get started with the code because you're no doubt itching to see this program in action.

Writing the Program Code

As you know by now, every Windows program has a header file that includes other important header files, as well as declares global variables used by the program. Listing 10.5 contains the code for the Fore.h header file.

LISTING 10.5   The Fore.h Header File Imports Several Header Files and Declares Global Variables Required for the Golf Ball Sprites

```
 1: #pragma once
 2:
 3: //------------------------------------------------------------------
 4: // Include Files
 5: //------------------------------------------------------------------
 6: #include <windows.h>
 7: #include "Resource.h"
 8: #include "GameEngine.h"
 9: #include "Bitmap.h"
10: #include "Sprite.h"
11:
12: //------------------------------------------------------------------
13: // Global Variables
14: //------------------------------------------------------------------
15: HINSTANCE     _hInstance;
16: GameEngine*   _pGame;
17: Bitmap*       _pForestBitmap;
18: Bitmap*       _pGolfBallBitmap;
19: Sprite*       _pGolfBallSprite[3];
20: BOOL          _bDragging;
21: int           _iDragBall;
```

A quick look at this code reveals two bitmaps—one for the forest background (line 17) and another for the golf balls (line 18). Each ball sprite uses the same bitmap. The golf ball sprites are stored in an array to make it a little easier to access them (line 19). The last two member variables are used to allow you to drag a golf ball around with the mouse. The bDragging variable determines whether a ball is currently being dragged (line 20). If a ball is indeed being dragged, the iDragBall variable keeps track of which ball it is (line 21); this variable is actually an index into the _pGolfBallSprite array.

With the global variables for the Fore program in mind, you can now press on and examine the specific game functions for the program. The GameInitialize() function is virtually identical to the version of it that you've seen in other examples. The only point to make is that it sets the frame rate to 30 frames per second, which is relatively standard for the programs that use sprite animation throughout the book.

The GameStart() and GameEnd() functions are where the interesting things start taking place in the Fore program, as shown in Listing 10.6.

10

LISTING 10.6 The GameStart() Function Creates and Loads the Bitmaps and Sprites, While the GameEnd() Function Cleans Them Up

```
 1: void GameStart(HWND hWindow)
 2: {
 3:    // Seed the random number generator
 4:    srand(GetTickCount());
 5:
 6:    // Create and load the bitmaps
 7:    HDC hDC = GetDC(hWindow);
 8:    _pForestBitmap = new Bitmap(hDC, IDB_FOREST, _hInstance);
 9:    _pGolfBallBitmap = new Bitmap(hDC, IDB_GOLFBALL, _hInstance);
10:
11:    // Create the golf ball sprites
12:    RECT rcBounds = { 0, 0, 600, 400 };
13:    _pGolfBallSprite[0] = new Sprite(_pGolfBallBitmap, rcBounds);
14:    _pGolfBallSprite[1] = new Sprite(_pGolfBallBitmap, rcBounds, BA_WRAP);
15:    _pGolfBallSprite[2] = new Sprite(_pGolfBallBitmap, rcBounds, BA_BOUNCE);
16:    _pGolfBallSprite[0]->SetVelocity(2, 1);
17:    _pGolfBallSprite[1]->SetVelocity(3, -2);
18:    _pGolfBallSprite[2]->SetVelocity(7, 4);
19:
20:    // Set the initial drag info
21:    _bDragging = FALSE;
22:    _iDragBall = -1;
23: }
24:
25: void GameEnd()
26: {
```

LISTING 10.6   Continued

```
27:   // Cleanup the bitmaps
28:   delete _pForestBitmap;
29:   delete _pGolfBallBitmap;
30:
31:   // Cleanup the sprites
32:   for (int i = 0; i < 3; i++)
33:     delete _pGolfBallSprite[i];
34:
35:   // Cleanup the game engine
36:   delete _pGame;
37: }
```

The GameStart() function does several important things, beginning with the loading of the forest and golf ball bitmaps (lines 8 and 9). A bounding rectangle for the game screen is then created (line 12), which is important because it serves as the bounding rectangle for all the golf ball sprites. The three golf ball sprites are then created and stored in the _pGolfBallSprite array (lines 13–15), and their velocities are set to differing values (lines 16–18). The function ends by initializing the global variables that keep track of a sprite being dragged with the mouse (lines 21 and 22). The GameEnd() function simply cleans up the bitmaps and sprites, as well as the game engine itself (lines 25–37).

The GamePaint() function is next on the agenda, and you might be surprised by its simplicity (Listing 10.7).

LISTING 10.7   The GamePaint() Function Draws the Forest Background and the Golf Ball Sprites

```
1: void GamePaint(HDC hDC)
2: {
3:   // Draw the background forest
4:   _pForestBitmap->Draw(hDC, 0, 0);
5:
6:   // Draw the golf ball sprites
7:   for (int i = 0; i < 3; i++)
8:     _pGolfBallSprite[i]->Draw(hDC);
9: }
```

The GamePaint() function simply draws the forest bitmap (line 4) followed by the three golf ball sprites (lines 7 and 8). The Draw() method in the Sprite class makes drawing the sprites painfully easy (line 8).

Of course, the GamePaint() method alone wouldn't be too helpful in animating the golf ball sprites if the game screen wasn't told to repaint itself periodically. This is accomplished in the GameCycle() function, which also updates the sprites (Listing 10.8).

LISTING 10.8 The `GameCycle()` Function Updates the Golf Ball Sprites and Then Repaints the Game Screen

```
1: void GameCycle()
2: {
3:   // Update the golf ball sprites
4:   for (int i = 0; i < 3; i++)
5:     _pGolfBallSprite[i]->Update();
6:
7:   // Force a repaint to redraw the golf balls
8:   InvalidateRect(_pGame->GetWindow(), NULL, FALSE);
9: }
```

This function begins by updating the golf ball sprites, which simply involves calling the `Update()` method on each sprite (lines 4 and 5). After updating the sprites, the game screen is invalidated so that it gets repainted to show the new sprite positions (line 8). If you didn't invalidate the game screen, the `GamePaint()` method wouldn't get called and you wouldn't see any changes on the screen even though the sprites are being moved behind the scenes. In other words, in addition to changing the position of sprites, you must also make sure that they get repainted so that the changes are visualized.

I mentioned earlier in the hour that the Fore program allows you to click a golf ball sprite with the mouse and drag it around. This functionality is established in the `MouseButtonDown()`, `MouseButtonUp()`, and `MouseMove()` functions, which are shown in Listing 10.9.

LISTING 10.9 The `MouseButtonDown()`, `MouseButtonUp()`, and `MouseMove()` Functions Use the Left Mouse Button to Allow You to Click and Drag a Golf Ball Sprite Around on the Game Screen

```
1: void MouseButtonDown(int x, int y, BOOL bLeft)
2: {
3:   // See if a ball was clicked with the left mouse button
4:   if (bLeft && !_bDragging)
5:   {
6:     for (int i = 0; i < 3; i++)
7:       if (_pGolfBallSprite[i]->IsPointInside(x, y))
8:       {
9:         // Capture the mouse
10:        SetCapture(_pGame->GetWindow());
11:
12:        // Set the drag state and the drag ball
13:        _bDragging = TRUE;
14:        _iDragBall = i;
15:
16:        // Simulate a mouse move to get started
```

10

LISTING **10.9**   Continued

```
17:            MouseMove(x, y);
18:
19:            // Don't check for more balls
20:            break;
21:        }
22:    }
23: }
24:
25: void MouseButtonUp(int x, int y, BOOL bLeft)
26: {
27:    // Release the mouse
28:    ReleaseCapture();
29:
30:    // Stop dragging
31:    _bDragging = FALSE;
32: }
33:
34: void MouseMove(int x, int y)
35: {
36:    if (_bDragging)
37:    {
38:      // Move the sprite to the mouse cursor position
39:      _pGolfBallSprite[_iDragBall]->SetPosition(
40:        x - (_pGolfBallBitmap->GetWidth() / 2),
41:        y - (_pGolfBallBitmap->GetHeight() / 2));
42:
43:      // Force a repaint to redraw the golf balls
44:      InvalidateRect(_pGame->GetWindow(), NULL, FALSE);
45:    }
46: }
```

The MouseButtonDown() function starts the drag process by first checking to see if the left mouse button is being pressed, while making sure that a drag isn't somehow already in progress (line 4). The next check is to see if the mouse click actually occurred within a sprite. This involves looping through the sprites and seeing if the mouse coordinates lie within a sprite (lines 6 and 7). If so, the mouse is captured so that its input is routed to the Fore program even if it strays outside the game window (line 10). The drag state and ball being dragged are then stored away because the other mouse functions need to know about them (lines 13 and 14). The MouseMove() function is then called to simulate a mouse move so that the sprite is centered on the mouse cursor position (line 17). Finally, the sprite loop is broken out of because you don't want to check for more balls when one has been clicked with the mouse (line 20).

The MouseButtonUp() function ends a sprite drag by releasing the mouse capture (line 28), and then clearing the _bDragging global variable (line 31). This is sufficient to stop the sprite drag, while also allowing the user to initiate another drag by clicking a sprite and starting the process over.

The last of the mouse functions is `MouseMove()`, which moves a golf ball sprite so that it follows the location of the mouse cursor. The `_bDragging` global variable is first checked to make sure that a drag is taking place (line 36). If so, the position of the appropriate golf ball sprite is set to correspond to the position of the mouse cursor (lines 39–41). The program window is then invalidated so that the game screen is repainted (line 44), which is necessary so that the sprite is redrawn in the new position.

Testing the Finished Product

Although it isn't a game, the Fore program example is a quite interesting sample program in the sense that it demonstrates how powerful and straightforward sprite animation can be. After the Sprite class was created, it only took a few lines of code to create a few sprites and get them moving around the game screen. Figure 10.1 shows the golf ball sprites flying around on the forest background in the Fore program example.

FIGURE 10.1

The golf ball sprites in the Fore program move around thanks to the handy Sprite *class that you created in this hour.*

If you watch the sprites carefully, you'll notice that each of them responds differently when encountering the edge of the game screen, which happens to serve as their bounding rectangle. One of the balls will wrap around to the other side of the screen, another will bounce off the side of the screen like a game of Pong, whereas the last ball stops at the edge of the screen. The really neat thing about the program is that you can click and drag any of the balls on the screen, including the ones that are moving.

Granted, clicking and dragging a golf ball isn't exactly my idea of an exciting "game," but it does provide a good demonstration of the new Sprite class that you've now added to your game development toolkit.

10

Summary

This hour explained the basic kinds of animation used in games, including sprite animation, which is also known as cast-based animation. This hour took a significantly closer look at sprite animation by guiding you through the development of a sprite class that can be used to inject sprite animation into your games. The Sprite class that you created supports standard sprite features such as a bitmap, position, and velocity, as well as a handy bounding rectangle feature for controlling the area in which a sprite is allowed to travel. The hour concluded by putting the Sprite class to work in a program example that demonstrated how to create and use sprites.

Hour 11 builds on your newly created sprite code by beefing up the game engine to support interactions between sprites. More specifically, you develop a sprite manager that is capable of detecting and responding to collisions between sprites. You also improve upon the paint mechanism you've been using so that your future games don't suffer from the flicker that is inherent in sprite animation.

Q&A

Q Why is the position of a sprite stored as a rectangle, as opposed to a point?

A Although you might think of the position of a sprite as simply determining the location of the sprite on the game screen, it will eventually be used in other ways within the Sprite class. For example, the next hour adds collision detection capabilities to the Sprite class, which requires a sprite to support a collision rectangle. This rectangle is calculated as a percentage of the sprite's position rectangle. Of course, if a sprite's position was stored as a point, you could still come up with a position rectangle by looking at the width and height of the sprite's bitmap. However, this kind of lookup can be time-consuming when you consider that the Sprite class needs to be as efficient as possible.

Q If a sprite is hidden, does it continue to be updated?

A Yes. Just because a sprite is hidden from view doesn't mean that it is no longer updated. There might be situations in which you want a sprite to move around in the background unnoticed—in which case, it should be updated while it is hidden. A good example might be a torpedo fired by a submarine in a naval battle game. You might want the torpedo sprite to be invisible until just before impact, which means that it needs to be hidden from view while it continues to be updated.

Workshop

The Workshop is designed to help you anticipate possible questions, review what you've learned, and begin learning how to put your knowledge into practice. The answers to the quiz can be found in Appendix A, "Quiz Answers."

Quiz

1. What is the purpose of a bounding rectangle?
2. How does a bounds action work?
3. Why does the Sprite class contain a pointer to a Bitmap object?

Exercises

1. Try modifying the velocities of the golf ball sprites in the Fore program example to see how it changes their movements.

2. Create a new sprite of a bird that flies across the top of the screen in the Fore program example. (Hint: This isn't as hard as it sounds—just study the code for the golf ball sprites and take note of what it takes to incorporate a new sprite into the mix.)

10

HOUR 11

Managing a World of Sprites

When you think about it, the real world we live in is all about actions and reactions. If you kick a ball, the ball will respond to the impact by traveling a certain distance, where it might collide with another object or eventually come to rest thanks to air and ground friction. The real world is therefore a system of objects that physically interact with one another. You can think of a system of sprites as a similar system of objects that are capable of interacting with each other in a variety of ways. The primary manner in which sprites can interact is through collisions, which involve objects running into each other. This hour focuses on the design and development of a sprite manager that allows you to establish actions and reactions within a system of sprites.

In this hour, you'll learn:

- Why sprite management is important to games
- How to design a sprite manager
- How to modify the game engine to support the management of sprites

- How to eliminate animation flicker using a technique known as double buffering
- How to build a program example that takes advantage of new sprite features such as collision detection

Assessing the Need for Sprite Management

In the previous hour, you developed a sprite class that modeled the basic physical properties of a graphical object that can move. You then created a program example called Fore that involved several golf ball sprites co-existing in the same space. Although the sprites in the Fore program were visually sharing the same space, no actual connection existed between them. Unlike the real world, the golf ball sprites were unable to collide with each other and respond accordingly—in other words, the sprites didn't act very realistic. This limitation stems from the fact that the Sprite class alone can't account for the relationship between sprites. You need a sprite manager that is capable of overseeing a system of sprites and managing their interactions.

The idea behind a sprite manager is to group all the sprites in a system together so that they can be collectively updated and drawn. Additionally, a sprite manager must be able to compare the positions of sprites to each other and determine if any collisions have taken place. If so, the sprite manager must then somehow notify the program that the collision has occurred; in which case, the program can respond accordingly. This approach to sprite collision management is incredibly important in games, which makes the sprite manager an absolute necessity toward building games that use sprite animation.

Another benefit of a sprite manager is that it provides a means of supporting an additional bounds action, Die. The Die bounds action causes a sprite to be destroyed if it encounters a boundary. This might be useful in a shoot-em-up game in which the bullet sprites need to be killed upon hitting the edge of the game screen. It's difficult to support the Die bounds action directly in the Sprite class because the premise of the action is killing the sprite. This task is better left to an outside party whose job is to oversee all the sprites in a game—a sprite manager.

A moment ago, I mentioned that a sprite manager makes it possible to update and draw a system of sprites collectively. This is a significant feature as you move toward creating games that rely on several sprites. For example, it could quickly become a headache trying to update, draw, and generally keep tabs on 10 or 20 sprites. The sprite manager dramatically simplifies this situation by allowing you to simply update and draw all the sprites being managed at once, regardless of how many there are.

Designing a Sprite Manager

You now have a basic understanding of what is required of a sprite manager, so you can now move on to the specific design for it. You might think that the sprite manager would be created as a class similarly to the way that you created the Sprite class in the previous hour. However, the sprite manager is closely linked with the game engine, which makes it more beneficial to integrate the sprite manager directly with the game engine. So, the sprite manager will actually be created as a set of methods in the GameEngine class.

Even though the sprite manager is created as a modification on the game engine, it does require some changes outside of the GameEngine class. More specifically, some changes are required in the Sprite class in order for sprites to work smoothly with the sprite manager. The first of these changes involves supporting *sprite actions*, which are used to inform the sprite manager that it should take action in regard to a particular sprite. Sprite actions are sort of like bounds actions, except that they are somewhat more flexible. As an example, the first sprite action supported is Kill, which is used to inform the sprite manager that a sprite is to be destroyed. The Kill sprite action is similar to the Die bounds action, except that Kill can be issued for a variety of different reasons. Sprite actions are typically invoked when a collision occurs, which allows a missile to destroy a tank upon impact, for example.

Beyond sprite actions, another major requirement of the Sprite class and the sprite manager code is that of collision detection. You learned in Hour 9, "A Crash Course in Game Animation," that collision detection involves checking to see if two sprites have collided with each other. You also found out that a technique known as *shrunken rectangle collision detection* involves using a rectangle smaller than the sprite as the basis for detecting collisions. Because this form of collision detection requires its own rectangle, it only makes sense to add a collision rectangle as a member of the Sprite class, along with supporting methods to calculate the rectangle and test for a collision with another sprite.

That covers the changes required of the Sprite class in order to support the enhanced sprite animation features offered by the sprite manager. The sprite manager itself is integrated directly into the game engine, where it primarily involves adding a member variable to keep track of a list of sprites. This member variable could be an array with a fixed size representing the maximum number of sprites allowed, or it could be a more advanced data structure such as a vector that can grow dynamically to hold additional sprites.

Regardless of the specifics of how the sprite list is established, the sprite manager must provide several methods that can be used to interact with the sprites being managed.

11

Following are the major tasks the sprite manager needs to make available using the following methods:

- Add a new sprite to the sprite list
- Draw all the sprites in the sprite list
- Update all the sprites in the sprite list
- Clean up all the sprites in the sprite list
- Test to see if a point lies within a sprite in the sprite list

In addition to these tasks that must be capable of being invoked on the game engine, it is important to provide a function for a game that is called whenever a sprite collision occurs. When you think about it, handling a sprite collision is a very game-specific task, so it makes sense to let game code handle it, as opposed to including it in the game engine. So, a sprite collision notification function must be provided by any game that uses the sprite manager so that it can respond to sprite collisions. Of course, the sprite manager must make sure that this function gets called whenever a collision actually takes place.

Adding the Sprite Manager to the Game Engine

Throughout the hour thus far, I've drawn a distinction between the `Sprite` class and game engine, as if they were two different things. In reality, the `Sprite` class is part of the game engine even though it is a self-contained class. So, it's safe to say that you are upgrading the game engine even when you make changes to the `Sprite` class. The next couple of sections reveal the code changes required in both the `Sprite` class and the `GameEngine` class to add support for a sprite manager.

Improving the `Sprite` Class

The first piece of code required in the `Sprite` class is the addition of a collision rectangle, which is used to determine if one sprite has collided with another. This rectangle is added as a member variable of the `Sprite` class named m_rcCollision, as the following code reveals:

```
RECT m_rcCollision;
```

A single accessor method is required for the collision rectangle so that the sprite manager can access the rectangle for collision detections. This method is called GetCollision(), and looks like the following:

```
RECT& GetCollision() { return m_rcCollision; };
```

Although there are no surprises with the GetCollision() method, you might find the CalcCollisionRect()method to be a little more interesting. This method is used internally by the Sprite class to calculate a collision rectangle based on the position rectangle. The CalcCollisionRect()method is defined as virtual in the Sprite class so that derived classes can override it and use their own specific collision rectangle calculation:

```
virtual void CalcCollisionRect();
```

Listing 11.1 shows the code for the CalcCollisionRect() method, which calculates the collision rectangle of a sprite by subtracting one-sixth of the sprite's size off the position rectangle.

LISTING 11.1   The Sprite::CalcCollisionRect() Method Calculates a Collision Rectangle for a Sprite Based on the Sprite's Position Rectangle

```
1: inline void Sprite::CalcCollisionRect()
2: {
3:   int iXShrink = (m_rcPosition.left - m_rcPosition.right) / 12;
4:   int iYShrink = (m_rcPosition.top - m_rcPosition.bottom) / 12;
5:   CopyRect(&m_rcCollision, &m_rcPosition);
6:   InflateRect(&m_rcCollision, iXShrink, iYShrink);
7: }
```

11

This code is a little misleading because a shrink value for the X and Y dimensions of the sprite are first calculated as one-twelfth the size of the sprite (lines 3 and 4). These values are then passed into the Win32 InflateRect() function (line 6), which uses each value to shrink the sprite along each dimension. The end result is that the collision rectangle is one-sixth smaller than the position rectangle because the shrink values are applied to each side of the sprite.

Speaking of collision, the Sprite class provides a method called TestCollision() to see if the sprite has collided with another sprite:

```
BOOL TestCollision(Sprite* pTestSprite);
```

Listing 11.2 contains the code for the TestCollision() method, which simply checks to see if any part of the sprite's collision rectangles overlap.

LISTING 11.2   The Sprite::TestCollision() Method Compares the Collision Rectangles of Two Sprites to See if They Overlap

```
1: inline BOOL Sprite::TestCollision(Sprite* pTestSprite)
2: {
3:   RECT& rcTest = pTestSprite->GetCollision();
```

LISTING 11.2   Continued

```
4:    return m_rcCollision.left <= rcTest.right &&
5:           rcTest.left <= m_rcCollision.right &&
6:           m_rcCollision.top <= rcTest.bottom &&
7:           rcTest.top <= m_rcCollision.bottom;
8: }
```

If a collision has indeed occurred between the two sprites, the TestCollision() method returns TRUE; otherwise it returns FALSE (lines 4–7).

Getting back to the collision rectangle that was added to the Sprite class, it must be initialized in the Sprite() constructors. All three of these constructors include a call to CalcCollisionRect(), which sets the collision rectangle based on the position rectangle of the sprite. No other changes are required in the constructors to support collision detection in the Sprite class.

The other big change in the Sprite class involves the addition of sprite actions, which provide a means of allowing the sprite manager to manipulate sprites in response to events such as sprite collisions. A custom data type called SPRITEACTION is used to represent sprite actions, as follows:

```
typedef WORD        SPRITEACTION;
const SPRITEACTION  SA_NONE  = 0x0000L,
                    SA_KILL  = 0x0001L;
```

As you can see, only two sprite actions are defined for the SPRITEACTION data type, although the idea is to add new actions as necessary to expand the role of the sprite manager later. The SA_NONE sprite action indicates that nothing is to be done to any sprites. On the other hand, the SA_KILL sprite action indicates that a sprite is to be removed from the sprite list and destroyed. These sprite actions are given real meaning in the Update() method, which is now defined to return a SPRITEACTION value to indicate any actions to take with respect to the sprite.

The big change to the Update() method is that it now supports the BA_DIE bounds action, which causes a sprite to be destroyed when it encounters a boundary. This bounds action is made possible by the SA_KILL sprite action, which is returned by the Update() method in response to the BA_DIE bounds action occurring. So, the Update() method responds to the BA_DIE bounds action by returning SA_KILL, which results in the sprite being destroyed and removed from the sprite list. The remaining bounds actions return SA_NONE, which results in nothing happening to the sprite in terms of sprite actions.

Enhancing the Game Engine

The `Sprite` class is now whipped into shape in preparation for the new sprite manager support in the `GameEngine` class. Fortunately, managing a system of sprites isn't really all that difficult of a proposition. This is largely possible thanks to a suite of data collections known as the *Standard Template Library*, or *STL*. The STL is a suite of data collection classes that can be used to store any kind of data, including sprites. Rather than use an array to store a list of sprites in the game engine, it is much more convenient and flexible to use the `vector` collection class from the STL. The STL `vector` class allows you to store away and manage a list of objects of any type, and then manipulate them using a set of handy methods. The good news is that you don't have to know much about the `vector` class or the STL in order to put it to use in the game engine.

> The Standard Template Library is built in to most C++ compilers, and provides an extensive set of data collection classes that you can use in your programs. The STL is significant because it keeps you from having to spend time developing your own classes to perform common tasks. In other words, it saves you from having to reinvent the wheel.

The first step in using any data collection class in the STL is to properly include the header for the class, as well as its namespace. If you've never heard of namespaces, don't worry because they don't really impact the code you're writing here. The following two lines must be placed near the top of the header file for the `GameEngine` class, and they take care of including the vector class header file and establishing its namespace:

```
#include <vector>
using namespace std;
```

To use an STL collection class such as the `vector` class, you simply declare a variable of type `vector`, but you also include the data type that you want stored in the vector inside angle brackets (<>). The following code shows how to create a vector of `Sprite` pointers:

```
vector<Sprite*> m_vSprites;
```

This code creates a vector containing `Sprite` pointers, and is exactly what you need in the game engine to keep track of a list of sprites. You can now use the `m_vSprites` vector to manage a list of sprites and interact with them as necessary. It helps to set a property on the `vector` variable so that it operates a little more efficiently in games. I'm referring to the amount of memory reserved for the vector, which determines how many sprite pointers can be stored in the vector before it has to allocate more memory. This doesn't mean that you're setting a limit on the number of sprites that can be stored in the vector;

you're just determining how often the vector class will have to allocate memory for new sprites. Because memory allocation takes time, it's beneficial to keep it at a minimum. Given the requirements of most games, it's safe to say that reserving room for fifty sprites before requiring additional memory allocation is sufficient. This memory reservation takes place in the GameEngine::GameEngine() constructor.

The sprite manager support in the game engine prompts you to add a new game function that must be provided by games as part of their game-specific code. This function is called SpriteCollision(), and its job is to respond to sprite collisions in a game-specific manner. Following is the function prototype for the SpriteCollision() function:

```
BOOL SpriteCollision(Sprite* pSpriteHitter, Sprite* pSpriteHittee);
```

Keep in mind that the SpriteCollision() function must be provided by each game that you create. The SpriteCollision() function is called by the CheckSpriteCollision() method within the game engine, which steps through the sprite list (vector) and checks to see if any sprites have collided:

```
BOOL CheckSpriteCollision(Sprite* pTestSprite);
```

The CheckSpriteCollision() method calls the SpriteCollision() function to handle individual sprite collisions. The CheckSpriteCollision() method steps through the entire list of sprites and checks for collisions between all of them. The first thing required to step through the sprite vector is an *iterator*, which is a special object used to move forward or backward through a vector. The good thing about iterators is that they are objects that provide functions for easily looping through a vector. For example, the begin() and end() iterator methods are used to establish a loop that steps through each sprite in the sprite vector. The code for the CheckSpriteCollision() method is included in the GameEngine.cpp source code file, which is available on the accompanying CD-ROM, along with all of the source code for the examples in the book.

Within the loop, a check is first performed to make sure that you aren't comparing a sprite with itself. A collision test is then performed between the two sprites by calling the TestCollision() method. If a collision is detected, the SpriteCollision() function is called so that the game can respond appropriately to the collision. The return value of the SpriteCollision() function is also returned from the CheckSpriteCollision() method. This return value plays a vital role in determining how sprites react to collisions. More specifically, returning TRUE from CheckSpriteCollision() results in a sprite being restored to its original position prior to being updated, whereas a return value of FALSE allows the sprite to continue along its path. Without this mechanism for restoring the original position of a sprite, two sprites would tend to stick together instead of bouncing off each other when they collide. If there is no collision, FALSE is returned so that the sprite's new position isn't altered.

The CheckSpriteCollision() method is technically a helper method that is only used within the GameEngine class. It's also necessary to add a suite of public sprite management methods to the GameEngine class that are used to interact with the sprite manager. Following are the sprite manager methods that can be called on the game engine:

```
void    AddSprite(Sprite* pSprite);
void    DrawSprites(HDC hDC);
void    UpdateSprites();
void    CleanupSprites();
Sprite* IsPointInSprite(int x, int y);
```

The AddSprite() method is used to add a sprite to the sprite list, and must be called in order for a sprite to be taken under management by the sprite manager. Before adding a sprite, the AddSprite() method checks to make sure the pSprite argument is not set to NULL. If the sprite pointer is okay, the sprite vector is checked to see if any sprites are already in it. If sprites are in the vector, the AddSprite() method has to find a suitable spot to add the sprite because the sprite list is ordered so that the sprites are drawn in proper Z-order. In other words, the sprites are ordered in the list according to increasing Z-order. This allows you to simply draw the sprites as they appear in the sprite list, and they will properly overlap each other naturally.

> You might have noticed that I'm using the terms *list* and *vector* somewhat interchangeably. This is because the list of sprites in the game engine is technically stored in a vector, but conceptually you can just think of it as a list. So, I may use one term or the other, but they are both referring to the same thing.

The DrawSprites() method is responsible for drawing all the sprites in the sprite list. The method does this by obtaining an iterator for the vector, and then using the iterator to step through the vector and draw each sprite. The Draw() method in the Sprite class is used to draw each sprite, which makes the process of drawing the entire list of sprites relatively simple.

Rivaling the DrawSprites() method in terms of importance is the UpdateSprites() method, which updates the position of each sprite. The critical consideration in this method is that it must be careful to retain the old position of the sprite in case it needs to restore the sprite to that position. An iterator is created that allows the method to step through the sprite vector and update each sprite individually. The sprite is updated with a call to the Update() method, which returns a sprite action.

The sprite action returned from the `Sprite::Update()` method is checked to see if it corresponds to the `SA_KILL` action, which requires the sprite manager to kill the sprite being updated. In order to successfully destroy the sprite, it is first deleted from memory and then removed from the sprite vector. If the `SA_KILL` sprite action wasn't used on the sprite, the `CheckSpriteCollision()` method is called to see if the sprite has collided with any other sprites. The return value of this method determines whether the sprite's old position is restored; `TRUE` means that it should be restored, whereas `FALSE` means that the new position should stand.

Another sprite manager method is `CleanupSprites()`, which is responsible for freeing sprites from memory and emptying the sprite vector. The `CleanupSprites()` method steps through the sprite vector and deletes each sprite in the vector. It also makes sure to remove each sprite from the vector right after it frees the sprite memory. It is important for any game to call the `CleanupSprites()` method so that sprites aren't left hanging around in memory.

The last method in the `GameEngine` class pertaining to sprite management is the `IsPointInSprite()` method, which is used to see if a point lies within a sprite in the sprite list. This method is useful in situations in which you want to allow the user to click and somehow control a sprite. If the point lies within a sprite, the sprite is returned from the `IsPointInSprite()` method. Otherwise, `NULL` is returned, which indicates that the point doesn't lie within any sprites.

Eliminating Flicker with Double Buffering

The sprite manager is now complete and ready to use within a program example. However, one bit of unfinished business needs to be addressed before pressing onward with an example. You might have noticed an annoying flicker in all the animated examples throughout the book thus far. This flicker is caused by the fact that the background image on the game screen is repainted before painting the animated graphics. In other words, animated graphics objects are erased and repainted each time they are moved. Because the erase and repaint process is taking place directly on the game screen, the image appears to flicker. To better understand the problem, imagine a movie in which a blank background is displayed quickly in between each frame containing actors that move. Although the film is cooking along at a fast enough pace to give the illusion of movement, you would still see a noticeable flicker because of the blank backgrounds.

The flicker problem associated with sprite animation can be solved using a technique known as *double buffering*. In double buffering, you perform all of your erasing and drawing on an offscreen drawing surface that isn't visible to the user. After all the drawing is finished, the end result is painted straight to the game screen in one pass. Because no visible erasing is taking place, the end result is flicker-free animation. Figure 11.1 shows the difference between traditional single-buffer animation and double-buffer animation that eliminates flicker.

A *buffer* is simply an area in memory to which you are drawing graphics. The buffer in traditional single-buffer animation is the game screen itself, whereas double-buffer animation adds an offscreen memory buffer to the equation.

FIGURE 11.1

Double-buffer animation eliminates the annoying flicker associated with drawing directly to the game screen with a single buffer.

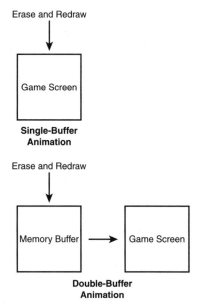

Erase and Redraw

Game Screen

Single-Buffer Animation

Erase and Redraw

Memory Buffer → Game Screen

Double-Buffer Animation

11

Figure 11.1 reveals how an offscreen memory buffer is used to perform all the incremental animation drawing, with only the finished image being drawn to the game screen. This might sound like a tricky programming problem, but double-buffering is really not very hard to incorporate into your games. The first step is to add two global variables to keep track of the offscreen device context and bitmap that serve as the offscreen buffer. Following is an example of how to create these global variables:

```
HDC     _hOffscreenDC;
HBITMAP _hOffscreenBitmap;
```

With these variables in place, you need to create the offscreen device context and then use it to create an offscreen bitmap the same size as the game screen. The offscreen bitmap then needs to be selected into the offscreen device context, and you're ready to go. The following code shows how these tasks are accomplished:

```
// Create the offscreen device context and bitmap
_hOffscreenDC = CreateCompatibleDC(GetDC(hWindow));
_hOffscreenBitmap = CreateCompatibleBitmap(GetDC(hWindow),
  _pGame->GetWidth(), _pGame->GetHeight());
SelectObject(_hOffscreenDC, _hOffscreenBitmap);
```

You now have an offscreen bitmap the same size as your game screen that is selected into an offscreen device context to which you can draw. The following code reveals how easy it is to use the offscreen device context and bitmap to add double-buffer support to the paint code in a game:

```
// Obtain a device context for repainting the game
HWND  hWindow = _pGame->GetWindow();
HDC   hDC = GetDC(hWindow);

// Paint the game to the offscreen device context
GamePaint(_hOffscreenDC);

// Blit the offscreen bitmap to the game screen
BitBlt(hDC, 0, 0, _pGame->GetWidth(), _pGame->GetHeight(),
  _hOffscreenDC, 0, 0, SRCCOPY);

// Cleanup
ReleaseDC(hWindow, hDC);
```

This code would fit in perfectly in a GameCycle() function. The familiar GamePaint() function is passed the offscreen device context, which means that all the game painting takes place offscreen. The resulting image is then painted, or *blitted*, to the game screen's device context at once, which eliminates the possibility of flicker. Notice that this code is structured so that you don't have to do anything special in the GamePaint() function.

It's still important to clean up after yourself, and the following code shows how to clean up the offscreen bitmap and device context:

```
// Cleanup the offscreen device context and bitmap
DeleteObject(_hOffscreenBitmap);
DeleteDC(_hOffscreenDC);
```

Although the double-buffer code isn't technically part of the sprite manager, it is nonetheless an important improvement to sprite animation, and a technique you should definitely use in all of your future sprite animation programs. The next sections build on what you've learned thus far in this hour to revamp the Fore program example from the previous hour to support the sprite manager and double-buffer animation.

Building the Fore 2 Program Example

If you recall from the previous hour, the Fore program example demonstrated how to use the Sprite class to create a few sprites and move them around on the game screen. You're now going to enhance that program example a little by reworking it to support the new sprite management features built in to the game engine, as well as double-buffer animation. The new version of the Fore program is called Fore 2, and it serves as a great test bed for exploring the sprite features you've now added to the game engine.

Writing the Program Code

As with most programs created using the game engine, the best place to start with the code is the GameStart() function, which is used to initialize global variables and get everything in place. Listing 11.3 shows the code for the GameStart() and GameEnd() functions in the Fore 2 program.

LISTING 11.3 The GameStart() Function Initializes the Offscreen Buffer Variables and Adds Sprites to the Game Engine, Whereas the GameEnd() Function Cleans Up the Offscreen Buffer

```
 1: void GameStart(HWND hWindow)
 2: {
 3:   // Seed the random number generator
 4:   srand(GetTickCount());
 5:
 6:   // Create the offscreen device context and bitmap
 7:   _hOffscreenDC = CreateCompatibleDC(GetDC(hWindow));
 8:   _hOffscreenBitmap = CreateCompatibleBitmap(GetDC(hWindow),
 9:     _pGame->GetWidth(), _pGame->GetHeight());
10:   SelectObject(_hOffscreenDC, _hOffscreenBitmap);
11:
12:   // Create and load the bitmaps
13:   HDC hDC = GetDC(hWindow);
14:   _pForestBitmap = new Bitmap(hDC, IDB_FOREST, _hInstance);
15:   _pGolfBallBitmap = new Bitmap(hDC, IDB_GOLFBALL, _hInstance);
16:
17:   // Create the golf ball sprites
18:   RECT    rcBounds = { 0, 0, 600, 400 };
19:   Sprite* pSprite;
20:   pSprite = new Sprite(_pGolfBallBitmap, rcBounds, BA_WRAP);
21:   pSprite->SetVelocity(5, 3);
22:   _pGame->AddSprite(pSprite);
23:   pSprite = new Sprite(_pGolfBallBitmap, rcBounds, BA_WRAP);
24:   pSprite->SetVelocity(3, 2);
25:   _pGame->AddSprite(pSprite);
26:   rcBounds.left = 265; rcBounds.right = 500; rcBounds.bottom = 335;
```

11

LISTING **11.3**   Continued

```
27:    pSprite = new Sprite(_pGolfBallBitmap, rcBounds, BA_BOUNCE);
28:    pSprite->SetVelocity(-6, 5);
29:    _pGame->AddSprite(pSprite);
30:    rcBounds.right = 470;
31:    pSprite = new Sprite(_pGolfBallBitmap, rcBounds, BA_BOUNCE);
32:    pSprite->SetVelocity(7, -3);
33:    _pGame->AddSprite(pSprite);
34:
35:    // Set the initial drag info
36:    _pDragSprite = NULL;
37: }
38:
39: void GameEnd()
40: {
41:    // Cleanup the offscreen device context and bitmap
42:    DeleteObject(_hOffscreenBitmap);
43:    DeleteDC(_hOffscreenDC);
44:
45:    // Cleanup the bitmaps
46:    delete _pForestBitmap;
47:    delete _pGolfBallBitmap;
48:
49:    // Cleanup the sprites
50:    _pGame->CleanupSprites();
51:
52:    // Cleanup the game engine
53:    delete _pGame;
54: }
```

The first big change in the GameStart() function, as compared to its previous version, is the creation of the offscreen device context and bitmap (lines 7–10). The other change has to do with how the golf ball sprites are created. Rather than use a global array of sprites to keep track of the sprites, they are now just created and added to the game engine via the AddSprite() method (lines 22, 25, 29, and 33). Actually, there is an extra golf ball sprite in the Fore 2 program example, which is helpful in demonstrating the collision detection features now built in to the game engine.

You might notice that two of the sprites have their bounding rectangles set differently than the others. More specifically, the third sprite has its bounding rectangle diminished in size, which limits the area in which the sprite can travel (line 26). Similarly, the last sprite's bounding rectangle is further reduced to limit its travel area even more (line 30). When you later test the program, you'll see that these diminished bounding rectangles give the balls the effect of bouncing between trees in the forest background image.

The GameEnd() function is similar to the previous version except that it now cleans up the offscreen bitmap and device context that are required for double-buffer animation (lines 42 and 43).

One of the areas where the new sprite manager really simplifies things is in the GamePaint() function, which is shown in Listing 11.4.

LISTING 11.4 The GamePaint() Function Draws the Forest Background and All the Sprites in the Sprite List

```
1: void GamePaint(HDC hDC)
2: {
3:   // Draw the background forest
4:   _pForestBitmap->Draw(hDC, 0, 0);
5:
6:   // Draw the sprites
7:   _pGame->DrawSprites(hDC);
8: }
```

Notice in this code that the entire list of sprites is drawn using a single call to the DrawSprites() method in the game engine (line 7). This is a perfect example of how a little work in the game engine can really help make your game code easier to manage and understand.

Unlike the GamePaint() function, the GameCycle()function is a little more complex in the Fore 2 program than in its predecessor. However, as Listing 11.5 reveals, the new code consists solely of the familiar double-buffer code that you saw in the previous section.

LISTING 11.5 The GameCycle() Function Updates the Sprites in the Sprite List, and Then Draws Them to an Offscreen Memory Buffer Before Updating the Game Screen

```
1: void GameCycle()
2: {
3:   // Update the sprites
4:   _pGame->UpdateSprites();
5:
6:   // Obtain a device context for repainting the game
7:   HWND  hWindow = _pGame->GetWindow();
8:   HDC   hDC = GetDC(hWindow);
9:
10:  // Paint the game to the offscreen device context
11:  GamePaint(_hOffscreenDC);
12:
```

11

LISTING 11.5   Continued

```
13:     // Blit the offscreen bitmap to the game screen
14:     BitBlt(hDC, 0, 0, _pGame->GetWidth(), _pGame->GetHeight(),
15:       _hOffscreenDC, 0, 0, SRCCOPY);
16:
17:     // Cleanup
18:     ReleaseDC(hWindow, hDC);
19: }
```

The GameCycle() function first updates the sprites in the sprite list with a call to the game engine's UpdateSprites() method (line 4). The remainder of the code in the function should look familiar to you because it is identical to the code you saw earlier when you learned about double-buffer animation. The GamePaint() method is called to paint the game graphics to the offscreen device context (line 11). The offscreen image is then blitted to the game screen's device context to finish the painting (lines 14 and 15).

If you recall from the previous hour, the left mouse button can be used to click and drag a golf ball sprite around on the game screen. Listing 11.6 contains the code for the three mouse functions that make sprite dragging possible.

LISTING 11.6   The MouseButtonDown(), MouseButtonUp(), and MouseMove() Functions Use New Game Engine Sprite Manager Features to Simplify the Process of Dragging a Sprite Around the Game Screen

```
 1: void MouseButtonDown(int x, int y, BOOL bLeft)
 2: {
 3:   // See if a ball was clicked with the left mouse button
 4:   if (bLeft && (_pDragSprite == NULL))
 5:   {
 6:     if ((_pDragSprite = _pGame->IsPointInSprite(x, y)) != NULL)
 7:     {
 8:       // Capture the mouse
 9:       SetCapture(_pGame->GetWindow());
10:
11:       // Simulate a mouse move to get started
12:       MouseMove(x, y);
13:     }
14:   }
15: }
16:
17: void MouseButtonUp(int x, int y, BOOL bLeft)
18: {
19:   // Release the mouse
20:   ReleaseCapture();
21:
```

LISTING 11.5 Continued

```
22:    // Stop dragging
23:    _pDragSprite = NULL;
24: }
25:
26: void MouseMove(int x, int y)
27: {
28:    if (_pDragSprite != NULL)
29:    {
30:      // Move the sprite to the mouse cursor position
31:      _pDragSprite->SetPosition(x - (_pDragSprite->GetWidth() / 2),
32:        y - (_pDragSprite->GetHeight() / 2));
33:
34:      // Force a repaint to redraw the sprites
35:      InvalidateRect(_pGame->GetWindow(), NULL, FALSE);
36:    }
37: }
```

The mouse functions in Fore 2 are simplified from their previous versions thanks to the new and improved game engine. For example, the MouseButtonDown() function now relies on the IsPointInSprite() method in the game engine to check and see if the mouse position is located within a sprite (line 6). The other two mouse functions are very similar to their previous counterparts, except that they now rely on a sprite pointer to keep track of the drag sprite, as opposed to an index into an array of sprites. For example, notice that when the mouse button is released, the _pDragSprite pointer is set to NULL (line 23). Similarly, the same pointer is used to set the position of the drag sprite in the MouseButtonUp() function (lines 31 and 32).

The last function in the Fore 2 program example is the SpriteCollision() function, which is called whenever two sprites collide with each other. Listing 11.7 contains the code for this function.

LISTING 11.7 The SpriteCollision() Function Swaps the Velocities of Sprites That Collide, Which Makes Them Appear to Bounce Off of Each Other

```
1: BOOL SpriteCollision(Sprite* pSpriteHitter, Sprite* pSpriteHittee)
2: {
3:    // Swap the sprite velocities so that they appear to bounce
4:    POINT ptSwapVelocity = pSpriteHitter->GetVelocity();
5:    pSpriteHitter->SetVelocity(pSpriteHittee->GetVelocity());
6:    pSpriteHittee->SetVelocity(ptSwapVelocity);
7:    return TRUE;
8: }
```

11

The `SpriteCollision()` function receives the two sprites that collided as its only arguments (line 1). The function handles the collision by swapping the velocities of the sprites (lines 4–6). This has the effect of making the sprites appear to bounce off of each other and reverse direction. Notice that the `SpriteCollision()` function returns TRUE at the end to indicate that the sprites should be restored to their old positions prior to the collision (line 7) .

Testing the Finished Product

The improvements you made in the Fore 2 program example are somewhat subtle, but they are significant in terms of adding functionality to the game engine that is required to create real games. For example, it is critical that you be able to detect collisions between sprites and react accordingly. The collision detection support in the game engine now makes it very easy to tell when two sprites have collided, and then take appropriate action. Although it's hard to show sprite collisions in a still image, Figure 11.2 shows the Fore 2 program example in action.

FIGURE **11.2**

The golf ball sprites in the Fore 2 program move around and bounce off of each other thanks to the new and improved sprite management features in the game engine.

If you pay close attention to the sprites, you'll notice that two of them appear to bounce between trees in the background. These two sprites are the ones whose bounding rectangles were reduced to limit their movement. You can see that bounding rectangles provide a simple yet effective way to limit the movement of sprites. Keep in mind that you can still click and drag any of the sprites with the left mouse button. Now that the sprites are sensitive to collisions, dragging them around with the mouse is considerably more interesting.

Summary

Sprites are undoubtedly a critical part of two-dimensional game programming because they allow you to create graphical objects that can move around independently of a background image. Not only that, but sprites can be designed so that they reside together in a system in which they can interact with one another. Most games represent a model of some kind of physical system, so a system of sprites becomes a good way of simulating a physical system in a game. This hour built on the sprite code that you developed in the previous hour by pulling sprites together into a system that is managed within the game engine. By actively managing the sprites in the game engine, you're able to ensure that they are layered properly according to Z-order, as well handle collisions between them.

Moving into the next hour, you'll quickly realize how important the new sprite features are to games. The next hour guides you through the development of a complete game called Henway, that is sort of a takeoff on the classic Frogger arcade game. You'll be using your newfound sprite knowledge to the maximum as you build Henway, so get ready!

Q&A

Q Why isn't the sprite manager created as its own class similar to `Sprite`?

A Although the sprite manager code has been created in a class of its own, its tight integration with the game engine made it simpler to just place the sprite management code directly in the engine. If the code resided in a separate class, you'd have to do a fair amount of work making sure that the game engine could communicate with the sprite manager, and vice versa. This is a situation in which it's easier to forego a strict OOP approach of sticking everything in its own class, with the benefit being a more simplistic design.

Q I'm still having trouble understanding how the `AddSprite()` function affects the order of sprites in the sprite list according to their Z-order. What gives?

A It works like this: The Z-order of a sprite determines its depth on the screen, with higher Z-order values resulting in sprites that are more visible. In other words, a sprite with a Z-order of 3 would appear to be sitting on top of a sprite with a Z-order of 2. The practical way to achieve this effect is to draw the topmost sprite last. Or to put it another way, you draw all the sprites in order of increasing Z-order, which naturally means that the higher Z-order sprites appear to be on top of the others. The `AddSprite()` function enforces this system by making sure that the sprite list remains sorted by increasing Z-order as new sprites are added. The Z-order of the sprites is then automatically factored in when drawing the sprites because the sprite list is already sorted accordingly.

11

Workshop

The Workshop is designed to help you anticipate possible questions, review what you've learned, and begin learning how to put your knowledge into practice. The answers to the quiz can be found in Appendix A, "Quiz Answers."

Quiz

1. What is the purpose of the `vector` class in the Standard Template Library?

2. What is the purpose of the `SA_KILL` sprite action?

3. What is double buffering, and why is it important?

Exercises

1. Modify the `SpriteCollision()` function in the Fore 2 example program so that the velocities of the sprites are not only swapped, but also increased slightly with each collision. Then run the program and notice how the balls speed up with each new collision.

2. Create a couple of new sprites in the Fore 2 program example that use an image other than the golf ball image. Pay close attention to how you set the Z-order of the new sprites, and then watch as they move with respect to the golf ball sprites. You should quickly be able to tell how useful Z-order can be in providing depth to games.

HOUR 12

Example Game: Henway

You've spent a great deal of time throughout the book thus far assembling a game engine and learning the ropes of what it takes to build games. You've even created a complete game, although it didn't involve any animation. In this hour, you embark on your next complete game, which takes what you've learned about sprites and puts it to use. The Henway game developed in this hour uses several sprites and most of the sprite features built in to the game engine. The game is somewhat of a takeoff on the classic Frogger game, and it represents a significant milestone in your game programming quest because it is such an interesting little game. This is the kind of game that you can use as the basis for your own game development efforts.

In this hour, you'll learn:

- Why modeling a game on a classic arcade game is sometimes a good idea
- How to design a game called Henway that is somewhat of a takeoff on Frogger
- How to write the code for the Henway game
- Why testing a game of your own is often the most fun part of the development process

How Does the Game Play?

The original Frogger arcade game involved a frog whose goal was to make it across a highway and a river safely. Several obstacles appeared in the frog's path, including speeding cars, treacherous rushing water, and alligators, to name a few. Frogger played vertically, which means that you guided the frog from the bottom of the game screen to the top of the screen in order to reach safety. As you guided more and more frogs safely across, the game progressed to get more difficult by adding more cars and other obstacles to the mix. Although Frogger is certainly an incredibly simple game by modern gaming standards, it's a perfect example of a classic game with fun game play. This makes it a perfect candidate for creating a game of your own—just put a twist on the concept, and you can create your own Frogger-like masterpiece.

In case you're wondering, I don't generally encourage basing all of your games on existing classics, but I have found that popular games of the past can provide good ideas for new games. These days everyone is busy trying to model computer games after movies, but not everyone is interested in playing a heavily scripted drama. Sometimes it's fun to fire up a game and play for a few minutes as a light diversion; in which case, the classics are perfect.

The popularity of Frogger resulted in a variety of knock-off games being created to coat-tail Frogger's success. One of these games was called Freeway, and it involved a chicken trying to cross a busy highway. Freeway was made by Activision for the Atari 2600 game system, which was the first console system to really hit it big. As a proud owner and player of Freeway, I thought it would be fun to create a similar game in this hour. However, the game you create is called Henway, which comes from an old joke. If you've never heard the joke, it goes like this: You mention the word "henway" a few times in a conversation with a friend, and eventually he'll get up the nerve to say, "What's a henway?" And you immediately respond, "Oh, about three pounds." I know, it's a very bad joke, but it makes for a fun name for a game involving a chicken and a highway.

Unlike Frogger, the hero in Henway is a chicken who desperately needs to get from one side of a busy highway to the other. Also unlike Frogger, Henway plays horizontally, which means that you guide the chicken from the left side of the screen to the right side. So, the game screen looks something like the drawing in Figure 12.1.

FIGURE 12.1

The Henway game consists of a Start Area, a Highway, and a Finish Area, along with chicken and car sprites.

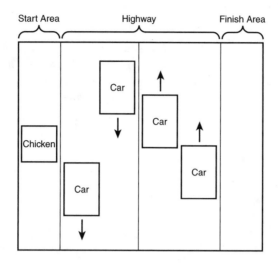

As you can see, the obstacles working against the chicken are four sprites that are cruising up and down four lanes of highway. The cars move at varying speeds, which makes it a little trickier to time the chicken's crossing. Unlike Frogger, which requires you to guide the frog into specific zones of the Finish Area, Henway just requires you to get the chicken across the road.

You'll notice that a common thread throughout all of the game examples in the book is simplicity. Although there are all kinds of neat ways to improve on the games, I opted to leave it up to you to make the improvements. My goal is to provide you with a working game that is simple enough to understand, and then you can jazz it up with extra features.

12

You start the Henway game with a limited number of chickens: three. When all of your chickens get run over, the game is over. It's important to show somewhere on the screen how many chickens you have remaining. Additionally, some kind of notification should take place to inform you when you lose a chicken, as well as when you successfully make it across the highway. It also wouldn't hurt to have some kind of scoring system for rewarding good game play.

The Henway game is well suited for both keyboard and joystick input, although there isn't really a good way to use the mouse in the game. For this reason, you'll focus on supporting the keyboard and joystick, and skip the mouse entirely.

Designing the Game

The overview of the Henway game has already given you a leg up on the game's design, even if you don't realize it. For example, you already know how many sprites are required for the game. Can you hazard a guess? There are five sprites in the game: one chicken sprite and four car sprites. There is certainly the opportunity to include additional car sprites if desired, but the basic game only uses four.

Beyond the sprites, can you guess how many bitmap images the game needs? If you guessed six, you're very close. Following are the seven bitmap images required of the game:

- Background highway image
- Chicken image
- Four car images
- Small chicken image

You probably factored in all these images except the last one. The small chicken image is used to convey to the player how many chickens are left. As an example, when the game starts, three small chickens are displayed in the lower right edge of the screen. As you sacrifice your chickens to the highway, the small chickens disappear until you have none left and the game is over.

Now that you have a feel for the graphical objects involved in the game, let's consider other data that must be maintained by the game. First, it's pretty obvious that you'll need to keep track of how many chicken lives are remaining. You'll also want to keep a running score that is added to each time a chicken makes it safely across the highway. A Boolean variable keeping track of whether the game is over is also required.

There is one last variable that would be hard for you to anticipate without actually developing the game and testing it out. I'm referring to an input delay variable, which helps to alter the keyboard and joystick input response to improve the playability of the game. If you directly responded to the keyboard and joystick in every game cycle, which is how you would logically support input in the game, the chicken would zip around the game screen too fast. There are just too many game cycles taking place to give input devices that much attention. In order to slow down the input a little, you can use a delay variable and only check for keyboard and joystick input every third game cycle. Determining the appropriate delay is somewhat of a trial and error process, so you're free to tinker with it and see what you like best. The point is that the game benefits dramatically from putting a leash on the speed of the user input handling.

To recap, the design of the Henway game has led us to the following pieces of information that must be managed by the game:

- The number of chicken lives
- The score
- A Boolean game over variable
- A delay variable

With this information in mind, you're now ready to move on and put the code together for the Henway game.

Building the Game

Hopefully by now you're getting antsy to see how the Henway game is put together. The next couple of sections explore the code development for the Henway game, which is relatively simple when you consider that this is the first fully functioning game you've created that supports double-buffer sprite animation. The revamped game engine with sprite management really makes the Henway game a smooth game to develop.

Writing the Game Code

The code for the Henway game begins with the Henway.h header file, which is shown in Listing 12.1.

LISTING 12.1   The Henway.h Header File Declares Global Variables that Are Used to Manage the Game, as well as a Helper Function

```
 1: #pragma once
 2:
 3: //-------------------------------------------------------------
 4: // Include Files
 5: //-------------------------------------------------------------
 6: #include <windows.h>
 7: #include "Resource.h"
 8: #include "GameEngine.h"
 9: #include "Bitmap.h"
10: #include "Sprite.h"
11:
12: //-------------------------------------------------------------
13: // Global Variables
14: //-------------------------------------------------------------
15: HINSTANCE   _hInstance;
16: GameEngine* _pGame;
17: HDC         _hOffscreenDC;
```

12

LISTING 12.1 Continued

```
18: HBITMAP      _hOffscreenBitmap;
19: Bitmap*      _pHighwayBitmap;
20: Bitmap*      _pChickenBitmap;
21: Bitmap*      _pCarBitmaps[4];
22: Bitmap*      _pChickenHeadBitmap;
23: Sprite*      _pChickenSprite;
24: int          _iInputDelay;
25: int          _iNumLives;
26: int          _iScore;
27: BOOL         _bGameOver;
28:
29: //-------------------------------------------------------------
30: // Function Declarations
31: //-------------------------------------------------------------
32: void MoveChicken(int iXDistance, int iYDistance);
```

The global variables for the Henway game consist largely of the different bitmaps used throughout the game. The offscreen device context and bitmap are declared (lines 17 and 18), as well as the different bitmaps that comprise the game's graphics (lines 19–22). Even the sprite management features of the game engine are being used in this game; it's necessary to keep a pointer to the chicken sprite so that you can change its position in response to user input events. The _pChickenSprite member variable is used to store the chicken sprite pointer (line 23). The input delay for the keyboard and joystick is declared next (line 24), along with the number of chicken lives remaining (line 25) and the score (line 26). The last variable is the Boolean game over variable, which simply keeps track of whether the game is over (line 27).

You'll notice that a helper function named MoveChicken() is declared in the Henway.h file. This function is called by other game functions within the game to move the chicken sprite in response to user input events. The two arguments to the MoveChicken() function are the X and Y amounts to move the chicken.

The actual game functions appear in the Henway.cpp source code file, which is located on the accompanying CD-ROM. The first game function worth mentioning is the GameInitialize() function, which creates the game engine, establishes the frame rate, and initializes the joystick.

The GameStart() function is a little more interesting than GameInitialize(). This function is responsible for initializing the game data, as shown in Listing 12.2.

LISTING 12.2   The GameStart() Function Creates the Offscreen Buffer, Loads the
Game Bitmaps, Creates the Game Sprites, and Initializes Game State Member
Variables

```
 1: void GameStart(HWND hWindow)
 2: {
 3:   // Seed the random number generator
 4:   srand(GetTickCount());
 5:
 6:   // Create the offscreen device context and bitmap
 7:   _hOffscreenDC = CreateCompatibleDC(GetDC(hWindow));
 8:   _hOffscreenBitmap = CreateCompatibleBitmap(GetDC(hWindow),
 9:     _pGame->GetWidth(), _pGame->GetHeight());
10:   SelectObject(_hOffscreenDC, _hOffscreenBitmap);
11:
12:   // Create and load the bitmaps
13:   HDC hDC = GetDC(hWindow);
14:   _pHighwayBitmap = new Bitmap(hDC, IDB_HIGHWAY, _hInstance);
15:   _pChickenBitmap = new Bitmap(hDC, IDB_CHICKEN, _hInstance);
16:   _pCarBitmaps[0] = new Bitmap(hDC, IDB_CAR1, _hInstance);
17:   _pCarBitmaps[1] = new Bitmap(hDC, IDB_CAR2, _hInstance);
18:   _pCarBitmaps[2] = new Bitmap(hDC, IDB_CAR3, _hInstance);
19:   _pCarBitmaps[3] = new Bitmap(hDC, IDB_CAR4, _hInstance);
20:   _pChickenHeadBitmap = new Bitmap(hDC, IDB_CHICKENHEAD, _hInstance);
21:
22:   // Create the chicken and car sprites
23:   Sprite* pSprite;
24:   RECT    rcBounds = { 0, 0, 465, 400 };
25:   _pChickenSprite = new Sprite(_pChickenBitmap, rcBounds, BA_STOP);
26:   _pChickenSprite->SetPosition(4, 175);
27:   _pChickenSprite->SetVelocity(0, 0);
28:   _pChickenSprite->SetZOrder(1);
29:   _pGame->AddSprite(_pChickenSprite);
30:   pSprite = new Sprite(_pCarBitmaps[0], rcBounds, BA_WRAP);
31:   pSprite->SetPosition(70, 0);
32:   pSprite->SetVelocity(0, 7);
33:   pSprite->SetZOrder(2);
34:   _pGame->AddSprite(pSprite);
35:   pSprite = new Sprite(_pCarBitmaps[1], rcBounds, BA_WRAP);
36:   pSprite->SetPosition(160, 0);
37:   pSprite->SetVelocity(0, 3);
38:   pSprite->SetZOrder(2);
39:   _pGame->AddSprite(pSprite);
40:   pSprite = new Sprite(_pCarBitmaps[2], rcBounds, BA_WRAP);
41:   pSprite->SetPosition(239, 400);
42:   pSprite->SetVelocity(0, -5);
43:   pSprite->SetZOrder(2);
44:   _pGame->AddSprite(pSprite);
45:   pSprite = new Sprite(_pCarBitmaps[3], rcBounds, BA_WRAP);
46:   pSprite->SetPosition(329, 400);
```

12

LISTING **12.2**   Continued

```
47:    pSprite->SetVelocity(0, -10);
48:    pSprite->SetZOrder(2);
49:    _pGame->AddSprite(pSprite);
50:
51:    // Initialize the remaining global variables
52:    _iInputDelay = 0;
53:    _iNumLives = 3;
54:    _iScore = 0;
55:    _bGameOver = FALSE;
56: }
```

The GameStart() function contains a fair amount of code, which primarily has to do with the fact that creating each sprite requires a few lines of code. The function starts out by creating the offscreen device context and bitmap (lines 7–10). All the bitmaps for the game are then loaded (lines 13–20). Finally, the really interesting part of the function involves the creation of the sprites, which you should be able to follow without too much difficulty. The chicken sprite is first created at a position in the Start Area of the game screen, and with 0 velocity (lines 25–29). The car sprites are then created at different positions and with varying velocities (lines 30–49). Notice that the bounds actions for the car sprites are set so that the cars wrap around the game screen, whereas the chicken sprite stops when it encounters a boundary. Also, the Z-order of the cars is set higher than the chicken so that the chicken will appear under the cars when it gets run over.

The remaining member variables in the Henway game are initialized in the GameStart() function after the sprites are created. The input delay is set to 0 (line 52), whereas the number of chicken lives is set to 3 (line 53). The score is also set to 0 (line 54), and the game over variable is set to FALSE to indicate that the game isn't over (line 55).

The Henway game relies on the keyboard and joystick for user input. In order to support joystick input, it's important to capture and release the joystick whenever the game window is activated and deactivated. Listing 12.3 shows the code for the GameActivate() and GameDeactivate() functions, which are responsible in this case for capturing and releasing the joystick.

LISTING **12.3**   The GameActivate() and GameDeactivate() Functions Capture and Release the Joystick, Respectively

```
1: void GameActivate(HWND hWindow)
2: {
3:    // Capture the joystick
4:    _pGame->CaptureJoystick();
5: }
```

LISTING 12.3 Continued

```
 6:
 7: void GameDeactivate(HWND hWindow)
 8: {
 9:   // Release the joystick
10:   _pGame->ReleaseJoystick();
11: }
```

The GameActivate() function calls the CaptureJoystick() method on the game engine to capture the joystick (line 4), whereas the GameDeactivate() function calls ReleaseJoystick() to release the joystick (line 10).

As you know, the GamePaint() function is responsible for painting games. Listing 12.4 contains the code for the Henway game's GamePaint() function.

LISTING 12.4 The GamePaint()Function Draws the Highway Background Image, the Game Sprites, and the Number of Remaining Chicken Lives

```
 1: void GamePaint(HDC hDC)
 2: {
 3:   // Draw the background highway
 4:   _pHighwayBitmap->Draw(hDC, 0, 0);
 5:
 6:   // Draw the sprites
 7:   _pGame->DrawSprites(hDC);
 8:
 9:   // Draw the number of remaining chicken lives
10:   for (int i = 0; i < _iNumLives; i++)
11:     _pChickenHeadBitmap->Draw(hDC,
12:       406 + (_pChickenHeadBitmap->GetWidth() * i), 382, TRUE);
13: }
```

12

This GamePaint() function must draw all the game graphics for the Henway game. The function begins by drawing the background highway image (line 4), and then it draws the game sprites (line 7). The remainder of the function draws the number of remaining chicken lives in the lower right corner of the game screen using small chicken head bitmaps (lines 10–12). A small chicken head is drawn for each chicken life remaining, which helps you to know how many times you can get run over before the game ends.

The GameCycle() function works hand in hand with GamePaint() to update the game's sprites and then reflect the changes onscreen. Listing 12.5 shows the code for the GameCycle() function.

LISTING 12.5   The `GameCycle()` Function Updates the Game Sprites and Repaints the Game Screen Using an Offscreen Buffer to Eliminate Flicker

```
 1: void GameCycle()
 2: {
 3:   if (!_bGameOver)
 4:   {
 5:     // Update the sprites
 6:     _pGame->UpdateSprites();
 7:
 8:     // Obtain a device context for repainting the game
 9:     HWND  hWindow = _pGame->GetWindow();
10:     HDC   hDC = GetDC(hWindow);
11:
12:     // Paint the game to the offscreen device context
13:     GamePaint(_hOffscreenDC);
14:
15:     // Blit the offscreen bitmap to the game screen
16:     BitBlt(hDC, 0, 0, _pGame->GetWidth(), _pGame->GetHeight(),
17:       _hOffscreenDC, 0, 0, SRCCOPY);
18:
19:     // Cleanup
20:     ReleaseDC(hWindow, hDC);
21:   }
22: }
```

The `GameCycle()` function first checks to make sure that the game isn't over (line 3); in which case, there would be no need to update anything. The function then updates the sprites (line 6) and goes about redrawing the game graphics using double-buffer animation. This double-buffer code should be fairly familiar to you by now, so I won't go into the details. The main thing to notice is that the `GamePaint()` function is ultimately being used to draw the game graphics (line 13).

I mentioned earlier that the Henway game supports both keyboard and joystick input. Listing 12.6 contains the code for the `HandleKeys()` function, which takes care of processing and responding to keyboard input in the game.

LISTING 12.6   The `HandleKeys()` Function Responds to the Arrow Keys on the Keyboard by Moving the Chicken

```
 1: void HandleKeys()
 2: {
 3:   if (!_bGameOver && (++_iInputDelay > 2))
 4:   {
 5:     // Move the chicken based upon key presses
 6:     if (GetAsyncKeyState(VK_LEFT) < 0)
```

LISTING 12.6   Continued

```
 7:        MoveChicken(-20, 0);
 8:      else if (GetAsyncKeyState(VK_RIGHT) < 0)
 9:        MoveChicken(20, 0);
10:      if (GetAsyncKeyState(VK_UP) < 0)
11:        MoveChicken(0, -20);
12:      else if (GetAsyncKeyState(VK_DOWN) < 0)
13:        MoveChicken(0, 20);
14:
15:      // Reset the input delay
16:      _iInputDelay = 0;
17:    }
18: }
```

The HandleKeys() function begins by making sure that the game isn't over, as well as incrementing and testing the input delay (line 3). By testing the input delay before processing any keyboard input, the HandleKeys() function effectively slows down the input so that the chicken is easier to control. The chicken is actually controlled via the arrow keys, which are checked using the Win32 GetAsyncKeyState() function. Each arrow key is handled by calling the MoveChicken() function, which moves the chicken by a specified amount (lines 6–13). After processing the keys, the input delay is reset so that the input process can be repeated (line 16).

The joystick is handled in the Henway game in a similar manner as the mouse, as Listing 12.7 reveals.

LISTING 12.7   The HandleJoystick() Function Responds to Joystick Movements by Moving the Chicken, and also Supports Using the Primary Joystick Button to Start a New Game

```
 1: void HandleJoystick(JOYSTATE jsJoystickState)
 2: {
 3:   if (!_bGameOver && (++_iInputDelay > 2))
 4:   {
 5:     // Check horizontal movement
 6:     if (jsJoystickState & JOY_LEFT)
 7:         MoveChicken(-20, 0);
 8:     else if (jsJoystickState & JOY_RIGHT)
 9:         MoveChicken(20, 0);
10:
11:     // Check vertical movement
12:     if (jsJoystickState & JOY_UP)
13:         MoveChicken(0, -20);
14:     else if (jsJoystickState & JOY_DOWN)
15:         MoveChicken(0, 20);
```

12

LISTING 12.7   Continued

```
16:
17:     // Reset the input delay
18:     _iInputDelay = 0;
19:   }
20:
21:   // Check the joystick button and start a new game, if necessary
22:   if (_bGameOver && (jsJoystickState & JOY_FIRE1))
23:   {
24:     _iNumLives = 3;
25:     _iScore = 0;
26:     _bGameOver = FALSE;
27:   }
28: }
```

The `HandleJoystick()` function performs the same check on the `_bGameOver` and `_iInputDelay` variables to make sure that it is time to check the joystick for input (line 3). If so, the joystick is first checked for horizontal movement by examining the `jsJoystickState` argument passed in to the function. The chicken is then moved left or right, if necessary, by calling the `MoveChicken()` function (lines 6–9). A similar process is then repeated for vertical joystick movement (lines 12–15). After handling joystick movement, the `HandleJoystick()` function resets the `_iInputDelay` variable (line 18). The function then concludes by checking to see if the primary joystick button was pressed (line 22); in which case, a new game is started (lines 24–26).

Speaking of starting a new game, the mouse is used in the Henway game solely to start a new game if the current game has ended. Listing 12.8 shows the code for the `MouseButtonDown()` function, which starts a new game in response to a mouse button click.

LISTING 12.8   The `MouseButtonDown()` Function Starts a New Game if the Current Game Is Over

```
 1: void MouseButtonDown(int x, int y, BOOL bLeft)
 2: {
 3:   // Start a new game, if necessary
 4:   if (_bGameOver)
 5:   {
 6:     _iNumLives = 3;
 7:     _iScore = 0;
 8:     _bGameOver = FALSE;
 9:   }
10: }
```

If a mouse button is clicked and the current game is over, the MouseButtonDown() function starts a new game by clearing the game state variables (lines 6–8).

The game play of the Henway game is largely dictated by the sprites in the game. These sprites are capable of colliding; in which case, the SpriteCollision() function gets called. Of course, the car sprites are designed to only move vertically up and down the screen, so they'll never hit each other. This means that the SpriteCollision() function only gets called when a car hits the chicken, or vice versa. Listing 12.9 shows how this collision is handled in the SpriteCollision() function.

LISTING 12.9 The SpriteCollision() Function Checks to See if the Chicken Was Hit by a Car, and Then Responds Accordingly

```
 1: BOOL SpriteCollision(Sprite* pSpriteHitter, Sprite* pSpriteHittee)
 2: {
 3:   // See if the chicken was hit
 4:   if (pSpriteHittee == _pChickenSprite)
 5:   {
 6:     // Move the chicken back to the start
 7:     _pChickenSprite->SetPosition(4, 175);
 8:
 9:     // See if the game is over
10:     if (--_iNumLives > 0)
11:       MessageBox(_pGame->GetWindow(), TEXT("Ouch!"), TEXT("Henway"), MB_OK);
12:     else
13:     {
14:       // Display game over message
15:       TCHAR szText[64];
16:       wsprintf(szText, "Game Over! You scored %d points.", _iScore);
17:       MessageBox(_pGame->GetWindow(), szText, TEXT("Henway"), MB_OK);
18:       _bGameOver = TRUE;
19:     }
20:
21:     return FALSE;
22:   }
23:
24:   return TRUE;
25: }
```

Most of the game logic in the Henway game is located in the SpriteCollision() function. First, a check is made to ensure that the chicken was indeed involved in the collision (line 4). If so, you can safely assume that the chicken was hit by a car, so the chicken's position is restored to its starting position in the Start Area (line 7). The number of chicken lives is then decremented and checked to see if the game is over (line 10). If the game isn't over, a message is displayed indicating that you lost a chicken (line 11),

12

but the game ultimately continues on. If the game is over, however, a special "Game Over" message is displayed and the _bGameOver variable is set to TRUE (lines 15–18).

If you recall from the design of the sprite manager, the return value of the SpriteCollision() function determines whether the sprite's old position is restored; a value of TRUE restores the old position, whereas FALSE allows the sprite to keep its newly updated position. In this case, the sprite keeps its new position when it collides with a car (line 21). Because the position was just set to the Start Area in line 7, the effect is that the chicken is allowed to move to the start area, which gives the appearance of a new chicken appearing.

The final function in the Henway game is the MoveChicken() function, which you've used several times throughout the game code. Listing 12.10 shows the code for the MoveChicken() function.

LISTING 12.10   The MoveChicken() Function Moves the Chicken Sprite by a Specified Distance While Checking to See if the Chicken Made It Across the Highway

```
 1: void MoveChicken(int iXDistance, int iYDistance)
 2: {
 3:   // Move the chicken to its new position
 4:   _pChickenSprite->OffsetPosition(iXDistance, iYDistance);
 5:
 6:   // See if the chicken made it across
 7:   if (_pChickenSprite->GetPosition().left > 400)
 8:   {
 9:     // Move the chicken back to the start and add to the score
10:     _pChickenSprite->SetPosition(4, 175);
11:     _iScore += 150;
12:     MessageBox(_pGame->GetWindow(), TEXT("You made it!"), TEXT("Henway"),
13:       MB_OK);
14:   }
15: }
```

The MoveChicken() function is a helper function that simplifies the task of moving the chicken around on the game screen. The iXDistance and iYDistance arguments specify how many pixels to move the chicken in the X and Y directions (line 1). These arguments are used to move the chicken by calling the OffsetPosition() method on the Sprite class (line 4). If you didn't care what happened to the chicken, this is all the code you would need in the MoveChicken() function. However, you need to know when the chicken makes it across the highway, and this is a perfect place to perform the check (line 7). If the chicken made it safely across, its position is set back to the Start Area (line 10) and the score is increased (11). A message is also displayed that notifies the player of a successful highway crossing (lines 12–13) .

Testing the Game

Unless you just happen to be a fan of memory games, you'll hopefully find the Henway game to be much more fun to test than the Brainiac game from Hour 8, "Example Game: Brainiac." The Henway is the first legitimate action game that you've created, which makes it considerably more interesting from a playability perspective. Keep in mind that action games often require a greater deal of testing because it's hard to predict how sprites will react in every little situation. You should play your games a great deal to make sure that nothing out of the ordinary ever happens, or at least nothing detrimental that's out of the ordinary.

Figure 12.2 shows the Henway game at the start, with your lion-hearted chicken poised for a trip across the highway.

FIGURE 12.2

The Henway game begins with the chicken in the Start Area, ready to make an attempt at crossing the busy highway.

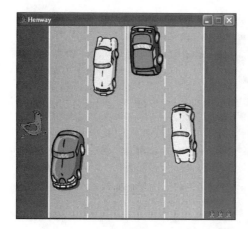

If the chicken immediately starts moving when you start the game, there's a good chance that your joystick needs calibrating. Refer back to the section titled "Calibrating Joysticks" in Hour 7, "Improving Input with Joysticks," if you've forgotten how to calibrate your joystick.

To get started with the game, just begin guiding your chicken through traffic using the keyboard or joystick. If you successfully navigate the chicken across the highway, the game will display a message and award you with 150 points. Figure 12.3 shows the message that appears when you succeed in crossing the highway.

12

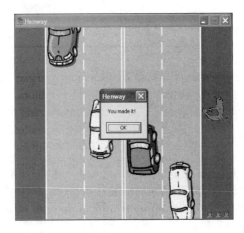

Of course, even the best Henway player will eventually get careless and steer the chicken into the path of an oncoming car. Figure 12.4 shows the message displayed after a chicken is hit by a car.

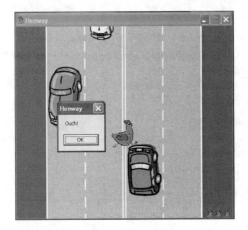

After you lose a chicken, the number of chicken lives in the lower right corner of the screen will reduce by one to show the remaining lives. When you eventually lose all three chickens, the game ends. Figure 12.5 shows the end of the game, which simply involves a message being displayed that notifies you of your final score.

Although it might be sad to steer three chickens to their demise in a highway full of busy traffic, it's all just a game. Despite it's relative simplicity, hopefully you can appreciate the Henway game in terms of it representing a culmination of much of what you've learned throughout the book thus far. Even so, there is much ahead as you continue to build more exciting games from here on.

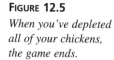

FIGURE 12.5

When you've depleted all of your chickens, the game ends.

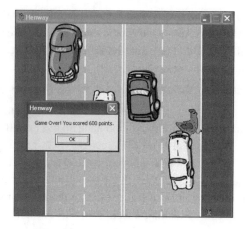

Summary

It is a fact of life that book knowledge can only get you so far before you have to experience something yourself. This hour is an example of how book knowledge was made real when you assembled a game that relied on what you've learned about game programming. The Henway game made use of the sprite animation code that you developed in the previous two hours, as well as a great deal of the user input code that you built in to the game engine earlier in the book. Hopefully, you're feeling a sense of gratification that the work you've spent constructing the game engine is starting to pay off in the development of a complete game with a surprisingly small amount of code.

This hour concludes the current part of the book. The next part, "Making Noise with Sound and Music," introduces you to digital sound effects and music, as well as the role they play in games. Not surprisingly, you learn how to add sound and music to games. In fact, you'll encounter the Henway game once more in the next part when you add sound effects and music to it.

12

Q&A

Q **Why doesn't the Henway game take advantage of the SA_KILL sprite action to kill the chicken sprite when the chicken gets run over?**

A It's logical that because the chicken is getting run over, you might think that the chicken sprite should go away. However, you have to consider that the chicken sprite immediately gets used again if the player has more lives left. And even if the game is over, it doesn't hurt to keep the chicken sprite around because it will undoubtedly be used again if a new game is started. For these reasons, it makes sense to keep the chicken sprite around throughout the entire game, and simply move it back to the Start Area whenever a chicken is run over in the game. Don't worry: You'll still get around to using the SA_KILL sprite action to kill off some sprites a little later in the book.

Q Why is the input delay variable necessary in the Henway game?

A The best way to answer this question is to just have you change the line of code that checks the input delay variable in the HandleKeys() and HandleJoystick() functions. Where the code says ++_iInputDelay > 2, just change the code to be **++_iInputDelay > 0**. This will remove the effect of the _iInputDelay variable and will cause the keyboard and joystick to be checked in every game cycle, as opposed to every third cycle. You'll find out that the keyboard and joystick are way too responsive and end up making the chicken move around too fast. This is one of those rare instances in which you actually want to slow down an aspect of a game to improve its playability.

Workshop

The Workshop is designed to help you anticipate possible questions, review what you've learned, and begin learning how to put your knowledge into practice. The answers to the quiz can be found in Appendix A, "Quiz Answers."

Quiz

1. What is the purpose of the _pChickenSprite member variable in the Henway game?

2. How is the SpriteCollision() function used in the Henway game?

3. How does the Henway game know when the chicken makes it across the highway?

Exercises

1. Modify the Henway game so that additional car sprites are added to make the game harder. (Hint: You can use the score as the basis for adding these sprites and making the game harder over time.)

2. Modify the background image for the Henway game so that there are limited spaces in the Finish Area for the chicken to finish. Then modify the code in the game so that the chicken is only allowed to move into the new spaces. This change effectively makes Henway play more like Frogger, and adds a bit more challenge to the game.

PART IV
Making Noise with Sound and Music

Hours

HOUR 13

Getting Acquainted with Digital Sound and Music

It's hard to argue the impact of compelling sound effects and music on video games of all types. Even the video game classics with their limited sound-making capabilities often incorporated music that you simply couldn't get out of your head, not to mention highly entertaining sound effects. Modern games now have the capability to use extremely realistic sound effects and intricate musical compositions. Even if you aren't musically inclined, you owe it to yourself to figure out a way to incorporate sound and music into your games. This hour lays the conceptual groundwork for understanding how sound and music are used in computer games, as well as how to create sound effects, and how to find sounds and music for games.

In this hour, you'll learn:

- The basics of digital sound
- How digital sound in Windows is represented by waves
- What MIDI means, and how it relates to computer music
- About some of the more powerful sound editing tools available
- How to create and edit your own sound effects for games

Understanding Digital Sound

Although you could probably get away with playing sounds in games without understanding how digital sound works, I'm not going to let you off the hook that easy. It's
important to at least have a basic understanding of digital sound, and how it relates to
physical sound that we hear in the real world. A physical sound is a wave that moves
through the air, kind of like an air equivalent of an ocean wave. A *sound wave* is actually
a result of the pressure of air expanding and contracting. In other words, a sound wave is
a series of traveling pressure changes in the air. You hear sound because the traveling
sound wave eventually gets to your ears, where the pressure changes are processed and
interpreted by your eardrums. If your eardrums are rocky outcroppings on a beach, you
hear sound when an ocean wave crashes against the rocks. The softness or loudness of a
sound is determined by the amount of energy in the wave, which corresponds to the
height and force of an ocean wave. Because sound waves lose energy as they travel, you
hear sounds louder up close and softer from a distance. Eventually, sound waves travel
far enough to be completely absorbed by the air or some other object such as a wall in
your house.

When I refer to the energy of a sound wave, I'm really talking about the *amplitude* of the
wave. Amplitudes of sound waves are usually measured in decibels (dB). Decibels are
logarithmic units of measurement, meaning that 80dB is 10 times louder than 79dB. This
type of measurement is used because it reflects the hearing characteristics of the human
ear. The threshold of human hearing is 0dB, which means that anything less is too soft to
be heard by humans. Likewise, the threshold of pain is 120dB, which is the amplitude
level at which humans experience physical pain. Prolonged exposure to sound this loud
can cause permanent hearing damage.

> Many rock concerts over the years have hit the 120dB sound level. In 1976,
> The Who made it into the Guinness Book of World Records with a 125dB
> concert that is now considered the loudest concert of all time.

When a microphone converts sound waves to voltage signals, the resulting signal is an
analog (or continuous) signal. Because computers are *digital* machines, it is necessary to
convert this analog signal to a digital signal for a computer to process. Analog to digital
(A/D) converters handle the task of converting analog signals to digital signals, which is
also referred to as *sampling*. The process of converting an analog signal to a digital signal doesn't always yield exact results. How closely a digital wave matches its analog
counterpart is determined by the frequency at which it is sampled, as well as the amount
of information stored at each sample.

To sample a sound, you just store the amplitude of the sound wave at regular intervals. Taking samples at more frequent intervals causes the digital signal to more closely approximate the analog signal and, therefore, sound more like the analog wave when played. So, when sampling sounds the rate (*frequency*) at which the sound is sampled is very important, as well as how much data is stored for each sample. The unit of measurement for frequency is Hertz (Hz), which specifies how many samples are taken per second. As an example, CD-quality audio is sampled at 44,000Hz (44kHz), which means that when you're listening to a music CD you're actually hearing 44,000 digital sound samples every second.

In addition to the frequency of a sampled sound, the number of bits used to represent the amplitude of the sound impacts the sound quality, as well as whether the sound is a stereo or mono sound. Knowing this, it's possible to categorize the quality of a digital sound according to the following properties:

- Frequency
- Bits-per-sample
- Mono/stereo

The frequency of a sampled sound typically falls somewhere in the range of 8kHz to 44kHz, with 44kHz representing CD-quality sound. The bits-per-sample of a sound is usually either 8bps (bits per sample) or 16bps, with 16bps representing CD-quality audio; this is also known as 16-bit audio. A sampled sound is then classified as being either mono or stereo, with mono meaning that there is only one channel of sound, whereas stereo has two channels. As you might expect, a stereo sound contains twice as much information as a mono sound. Not surprisingly, CD-quality audio is always stereo. Therefore, you now understand that a CD-quality sound is a 44kHz 16-bit stereo sound.

Although it would be great to incorporate sounds that are CD-quality into all of your games, the reality is that high-quality sounds take up a lot of memory and can therefore be burdensome to play if your game already relies on a lot of images and other memory-intensive resources. Granted, most computers these days are capable of ripping through memory-intensive multimedia objects such as MP3 songs like they are nothing, but games must be designed for extreme efficiency. Therefore, it's important to consider ways to minimize the memory and processing burden on games every chance you get. One way to minimize this burden is to carefully choose a sound quality that sounds good without hogging too much memory.

Another issue you should consider in regard to using sound in games is that of copyrighted sounds—you can't use copyrighted sounds without written permission from the owner of the copyright. For example, sounds sampled from copyrighted movies or audio

13

recordings can't be used without permission. It is technically no different than using copyrighted software without permission or a licensing agreement. So be careful when sampling sounds from copyrighted sources.

> Some seemingly public domain sound collections are actually copyrighted and can get you into trouble. Most of these types of collections come in the form of an audio CD containing a variety of sound effects. Be sure to read the fine print on these CDs, and make sure that you can legally reuse the sounds or get explicit permission from the publisher.

Getting to Know Windows Waves

Digital sounds in Windows are known as *waves*, which refer to the physical sound waves from which digital sounds originate. Windows waves are stored in files with a .WAV file extension, and can be stored in a wide range of formats to accommodate different sound qualities. More specifically, you can save waves in frequencies from 8kHz to 44kHz with either 8 or 16 bits per sample and as either mono or stereo. Just as with any other sampled digital audio, the size of a wave file is directly proportional to the quality of the wave sound. So, higher quality waves take up more memory than lower quality waves.

You might be surprised to find out that waves are really just Windows resources like bitmaps, icons, and cursors. This means that you can specify waves as resources in the resource script for your games and compile them directly into the executable program files. The benefit is that you don't have to worry about distributing a bunch of extra files when you make your game available to the public; all the wave files are included in the game's executable program file.

If you want to experiment a little with Windows waves and how they work, you'll be glad to know that Windows includes a built-in tool for working with waves. It's called Sound Recorder, and you'll find it by following these steps in Windows XP:

1. Click the Start button.
2. Select All Programs, followed by Accessories, and then Entertainment.
3. Select Sound Recorder to launch the program.

> If you aren't using Windows XP, don't worry because Sound Recorder is included with all versions of Windows. Just poke around within the Accessories folder, and you'll be able to find it.

The Sound Recorder program is shown in Figure 13.1.

FIGURE 13.1

The Sound Recorder program allows you to record sounds and then manipulate them to some degree.

You'll notice that the Sound Recorder tool includes a series of buttons that look like the buttons on a VCR. These buttons allow you to record new sounds using your computer's microphone or CD-ROM drive, as well as play, stop, rewind, and fast forward sounds. Feel free to try your hand at recording a sound with the microphone and playing it back with Sound Recorder. You might also want to experiment with some of the effects that can be applied to the sound, such as reversing it and hearing the sound backwards. Remember all of the rumors about hidden messages in rock music when you play it backwards? Now you can create your own!

Although Sound Recorder is a fairly primitive tool in terms of features, it does give you capability to tinker with waves and even apply effects to them. Before you invest in a higher-powered sound tool, be sure to take some time to experiment with Sound Recorder. Later this hour in the section "Creating and Editing Sounds," you'll learn some interesting techniques used to create wave sound effects; you can certainly use Sound Recorder as the tool for creating these effects. If Sound Recorder ends up feeling too limited for you, you also learn about other sound tools in the later section "Exploring Sound Tools."

Feeling the Music with MIDI

Musical Instrument Digital Interface, or *MIDI*, started out in the early 80s as an attempt to establish a standard interface between musical instruments. The main use for MIDI back then was to enable a dedicated keyboard to control a synthesizer. Keyboard synthesizers consist of two main components: the keyboard and the synthesizer. The keyboard is responsible for keeping up with input information such as which musical note is being generated and how hard the key is being pressed on the keyboard. The synthesizer, on the other hand, is responsible for generating sounds based on the input information provided by the keyboard. So, the original goal of MIDI was to provide a standardized approach to controlling a synthesizer with a keyboard. MIDI eventually expanded to support an incredibly wide range of musical instruments and devices, but the keyboard/synthesizer relationship is significant to MIDI as it applies to computers.

13

One way to view a MIDI device is as a note generator in the input sense and as a sound generator in the output sense. It isn't important how a MIDI device works internally as long as it adheres to a MIDI interface for generating or outputting notes. You might be thinking that the design of MIDI sounds somewhat reminiscent of the device-independent design of Windows, and in many ways this comparison is accurate. Just as Windows makes it possible to mix and match different kinds of hardware and have them work together, MIDI makes it possible to connect different kinds of musical devices together and have them work together as well. Most electronic musical equipment now comes standard with MIDI interface ports. In fact, the sound card on your computer has a MIDI-compatible interface through which a MIDI device can communicate with your computer.

Similar to waves, MIDI music is digital. However, unlike waves, which are just approximations of analog sound waves, MIDI music consists of musical notes. In other words, a MIDI song consists of a series of carefully timed musical notes. This means that you can create a MIDI song much like you might write out a musical composition on paper. This task requires special software, but it is possible if you have the knowledge and skill to write music. Because MIDI music is composed of notes rather than wave data, the resulting output sound quality is entirely dependent on the MIDI output device used to play the music. In the case of your computer, your sound card likely includes a MIDI synthesizer that can be used to play MIDI music. It's up to the synthesizer and Windows multimedia features to decide how the specific music sounds when played.

The main benefit of MIDI is that it allows you to use one MIDI device to control others. You can use a MIDI keyboard to play notes through another MIDI device, such as a MIDI sequencer. Even though you're generating notes by playing them on the keyboard, the actual instrument sounds are processed and output by the sequencer. In other words, you are *triggering* the sequencer with the keyboard. A similar situation occurs when you play MIDI music on your computer. The notes contained within the music are sent to the sound card where they trigger the synthesizer to play the actual sound.

I've mentioned MIDI music several times throughout this discussion, but I haven't really clarified how it is stored or how you work with it. Similar to waves, MIDI music is stored in files, but MIDI files have the file extension .MID. Unlike waves, MIDI music files are typically fairly small because musical notes simply don't take up a whole lot of space. Like waves, you can play MIDI files using Windows Media Player (see Figure 13.2). There is no built-in Windows tool for creating or editing MIDI files because creating MIDI music is more difficult than recording waves, and it involves a fair amount of music knowledge.

FIGURE 13.2

Windows Media Player can be used to play MIDI files, as well as wave files.

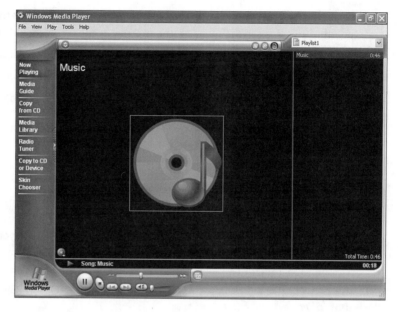

Playing a MIDI file in Windows Media Player is as simple as double-clicking the file in Windows Explorer. This works because MIDI files are automatically associated with Windows Media Player. You will likely use Windows Media Player to screen MIDI files for use in your games. Or, if you're ambitious enough to create your own game music, you'll likely use Windows Media Player as a final means of testing a MIDI file before incorporating it into a game.

Exploring Sound Tools

To be able to create and modify your own sounds, you need some type of software sound editing utility. Sound editing utilities usually provide a means of sampling sounds from a microphone, CD-ROM, or line input. From there, each utility varies as to what degree of editing it provides. Some sound editing utilities include very advanced signal processing features, in addition to the relatively standard amplification and echoing features. Other sound utilities, such as Sound Recorder that you learned about earlier in the hour, are fairly bare bones tools for working with wave sounds.

The most important component of a good sound editor in regard to Windows games is the capability to save sounds in the wave audio format. It doesn't matter how cool the sounds are if you can't play them in your games. Fortunately, the wave audio standard is quite popular, and is supported in most sound tools. Another key feature is the capability

13

to zoom in and clip sounds down to exactly the portions you want to use. Because the length of sounds is of the utmost importance in games, you should always clip sounds down to the absolute minimum length possible.

The next two sections focus on a couple of popular sound editors that you can use to edit sounds for games. They both support the wave sound format and provide a high degree of sound effects processing. You might also be able to find shareware sound utilities out there that are cheaper, possibly even free, but they likely won't compare in terms of features with commercial sound editors.

Sound Forge

Sound Forge, by Sonic Foundry, is in many ways the Adobe Photoshop of sound editing. What this means is that Sound Forge represents the high-end professional approach to sound editing, and is likely the most powerful option out there if you want to become a master of sounds. Of course, with power comes both price and complexity, which are two things that might be more than you're ready for at the moment. Even so, you might still consider downloading the free Sound Forge demo from the Sonic Foundry Web site at `http://www.sonicfoundry.com/`.

Cool Edit

Cool Edit, by Syntrillium Software, is a more affordable sound editor for Windows that is loaded with features. Its creators have suggested thinking of it as a paint program for audio. Just as a paint program enables you to create images with colors, brush strokes, and a variety of special effects, Cool Edit enables you to "paint" with sound: tones, pieces of songs with voices and other noises, sine and sawtooth waves, noise, or just pure silence. Cool Edit provides a wide variety of special effects for manipulating sounds, such as reverberation, noise reduction, echo and delay, flanging, filtering, and many others. Several different versions of Cool Edit are available to fit just about any budget. You can get additional information about Cool Edit from the Syntrillium Software Web site, which is located at `http://www.syntrillium.com/`.

Creating and Editing Sounds

After you've decided on a sound utility, you're ready to start creating and editing sounds. The first decision to make is how you will create the sounds. For example, are you planning to record sounds yourself with a microphone or sample sounds from a stereo cassette deck or VCR? The microphone is probably the easiest route because many multimedia computers come equipped with one. It's also the most creative route. However, you might already have some sounds in mind from a prerecorded cassette or movie, which means that you need to look into connecting an external sound source to your computer. This is covered in detail a little later in the hour.

Regardless of where you sample sounds from, the process of getting a sampled sound cleaned up for use in a game is basically the same. After you've sampled a sound, play it back to make sure that it sounds okay. It's likely that the sound will either be too loud or too soft. You can judge whether the volume of the sound is acceptable by looking at the waveform displayed in the sound editor; the *waveform* of a sound is the graphical appearance of the sound when plotted over time. If the sound amplitude goes beyond the top or bottom of the waveform display, you know it's definitely too loud. If you can barely hear it, it's probably too soft. To remedy this problem, you can either adjust the input level for the sound device and resample the sound or try to use amplification effects provided by the sound utility.

The best way to fix the volume problem is to adjust the input level of the sound device and resample the sound. For example, in Windows XP you can easily adjust the microphone or line input level from the Control Panel. After you have the volume of the sound at a level you like, you need to clip the sound to remove unwanted portions of it. *Clipping* a sound involves zooming in on the waveform in a sound editor and cutting out the silence that appears before and after the sound. This helps shorten the length of the sound and prevents unnecessary latency.

Latency is the amount of time between when you queue a sound for playing and when the user actually hears it. Latency should be kept to a minimum so that sounds are heard when you want them to be heard without any delay. Unnecessary silence at the beginning of a sound is a common cause of latency problems.

Once you have a sound clipped, it should be ready for prime time. You might want to check out the kinds of effects that are available with the sound utility you are using. Some simple effects range from reverse to echo, with more advanced effects including fading and phase shifts. It's all up to your imagination and your discerning ears.

13

Finding Sounds and Music

If you've decided that you don't have what it takes to create your own sounds, you still have options. In this case, you need to seek an outside source for your sounds and probably for your music as well. The best source for finding prerecorded sounds and music is in sound archives on the Web. Many different archives are out there with a vast amount of sounds and music from which to choose. Many are even available already in the wave and MIDI audio formats. Even if you get sounds and music from an online archive, be very careful about the copyright issues surrounding using them.

A good starting point for finding sounds and music is the World Wide Web Virtual Library, which maintains an Audio page with links to archives. This Audio Web site is located at `http://archive.museophile.sbu.ac.uk/audio/`.

Summary

Just as tiny colored squares called pixels allow you to represent images digitally, it is possible to represent a physical sound digitally by sampling it several thousand times a second. Sampled digital audio can be recorded in a variety of different sound qualities, which dramatically impact the size and memory requirements of the digital sounds. Digital sounds in Windows are known as waves, and are stored in files with a .WAV file extension. In addition to learning how waves work, you also learned in this hour how MIDI music is used to represent music in computers. The hour concluded by giving you some practical tips regarding creating your own digital sound effects.

The next hour takes what you learned in this hour and applies it to game programming. More specifically, you find out how to write code to play digital sounds in games.

Q&A

Q **Is an MP3 song an example of a digital sound?**

A Yes, an MP3 song is very much like a wave file except that the MP3 audio format uses a technique known as compression to crunch the raw sound data into a smaller size. Audio compression is a complex topic that I'd rather steer clear of here, but the idea is that you analyze the data in a digital sound and figure out how to use less data to represent roughly the same sound. As a comparison, CD-quality sounds don't use any compression, which is why a song on a music CD takes up way more space than an MP3 song. If you listen closely, you might be able to notice a reduction in sound quality between a song on a CD and an MP3 song. On the other hand, the MP3 format makes sound files so much smaller that it's worth the reduction in quality in most cases.

Q **Can I record music as a wave file instead of using MIDI?**

A Absolutely. In fact, many commercial games use sampled music instead of MIDI music because it can be sampled directly from a music recording and will sound exactly like the original. A good example of a game that uses this approach is Tony

Hawk's Pro Skater 4, which includes several sampled music tracks from popular music groups as background music for the game. Unfortunately, this approach won't work for the games you develop in this book because you're going to be limited in terms of how you can play waves. You learn more about why this is so in the next hour, but the limitation basically means that you can only play one wave sound at a time. So, if you play background music as a wave sound, you won't be able to add any sound effects.

Workshop

The Workshop is designed to help you anticipate possible questions, review what you've learned, and begin learning how to put your knowledge into practice. The answers to the quiz can be found in Appendix A, "Quiz Answers."

Quiz

1. What is a decibel?
2. What sound properties are associated with a CD-quality sound?
3. What does MIDI stand for, and why?

Exercises

1. Try your hand at recording a few wave sounds using the microphone or CD-ROM on your computer. Feel free to use the Sound Recorder utility if you don't want to invest in a commercial sound editor. As you create these sounds, think about how they might be incorporated into games of your own.
2. Spend some time getting familiar with MIDI music by searching for .MID files on your hard drive. I also encourage you to perform a search on the Web and see if you can find any MIDI songs available for download. The main goal is to get comfortable dealing with .MID files and playing MIDI songs with Windows Media Player.

13

HOUR 14

Playing Wave Sounds

In the previous hour, you learned that digital sounds are called waves in Windows, and that they can be easily recorded and edited using a sound utility such as Sound Recorder, which ships with Windows. What you didn't learn was how to play wave sounds in the context of a game. This hour picks up where the previous hour left off by showing you exactly how to play wave sounds. You might be thinking that if wave sounds are anything like bitmaps, this hour will be fairly technical and include a lot of messy code for loading and interacting with wave data. You'll be glad to know that waves are actually quite easy to play, and adding wave sound effects to a game is unbelievably simple to do. This hour shows you how!

In this hour, you'll learn:

- The two different ways to access wave sounds for playback
- How to play wave sounds using the Win32 API
- How to play a looped wave sound, and then stop it
- How to incorporate wave sounds into an existing game

Accessing Wave Sounds

You learned in the previous hour that wave sounds are stored in files with a .WAV file extension. So, if you record a wave using Sound Recorder or some other sound utility, the end result will be a file with a .WAV file extension. Hopefully by now you've already recorded a few sounds or maybe found a few on the Internet. Either way, you understand that a wave sound is stored in a file on disk, kind of like how bitmap images are stored. Similar to bitmaps, it's possible to load a wave directly from a file in a game. However, this isn't the most advantageous way to use waves in games.

If you recall from earlier in the book, I showed you how to include bitmaps as resources in your games. In fact, every program example you've seen thus far that uses bitmaps, such as the Henway game in Hour 12, has included them as resources that are stored directly in the executable program file. Waves are also resources, and can therefore be included in the resource script of a program and compiled into the executable program file. Playing the wave sound is slightly different depending on whether the wave is stored in a file or placed directly within the program as a resource. It's ultimately up to you how you want to access waves, but organizationally I think it's much better to use them as resources so that you don't have to worry about distributing separate wave files with your games.

Playing Wave Sounds

The Win32 API provides high-level support for playing wave sounds, which is extremely good news for you and me. One drawback with the high-level wave support in the Win32 API is that it doesn't allow for *wave mixing*, which is the process of mixing wave sounds so that multiple sounds can be played at once. Unfortunately, this means that only one wave sound can be played at any given moment. You'll have to decide how you want this to impact your games because there are certainly going to be situations in which two or more sounds need to be played at once. You have the following options when it comes to resolving the problem of being able to play only one sound among several:

- Interrupt the currently playing sound to play the next sound.
- Allow every sound to play to completion, and reject sounds that attempt to interrupt the currently playing sound.

Wave mixing is made possible by the DirectX game programming API, which I've mentioned a few times throughout the book. DirectX is incredibly powerful, especially when it comes to its digital sound capabilities, but it has a very steep learning curve. If you should decide to tackle DirectX after reading this book, by all means go for it. However, for the purposes of creating your own games without spending a great deal of time and energy learning the inner workings of DirectX, the high-level Win32 API approach to playing wave sounds is sufficient.

Until you actually experiment with these two wave playing approaches, you might think that the first approach sounds appealing because it gives every sound a chance to play. However, in some situations you'll find that sounds interrupting each other can be as annoying as a bunch of people interrupting each other in a heated debate. If you've ever seen the political television show *Crossfire*, you know what I'm talking about. On the other hand, when you let sounds play to completion, you will inevitably be disallowing other sounds their chance at playing—some of which might be important to the game play. So, it ultimately depends on the kind of game as to whether it makes sense to interrupt sounds or allow them to play out.

Regardless of how you address the limitation of only being able to play one sound, the Win32 API function that makes wave playing possible is called `PlaySound()`, and it looks like this:

```
BOOL PlaySound(LPCSTR szSound, HMODULE hModule, DWORD dwSound);
```

The three arguments to the `PlaySound()` function determine a variety of different things such as whether the sound is being played from a wave file or from memory as a wave resource. Additionally, the function allows you to control whether a sound may be interrupted while playing, as well as whether it should be looped repeatedly. The next few sections examine the `PlaySound()` function in more detail, and show you how to control the playback of wave sounds.

Playing a Wave from a File

The simplest way to use the `PlaySound()` function is to play a wave file directly from the local hard drive. When playing a wave from a file, the first argument to the `PlaySound()` function, szSound, identifies the name of the wave file. The second argument, hModule, applies only to playing wave resources, so you can pass NULL as the second argument when playing wave files. The third argument, dwSound, is used to determine the specific manner in which the wave is played.

14

The dwSound argument can contain one or more of several different flags that control various facets of the wave playback. For example, the SND_FILENAME flag indicates that you're playing the wave from a file. There are two other flags, SND_SYNC and SND_ASYNC, that determine whether a wave is played synchronously or asynchronously. A *synchronous* wave is a wave that doesn't allow a program to resume operation until it finishes playing, whereas an *asynchronous* wave allows a program to continue its business while the wave plays in the background. As you might be guessing, synchronous waves are pretty much out of the question in games because you don't want the whole game to pause while a wave is playing. So, you'll need to use the SND_ASYNC flag when playing waves using the PlaySound() function.

Following is an example of playing a wave file using the PlaySound() function:

```
PlaySound("Boo.wav", NULL, SND_ASYNC | SND_FILENAME);
```

As you can see, this is a pretty simple line of code when you think about everything it is accomplishing. A wave file is being loaded from disk and played through the speakers on your computer while your program is allowed to continue operating.

Another PlaySound() flag worth mentioning is the SND_NOSTOP flag, which causes a sound to be more respectful of a sound that is already playing. More specifically, if you specify the SND_NOSTOP flag when playing a wave sound, the sound will not interrupt another wave if it is already playing. The downside to this flag is that the sound will end up never getting played. If you want to make sure that a sound is played no matter what, be sure not to specify the SND_NOSTOP flag. When you don't specify the SND_NOSTOP flag, the sound you're playing will interrupt the currently playing sound no matter what.

Playing a Wave from a Resource

Earlier in the hour, I mentioned that playing a wave sound as a resource has advantages over playing a wave file because you can combine the wave resource into the main program file. The PlaySound() function includes a flag that allows you to specify that you're playing a wave resource, as opposed to a wave file. The SND_RESOURCE flag indicates that the wave is a resource and that the hInstance argument to PlaySound() is a resource identifier. Because a wave resource must be loaded from an executable program file, you must provide the module handle for the program in the second argument to PlaySound(). The games and program examples you've seen throughout the book store away this handle in the _hInstance global variable.

Following is an example of playing a wave sound as a resource using the PlaySound() function:

```
PlaySound((LPCSTR)IDW_BOO, _hInstance, SND_ASYNC | SND_RESOURCE);
```

Wave resource IDs are typically named so that they begin with IDW_, which indicates that the ID is associated with a wave.

In this example, the resource ID of the wave sound is IDW_BOO, whereas the module handle of the program is the global variable _hInstance. Also, the SND_RESOURCE flag is used to indicate that this is indeed a wave resource, as opposed to a wave file. One important thing to note about this code is that it assumes you've already declared the IDW_BOO resource ID and placed a reference to the wave resource in the resource script for the program. Just as when you add new bitmaps to a game, you'll need to create a resource ID and an entry in the resource script for each wave sound you use in a game.

Looping a Wave Sound

In some situations, you might want to play a sound repeatedly. For example, if you opt to use sampled music in a game, it probably will make sense to use a wave sound that can be *looped* over and over and sound like one continuous piece of music. The PlaySound() function supports a flag for playing a wave sound looped, which means that the sound is played repeatedly until you interrupt it with another sound or until you explicitly stop it using the PlaySound() function (more on stopping waves in a moment). The flag to which I'm referring is SND_LOOP, and specifying it results in a wave being repeated over and over.

Following is an example of playing a looped wave resource:

```
PlaySound((LPCSTR)IDW_BACKBEAT, _hInstance, SND_ASYNC | SND_RESOURCE |
  SND_LOOP);
```

The SND_LOOP flag requires you to also use the SND_ASYNC flag because it wouldn't make sense to loop a sound synchronously. Keep in mind that a looped sound will continue to loop indefinitely unless you stop it by playing another wave or by stopping the looped wave with another call to PlaySound().

Stopping a Wave Sound

If you ever use a looped wave, you will undoubtedly want to know how to stop it from playing at some point. Additionally, you might have a fairly lengthy wave sound that you'd like to be able to stop in case your game is deactivated or otherwise needs to slip into silent mode. You stop a wave from playing by using the SND_PURGE flag in the PlaySound() function. The SND_PURGE flag requires the first two arguments to PlaySound() to be used just as when you first played the sound. For example, if you

14

provided a module handle as part of playing a wave resource, you'll still need to provide the handle when purging the wave.

Following is an example of stopping the looped sound played in the previous section:

```
PlaySound((LPCSTR)IDW_BACKBEAT, _hInstance, SND_PURGE | SND_RESOURCE);
```

This example reveals how to stop a single wave from playing. It's also possible to stop any waves from playing so that you don't have to be so specific about what you're doing. This is accomplished by passing NULL as the first argument to PlaySound(), like this:

```
PlaySound(NULL, NULL, SND_PURGE);
```

This line of code results in the currently playing sound being stopped, regardless of what it is and how it was played.

Building the Brainiac 2 Program Example

You now have enough wave playing skills to see how waves are played in the context of a real game. In fact, instead of embarking on an entirely new game project, it makes sense to revisit a game you've already created and examine how to spiff it up with wave sounds. I'm referring to the Brainiac game from Hour 8, which is a simple tile matching memory game if you recall.

The Brainiac game isn't necessarily suffering from a lack of sound support, but it could definitely be made more interesting with some carefully injected waves. Think about how the game plays and how playing a wave sound here and there might improve its playability. After playing the game a few times and thinking about what would make it more fun, I came up with the following list of game events that could benefit from having sound effects associated with them:

- Selecting a tile
- Matching a pair of tiles
- Mismatching a pair of tiles
- Winning the game by matching all the tiles

If you play the game again and pay attention to each of these game events, you can start to see how a brief sound could add some interest to the game and make it a little more fun. The next few sections explore how to create a new version of the Brainiac game called Brainiac 2 that plays wave sounds in response to each of these game events.

Writing the Program Code

If you recall, the bulk of the code for the game logic in the Brainiac game resides in the
MouseButtonDown() function. This function is called whenever the player clicks the
mouse on the game screen, and is therefore where all of the tile matching takes place.
Not surprisingly, this function is where you'll find all the game events for the Brainiac
game, such as tile selections, matches, and mismatches. Listing 14.1 shows the new
MouseButtonDown() function, which includes several calls to the PlaySound() function
to play sounds responding to game events.

LISTING 14.1   The MouseButtonDown() Function Plays Wave Sounds in Response
to Several Important Game Events

```
 1: void MouseButtonDown(int x, int y, BOOL bLeft)
 2: {
 3:   // Determine which tile was clicked
 4:   int iTileX = x / _pTiles[0]->GetWidth();
 5:   int iTileY = y / _pTiles[0]->GetHeight();
 6:
 7:   // Make sure the tile hasn't already been matched
 8:   if (!_bTileStates[iTileX][iTileY])
 9:   {
10:     // See if this is the first tile selected
11:     if (_ptTile1.x == -1)
12:     {
13:       // Play a sound for the tile selection
14:       PlaySound((LPCSTR)IDW_SELECT, _hInstance, SND_ASYNC | SND_RESOURCE);
15:
16:       // Set the first tile selection
17:       _ptTile1.x = iTileX;
18:       _ptTile1.y = iTileY;
19:     }
20:     else if ((iTileX != _ptTile1.x) || (iTileY != _ptTile1.y))
21:     {
22:       if (_ptTile2.x == -1)
23:       {
24:         // Play a sound for the tile selection
25:         PlaySound((LPCSTR)IDW_SELECT, _hInstance, SND_ASYNC |
26:           SND_RESOURCE);
27:
28:         // Increase the number of tries
29:         _iTries++;
30:
31:         // Set the second tile selection
32:         _ptTile2.x = iTileX;
33:         _ptTile2.y = iTileY;
34:
35:         // See if it's a match
```

14

LISTING 14.1   Continued

```
36:            if (_iTiles[_ptTile1.x][_ptTile1.y] ==
37:              _iTiles[_ptTile2.x][_ptTile2.y])
38:            {
39:              // Play a sound for the tile match
40:              PlaySound((LPCSTR)IDW_MATCH, _hInstance, SND_ASYNC |
41:                SND_RESOURCE);
42:
43:              // Set the tile state to indicate the match
44:              _bTileStates[_ptTile1.x][_ptTile1.y] = TRUE;
45:              _bTileStates[_ptTile2.x][_ptTile2.y] = TRUE;
46:
47:              // Clear the tile selections
48:              _ptTile1.x = _ptTile1.y = _ptTile2.x = _ptTile2.y = -1;
49:
50:              // Update the match count and check for winner
51:              if (++_iMatches == 8)
52:              {
53:                // Play a victory sound
54:                PlaySound((LPCSTR)IDW_WIN, _hInstance, SND_ASYNC |
55:                  SND_RESOURCE);
56:                TCHAR szText[64];
57:                wsprintf(szText, "You won in %d tries.", _iTries);
58:                MessageBox(_pGame->GetWindow(), szText, TEXT("Brainiac"),
59:                  MB_OK);
60:              }
61:            }
62:            else
63:              // Play a sound for the tile mismatch
64:              PlaySound((LPCSTR)IDW_MISMATCH, _hInstance, SND_ASYNC |
65:                SND_RESOURCE);
66:          }
67:          else
68:          {
69:            // Clear the tile selections
70:            _ptTile1.x = _ptTile1.y = _ptTile2.x = _ptTile2.y = -1;
71:          }
72:        }
73:
74:        // Force a repaint to update the tile
75:        InvalidateRect(_pGame->GetWindow(), NULL, FALSE);
76:      }
77: }
```

The first two calls to the PlaySound() function occur in response to tile selections (lines 14, 25, and 26). If you recall, two tiles must be selected in each turn of the game, so the IDW_SELECT sound is played in response to each of the two tile selections. The

IDW_MATCH sound is played whenever a pair of tiles is successfully matched (lines 40–41). Similarly, the IDW_MISMATCH sound is played whenever two mismatched tiles are selected (lines 64–65). Finally, the IDW_WIN wave is played whenever all the tiles have been matched (lines 54–55) .

Assembling the Resources

Because waves are resources similar to bitmaps and icons, you must declare resource IDs for them, as well as include them in the resource script for your games. In the case of the Brainiac 2 game, the wave resource IDs are declared in the Resource.h header file, which is shown in Listing 14.2.

LISTING 14.2 The Resource.h Header File Defines New Resource IDs for the Wave Sounds

```
 1: //-------------------------------------------------------
 2: // Icons                    Range : 1000 - 1999
 3: //-------------------------------------------------------
 4: #define IDI_BRAINIAC      1000
 5: #define IDI_BRAINIAC_SM   1001
 6:
 7: //-------------------------------------------------------
 8: // Bitmaps                  Range : 2000 - 2999
 9: //-------------------------------------------------------
10: #define IDB_TILEBLANK     2000
11: #define IDB_TILE1         2001
12: #define IDB_TILE2         2002
13: #define IDB_TILE3         2003
14: #define IDB_TILE4         2004
15: #define IDB_TILE5         2005
16: #define IDB_TILE6         2006
17: #define IDB_TILE7         2007
18: #define IDB_TILE8         2008
19:
20: //-------------------------------------------------------
21: // Wave Sounds              Range : 3000 - 3999
22: //-------------------------------------------------------
23: #define IDW_SELECT        3000
24: #define IDW_MATCH         3001
25: #define IDW_MISMATCH      3002
26: #define IDW_WIN           3003
```

The four wave resource IDs are declared in the Resource.h header file (lines 23–26), which means that you can now place them in the Brainiac.rc resource script. This script is shown in Listing 14.3.

14

LISTING 14.3   The Brainiac.rc Resource Script Includes Four New Wave Resources

```
 1: //------------------------------------------------------------
 2: // Include Files
 3: //------------------------------------------------------------
 4: #include "Resource.h"
 5:
 6: //------------------------------------------------------------
 7: // Icons
 8: //------------------------------------------------------------
 9: IDI_BRAINIAC        ICON            "Brainiac.ico"
10: IDI_BRAINIAC_SM     ICON            "Brainiac_sm.ico"
11:
12: //------------------------------------------------------------
13: // Bitmaps
14: //------------------------------------------------------------
15: IDB_TILEBLANK       BITMAP          "TileBlank.bmp"
16: IDB_TILE1           BITMAP          "Tile1.bmp"
17: IDB_TILE2           BITMAP          "Tile2.bmp"
18: IDB_TILE3           BITMAP          "Tile3.bmp"
19: IDB_TILE4           BITMAP          "Tile4.bmp"
20: IDB_TILE5           BITMAP          "Tile5.bmp"
21: IDB_TILE6           BITMAP          "Tile6.bmp"
22: IDB_TILE7           BITMAP          "Tile7.bmp"
23: IDB_TILE8           BITMAP          "Tile8.bmp"
24:
25: //------------------------------------------------------------
26: // Wave Sounds
27: //------------------------------------------------------------
28: IDW_SELECT          WAVE            "Select.wav"
29: IDW_MATCH           WAVE            "Match.wav"
30: IDW_MISMATCH        WAVE            "Mismatch.wav"
31: IDW_WIN             WAVE            "Win.wav"
```

The resource script for the Brainiac 2 game is very similar to the original Brainiac resource script, except that it now includes wave resources (lines 28–31). Notice that the resource type WAVE is used when listing each of the wave resources in the script. This script successfully maps the wave sounds to resource identifiers that can then be used with the PlaySound() function, as you saw in the previous section.

If you happen to get a "multiple initialization" compiler error while compiling the Brainiac 2 program, you can easily fix it by removing the int variable declaration in the second for loop of the GameStart() function. This error stems from the fact that some compilers don't fully support the standard C++ approach of declaring loop initializer variables local to the loop. So, the int variable i is mistakenly interpreted as being declared twice.

Testing the Finished Product

You already have a pretty good idea how to play the Brainiac game, so testing out the new wave sounds is very straightforward. Just take the game for a spin and pay attention to how sounds are played in response to different game events such as selecting and matching tiles. Figure 14.1 shows the game in action.

FIGURE 14.1

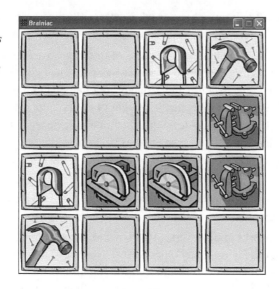

FIGURE **14.1**

The Brainiac 2 game is made more interesting than its predecessor by playing wave sounds in response to game events.

Believe it or not, a sound is being played in this figure. Because I couldn't convince the publisher to include an audio tape with the book, you'll just have to imagine the sound as you look at the figure. Or just fire up the game yourself and experience the sounds on your own!

Summary

This hour took what you learned in the previous hour about digital sound and gave it a practical face. More specifically, you learned how to play wave sounds using a high-level Win32 API function called `PlaySound()`. Although this function certainly has its limitations, you can't beat it when it comes to sheer simplicity; a single line of code is all it takes to play a wave sound. You found out how to play wave sounds from a file or as a resource, as well as how to play looped wave sounds and how to stop a sound once it has started playing.

You might be wondering about the fact that this hour focused solely on sampled digital audio, as opposed to MIDI music. The playback of wave sounds is in fact dramatically

14

different than the playback of MIDI music at the programming level, which is why this hour dodged the topic of playing MIDI music. However, the next hour digs right into the playback of MIDI music, and how to add music to games.

Q&A

Q Why doesn't Windows keep track of waves that weren't allowed to play because of interruption, and then play them as soon as it gets a chance?

A Windows doesn't get into the business of tracking waves because it would be very difficult, if not impossible, to ever play them all when you consider that only one can play at a time. Additionally, sounds are often tied to program events that are time critical, which means that it wouldn't be very helpful to play the sound late. For example, if you were developing a military game and a bullet sound was postponed because an explosion sound was being played, it wouldn't really help for the bullet sound to be played later when the bullet might not even be on the screen anymore.

Q Is it possible to prioritize waves so that only some waves are interrupted, while others are not?

A Yes, but it works in the reverse. If you recall, when you play a wave, you indicate whether it can interrupt any other waves. So, instead of identifying a high-priority wave as not being able to be interrupted, you instead indicate that a high-priority wave has the ability to interrupt other waves. Practically speaking, this means that you can have two levels of priority for waves. Low-priority waves would use the SND_NOSTOP flag to indicate that they aren't allowed to interrupt other waves. On the other hand, high-priority waves would simply not use the SND_NOSTOP flag, which means that they will interrupt any currently playing wave.

Workshop

The Workshop is designed to help you anticipate possible questions, review what you've learned, and begin learning how to put your knowledge into practice. The answers to the quiz can be found in Appendix A, "Quiz Answers."

Quiz

1. Why is it a problem that the Win32 PlaySound() function doesn't support wave mixing?

2. What is the difference between synchronous and asynchronous wave playback?

3. How do you stop a wave from playing once it has started?

Exercises

1. Try replacing a couple of the wave sounds in the Brainiac 2 game with some sounds of your own.

2. Think of another game event in the Brainiac 2 game that doesn't currently have a sound, and then add a wave sound for it. This isn't necessarily as difficult as you might think. For example, how about a new wave sound to indicate that the player made two matches in a row? Or maybe a wave sound to reward the player for beating the previous score?

14

HOUR 15

Playing MIDI Music

Jaws is probably my favorite movie of all time, and few people who have
seen the movie will ever forget the nerve-racking music used to communicate that the shark was about to strike. This is just one example of how simple music was able to establish a very specific mood. Video games are
capable of using music in the same way. In fact, seeing as how movies are
generally capable of being more expressive visually, it becomes more important for games to take advantage of music as a means of reinforcing a mood
or enhancing the reality of a virtual environment. MIDI music is one of the
best ways to incorporate music into games, and this hour shows you exactly
how to play MIDI music with a relatively small amount of code.

In this hour, you'll learn:

- About the Media Control Interface (MCI) and how it relates to MIDI
  music
- How to use the MCI to play MIDI music
- How to add MIDI music to a game

Understanding the Windows Media Control Interface

In the previous hour, you found out that the Win32 API provides a single function, PlaySound(), that makes it possible to play wave sounds with very little effort. Unfortunately, there is no such function available for playing MIDI music. The Win32 API groups MIDI music with other kinds of multimedia objects such as video clips. In order to play a MIDI song in a Windows program, you have to work with a special multimedia API known as the *Media Control Interface*, or *MCI*. The Media Control Interface is a high-level API that allows you to control multimedia devices such as a MIDI synthesizer or a video player. Because the MCI is so versatile in supporting a lot of different multimedia objects and devices, the MCI API is somewhat complex. The good news is that I'm going to carefully steer you through the MCI API and highlight only the portions you need in order to play MIDI music in games.

The idea behind the MCI is that you communicate with a multimedia device by sending it commands. A command is simply an instruction to carry out a particular action such as playing, pausing, or stopping a song or video clip. Two kinds of commands are actually supported by the MCI: command messages and command strings. Both approaches work equally well, but for the sake of simplicity, I opted to use command messages to communicate with the MIDI synthesizer device throughout this hour. A *command message* basically allows you to have a conversation with a multimedia device by sending it a message that tells it what to do. So, if you want to play a song, you would send a command message that includes the name of the song file along with the *play* command. I'm simplifying things a little here, but hopefully you get the idea.

Keep in mind that the Win32 API also supports a low-level programming interface that allows you to dig really deep into the details of multimedia programming. For example, you could use low-level multimedia functions to develop your own music editing software. However, the low-level multimedia API is extremely complex, so I don't recommend working with it until you have considerable experience with multimedia programming. Fortunately, you can accomplish everything you need for games without having to resort to low-level multimedia programming. Just use the MCI.

Using the MCI to Play MIDI Music

The device used to play MIDI music in a game is called the MIDI synthesizer, and its job is to take notes of music and play them aloud. The MIDI synthesizer isn't a physical device that you plug in to your computer—it's built in to your sound card. Just about every sound card these days includes a MIDI synthesizer, so you shouldn't have any trouble playing MIDI music. A big part of using the MCI to play MIDI music is establishing a line of communication with the MIDI synthesizer device. For example, you must first open the device before you can issue a command such as playing a MIDI song. The next section shows you how to open the MIDI sequencer device for playing MIDI music, and subsequent sections reveal how to play MIDI songs.

Opening the MIDI Device

When working with MIDI devices using the MCI, it's important to understand that a device is referenced using a unique device identifier. So, when you open a MIDI device to play MIDI music, you'll want to keep track of the device ID that is returned when you first open the device. This ID is your ticket for communicating with the device from then on. You can think of the device ID as the phone number you need in order to call the device and tell it what you want it to do.

To perform any MIDI tasks with the MCI, you must get comfortable with the mciSendCommand() function, which sends a command string to a MIDI device. This function is described in the Win32 API as follows:

```
MCIERROR mciSendCommand(MCIDEVICEID IDDevice, UINT uiMsg, DWORD dwCommand,
  DWORD_PTR pdwParam);
```

The mciSendCommand() function is used to send command messages to a MIDI device. The arguments to this function vary depending on what kind of message you're sending, so we'll analyze them on a message-by-message basis. Before you can send a message to play a MIDI song, you must first open a MIDI device by sending an *open* message using the mciSendCommand() function. The *open* message is called MCI_OPEN, and it requires the use of a special data structure called MCI_OPEN_PARMS, which is defined as follows:

```
typedef struct {
  DWORD_PTR    dwCallback;
  MCIDEVICEID  wDeviceID;
  LPCSTR       lpstrDeviceType;
  LPCSTR       lpstrElementName;
  LPCSTR       lpstrAlias;
} MCI_OPEN_PARMS;
```

The only members of this structure that we're interested in are the middle three: wDeviceID, lpstrDeviceType, and lpstrElementName. The wDeviceID member stores the device ID for the MIDI sequencer, and in our case will be used to retrieve this ID. In other words, the wDeviceID member gets filled in with the device ID when you open the device. The other two fields have to be specified when you open the device. The lpstrDeviceType field must be set to the string "sequencer" to indicate that you want

15

to open the MIDI sequencer. The lpstrElementName field must contain the name of the MIDI file that you want to play. This reveals an interesting aspect of the MCI—you must specify a multimedia object when you open a device. In other words, you don't just open a device and then decide what multimedia file you want to play.

Although I could go on and on about how interesting the mciSendCommand() function is, I'd rather just show you the code for opening the MIDI sequencer device, so here goes:

```
UINT uiMIDIPlayerID;
MCI_OPEN_PARMS mciOpenParms;
mciOpenParms.lpstrDeviceType = "sequencer";
mciOpenParms.lpstrElementName = "Music.mid";
if (mciSendCommand(NULL, MCI_OPEN, MCI_OPEN_TYPE | MCI_OPEN_ELEMENT,
  (DWORD_PTR)&mciOpenParms) == 0)
  // Get the ID for the MIDI player
  uiMIDIPlayerID = mciOpenParms.wDeviceID;
```

Hopefully this code isn't too terribly shocking considering that I just primed you with a brief explanation of the MCI_OPEN_PARMS data structure. This code initializes the two important fields of this structure (lpstrDeviceType and lpstrElementName), and then passes the entire structure as the last argument to the mciSendCommand() function. Notice that the MIDI music file in this example is named Music.mid. The first argument to the mciSendCommand() function is set to zero because you don't yet know the ID of the device. The second argument, MCI_OPEN, is the message you're sending to the MIDI sequencer. Finally, the third argument identifies the fields of the MCI_OPEN_PARMS data structure that are to be taken into consideration for the message.

You might have noticed that the MCI approach to playing MIDI songs involves opening and playing a MIDI file, as opposed to using MIDI songs as resources. Unfortunately, there is no good workaround for this problem, so you won't be able to compile .MID music files into your executable game files as you've done with bitmaps and wave sounds. This means that you'll have to provide separate .MID files with your games when you distribute the games.

If all goes well, the mciSendCommand() function returns 0 to indicate that the MIDI sequencer was successfully opened. You can then store away the device ID since it is now available in the wDeviceID field of the MCI_OPEN_PARMS data structure.

Playing a MIDI Song

Now that you have the MIDI sequencer opened for a specific MIDI song, you're ready to issue a play command and start the song playing. This is accomplished with the same mciSendCommand() function, but this time you provide a different command. In this case, the command is MCI_PLAY, and its required arguments are somewhat simpler than those for the MCI_OPEN command. However, the MCI_PLAY command does involve another data structure, MCI_PLAY_PARMS, although you can leave it uninitialized when you're just playing a song from start to finish.

The MCI_PLAY_PARMS data structure comes into play whenever you want a finer degree of control over how a MIDI song is played, such as selecting a different starting and ending point for the song.

Unlike the MCI_OPEN command, which doesn't require a device ID, the MCI_PLAY command requires a device ID in order to successfully play a MIDI song. Following is code to play a song based on the previous code that opened the MIDI sequencer for the Music.mid song:

```
MCI_PLAY_PARMS mciPlayParms;
mciSendCommand(uiMIDIPlayerID, MCI_PLAY, 0, (DWORD_PTR)&mciPlayParms);
```

You're probably thinking that there must be a catch because this code looks way too simple. Unless you're wanting to do something tricky like skip the first three seconds of a MIDI song, this is all that's required to play a song from start to finish using the MCI. Notice that the device ID is provided in the first argument to mciSendCommand(), while the MCI_PLAY command is provided as the second argument. The third argument isn't necessary, so you simply pass 0. And finally, the fourth argument isn't really necessary either, but you must still pass a legitimate structure, even if it's just left uninitialized.

Pausing a MIDI Song

There are situations in which you will definitely want to pause a MIDI song while it's being played. For example, you don't want the music to continue playing when the main game window is deactivated. So, you need a way to pause a MIDI song. This is accomplished with the MCI_PAUSE command, which is surprisingly simple to use. Following is an example of pausing a MIDI song using the MCI_PAUSE command and the mciSendCommand() function:

```
mciSendCommand(uiMIDIPlayerID, MCI_PAUSE, 0, NULL);
```

Notice that the only two arguments of significance in this code are the device ID (the first argument) and the *pause* message (the second argument). The remaining two arguments have no bearing on the MCI_PAUSE command, so you can pass empty values for them. In order to play a MIDI song that has been paused, you just issue another *play* command.

Closing the MIDI Device

Of course, all good things must come to an end, and eventually you'll want to close the MIDI sequencer device because you're finished with it or because you want to stop playing a song. The MCI_CLOSE command is used to close a MIDI device with the mciSendCommand() function. Following is an example of closing the MIDI sequencer by issuing an MCI_CLOSE command:

```
mciSendCommand(uiMIDIPlayerID, MCI_CLOSE, 0, NULL);
```

Similar to the MCI_PAUSE command, the only two arguments of significance in this code are the device ID (the first argument) and the *close* message (the second argument).

One point I haven't clarified in regard to playing and closing devices is that it's possible to encounter a problem when you attempt to play a MIDI song—in which case, the mciSendCommand() function will return a value other than 0 when you issue the MCI_PLAY command. In the earlier play example, I didn't bother looking at the return value of the mciSendCommand() function. But, it's a good idea to check and see if the song was successfully played because you should close the device if a problem occurred while playing the song. Following is revised play code that shows how to close the MIDI sequencer device if an error took place while playing the song:

```
MCI_PLAY_PARMS mciPlayParms;
if (mciSendCommand(uiMIDIPlayerID, MCI_PLAY, 0, (DWORD_PTR)&mciPlayParms) != 0)
{
  mciSendCommand(uiMIDIPlayerID, MCI_CLOSE, 0, NULL);
  uiMIDIPlayerID = 0;
}
```

This code checks the return value of the mciSendCommand() function for the *play* command, and then closes the device if an error occurred. Notice that the device ID is also cleared after closing the device. This helps to make sure that you don't try to send any more commands to the device since the ID is no longer valid.

Adding MIDI Music Support to the Game Engine

Now that you're an MCI programming expert, you're no doubt ready to find out how to incorporate MIDI music capabilities into the game engine. You might not realize it, but you've already seen the majority of the MIDI code required to add music support to the game engine. It's mainly just a matter of creating a clean user interface for opening and closing the MIDI sequencer device, as well as playing MIDI songs. Keep in mind that the entire source code for the game engine and all example programs is included on the accompanying CD-ROM.

The first step required for adding MIDI support to the game engine is to keep track of the MIDI sequencer device ID. This is easily accomplished with a new member variable, which looks like this:

```
UINT m_uiMIDIPlayerID;
```

The m_uiMIDIPlayerID member variable contains the device ID for the MIDI sequencer. Any time the ID is not 0, you will know that you have the device open and ready for playing music. If this member variable is set to 0, the device is closed. This means that you need to initialize the m_uiMIDIPlayerID member variable to 0 in the GameEngine() constructor, like this:

```
m_uiMIDIPlayerID = 0;
```

This is the only change required in the GameEngine() constructor to support MIDI music, and it simply involves setting the m_uiMIDIPlayerID member variable to 0.

I mentioned earlier that the most important requirement for the game engine is to establish an interface for carrying out MIDI music tasks. Following are three new methods in the game engine that carry out important MIDI music playback tasks:

```
void PlayMIDISong(LPTSTR szMIDIFileName = TEXT(""), BOOL bRestart = TRUE);
void PauseMIDISong();
void CloseMIDIPlayer();
```

The roles of these methods hopefully are somewhat self-explanatory in that they are used to play a MIDI song, pause a MIDI song, and close the MIDI player (sequencer). You might be wondering why there isn't a method for opening the MIDI player. The opening of the player is actually handled within the PlayMIDISong() method. In fact, you'll notice that the PlayMIDISong() method has a string parameter that is the filename of the MIDI file to be played. This filename is used as the basis for opening the MIDI player. It might seem strange that the MIDI filename has a default value, meaning that you don't have to provide it if you don't want to. Calling the PlayMIDISong() method with no filename only works if you've already begun playing a song and it is now paused.

The purpose for allowing you to pass an empty filename to the PlayMIDISong() method is to allow you to restart or resume the playback of a song that has already started playing. In this case, the second parameter to the method, bRestart, is used to determine how the song is played. Resuming playback would be useful if you had simply paused the music in a game, whereas restarting the playback would be useful if you were starting a new game and wanted to start the music over.

The PlayMIDISong() method is responsible for opening the MIDI player if it isn't already open. The method first checks to see if the player isn't yet open, and if it isn't, an *open* command is issued to open the MIDI sequencer device. The device ID for the MIDI sequencer is stored in the `m_uiMIDIPlayerID` variable. The `PlayMIDISong()` method continues by restarting the song if the `bRestart` argument is `TRUE`. The MIDI song is then played by issuing a *play* command via MCI. If the *play* command fails, the MIDI sequencer device is closed.

It's likely that you might at some point want to pause a MIDI song once it has started playing. This is accomplished with the `PauseMIDISong()` method, which simply issues a *pause* command to the MIDI player, providing the device ID isn't set to `0`.

The `CloseMIDIPlayer()` method is used to close the MIDI device and clear the device ID. This method first checks to make sure that the device is indeed open by checking to see if the device ID is not equal to `0`. If the device is open, the `CloseMIDIPlayer()` method proceeds to close the device by issuing a *close* command, and then clearing the device ID member variable.

Building the Henway 2 Program Example

You've spent the better part of this hour adding MIDI music support to the game engine. By adding the code to the game engine, you've made it possible to put a very small burden on the code for a game. In other words, the new and improved game engine now makes it painfully easy to add MIDI music support to any game. The remainder of this hour proves my point by showing you how to add MIDI music to the Henway game that you developed back in Hour 12, "Example Game: Henway." In fact, the Henway 2 game that you're about to develop not only includes MIDI music, but it also uses wave sounds to incorporate some sound effects into the game. The MIDI music added to the game simply serves as background music to make the game a little more interesting. You'll no doubt find the game to be a major improvement over its earlier version.

Writing the Program Code

The code for the audio supercharged Henway 2 game begins with the `GameStart()` function, which now includes a single line of code near the end that plays the MIDI song stored in the file Music.mid:

```
_pGame->PlayMIDISong(TEXT("Music.mid"));
```

There isn't too much to say about this code because it simply passes the name of the MIDI song file to the `PlayMIDISong()` method in the game engine.

Just as the `GameStart()` function opens the MIDI player by starting the playback of a MIDI song, the `GameEnd()` function is responsible for cleaning up by closing the MIDI player. The following line of code appears near the beginning of the `GameStart()` function:

```
_pGame->CloseMIDIPlayer();
```

The GameEnd() function performs the necessary MIDI music cleanup by calling the CloseMIDIPlayer() method to close the MIDI player.

Earlier in the hour, I mentioned how it wouldn't be good for a MIDI song to continue playing if the game window is deactivated. In order to keep this from happening, it's important to pause the MIDI song when a window deactivation occurs, and then play it again when the window regains activation. Listing 15.1 contains the code for the GameActivate() and GameDeactivate() functions, which are responsible for carrying out these tasks.

LISTING 15.1 The GameActivate() and GameDeactivate() Functions Are Used to Pause and Play the MIDI Song Based on the State of the Game Window

```
 1: void GameActivate(HWND hWindow)
 2: {
 3:   // Capture the joystick
 4:   _pGame->CaptureJoystick();
 5:
 6:   // Resume the background music
 7:   _pGame->PlayMIDISong(TEXT(""), FALSE);
 8: }
 9:
10: void GameDeactivate(HWND hWindow)
11: {
12:   // Release the joystick
13:   _pGame->ReleaseJoystick();
14:
15:   // Pause the background music
16:   _pGame->PauseMIDISong();
17: }
```

The GameActivate() function is responsible for continuing the playback of a paused MIDI song, and it does so by calling the PlayMIDISong() method and specifying FALSE as the second argument (line 7). If you recall from earlier in the hour, the second argument determines whether the MIDI song is rewound before it is played. So, passing FALSE indicates that the song shouldn't be rewound, which has the effect of continuing playback from the previously paused position. The GameDeactivate() function performs an opposite task by pausing the MIDI song with a call to the PauseMIDISong() method (line 16).

The GameCycle() function doesn't have any MIDI-related code, but it does include some new sound effects code. More specifically, the GameCycle() function now plays car horn sounds at random intervals to help add some realism to the game (see Listing 15.2).

LISTING 15.2   The GameCycle() Function Randomly Plays Car Horn Sounds

```
 1: void GameCycle()
 2: {
 3:   if (!_bGameOver)
 4:   {
 5:     // Play a random car sound randomly
 6:     if (rand() % 100 == 0)
 7:       if (rand() % 2 == 0)
 8:         PlaySound((LPCSTR)IDW_CARHORN1, _hInstance, SND_ASYNC |
 9:           SND_RESOURCE);
10:       else
11:         PlaySound((LPCSTR)IDW_CARHORN2, _hInstance, SND_ASYNC |
12:           SND_RESOURCE);
13:
14:     // Update the sprites
15:     _pGame->UpdateSprites();
16:
17:     // Obtain a device context for repainting the game
18:     HWND  hWindow = _pGame->GetWindow();
19:     HDC   hDC = GetDC(hWindow);
20:
21:     // Paint the game to the offscreen device context
22:     GamePaint(_hOffscreenDC);
23:
24:     // Blit the offscreen bitmap to the game screen
25:     BitBlt(hDC, 0, 0, _pGame->GetWidth(), _pGame->GetHeight(),
26:       _hOffscreenDC, 0, 0, SRCCOPY);
27:
28:     // Cleanup
29:     ReleaseDC(hWindow, hDC);
30:   }
31: }
```

The modified GameCycle() function establishes a 1 in 100 chance of playing a car horn in every game cycle (line 6). Because the game cycles are flying by at 30 per second, these really aren't as bad odds as they sound. Whenever the odds do work out and a car horn is played, another random number is selected to see which car horn is played (lines 7–12). You could have just as easily played a single car horn, but having two horns with different sounds makes the game much more interesting. It's the little touches like this that make a game more intriguing to players.

If you recall from the earlier design of the Henway game, you can start a new game by clicking the mouse anywhere on the game screen after the game is over. Listing 15.3 contains code for a new MouseButtonDown() function that restarts the MIDI song as part of starting a new game.

LISTING 15.3   The `MouseButtonDown()` Function Restarts the MIDI Song to Coincide with a New Game

```
 1: void MouseButtonDown(int x, int y, BOOL bLeft)
 2: {
 3:   // Start a new game, if necessary
 4:   if (_bGameOver)
 5:   {
 6:     // Restart the background music
 7:     _pGame->PlayMIDISong();
 8:
 9:     // Initialize the game variables
10:     _iNumLives = 3;
11:     _iScore = 0;
12:     _bGameOver = FALSE;
13:   }
14: }
```

It obviously makes sense to start the background music over when a new game starts. Because the default action of the `PlayMIDISong()` method is to rewind a song before playing it, it isn't necessary to pass any arguments to the method in this particular case (line 7).

Speaking of restarting the MIDI song, Listing 15.4 contains the code for the `HandleJoystick()` function, which also restarts the song as part of starting a new game.

LISTING 15.4   The `HandleJoystick()` Function Also Restarts the MIDI Song to Signal a New Game

```
 1: void HandleJoystick(JOYSTATE jsJoystickState)
 2: {
 3:   if (!_bGameOver && (++_iInputDelay > 2))
 4:   {
 5:     // Check horizontal movement
 6:     if (jsJoystickState & JOY_LEFT)
 7:         MoveChicken(-20, 0);
 8:     else if (jsJoystickState & JOY_RIGHT)
 9:         MoveChicken(20, 0);
10:
11:     // Check vertical movement
12:     if (jsJoystickState & JOY_UP)
13:         MoveChicken(0, -20);
14:     else if (jsJoystickState & JOY_DOWN)
15:         MoveChicken(0, 20);
16:
```

LISTING 15.4   Continued

```
17:     // Reset the input delay
18:     _iInputDelay = 0;
19:   }
20:
21:   // Check the joystick button and start a new game, if necessary
22:   if (_bGameOver && (jsJoystickState & JOY_FIRE1))
23:   {
24:     // Play the background music
25:     _pGame->PlayMIDISong();
26:
27:     // Initialize the game variables
28:     _iNumLives = 3;
29:     _iScore = 0;
30:     _bGameOver = FALSE;
31:   }
32: }
```

The call to the PlayMIDISong() method again occurs with no arguments, which results in the MIDI song being started over at the beginning (line 25).

You've now seen all the MIDI music-related code in the Henway 2 game, but there are still some wave sound effects left to be played. Two of these sound effects are played in the SpriteCollision() function, which is shown in Listing 15.5.

LISTING 15.5   The SpriteCollision() Function Plays Sound Effects in Response to the Chicken Getting Run Over and the Game Ending

```
 1: BOOL SpriteCollision(Sprite* pSpriteHitter, Sprite* pSpriteHittee)
 2: {
 3:   // See if the chicken was hit
 4:   if (pSpriteHittee == _pChickenSprite)
 5:   {
 6:     // Move the chicken back to the start
 7:     _pChickenSprite->SetPosition(4, 175);
 8:
 9:     // See if the game is over
10:     if (--_iNumLives > 0)
11:       // Play a sound for the chicken getting hit
12:       PlaySound((LPCSTR)IDW_SQUISH, _hInstance, SND_ASYNC |
13:         SND_RESOURCE);
14:     else
15:     {
16:       // Play a sound for the game ending
17:       PlaySound((LPCSTR)IDW_GAMEOVER, _hInstance, SND_ASYNC |
18:         SND_RESOURCE);
19:
```

LISTING 15.5 Continued

```
20:       // Display game over message
21:       TCHAR szText[64];
22:       wsprintf(szText, "Game Over! You scored %d points.", _iScore);
23:       MessageBox(_pGame->GetWindow(), szText, TEXT("Henway 2"), MB_OK);
24:       _bGameOver = TRUE;
25:
26:       // Pause the background music
27:       _pGame->PauseMIDISong();
28:     }
29:
30:   return FALSE;
31:   }
32:
33:   return TRUE;
34: }
```

If you remember, the SpriteCollision() function is where you detect a collision between the chicken and a car. This makes it an ideal place to play a squish sound when the chicken is run over (lines 12 and 13). Similarly, the SpriteCollision() function also knows when the game ends, so it only makes sense to play a sound whenever the player runs out of chickens (lines 17 and 18).

The final sound effect in the Henway 2 game occurs in the MoveChicken() function, which is where the game determines when the chicken has made it across the road. Listing 15.6 shows how a celebration sound is played each time the chicken makes it across.

LISTING 15.6 The MoveChicken() Helper Function Plays a Celebration Sound Whenever the Chicken Makes It Safely Across the Road

```
 1: void MoveChicken(int iXDistance, int iYDistance)
 2: {
 3:   // Move the chicken to its new position
 4:   _pChickenSprite->OffsetPosition(iXDistance, iYDistance);
 5:
 6:   // See if the chicken made it across
 7:   if (_pChickenSprite->GetPosition().left > 400)
 8:   {
 9:     // Play a sound for the chicken making it safely across
10:     PlaySound((LPCSTR)IDW_CELEBRATE, _hInstance, SND_ASYNC | SND_RESOURCE);
11:
12:     // Move the chicken back to the start and add to the score
13:     _pChickenSprite->SetPosition(4, 175);
14:     _iScore += 150;
15:   }
16: }
```

This function makes sure that a celebration wave sound is played whenever the chicken successfully crosses the road (line 10). This might be a small concession for working so hard to get the chicken across, but keep in mind that the previous version of the game offered no audible reward at all!

Testing the Finished Product

You'll find that testing sounds and music in games is initially one of the most exciting test phases of a game, but eventually becomes quite monotonous. The music in the Henway 2 game will no doubt haunt me for years when you consider that I had to listen to it over and over as I developed and debugged the game. You will likely experience the same joy and frustration when developing and testing your own games that take advantage of wave sounds and music.

To test the Henway 2 game, just launch the game and listen. The music will immediately start playing, and you'll quickly begin hearing random car horns that help create the atmosphere of busy traffic buzzing by the chicken. You will notice the new sound effects as you safely navigate the chicken across the road, as well as when you get run over. More important from the perspective of the MIDI music is to test the game as it is deactivated and then reactivated. Just minimize the game or activate a different program to see how the game responds. The music should immediately stop playing. Reactivating the game results in the music continuing to play from where it left off.

Summary

Just as sound effects add interest and excitement to specific events that take place in a game, music can be extremely effective in establishing a mood or simply making a game more fun. This hour explored MIDI music and how to work with it at the programming level. You learned about the Media Control Interface, or MCI, which is used to play MIDI songs without having to get into a bunch of messy low-level code. You then took your new MCI programming knowledge and used it to add MIDI music support to the game engine. Finally, you revisited the Henway game from Hour 12, and added both MIDI music and wave sound effects to it.

The next hour pulls together everything you've learned throughout the book thus far in the creation of another complete game. The game is called Battle Office, and I think you'll find it to be a pretty neat little game.

Q&A

15

Q Why isn't it possible to store MIDI songs as resources in the executable game file like I've done with bitmaps and wave sounds?

A This limitation has to do with the fact that the MCI simply doesn't support the playback of MIDI songs from any source other than a file. So, although you could certainly include a MIDI song as a resource in a game, you wouldn't be able to play it using the MCI. You could, however, play it using low-level multimedia functions, assuming that you had the desire to learn low-level Windows multimedia programming. Assuming that you don't, being limited to playing a MIDI song from a file is a relatively small concession when you consider how easy it makes it to play songs.

Q Can the MCI be used to do other things with MIDI files?

A Yes, the MCI is flexible in allowing you to carry out other tasks related to the playback of MIDI files. For example, you can get more detailed about how you want a song played, such as playing only the beginning or end of a song. However, there are certainly still limitations when it comes to using the MCI to play MIDI songs because it is a high-level API. For complete control over the playback of MIDI music, you'll have to use the low-level Windows multimedia API, which is considerably more complex than the MCI.

Workshop

The Workshop is designed to help you anticipate possible questions, review what you've learned, and begin learning how to put your knowledge into practice. The answers to the quiz can be found in Appendix A, "Quiz Answers."

Quiz

1. What is the purpose of an MCI command message?
2. What is the device in your computer that is responsible for playing MIDI music?
3. When is it important to pause a MIDI song in a game?

Exercises

1. Find a different MIDI song and use it in place of the Music.mid song that is currently being used in the Henway 2 game.
2. Add some more wave sound effects to the Henway 2 game that are played randomly along with the car horn sounds. Sounds you might consider adding include a chicken sound (Bok!), the sound of a car passing by, and maybe the sound of tires screeching.

HOUR 16

Example Game: Battle Office

Well here you are, ready to embark on your third complete game. At this point in the book, you've successfully added wave sound effects and MIDI music programming to your repertoire of game development skills. What better way to celebrate than to design and develop another game to put the skills to good use? This hour leads you through the construction of a game called Battle Office that chronicles an interoffice war between co-workers. Don't worry: It's not as violent as it sounds. The job of the player in the game is to use the mouse to fire at co-workers as they appear in various places on the game screen. The game makes interesting use of the sprite classes, as well as wave sound effects and music.

In this hour, you'll learn:

- How to design a game called Battle Office that simulates a battle between co-workers within an office
- How to write the code for the Battle Office game
- About the joys of testing a completely new game

How Does the Game Play?

I once worked at a software company where it was fairly common for balls and other objects to be thrown around for fun while taking a break from the seriousness of programming. On some rare occasions, the speed of the throws would increase to the point where an all-out game of dodge ball erupted. Sometimes the games were friendly, and sometimes they progressed to being almost dangerous. In fact, prior to me joining the company, there was a story of a guy being knocked out because someone threw a small bag of change that caught him in the head. Not a good idea! And in case you're thinking about starting your own interoffice dodge ball game, I encourage you to use soft balls and make sure that everyone is up for it before firing the first shot.

My experience hurling balls and other objects at people in my former job serves as the inspiration for the Battle Office game, which involves firing at co-workers in an office environment. The game screen in Battle Office consists of an office space with several desks and a doorway in the back. Co-workers will periodically pop up from behind their desks, as well as run by in the background through the doorway. Your job is simple: bean every co-worker who appears onscreen.

Although the Battle Office game does simulate a battle, it's safe to say that it's a friendly battle. In fact, the specifics of what is being fired at the co-workers are deliberately left vague so that the player can imagine what is being fired. It could be paper wads, Koosh balls, rubber bands, or dinner rolls—it's up to your imagination to fill in the blank here.

If the object of the game is to shoot every person who appears on the screen, you might be wondering how you lose. Well, the Battle Office game is all about efficiency and perfection, so you are only allowed so many misses. In other words, each time a person on the screen escapes, it is considered a miss because he got away. When you run out of misses, the game ends. On the other hand, the game keeps track of how many people you successfully hit, so there is a score to keep track of how well you're playing.

Designing the Game

The design of the Battle Office game flows fairly smoothly from the overview of the game that you just went through. You know that there is a background image required to show the office inhabited by the people you're shooting at. You also know that the people themselves can probably be represented by sprites. Granted, not all the people are moving, but keep in mind that sprites can be used in a variety of different ways. For example, you can use a sprite to simply show and hide an image of a person, as well as perform *hit testing* on the sprite to see if it has been clicked with the mouse. This approach works well for the people hiding behind desks. Similarly, sprites can be used to represent the people running in the back of the office.

To help you get a feel for how the Battle Office game is laid out, take a look at Figure 16.1.

16

FIGURE 16.1

The Battle Office game consists of an office with desks that people can hide behind, as well as a hallway that people can run back and forth through.

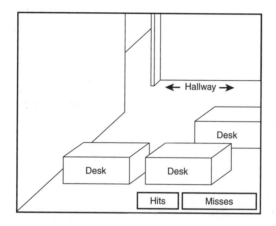

Notice that the office in the figure includes three desks that are suitable for people to hide behind, along with a hallway. The hallway provides a way for people to run back and forth, which provides you with moving targets to shoot at. Again, the main premise of the game is to shoot at the office workers as they pop up from behind desks and run back and forth down the hallway. In the lower right corner of the game screen, you'll notice that there are boxes to display the number of hits and misses in the game.

As I mentioned earlier, your weapon is up to your imagination; all you use to shoot people is a special bull's-eye sprite designed to follow the mouse pointer. It's probably a little healthier to think in terms of using a "friendly" weapon such as a wad of paper, but this is ultimately up to each individual player. Rather than focus on a weapon, the game instead displays a red bull's-eye that you control with the mouse and use to shoot the people in the office. When you score a hit, a "pow" image is displayed to indicate that you hit the target.

Now that you understand the basics of the game and how it is played, it's time to examine what kinds of sprites need to be used. Following is a list of the sprites that go into the Battle Office game:

- Five office worker sprites
- Target sprite
- Pow sprite

The five office worker sprites represent the people in the office who you are shooting at when you play the game. Three of these people sprites are stationary behind desks and simply appear and disappear, while the two others run across the hallway near the back of the office. The target sprite is the bull's-eye that you use to aim with the mouse. Finally, the pow sprite is used to indicate that you've scored a hit, and it is placed directly over the person you've hit. Although you can certainly score multiple hits throughout the game, a single pow sprite is sufficient to represent each hit; the sprite is simply moved to the new hit location when a new hit occurs.

Beyond the sprites, the Battle Office game also requires several bitmaps. Following are the ten bitmap images required of the game:

- Background office image
- Bull's-eye target image
- Pow image
- Five office worker images
- Small office worker image
- Game over image

Most of these images should be pretty obvious given the game design thus far. However, you're probably curious about the small office worker image, which is used to indicate how many people you've missed. When the game begins, there are no misses, so none of the small worker images are displayed. As the game progresses and some of the people get away, the small worker image is drawn repeatedly to indicate each miss. Five misses results in the game ending; in which case, the game over image is displayed.

Now that you have a feel for the graphical objects involved in the game, let's consider other data that must be maintained by the game. First, it's pretty obvious that you'll need to keep track of how many misses you've had because it determines when the game ends. It's also important to keep track of the number of hits so that you'll have a means of keeping score—the number of hits is the score in the Battle Office game. A Boolean variable to keep track of whether the game is over is also required.

A couple of other pieces of information that aren't immediately obvious involve the manner in which the office workers are displayed. By the way, when you see the bitmaps, you'll realize that all the workers are men, so I've opted to refer to them as "guys" in the game code. So, I might as well start using the same terminology in this discussion. The game displays the five different guys at random time intervals, which gives the game a more spontaneous feel. In order to establish these intervals, you need to keep track of each guy's time delay. Additionally, the game is much better if it gradually gets harder the longer you play. So, a master delay is used to provide a means of slowly reducing the length of time that the stationary guys appear on screen. In other words, the guys behind the desks slowly begin appearing for shorter periods of time, which makes it harder to shoot them.

To recap the data requirements of the Battle Office game, the game design has led us to the following pieces of information that must be managed by the game:

- The number of guys missed
- The number of guys hit
- A Boolean game over variable
- A delay variable for each guy
- A master delay variable for controlling the game's difficulty level

With this information in mind, you're now ready to move on and assemble the code for the Battle Office game.

Building the Game

The construction of the Battle Office game follows the same pattern you've grown accustomed to in other programs' examples and games. The next few sections guide you through the development of the game's code and resources.

Writing the Program Code

The code for the Battle Office game begins in the BattleOffice.h header file, which is responsible for declaring the global variables used throughout the game. Listing 16.1 contains the code for this file.

LISTING 16.1 The BattleOffice.h Header File Declares Global Variables That Are Used to Manage the Game

```
1: #pragma once
2:
3: //-----------------------------------------------------------
4: // Include Files
5: //-----------------------------------------------------------
6: #include <windows.h>
```

LISTING 16.1   Continued

```
 7: #include "Resource.h"
 8: #include "GameEngine.h"
 9: #include "Bitmap.h"
10: #include "Sprite.h"
11:
12: //-------------------------------------------------------------
13: // Global Variables
14: //-------------------------------------------------------------
15: HINSTANCE    _hInstance;
16: GameEngine*  _pGame;
17: HDC          _hOffscreenDC;
18: HBITMAP      _hOffscreenBitmap;
19: Bitmap*      _pOfficeBitmap;
20: Bitmap*      _pTargetBitmap;
21: Bitmap*      _pPowBitmap;
22: Bitmap*      _pGuyBitmaps[5];
23: Bitmap*      _pSmallGuyBitmap;
24: Bitmap*      _pGameOverBitmap;
25: Sprite*      _pTargetSprite;
26: Sprite*      _pPowSprite;
27: Sprite*      _pGuySprites[5];
28: int          _iGuyDelay[5];
29: int          _iGuyMasterDelay;
30: int          _iHits;
31: int          _iMisses;
32: BOOL         _bGameOver;
```

As the listing reveals, the global variables for the Battle Office game largely consist of
the different bitmaps that are used throughout the game. The offscreen device context
and bitmap are declared first (lines 17 and 18), as well as the different bitmaps that make
up the game's graphics (lines 19–24). The sprite variables for the game are declared after
the bitmaps, and include the target sprite, the pow sprite, and the five guy sprites (lines
25–27). The delays for each of the five guys are then declared (line 28), along with the
master delay that controls the game's difficulty level (line 29). Finally, the number of hits
and misses are declared (lines 30 and 31), as well as the familiar game over Boolean
variable (line 32).

The initialization of the game variables primarily takes place in the GameStart() function, which is shown in Listing 16.2.

LISTING 16.2   The `GameStart()` Function Initializes the Bitmaps, Sprites, and Game State Variables

```
 1: void GameStart(HWND hWindow)
 2: {
 3:     // Seed the random number generator
 4:     srand(GetTickCount());
 5:
 6:     // Create the offscreen device context and bitmap
 7:     _hOffscreenDC = CreateCompatibleDC(GetDC(hWindow));
 8:     _hOffscreenBitmap = CreateCompatibleBitmap(GetDC(hWindow),
 9:       _pGame->GetWidth(), _pGame->GetHeight());
10:     SelectObject(_hOffscreenDC, _hOffscreenBitmap);
11:
12:     // Create and load the bitmaps
13:     HDC hDC = GetDC(hWindow);
14:     _pOfficeBitmap = new Bitmap(hDC, IDB_OFFICE, _hInstance);
15:     _pTargetBitmap = new Bitmap(hDC, IDB_TARGET, _hInstance);
16:     _pPowBitmap = new Bitmap(hDC, IDB_POW, _hInstance);
17:     _pGuyBitmaps[0] = new Bitmap(hDC, IDB_GUY1, _hInstance);
18:     _pGuyBitmaps[1] = new Bitmap(hDC, IDB_GUY2, _hInstance);
19:     _pGuyBitmaps[2] = new Bitmap(hDC, IDB_GUY3, _hInstance);
20:     _pGuyBitmaps[3] = new Bitmap(hDC, IDB_GUY4, _hInstance);
21:     _pGuyBitmaps[4] = new Bitmap(hDC, IDB_GUY5, _hInstance);
22:     _pSmallGuyBitmap = new Bitmap(hDC, IDB_SMALLGUY, _hInstance);
23:     _pGameOverBitmap = new Bitmap(hDC, IDB_GAMEOVER, _hInstance);
24:
25:     // Create the target, pow, and guy sprites
26:     RECT    rcBounds = { 0, 0, 500, 400 };
27:     _pTargetSprite = new Sprite(_pTargetBitmap, rcBounds, BA_STOP);
28:     _pTargetSprite->SetZOrder(4);
29:     _pGame->AddSprite(_pTargetSprite);
30:     _pPowSprite = new Sprite(_pPowBitmap, rcBounds, BA_STOP);
31:     _pPowSprite->SetZOrder(3);
32:     _pPowSprite->SetHidden(TRUE);
33:     _pGame->AddSprite(_pPowSprite);
34:     _pGuySprites[0] = new Sprite(_pGuyBitmaps[0], rcBounds);
35:     _pGuySprites[0]->SetPosition(92, 175);
36:     _pGuySprites[0]->SetZOrder(2);
37:     _pGuySprites[0]->SetHidden(TRUE);
38:     _pGame->AddSprite(_pGuySprites[0]);
39:     _pGuySprites[1] = new Sprite(_pGuyBitmaps[1], rcBounds);
40:     _pGuySprites[1]->SetPosition(301, 184);
41:     _pGuySprites[1]->SetZOrder(2);
42:     _pGuySprites[1]->SetHidden(TRUE);
43:     _pGame->AddSprite(_pGuySprites[1]);
44:     _pGuySprites[2] = new Sprite(_pGuyBitmaps[2], rcBounds);
45:     _pGuySprites[2]->SetPosition(394, 61);
46:     _pGuySprites[2]->SetZOrder(2);
47:     _pGuySprites[2]->SetHidden(TRUE);
```

16

LISTING 16.2 Continued

```
48:    _pGame->AddSprite(_pGuySprites[2]);
49:    rcBounds.left = 340;
50:    _pGuySprites[3] = new Sprite(_pGuyBitmaps[3], rcBounds, BA_WRAP);
51:    _pGuySprites[3]->SetPosition(500, 10);
52:    _pGuySprites[3]->SetVelocity(-3, 0);
53:    _pGuySprites[3]->SetZOrder(1);
54:    _pGuySprites[3]->SetHidden(TRUE);
55:    _pGame->AddSprite(_pGuySprites[3]);
56:    rcBounds.left = 385;
57:    _pGuySprites[4] = new Sprite(_pGuyBitmaps[4], rcBounds, BA_WRAP);
58:    _pGuySprites[4]->SetPosition(260, 60);
59:    _pGuySprites[4]->SetVelocity(5, 0);
60:    _pGuySprites[4]->SetZOrder(1);
61:    _pGuySprites[4]->SetHidden(TRUE);
62:    _pGame->AddSprite(_pGuySprites[4]);
63:
64:    // Initialize the remaining global variables
65:    _iGuyMasterDelay = 50;
66:    _iHits = 0;
67:    _iMisses = 0;
68:    _bGameOver = FALSE;
69:
70:    // Play the background music
71:    _pGame->PlayMIDISong(TEXT("Music.mid"));
72: }
```

I know; that's a heck of a lot of code for a function whose only job is to get the game started. However, you have to consider what all it takes to start a game like this. The bitmaps must be loaded (lines 14–23) and the sprites created (lines 26–62)—not to mention initializing the other global variables in the game (lines 65–68) and starting the background music (line 71). Of course, a few specific parts of this function are worth closer attention.

First, notice that the target sprite is set so that it stops when it reaches the boundary of the game screen (line 27). This ensures that the bull's-eye target is always visible on the screen no matter where you drag the mouse. Similarly, the pow sprite is also given the stop bounds action, as well as being hidden when the game first starts (line 32). This sprite is only displayed when a successful hit is made, which is why it begins the game hidden. At this point it's worth pointing out that the Z-order of the target sprite is set higher than the pow sprite (line 28), whereas the pow sprite's Z-order is set higher than the guy sprites (line 31). This results in the target sprite always appearing on top of the other sprites, while the pow sprite appears on top of the guys.

The first three guy sprites are created at fixed positions on the screen and are also hidden (lines 34–48). The fixed positions are already calculated to display each guy so that he appears to be standing behind the desks in the background office image. The remaining two guy sprites are designed to move across the hallway section of the office background. For this reason, the sprites are given velocities that cause them to move horizontally across the screen (lines 52 and 59). These sprites are also hidden, which allows the game to start with no guys in the office.

The other global variables in the Battle Office game are initialized with values suitable for the game's start. For example, the master delay for the guys is set to 50 (line 65), which is a value that you'll get a better understanding of a little later in the hour. The hits and misses are then zeroed out (lines 66 and 67), and the game over variable is set to FALSE (line 68). Finally, the PlayMIDISong() method of the game engine is used to start playing the background music for the game (line 71).

Although it is longer than what you've seen in most of the examples throughout the book thus far, the GameEnd() function is still much smaller than the GameStart() function that you just saw. Listing 16.3 contains the code for the GameEnd() function.

LISTING 16.3   The GameEnd() Function Cleans Up After the Game

```
 1: void GameEnd()
 2: {
 3:   // Close the MIDI player for the background music
 4:   _pGame->CloseMIDIPlayer();
 5:
 6:   // Cleanup the offscreen device context and bitmap
 7:   DeleteObject(_hOffscreenBitmap);
 8:   DeleteDC(_hOffscreenDC);
 9:
10:   // Cleanup the bitmaps
11:   delete _pOfficeBitmap;
12:   delete _pTargetBitmap;
13:   delete _pPowBitmap;
14:   for (int i = 0; i < 5; i++)
15:     delete _pGuyBitmaps[i];
16:   delete _pSmallGuyBitmap;
17:   delete _pGameOverBitmap;
18:
19:   // Cleanup the sprites
20:   _pGame->CleanupSprites();
21:
22:   // Cleanup the game engine
23:   delete _pGame;
24: }
```

As you can see, this function is responsible for performing a variety of different cleanup tasks for the Battle Office game. The first step is to close the MIDI player (line 4). The bitmaps and sprites are then wiped away (lines 7–20), and the game engine is deleted (line 23).

Because the Battle Office game plays MIDI music, you know that it's important to pause and resume the music appropriately when the game is deactivated and reactivated. This takes place in the familiar GameActivate() and GameDeactivate() functions, which you've already seen performing this task in other examples.

The game screen in the Battle Office game is painted entirely by the GamePaint() function, which is shown in Listing 16.4.

LISTING 16.4 The GamePaint() Function Draws the Office Background Bitmap, the Sprites, and the Number of Hits and Misses

```
 1: void GamePaint(HDC hDC)
 2: {
 3:    // Draw the background office
 4:    _pOfficeBitmap->Draw(hDC, 0, 0);
 5:
 6:    // Draw the sprites
 7:    _pGame->DrawSprites(hDC);
 8:
 9:    // Draw the number of guys who were hit
10:    TCHAR szText[64];
11:    RECT  rect = { 237, 360, 301, 390 };
12:    wsprintf(szText, "%d", _iHits);
13:    DrawText(hDC, szText, -1, &rect, DT_SINGLELINE | DT_CENTER | DT_VCENTER);
14:
15:    // Draw the number of guys who were missed (got away)
16:    for (int i = 0; i < _iMisses; i++)
17:      _pSmallGuyBitmap->Draw(hDC, 389 + (_pSmallGuyBitmap->GetWidth() * i),
18:        359, TRUE);
19:
20:    // Draw the game over message, if necessary
21:    if (_bGameOver)
22:      _pGameOverBitmap->Draw(hDC, 120, 110, TRUE);
23: }
```

This GamePaint() function is responsible for drawing all the game graphics for the game. The function begins by drawing the background office image (line 4), and then it draws the game sprites (line 7). The remainder of the function primarily draws the number of hits and misses in the lower right corner of the game screen. The hits are drawn as a number using the Win32 DrawText() function (lines 10–13). The misses, on the other hand, are drawn using small guy bitmaps (lines 16–18). A small guy is drawn for each guy who was missed, which helps you to know how many guys can escape before the game ends.

The GameCycle() function controls most of the game play in the Battle Office game, and also works closely with GamePaint() to update the game's sprites and reflect the changes onscreen. Listing 16.5 shows the code for the GameCycle() function.

16

LISTING 16.5 The GameCycle() Function Randomly Controls the Guys in the Office and Determines if the Game Has Ended

```
 1: void GameCycle()
 2: {
 3:   if (!_bGameOver)
 4:   {
 5:     // Randomly show and hide the guys
 6:     for (int i = 0; i < 5; i++)
 7:       if (_pGuySprites[i]->IsHidden())
 8:       {
 9:         if (rand() % 60 == 0)
10:         {
11:           // Show the guy
12:           _pGuySprites[i]->SetHidden(FALSE);
13:
14:           // Start the countdown delay
15:           if (i == 3)
16:           {
17:             // Start the guy running left
18:             _iGuyDelay[i] = 80;
19:             _pGuySprites[i]->SetPosition(500, 10);
20:           }
21:           else if (i == 4)
22:           {
23:             // Start the guy running right
24:             _iGuyDelay[i] = 45;
25:             _pGuySprites[i]->SetPosition(260, 60);
26:           }
27:           else
28:             // Start the stationary guys
29:             _iGuyDelay[i] = 20 + (rand() % _iGuyMasterDelay);
30:         }
31:       }
32:       else
33:       {
34:         if (--_iGuyDelay[i] == 0)
35:         {
36:           // Play a sound for the guy getting away
37:           PlaySound((LPCSTR)IDW_TAUNT, _hInstance, SND_ASYNC |
```

LISTING 16.5   Continued

```
38:               SND_RESOURCE);
39:
40:           // Hide the guy
41:           _pGuySprites[i]->SetHidden(TRUE);
42:
43:           // Increment the misses
44:           if (++_iMisses == 5)
45:           {
46:             // Play a sound for the game ending
47:             PlaySound((LPCSTR)IDW_BOO, _hInstance, SND_ASYNC |
48:               SND_RESOURCE);
49:
50:             // End the game
51:             for (int i = 0; i < 5; i++)
52:               _pGuySprites[i]->SetHidden(TRUE);
53:             _bGameOver = TRUE;
54:
55:             // Pause the background music
56:             _pGame->PauseMIDISong();
57:           }
58:         }
59:       }
60:
61:     // Update the sprites
62:     _pGame->UpdateSprites();
63:
64:     // Obtain a device context for repainting the game
65:     HWND  hWindow = _pGame->GetWindow();
66:     HDC   hDC = GetDC(hWindow);
67:
68:     // Paint the game to the offscreen device context
69:     GamePaint(_hOffscreenDC);
70:
71:     // Blit the offscreen bitmap to the game screen
72:     BitBlt(hDC, 0, 0, _pGame->GetWidth(), _pGame->GetHeight(),
73:       _hOffscreenDC, 0, 0, SRCCOPY);
74:
75:     // Cleanup
76:     ReleaseDC(hWindow, hDC);
77:   }
78: }
```

The GameCycle() function is one of the heftiest functions you've seen thus far in the
book, and there's a good reason for it. This function is carrying out a great deal of the
Battle Office game logic by determining when and how the office guys appear. The function first loops through the five guy sprites (line 6), checking to make sure that each one

is hidden before attempting to show it (line 7). If the guy is hidden, he is first made visible (line 12). And then some interesting things take place, depending on which guy is being shown. If one of the moving guys is being shown, which is indicated by an array index value of 3 or 4, a countdown delay is started and the sprite position is set (lines 15–26). The position makes sure that the guy starts moving from the edge of the game screen, while the delay gives them just enough time to run across the hallway before being hidden again. If the guy sprite is not one of the moving guys, a delay is set that is based on the master delay, which gets shorter as the game progresses (line 29). The idea is that the stationary guys will be displayed for shorter and shorter periods of time as the game continues.

If the first sprite check inside the loop showed that the guy sprite was already being displayed, the delay is decreased and checked to see if the guy has been shown long enough to hide him again (line 34). In other words, this is the part of the game logic that counts down the delay and results in each guy only being on the screen for a limited amount of time before hiding again. If the delay gets to 0 before the guy is shot, he gets away. If a guy gets away, the first step is to play a sound effect to let the player know (lines 37 and 38). The guy sprite is then hidden (line 41), and the number of misses is increased by one (line 44).

Because the number of misses is being increased, this is a good spot to check and see if the game is over (line 44 also). If there have been five misses, the game is over. A sound effect is played to let the player know that the game is over (lines 47 and 48), and the guy sprites are all hidden (lines 51 and 52). Ending the game also involves setting the _bGameOver variable (line 53), as well as stopping the MIDI music (line 56). In this case, the music is only paused—there is no reason to close the MIDI device just yet because the player might decide to start another game.

The remaining code in the GameCycle() function should be familiar to you because it is fairly generic game code. More specifically, it updates the sprites (line 62), and then draws the game graphics using double-buffer animation (line 65–76).

You survived the GameCycle() function, which was about as messy as the code in this book gets. Listing 16.6 contains another important function in the Battle Office game, MouseButtonDown().

LISTING 16.6   The MouseButtonDown() Function Checks to See if a Guy Was Clicked with the Mouse

```
1: void MouseButtonDown(int x, int y, BOOL bLeft)
2: {
3:   // Only check the left mouse button
```

LISTING **16.6**   Continued

```
 4:    if (!_bGameOver && bLeft)
 5:    {
 6:      // Temporarily hide the target and pow sprites
 7:      _pTargetSprite->SetHidden(TRUE);
 8:      _pPowSprite->SetHidden(TRUE);
 9:
10:      // See if a guy sprite was clicked
11:      Sprite* pSprite;
12:      if ((pSprite = _pGame->IsPointInSprite(x, y)) != NULL)
13:      {
14:        // Play a sound for hitting the guy
15:        PlaySound((LPCSTR)IDW_WHACK, _hInstance, SND_ASYNC | SND_RESOURCE);
16:
17:        // Position and show the pow sprite
18:        _pPowSprite->SetPosition(x - (_pPowSprite->GetWidth() / 2),
19:          y - (_pPowSprite->GetHeight() / 2));
20:        _pPowSprite->SetHidden(FALSE);
21:
22:        // Hide the guy that was clicked
23:        pSprite->SetHidden(TRUE);
24:
25:        // Increment the hits and make the game harder, if necessary
26:        if ((++_iHits % 5) == 0)
27:          if (--_iGuyMasterDelay == 0)
28:            _iGuyMasterDelay = 1;
29:      }
30:
31:      // Show the target sprite again
32:      _pTargetSprite->SetHidden(FALSE);
33:    }
34:    else if (_bGameOver && !bLeft)
35:    {
36:      // Start a new game
37:      _bGameOver = FALSE;
38:      _iHits = 0;
39:      _iMisses = 0;
40:
41:      // Restart the background music
42:      _pGame->PlayMIDISong();
43:    }
44:  }
```

The MouseButtonDown() function responds to mouse clicks in the game and serves as a means of determining if the player scored a hit on one of the office guys. The function first checks to make sure that the game isn't over and that the player clicked the left mouse button (line 4). If so, the target and pow sprites are temporarily hidden so that they don't interfere with performing a hit test on the mouse position (lines 7 and 8). This is necessary because the next task in the function is to see if the mouse position lies within any of the guy sprites. Because the target and pow sprites have a higher Z-order than the guys, they would always supercede the guys. In other words, the hit test would always return either the target or pow sprites and would never detect any of the guys.

The MouseButtonDown()function checks to see if one of the guy sprites was clicked by calling the IsPointInSprite() method on the game engine and passing in the mouse coordinates (line 12). If one of the guys was hit, a sound effect is played (line 15) and the pow sprite is positioned and displayed to indicate the successful hit (lines 18–20). The guy sprite who was hit is then hidden (line 23), which makes sense considering that he's been shot. The number of hits is then increased and checked to see if the difficulty level of the game needs to increase (line 26). The difficulty level is raised by decreasing the master delay for the guys (lines 27 and 28), which determines how long the stationary guys appear on the screen. Regardless of whether a hit was detected on a guy sprite, the target sprite is made visible after performing the test (line 32).

16

The last block of code in the function allows you to right-click to start a new game (lines 34–43). A new game is started by resetting the game state variables (lines 37–39) and restarting the background MIDI music (line 42).

Another mouse-related function used in the Battle Office game is MouseMove(), which is used to move the target sprite so that it tracks the mouse pointer. This is necessary so that you are always in control of the target sprite with the mouse. Listing 16.7 shows the code for the MouseMove() function.

LISTING 16.7   The MouseMove() Function Tracks the Mouse Cursor with the Target Sprite

```
1: void MouseMove(int x, int y)
2: {
3:   // Track the mouse with the target sprite
4:   _pTargetSprite->SetPosition(x - (_pTargetSprite->GetWidth() / 2),
5:     y - (_pTargetSprite->GetHeight() / 2));
6: }
```

The target sprite is made to follow the mouse pointer by simply calling the SetPosition() method on the sprite and passing in the mouse coordinates (lines 4 and 5). The position of the target sprite is actually calculated so that the mouse pointer points at the center of the sprite.

The last function of interest in the Battle Office game is the SpriteCollision() function, which is called in response to sprites colliding. Listing 16.8 shows how uneventful the SpriteCollision() function is in this game.

LISTING 16.8   The SpriteCollision() Function Does Nothing Because There is No Need to Respond to Sprite Collisions

```
1: BOOL SpriteCollision(Sprite* pSpriteHitter, Sprite* pSpriteHittee)
2: {
3:   return FALSE;
4: }
```

When you think about how the Battle Office game works, there is no reason to respond to any sprite collisions. Therefore, the SpriteCollision() function simply returns FALSE to indicate that nothing special is to take place in response to a collision (line 3) .

Testing the Game

You've finally arrived at the most fun step in the construction of a game: testing! Testing the Battle Office game is quite interesting because a fair amount of things are going on in the game. Figure 16.2 shows the game at the start, with one guy jumping from behind his desk to give you a quick scare. Notice that your bull's-eye target is near the guy ready for you to click and fire at him.

FIGURE 16.2

The Battle Office game gets started quickly with a guy jumping from behind an office desk.

Clicking the mouse with the target over the guy results in a hit, which causes the pow sprite to be displayed on the screen, as shown in Figure 16.3.

FIGURE 16.3

The pow sprite is displayed whenever you score a hit.

It won't take long for one of the moving guys to appear in the hallway near the top of the game screen. These guys are a little tougher to hit because they are moving, but it's still not too hard. Of course, the game doesn't really get tough until all the guys start appearing at the same time. Figure 16.4 shows an example of how the guys can start getting overwhelming.

FIGURE 16.4

As the game progresses, the guys will start overwhelming you, which makes it harder to hit them all.

Once five guys get away, the game ends. Figure 16.5 shows the end of the game, which involves displaying the game over image on the screen on top of the other game graphics.

I really don't encourage you to think of office co-workers as targets, but hopefully you can see the humor in the Battle Office game. If not, at least you can appreciate the game development techniques that went into making the game a reality.

FIGURE 16.5

When five guys get away, the game ends and the game over image is displayed.

Summary

Any time you're learning a new skill, it's helpful to put it into practice as much as possible to reinforce what you've learned. This hour helped to reinforce the game programming knowledge you've learned thus far throughout the book by guiding you through the design and development of the Battle Office game. The game made interesting use of the sprite features in the game engine—not to mention wave sound effects and MIDI music. Hopefully you're starting to get some confidence that you're capable of constructing a complete game of your own creation.

This hour concludes this part of the book. The next part revisits animation and explores some ways to enhance the animation features in the game engine so that you can create even more interesting games than those you've seen thus far.

Q&A

Q Exactly how do the moving guy sprites work in the Battle Office game?

A The moving guy sprites are both created with velocities that cause them to move across the game screen in the area where the office hallway is located. Their bounds actions are set to wrap, which means that they are constantly moving across the screen and wrapping around. In the context of the game, you don't want to see the wrapping motion of the guys, so there is a delay that gives them just enough time to get across the screen and then disappear. Because each guy is moving at a different speed, their delays are different. Keep in mind that the guys are constantly moving, even when they aren't visible. However, when it's time to make them visible for a pass across the screen, the game sets their positions so that they appear to walk onscreen from outside of the office.

Q I'm still a little confused by the master delay in the Battle Office game. How does it control the difficulty level of the game?

A The master delay impacts how long the stationary guys appear on the screen before disappearing. When this delay is shortened, the amount of time the guys appear on the screen is diminished, which makes it harder to shoot the guys. So, the master delay makes the game more difficult by causing the guys to appear for shorter periods of time as the game goes on.

16

Workshop

The Workshop is designed to help you anticipate possible questions, review what you've learned, and begin learning how to put your knowledge into practice. The answers to the quiz can be found in Appendix A, "Quiz Answers."

Quiz

1. Why is it necessary to first hide the target sprite before checking to see if the player clicked the mouse on a guy sprite in the Battle Office game?

2. What is the purpose of the `MouseMove()` function in the Battle Office game?

3. Why isn't it necessary to respond to sprite collisions in the Battle Office game?

Exercises

1. Modify the `_iGuyMasterDelay` global variable in the Battle Office game, and notice how it impacts the difficulty level of the game. Keep in mind that this variable only affects the period of time that the stationary guys appear in the game.

2. Modify the Battle Office game so that the velocities of the moving guys increase as the game progresses, effectively making them harder to shoot. You'll find out that you'll also have to modify the delay for each of the moving guys as you modify their velocities because their delay keeps them from wrapping around the screen and appearing again on the other side.

PART V

Taking Animation to the Next Level

Hours

HOUR 17

Animating the Appearance of Sprites

You're hopefully fairly comfortable with using sprites to create graphical objects that can move around the game screen and interact with each other. You've seen sprites in action in several programs' examples and a couple of complete games. One thing you might have found missing in the sprites that you've worked with is that they don't have any capability to change their appearance. Granted, being able to move around is certainly a huge benefit, but it would also be nice for some sprites to change their appearances every so often. For example, the guys moving across the screen in the Battle Office game would look much better if their legs were moving to give a more realistic impression that they were running. This hour takes a look at how to add frame animation features to your sprites so that their appearances can change.

In this hour, you'll learn:

- How frame animation can be incorporated into sprite animation
- How to design and integrate frame animation support into the existing game engine
- How to modify an existing game to take advantage of frame-animated sprites

Frame Animation Revisited

Back in Hour 9, "A Crash Course in Game Animation," you learned all about animation, including the two fundamental types of animation: frame-based animation and cast-based (sprite) animation. Although you learned that both types of animation are equally useful, you've focused solely on sprite animation since Hour 9 because it is more immediately useful in terms of allowing you to move objects around on the game screen. However, frame-based animation, or *frame animation* for short, is still very important to games. In fact, you'll find that the ideal usage of frame animation in games is when you combine it with sprite animation.

To better understand how frame animation fits in with sprite animation, consider a simple maze game such as Pac-Man. In Pac-Man, the main character moves around the game screen eating dots. To convey the effect of the main character eating, his mouth opens and closes as he moves around. The simple movement of the character is made possible with sprite animation, but the change in his appearance brought on by his mouth moving is made possible by frame animation. In other words, frame animation makes it possible to change the appearance of a sprite, independent of whether the sprite is moving with respect to the game screen.

Okay, so frame animation makes it possible to change the appearance of a sprite, but how does it work? If you recall, a basic sprite without frame animation uses a single bitmap image to reflect its appearance; when you draw the sprite, you are just drawing the bitmap image. A frame-animated sprite relies on a series of bitmap images to represent more than one appearance for the sprite. You can think of this series of images as a roll of film on a traditional film projector. The illusion of frame animation is made possible by cycling through the images on the roll of film. Figure 17.1 shows how this concept applies to adding animation to the Pac-Man character.

In the figure, the Pac-Man character consists of a series of four images. When this image series is incorporated into a game and played in sequence, the effect will be that Pac-Man is moving his mouth and eating something. If you look carefully, you'll notice that frame 4 is the same as frame 2. This is necessary because the animation sequence cycles back to frame 1 when it finishes, so duplicating frame 2 provides a smooth transition back to the first frame. Just visualize the frames being displayed in succession to see what I'm talking about.

FIGURE 17.1

A series of images shows how frame animation can make Pac-Man appear to be eating something.

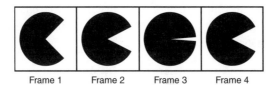

Frame 1   Frame 2   Frame 3   Frame 4

One problem associated with frame animation is that of controlling how fast the frame images are cycled through. For example, a frame-animated Pac-Man sprite might need to change its appearance slower than an animated sprite of an explosion, for example. For this reason, there needs to be a way to establish a timing delay that controls how fast the frames change. Increasing the delay would slow down the frame animation, which in some cases would be a desirable effect. You will definitely take a frame delay into consideration as you design and develop frame animation support for the game engine throughout the remainder of this hour.

Designing an Animated Sprite

Even though sprites are already animated in the sense that they can move around on the game screen, for the purposes of this discussion I'm going to refer to a frame-animated sprite as simply an *animated sprite*. The animation, in this case, means that the sprite's appearance is being animated. The first place to start in designing an animated sprite is its bitmap image.

You learned in the previous section how a series of images is used to represent an animated sprite because the images can be cycled through to give the effect of animation. There are a variety of different ways to store a series of images for an animated sprite, but the easiest I've found is to store the frame images horizontally in a single image. For example, the series of Pac-Man images you saw in Figure 17.1 shows several frame images appearing next to each other. These four frame images could be stored together just as they appear in the figure as a single image. It then becomes the responsibility of the animated sprite to draw only the frame image representing the current frame. You can think of the sprite image at any given moment as being a little window that moves from one frame image to the next to reveal only one frame image at a time. Figure 17.2 shows what I'm talking about.

This figure shows how the second frame of the Pac-Man sprite is currently being displayed. The figure also reveals how the bitmap image for an animated sprite is put together. The image is the same height as a normal unanimated sprite image, but its width is determined by the number of frames. So, if a single frame is 25 pixels wide and

there are a total of four frames of animation, the entire image is 100 pixels wide. To create an image like this, you just place the frame images immediately next to each other
with no space in between them.

FIGURE 17.2

The current sprite image is drawn from within the series of frame images.

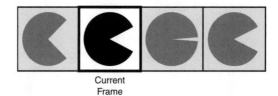

Current
Frame

With the animated sprite image in place, you can now turn your attention to the actual
data for the sprite that is used to manage frame animation. First of all, you know that the
sprite needs to understand how many frame images there are because this is crucial in
determining how to cycle through the frames of the sprite's bitmap image. In addition to
knowing the total number of animation frames, it's also necessary to keep track of the
currently selected frame—this is the frame image currently being displayed.

Earlier in the hour, I talked about how it's important to be able to control the speed at
which an animated sprite cycles through its frame images. This speed is controlled by a
piece of information known as a *frame delay*. The frame delay for a sprite basically
determines how many game cycles must elapse before the frame image is changed. In
order to carry out the frame delay feature for an animated sprite, you must keep up with
a trigger (counter) that counts down the delay and indicates that it's time to move to the
next frame. So, when an animated sprite first starts out, the trigger is set to the frame
delay, and it begins counting down with each game cycle. When the trigger reaches zero,
the sprite moves to the next frame and resets the trigger to the frame delay again.

To recap, the following pieces of information are required of the new animated sprite, in
addition to the bitmap image that contains the horizontal frame images:

- Total number of frames
- Current frame
- Frame delay
- Frame trigger

The next section puts code behind this sprite data as you add animated sprite support to
the game engine.

Adding Animated Sprite Support to the Game Engine

In order to add animated sprite support to the game engine, a few changes have to be made to existing code. These changes impact the `Bitmap` and `Sprite` classes, but strangely enough they don't directly impact the `GameEngine` class at all. The next couple of sections show you exactly what changes need to be made to the `Bitmap` and `Sprite` classes to integrate frame-animated sprites into the game engine.

Drawing Only Part of a Bitmap

The first change is related to the `Bitmap` class, which represents a bitmap image. As you know, the `Sprite` class already relies on the `Bitmap` class to handle the details of storing and drawing a sprite's visual appearance. However, the `Bitmap` class is currently only designed to draw a complete image. This presents a problem for animated sprites because the frame images are all stored in a single bitmap image. It is therefore necessary to modify the `Bitmap` class so that it supports drawing only a part of the bitmap.

If you recall, the `Bitmap` class includes a `Draw()` method that accepts a device context and an XY coordinate to indicate where the bitmap is to be drawn. The new method you now need is called `DrawPart()`, and it accepts the familiar device context and XY coordinate, as well as the XY position and width and height of the frame image within the overall sprite bitmap. So, the new `DrawPart()` method basically allows you to select and draw a rectangular subsection of a bitmap image. Listing 17.1 contains the code for the `Bitmap::DrawPart()` method.

LISTING 17.1 The `Bitmap::DrawPart()` Method Supports Frame Animation by Allowing You to Draw Only a Part of a Sprite's Bitmap Image

```
 1: void Bitmap::DrawPart(HDC hDC, int x, int y, int xPart, int yPart,
 2:   int wPart, int hPart, BOOL bTrans, COLORREF crTransColor)
 3: {
 4:   if (m_hBitmap != NULL)
 5:   {
 6:     // Create a memory device context for the bitmap
 7:     HDC hMemDC = CreateCompatibleDC(hDC);
 8:
 9:     // Select the bitmap into the device context
10:     HBITMAP hOldBitmap = (HBITMAP)SelectObject(hMemDC, m_hBitmap);
11:
12:     // Draw the bitmap to the destination device context
13:     if (bTrans)
14:       TransparentBlt(hDC, x, y, wPart, hPart, hMemDC, xPart, yPart,
```

17

LISTING 17.1   Continued

```
15:          wPart, hPart, crTransColor);
16:      else
17:        BitBlt(hDC, x, y, wPart, hPart, hMemDC, xPart, yPart, SRCCOPY);
18:
19:      // Restore and delete the memory device context
20:      SelectObject(hMemDC, hOldBitmap);
21:      DeleteDC(hMemDC);
22:    }
23: }
```

This code is very similar to the original Draw() method in the Bitmap class, except that it doesn't take for granted the parameters of the source bitmap image. More specifically, the DrawPart() method uses the new arguments xPart, yPart, wPart, and hPart to single out a frame image within the bitmap image to draw. These arguments are passed in to the TransparentBlt() function to draw a frame image with transparency (lines 14 and 15) and the BitBlt() function to draw a frame image without transparency (line 17).

It's important to note that the Draw() method still works fine for drawing sprites that don't involve frame animation. In fact, the Draw() method has now been modified to use the DrawPart() method, which helps to conserve code since the methods are very similar. Listing 17.2 shows the code for the new Bitmap::Draw() method, which is surprisingly simple.

LISTING 17.2   The New Bitmap::Draw() Method Simply Calls the DrawPart() Method to Draw a Bitmap Image In Its Entirety

```
1: void Bitmap::Draw(HDC hDC, int x, int y, BOOL bTrans,
2:   COLORREF crTransColor)
3: {
4:   DrawPart(hDC, x, y, 0, 0, GetWidth(), GetHeight(), bTrans, crTransColor);
5: }
```

Notice that the new Draw() method just calls the DrawPart() method and passes in arguments that result in the entire bitmap image being drawn (line 4). You could've kept the original Draw() method without modifying it, but it's wasteful to duplicate code without a good reason. More importantly, if you ever need to change the manner in which a bitmap is drawn, you only have to modify one section of code, the DrawPart() method.

Animating the Sprite Class

Now that you've altered the Bitmap class to support the drawing of only part of a bitmap image, you're ready to make changes to the Sprite class to support frame animation.

Earlier in the hour, you worked through the design of a frame-animated sprite that involved adding several important pieces of information to a traditional unanimated sprite. The following new member variables of the Sprite class represent these pieces of information:

```
int m_iNumFrames, m_iCurFrame;
int m_iFrameDelay, m_iFrameTrigger;
```

These member variables correspond one-to-one with the pieces of animated sprite information mentioned earlier in the hour. They are all initialized in the Sprite() constructors, as the following code reveals:

```
m_iNumFrames = 1;
m_iCurFrame = m_iFrameDelay = m_iFrameTrigger = 0;
```

The default value of the m_iNumFrames variable is 1 because a normal sprite that doesn't use frame animation includes only one bitmap image. The other three variables are initialized with values of 0, which is suitable for a sprite without frame animation.

In order to create a sprite that takes advantage of frame animation, you must call the SetNumFrames() method and possibly even the SetFrameDelay() method. Listing 17.3 contains the code for the SetNumFrames() method.

LISTING 17.3   The Sprite::SetNumFrames() Method Turns a Normal Sprite Into an Animated Sprite by Setting Its Number of Frames

```
 1: void Sprite::SetNumFrames(int iNumFrames)
 2: {
 3:   // Set the number of frames
 4:   m_iNumFrames = iNumFrames;
 5:
 6:   // Recalculate the position
 7:   RECT rect = GetPosition();
 8:   rect.right = rect.left + ((rect.right - rect.left) / iNumFrames);
 9:   SetPosition(rect);
10: }
```

The listing shows how the number of frames is set by assigning the specified argument to the m_iNumFrames member variable (line 4). It's also important to recalculate the sprite's position because it is no longer based upon the entire image size (lines 7–9).

The SetFrameDelay() method goes hand in hand with the SetNumFrames() method, and it's even easier to follow:

```
void SetFrameDelay(int iFrameDelay) { m_iFrameDelay = iFrameDelay; };
```

17

As you can see, the SetFrameDelay() method is a simple accessor method that sets the m_iFrameDelay member variable. Setting the number of frames and the frame delay is all that is required to turn an ordinary sprite into a frame-animated sprite. Of course, you also need to make sure that you've laid out the frame images for the sprite in the sprite's single bitmap image.

Although the SetNumFrames() and SetFrameDelay() methods are all you need to worry about from the perspective of game code, work still needs to be done to get the Sprite class ready to use its new member variables. For example, the GetWidth() method needs to take into consideration the number of frames when calculating the width of the sprite image. This width is either the entire sprite image for an unanimated sprite, or the width of a single frame image for an animated sprite. Following is the code for the new GetWidth() method:

```
int GetWidth() { return (m_pBitmap->GetWidth() / m_iNumFrames); };
```

Notice that this code simply divides the width of the sprite image by the number of frames. For an unanimated sprite, the number of frames is one, which means that the normal bitmap width is returned. For animated sprites, the width returned reflects the width of an individual frame image.

A new helper method is included in the Sprite class to handle the details of updating the current animation frame. This method is called UpdateFrame() and is shown in Listing 17.4.

LISTING 17.4   The Sprite::UpdateFrame() Method Updates the Sprite's Current Animation Frame

```
 1: inline void Sprite::UpdateFrame()
 2: {
 3:   if ((m_iFrameDelay >= 0) && (--m_iFrameTrigger <= 0))
 4:   {
 5:     // Reset the frame trigger;
 6:     m_iFrameTrigger = m_iFrameDelay;
 7:
 8:     // Increment the frame
 9:     if (++m_iCurFrame >= m_iNumFrames)
10:       m_iCurFrame = 0;
11:   }
12: }
```

The UpdateFrame() method is called by the Update() method to update the frame image of the sprite, if necessary. The method starts off by making sure that the frame indeed needs to be updated. This check involves seeing if the frame delay is greater than or equal to 0, as well as if the frame trigger is less than or equal to 0 (line 3). If both of these conditions are met, the frame trigger is reset to the frame delay (line 6) and the current frame is moved to the next frame (lines 9 and 10).

The Update() method is responsible for calling the UpdateFrame() method to make sure that the frame is updated. Listing 17.5 shows how the UpdateFrame() method is now called in the Update() method.

LISTING 17.5 The Sprite::Update() Method Now Calls the UpdateFrame() Method to Update the Sprite's Animation Frame

```
1: SPRITEACTION Sprite::Update()
2: {
3:    // Update the frame
4:    UpdateFrame();
5:
6:    ...
7: }
```

17

The update of the frame is now taken care of first thing in the Update() method (line 4). I deliberately left out the remainder of the Update() code because none of it changed, and it's quite lengthy; the only code of importance to this discussion is the new call to UpdateFrame().

The last Sprite method impacted by the addition of animation support is the Draw()method, which must now take into account the current frame when drawing a sprite. Listing 17.6 shows the new and improved Draw() method—complete with frame animation support.

LISTING 17.6 The Sprite::Draw() Method Draws the Sprite Differently Depending on Whether It Is an Animated Sprite

```
 1: void Sprite::Draw(HDC hDC)
 2: {
 3:    // Draw the sprite if it isn't hidden
 4:    if (m_pBitmap != NULL && !m_bHidden)
 5:    {
 6:      // Draw the appropriate frame, if necessary
 7:      if (m_iNumFrames == 1)
 8:        m_pBitmap->Draw(hDC, m_rcPosition.left, m_rcPosition.top, TRUE);
 9:      else
10:        m_pBitmap->DrawPart(hDC, m_rcPosition.left, m_rcPosition.top,
11:          m_iCurFrame * GetWidth(), 0, GetWidth(), GetHeight(), TRUE);
12:    }
13: }
```

This version of the Draw() method now takes a look at the number of frames before deciding how to draw the sprite (line 7). If there is only one frame, the familiar Bitmap::Draw() method is called to draw the single bitmap image as you've been accustomed to doing (line 8). However, if there is more than one frame, the new Bitmap::DrawPart() method is used to draw only the current frame image within the sprite bitmap (lines 10 and 11). This is a critical piece of code that justifies why you needed to make the changes to the Bitmap class earlier in the hour.

Building the Battle Office 2 Program Example

You're now sitting there with a perfectly good game engine with a shiny new feature, so you're no doubt anxious to see how it works in a practical game. Fortunately, it's not too difficult to find a good application for animated sprites. I mentioned earlier in the book that the Battle Office game had a deficiency in that the guys moving across the hallway near the top of the game screen appear to slide, as opposed to run. It would only look as if they were running if their legs were moving as they moved across the game screen. This kind of visual effect is only possible through frame animation, which you now have the capability of carrying out within the game engine you've now grown to love. Okay, love might be too strong a word, but hopefully you've at least grown to appreciate what it can do.

The next couple of sections focus on what it takes to animate the two moving guys in the Battle Office game using frame-animated sprites. Because you've already built the animation logic into the game engine, modifying the Battle Office game takes very little effort. You'll call the new version of the game with the animated guys Battle Office 2.

Writing the Program Code

I mentioned earlier this hour that the only thing required from a programming perspective to add animated sprites to a game is setting the number of frames and the frame delay for each sprite. Of course, you'll also need to create a suitable bitmap image containing the frames for the sprite, but that doesn't directly impact the programming side of things. In the case of the Battle Office 2 game, the only two sprites being altered for frame animation are the two moving guy sprites. Both sprites use four frame images, which means that they each need to be set to use four frames. Listing 17.7 contains the sprite creation code for the first moving guy sprite.

If you set the number of frames for a sprite to a number greater than one but you don't change the sprite's bitmap image, you definitely will get strange results. This has to do with the fact that the sprite automatically assumes that the individual frame images are arranged horizontally across the sprite image.

LISTING 17.7   The Sprite Creation Code for the First Moving Guy Establishes the Number of Frames for the Animated Sprite

```
1: _pGuySprites[3] = new Sprite(_pGuyBitmaps[3], rcBounds, BA_WRAP);
2: _pGuySprites[3]->SetNumFrames(4);
3: _pGuySprites[3]->SetPosition(500, 10);
4: _pGuySprites[3]->SetVelocity(-3, 0);
5: _pGuySprites[3]->SetZOrder(1);
6: _pGuySprites[3]->SetHidden(TRUE);
7: _pGame->AddSprite(_pGuySprites[3]);
```

17

This code shows how easy it is to change a normal sprite into an animated sprite. A single call to the SetNumFrames() method is all it takes to inform the sprite that it is to use four frames of animation (line 2). It's important to note that the frame delay is not being set for this sprite, which means that it is cycling through the frames at maximum speed.

The second guy sprite is a little different in that it opts for a frame delay, as shown in Listing 17.8.

LISTING 17.8   The Sprite Creation Code for the Second Moving Guy Establishes the Number of Frames and the Frame Delay for the Animated Sprite

```
1: _pGuySprites[4] = new Sprite(_pGuyBitmaps[4], rcBounds, BA_WRAP);
2: _pGuySprites[4]->SetNumFrames(4);
3: _pGuySprites[4]->SetFrameDelay(5);
4: _pGuySprites[4]->SetPosition(260, 60);
5: _pGuySprites[4]->SetVelocity(5, 0);
6: _pGuySprites[4]->SetZOrder(1);
7: _pGuySprites[4]->SetHidden(TRUE);
8: _pGame->AddSprite(_pGuySprites[4]);
```

This code not only sets the number of frames for the sprite (line 2), but it also sets the frame delay for the sprite (line 3). Setting the frame delay to 5, as in this code, means that the sprite's animation frame will be updated in every fifth game cycle. In other words, the second guy sprite is animating at one-fifth the speed of the first sprite.

Testing the Finished Product

Testing the animated sprites in the Battle Office 2 game is not a very involved process, as you might imagine. Figure 17.3 shows the two guys moving across the hallway, and although it's difficult to see on the static page of a book, I promise you that they're kicking their legs like crazy!

FIGURE 17.3

The Battle Office 2 game shows off the new animated sprite features in the game engine.

Granted, the new animated sprites in the Battle Office 2 game don't really impact the play of the game very much. However, it's still hard to argue that a little more playful realism can never hurt a game. In fact, anything you can do to make a game more interesting will ultimately add to the satisfaction of game players, and ultimately the success of the game.

Summary

This hour built on your knowledge of sprite animation by expanding the sprite support in the game engine to support frame-animated sprites. Frame animation allows you to change the appearance of a sprite, which can be used to achieve a variety of different effects. This hour demonstrated how to use animated sprites to make the moving guys in the Battle Office game appear to run across the game screen. You could also make similar modifications to the Henway game so that the chicken appears to be running, or maybe change the car images so that their brake lights come on every once in a while. Regardless of how you use them, animated sprites can add significantly to the allure of games.

The next hour continues along the same path of improving games with better graphics effects by showing you how to create interesting backgrounds. You've grown accustomed to seeing backgrounds that are just a fixed image, but how about a space background complete with twinkling stars? Read on to find out how it's done.

Q&A

Q Is there some reason why all the examples in this hour use four frame images to demonstrate frame animation?

A No. In fact, there aren't any rules whatsoever regarding the number of frame images that are ideal for frame animation. It all comes down to what you're trying to accomplish with the animation. The more frames you use, the smoother and more realistic the movement will tend to be. On the other hand, creating a lot of frames requires a great deal of work and also tends to hog memory. So, it's worth striking a balance between nice visual effects and efficiency. Generally speaking, I'd try not to go over sixteen frames for most of your animated sprites. And quite likely you'll be able to achieve most effects in eight frames or fewer.

Q What is the unit of time measurement used by the frame delay of an animated sprite?

A Unfortunately, the frame delay of an animated sprite doesn't have a specific unit of measurement, such as seconds or milliseconds. The frame delay is expressed in game cycles, not time. So, if you set a frame delay of 10, it means that the frame of the sprite will be changed every 10 game cycles. This can therefore have a dramatically different impact on a game if you change the game's frame rate. For example, changing the frame rate from 30 to 15 will slow down the sprite's frame animation by half, which is actually what you would expect when you consider that the frame rate drives the speed of the entire game.

17

Workshop

The Workshop is designed to help you anticipate possible questions, review what you've learned, and begin learning how to put your knowledge into practice. The answers to the quiz can be found in Appendix A, "Quiz Answers."

Quiz

1. What does Pac-Man have to do with frame animation?
2. How are frame images stored in a frame-animated sprite?
3. What is the purpose of a frame delay?

Exercises

1. Modify the images for the moving guys in the Battle Office 2 game so that there are more animation frames that better convey the effect of the guys running.

2. Modify the images for the stationary guys in the Battle Office 2 game so that they wave their arms a little; it shouldn't take more than two or three frames to get this effect. Also, try altering the frame delay for these guys to see how you can speed up and slow down their motions.

HOUR 18

Creating Backgrounds for Your Sprites

If you've ever watched an animated movie, you are familiar with the importance of backgrounds. If you pay careful attention the next time you watch an animated movie, notice how the characters move on top of a background that doesn't tend to change much. This is because the characters are overlaid on the background, very much like sprites. Although you've already seen how to use an image as a background, this hour shows you how to create a general background class that you can use in your games. Not only that, but you learn how to create animated backgrounds that can be used to display a starry night complete with twinkling stars.

In this hour, you'll learn:

- Why backgrounds are so important in games
- About the three main types of backgrounds
- How to add support for backgrounds to the game engine
- How to use an animated background with animated sprites to simulate an asteroid field

Assessing the Significance of Game Backgrounds

It's hard to argue the significance of backgrounds in games, especially when you consider the example games that you've seen thus far. For example, picture the Henway game without the highway background, or the Battle Office game without the office background. Both of these backgrounds are critical in supporting the sprites in both games, and giving them context. Without the backgrounds, neither of the games would be as entertaining, and they certainly wouldn't make as much sense from a game play perspective.

In the two examples I mentioned, both backgrounds were created directly from bitmap images. The background image was drawn just before drawing the sprites, which gave the effect that the sprites appeared on top of the background. Although a stationary image was perfectly acceptable for these games, there are situations in which an animated background makes more sense. For example, consider a driving game where a sense of movement needs to be associated with objects passing by as you're driving. These objects could certainly be represented by sprites, which might even make more sense than using an animated background, but there are still aspects of the background that would need to be animated. For example, the lines painted on the road would need to move to some degree to give the illusion of movement.

Another good example of an animated background is the background of a space game, which might consist of a solid black region with stars drawn on it. The animation comes into play when you make the stars twinkle, which is a subtle but compelling enhancement to the background. A space background with twinkling stars adds considerably to the realism of a space game, and helps to immerse the player in the setting.

I could go through countless examples of how important backgrounds are in improving the visual feel of a game, but hopefully you're starting to get the idea. Most of the more interesting background effects involve animation of some sort. However, this animation typically isn't as simple as frame-based sprite animation; you typically must write custom animation code to handle each specific background. For example, a frame-based animation approach is overkill in the twinkling star background. For that background, it makes more sense to write custom code that varies the color of the stars over time. This is not only efficient, but also yields a more realistic effect than cycling through the same series of frame images over and over.

Understanding the Types of Game Backgrounds

Now that you have a basic understanding of how backgrounds fit into games, as well as why they are important, I'd like to spend a moment exploring the basic kinds of backgrounds that you'll encounter in game programming. Following are the three primary types of backgrounds:

- Solid backgrounds
- Image backgrounds
- Animated backgrounds
- Scrolling backgrounds

The next few sections explore these different types of backgrounds in more detail.

Solid Backgrounds

A *solid background* is a background consisting only of a solid color. This is by far the simplest of all backgrounds, and requires very little code to pull off. Not surprisingly, solid backgrounds are also the dullest of all backgrounds, and aren't used very often in games. Generally speaking, any time you could use a solid background, you could also use an image background and get a much better result. For example, if you were developing a football game, it might make sense to create a solid green background to represent the grass on the field. However, a grassy textured image would look much better in the same context, without a whole lot more development effort. So, although it's important to have the option of using a solid background, it's usually not your best option.

One situation in which you might find a solid background useful is in testing a game. For example, if you have a game that has a complex background image in which the sprites tend to blend in well, you might find it easier to fine-tune the sprites while viewing them against a stark background. By temporarily replacing a background image with a solid background of a contrasting color, you can easily make out what the sprites are doing and fix any problems with them.

Image Backgrounds

Image backgrounds are a step beyond solid backgrounds in that they use a bitmap image to represent the backdrop for a game, as opposed to a solid color. You've already used

18

image backgrounds in the games you've developed throughout the book, so hopefully you can appreciate their usefulness. The primary work involved in using an image background is creating the image itself; from a programming perspective, the Bitmap class in the game engine already handles most of the details of using an image background.

The problem with image bitmaps is that they are static, which means that they don't move or do anything interesting to convey that they are real. For example, the forest image background used in the Fore example from Hour 10, "Making Things Move with Sprites," would have been infinitely more realistic if the trees swayed a little and maybe dropped a leaf every now and then. Of course, such subtleties aren't always easy to add to a game, and you have to carefully weigh adding complexity for the sake of including small details in a game—sometimes it's worth it, sometimes not. One way to improve on the basic image background is to use an animated background.

Animated Backgrounds

An *animated background* is a background that somehow changes its appearance over time, which is similar in some ways to an animated sprite. However, an animated background doesn't necessarily have to involve a series of frame images. It's entirely possible to create an animated background whose animation is derived from custom code. The key to making an animated background work is providing some kind of mechanism for updating and drawing the background. Again, this is similar to sprites in that they must be updated periodically to convey a sense of motion.

Another reason why I hesitate to draw too close of a comparison between an animated background and an animated sprite is because backgrounds are usually much larger than sprites. Therefore, using a series of frame images for a background could quickly hog a lot of memory when you consider that backgrounds are typically hundreds of pixels in width and height. It is much more efficient to focus on coming up with interesting and more efficient ways of animating backgrounds. For example, the starry background I mentioned earlier could be created by changing the color of individual pixels in a background image.

Another approach to creating an animated background involves using several smaller images that are capable of moving around on the background. For example, if you wanted to enhance the starry background, you could feasibly add a few planets that are animated on the background by slightly changing their appearance every so often. It's debatable whether you should create these planets as sprites, as opposed to creating them as part of the background, but these are the kinds of decisions you have to make when creating a game.

Scrolling Backgrounds

The final type of background is the *scrolling background*, which involves an image or set of graphical objects that are capable of being shifted, or scrolled around on the screen. The best way to understand a scrolling background is to picture a background that is much larger than the game screen, which means that the game screen provides a view onto part of the background. To see other parts of the background, you have to scroll the view to another part. Figure 18.1 shows what I mean by a "view on a background."

FIGURE 18.1

When you use a scrolling background, the game screen provides a view on a portion of the background.

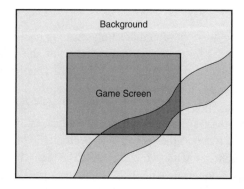

18

The figure shows how the game screen shows only a portion of a larger background. This type of background is used a lot in adventure games in which you control a character around a large virtual world. As you might have guessed, scrolling backgrounds are considerably more complex to develop than the other types of backgrounds because they involve a lot more game logic. For example, the background must respond to you moving the player, not to mention the fact that sprites have to be moved so that they appear to scroll with the background. Not only that, but scrolling backgrounds often must be capable of wrapping so that you don't encounter a boundary.

An interesting type of scrolling background that is commonly used in 2D games is a parallax scrolling background, which is a background that scrolls at differing rates. *Parallax scrolling* involves the use of multiple layered background images, such as buildings in the foreground, trees in the midground, and mountains in the background. The idea is to provide the illusion of depth by moving each image at a different speed. So, the mountains move slowest because they are furthest away, while the trees move a little faster, and the buildings move fastest. This simulates the effect of movement we perceive in the real world when passing by objects that are at different distances.

Creating a scrolling background certainly isn't impossible, but it is a formidable challenge when you approach it from the perspective of still learning the ropes of game development. Therefore, you won't be tackling scrolling backgrounds in this book. However, you do learn how to create animated backgrounds, which I think you will find to be plenty interesting for adding some pizzazz to your games.

Adding Background Support to the Game Engine

Because you're not going to worry about creating scrolling backgrounds, that leaves three types of backgrounds you're going to incorporate into the game engine: solid backgrounds, image backgrounds, and animated backgrounds. The first two background types can easily coexist in a single class, whereas the third requires a custom class of its own. So, you're going to be creating two new classes that will become part of the game engine. The first class is a basic background class that encompasses solid backgrounds and image backgrounds, whereas the second is a specific type of animated background that displays a starry night sky with twinkling stars. The starry background will serve as a good enough demonstration of how to create an animated background that you should be able to create your own custom animated backgrounds without any trouble.

Creating a Basic Background Class

The basic background that supports both solid and image backgrounds is contained within the Background class. The Background class is flexible in that the same class can be used to create both kinds of backgrounds—the decision regarding which kind of background you're creating is decided by which constructor you use. Listing 18.1 shows the code for the Background class, which reveals its overall design.

LISTING 18.1 The Background Class Is Used to Create Both Solid and Image Backgrounds

```
1: class Background
2: {
3: protected:
4:     // Member Variables
5:     int       m_iWidth, m_iHeight;
6:     COLORREF  m_crColor;
7:     Bitmap*   m_pBitmap;
8:
9: public:
```

LISTING **18.1**   Continued

```
10:    // Constructor(s)/Destructor
11:            Background(int iWidth, int iHeight, COLORREF crColor);
12:            Background(Bitmap* pBitmap);
13:    virtual ~Background();
14:
15:    // General Methods
16:    virtual void  Update();
17:    virtual void  Draw(HDC hDC);
18:
19:    // Accessor Methods
20:    int GetWidth()  { return m_iWidth; };
21:    int GetHeight() { return m_iHeight; };
22: };
```

The Background class contains several member variables that support both solid and image backgrounds. The m_iWidth and m_iHeight member variables keep track of the width and height of the background (line 5), which applies to any kind of background. The m_crColor variable stores the color of the background (line 6), and only applies to solid backgrounds. Similarly, the m_pBitmap variable stores a pointer to a Bitmap object (line 7), which is used to draw the bitmap image for an image background.

The Background class includes two constructors—each of which corresponds to one of the two basic background types. The first constructor accepts a width and height, along with a color for the solid background (line 11). The second constructor accepts a bitmap image (line 12), which it uses as the basis for calculating the width and height of the image background.

Two familiar methods are included in the Background class for updating and drawing the background. The Update() method is called to update the appearance of the background (line 16), and in the case of the solid and image backgrounds, this method does nothing. The purpose for having the Update() method is to allow derived animated background classes to use it to update themselves. The Draw() method applies to all kinds of backgrounds, and simply accepts a device context on which to draw the background (line 17). The last two methods in the Background class are the GetWidth() and GetHeight() accessor methods, which simply return the width and height of the background (lines 20 and 21).

Now that you have an understanding of how the Background class is assembled, you can take a look at the specific code that makes it work. Listing 18.2 shows the code for the Background() constructors.

18

LISTING 18.2   The Background::Background() Constructors Are Used to Create and Cleanup After a Background

```
 1: Background::Background(int iWidth, int iHeight, COLORREF crColor)
 2: {
 3:   // Initialize the member variables
 4:   m_iWidth = iWidth;
 5:   m_iHeight = iHeight;
 6:   m_crColor = crColor;
 7:   m_pBitmap = NULL;
 8: }
 9:
10: Background::Background(Bitmap* pBitmap)
11: {
12:   // Initialize the member variables
13:   m_crColor = 0;
14:   m_pBitmap = pBitmap;
15:   m_iWidth = pBitmap->GetWidth();
16:   m_iHeight = pBitmap->GetHeight();
17: }
```

The constructors for the Background class are pretty straightforward in that they simply initialize the member variables for the class based on the arguments provided. It is important to note that the bitmap pointer is set to NULL in the first constructor (line 7), which indicates that the background is a solid background, as opposed to an image background. Similarly, the background color is set to 0 in the second constructor (line 13) because an image background doesn't have a background color.

The Update() and Draw() methods in the Background class are responsible for updating and drawing the background. However, because neither a solid or image background is animated, the Update() method serves as more of a placeholder for future derived background classes. Listing 18.3 shows the code for these two methods.

LISTING 18.3   The Background::Update() and Background::Draw() Methods Handle the Updating and Drawing of a Background

```
 1: void Background::Update()
 2: {
 3:   // Do nothing since the basic background is not animated
 4: }
 5:
 6: void Background::Draw(HDC hDC)
 7: {
 8:   // Draw the background
 9:   if (m_pBitmap != NULL)
10:     m_pBitmap->Draw(hDC, 0, 0);
```

LISTING 18.3 Continued

```
11:    else
12:    {
13:      RECT    rect = { 0, 0, m_iWidth, m_iHeight };
14:      HBRUSH  hBrush = CreateSolidBrush(m_crColor);
15:      FillRect(hDC, &rect, hBrush);
16:      DeleteObject(hBrush);
17:    }
18: }
```

As I mentioned earlier, the Update() method is designed to be overridden with animation code in derived background classes, so it makes sense to leave it blank in this class (line 3). However, the Draw() method makes up for this lack of action by drawing a solid background or image background, depending on the state of the bitmap pointer (line 9). If the bitmap pointer is not NULL, you know that this is an image bitmap, so the Draw() method is called on the Bitmap object (line 10). Otherwise, you know this is a solid bitmap so a solid rectangle is drawn in the color of the background (lines 13–16). The code in the Draw() method reveals how two types of backgrounds are supported in a single class.

Creating an Animated Background Class

If the Background class didn't get you too excited, hopefully you'll be intrigued by the StarryBackground class, which represents an animated background of a starry sky. The starry sky could also be interpreted as a starry view of outer space, which makes the background more flexible in terms of how you use it in games.

The StarryBackground class is derived from the Background class, which means that it inherits member variables and methods from the Background class. However, the StarryBackground class requires its own constructor, as well as its own version of the Update() and Draw() methods. The StarryBackground class also adds some new member variables to the equation, which are used to manage the twinkling stars in the background. Listing 18.4 contains the code for the StarryBackground class.

LISTING 18.4 The StarryBackground Class Is Used to Create an Animated Background of a Starry Sky

```
1: class StarryBackground : Background
2: {
3: protected:
4:    // Member Variables
5:    int        m_iNumStars;
6:    int        m_iTwinkleDelay;
```

18

LISTING 18.4 Continued

```
 7:    POINT     m_ptStars[100];
 8:    COLORREF  m_crStarColors[100];
 9:
10: public:
11:    // Constructor(s)/Destructor
12:            StarryBackground(int iWidth, int iHeight, int iNumStars = 100,
13:                int iTwinkleDelay = 50);
14:    virtual ~StarryBackground();
15:
16:    // General Methods
17:    virtual void  Update();
18:    virtual void  Draw(HDC hDC);
19: };
```

The most important member variable in the StarryBackground class is m_iNumStars, which keeps track of how many stars appear on the background (line 5). This number is stored as a variable as opposed to a constant because you might want to vary the number of stars in different games. The m_iTwinkleDelay member variable is used to control how fast the stars twinkle (line 6)—the longer the delay, the slower they twinkle. So, setting a small value for the twinkle delay causes the stars to twinkle rapidly, which isn't very realistic. You'll find out in a moment that there is a default twinkle delay that I've found to be reasonably realistic in most situations.

The stars themselves are stored in two different member variables, m_ptStars and m_crStarColors. The m_ptStars variable is an array of points that stores the location of each individual star (line 7). You still need to keep track of the color of each star, which is a shade of gray that can vary between black and bright white. The m_crStarColors array stores the color of each star and corresponds directly to the stars stored in the m_ptStars array (line 8). Notice that both arrays are created with 100 elements, which means that you can't have more than 100 stars in the starry background.

Moving right along, the constructor for the StarryBackground class accepts several arguments to describe the starry background. More specifically, it allows you to provide the width, height, number of stars, and twinkle delay for the background (lines 12 and 13). It's important to note that the number of stars and twinkle delay arguments have default values, which you might find suitable for your games. You can also use your own trial and error approach to deciding exactly how many stars you like, as well as what kind of twinkle delay results in a good look for the twinkling stars.

The constructor for the StarryBackground class is shown in Listing 18.5 and reveals how the stars are created.

LISTING 18.5   The `StarryBackground::StarryBackground()` Constructor Is Used to Create a Starry Background

```
 1: StarryBackground::StarryBackground(int iWidth, int iHeight, int iNumStars,
 2:   int iTwinkleDelay) : Background(iWidth, iHeight, 0)
 3: {
 4:   // Initialize the member variables
 5:   m_iNumStars = min(iNumStars, 100);
 6:   m_iTwinkleDelay = iTwinkleDelay;
 7:
 8:   // Create the stars
 9:   for (int i = 0; i < iNumStars; i++)
10:   {
11:     m_ptStars[i].x = rand() % iWidth;
12:     m_ptStars[i].y = rand() % iHeight;
13:     m_crStarColors[i] = RGB(128, 128, 128);
14:   }
15: }
```

The `StarryBackground()` constructor first initializes the `m_iNumStars` member variable, making sure not to allow it to be set any higher than 100 (line 5). The twinkle delay is then set (line 6), and the star creation process begins. The creation of the stars involves looping through the number of stars (line 9), and then setting the position of each star to a random value (lines 11 and 12), as well as setting the color of each star to a neutral color (line 13). By neutral color, I mean a shade of gray that isn't too bright or too dark.

Once the stars are created in the constructor, you can turn your attention to the `Update()` and `Draw()` methods, which are really the most important part of the `StarryBackground` class. Listing 18.6 contains the code for these methods.

LISTING 18.6   The `StarryBackground::Update()` and `StarryBackground::Draw()` Methods Handle the Updating and Drawing of a Starry Background

```
 1: void StarryBackground::Update()
 2: {
 3:   // Randomly change the shade of the stars so that they twinkle
 4:   int iRGB;
 5:   for (int i = 0; i < m_iNumStars; i++)
 6:     if ((rand() % m_iTwinkleDelay) == 0)
 7:     {
 8:       iRGB = rand() % 256;
 9:       m_crStarColors[i] = RGB(iRGB, iRGB, iRGB);
10:     }
11: }
12:
13: void StarryBackground::Draw(HDC hDC)
```

18

LISTING 18.6 Continued

```
14: {
15:   // Draw the solid black background
16:   RECT    rect = { 0, 0, m_iWidth, m_iHeight };
17:   HBRUSH  hBrush = CreateSolidBrush(RGB(0, 0, 0));
18:   FillRect(hDC, &rect, hBrush);
19:   DeleteObject(hBrush);
20:
21:   // Draw the stars
22:   for (int i = 0; i < m_iNumStars; i++)
23:     SetPixel(hDC, m_ptStars[i].x, m_ptStars[i].y, m_crStarColors[i]);
24: }
```

The Update() method in this code is responsible for causing the stars to twinkle. This is accomplished by randomly changing the color of each star to a different shade of gray. The stars are looped through (line 5), and the twinkle delay is used as the basis for determining if the color of a star should be changed (line 6). If so, a random number is selected between 0 and 255 (line 8), and this color is used for each of the three color components to establish a new color for the star (line 9).

 When the three different components of a color (red, green, and blue) are set to the same number, the resulting color is a shade of gray. For example, the color (128, 128, 128) is medium gray. On the other hand, the color (0, 0, 0) is black, whereas (255, 255, 255) is white.

The Draw() method for the StarryBackground class is used to draw the background, and involves first drawing a solid black rectangle, followed by drawing the individual stars. The black rectangle is drawn with a call to FillRect() (line 18), which you saw earlier in the book. The more interesting code occurs near the end of the method, and consists of a loop that draws each individual star with a call to SetPixel() (lines 22 and 23). The SetPixel() function is a Win32 function that sets an individual pixel to a specified color.

Building the Roids Program Example

As with every new improvement to the game engine, new concepts only fully make sense when you see them in action. The remainder of the hour shows you how to put the new background classes to use in a program example called Roids. The Roids program example simulates an asteroid field by displaying several animated asteroid sprites over an animated starry background. Not surprisingly, the StarryBackground class is used as the basis for the background in the Roids program.

Writing the Program Code

The Roids program begins with the Roids.h header file, which declares global variables that are important to the program. Take a look at Listing 18.7 to see these variables.

LISTING 18.7   The Roids.h Header File Imports Several Header Files and Declares Global Variables Required for the Background and Asteroid Sprites

```
 1: #pragma once
 2:
 3: //-------------------------------------------------------------
 4: // Include Files
 5: //-------------------------------------------------------------
 6: #include <windows.h>
 7: #include "Resource.h"
 8: #include "GameEngine.h"
 9: #include "Bitmap.h"
10: #include "Sprite.h"
11: #include "Background.h"
12:
13: //-------------------------------------------------------------
14: // Global Variables
15: //-------------------------------------------------------------
16: HINSTANCE          _hInstance;
17: GameEngine*        _pGame;
18: HDC                _hOffscreenDC;
19: HBITMAP            _hOffscreenBitmap;
20: Bitmap*            _pAsteroidBitmap;
21: StarryBackground*  _pBackground;
```

The first variable unique to the Roids program is _pAsteroidBitmap (line 20), which is a bitmap for an asteroid image. This image is actually a series of frame images for an asteroid that appears to be tumbling when it is animated. A total of 14 frames are in the asteroid image, as you find out in a moment when you create the asteroid sprites. The other important global variable in the Roids program is the _pBackground variable, which stores a pointer to a StarryBackground object (line 21). This object serves as the background for the program, as you soon find out.

The GameStart() function is where the Roids program really gets rolling because it is responsible for creating bitmaps and sprites, not to mention the starry background. Listing 18.8 shows the code for this function.

18

LISTING 18.8   The `GameStart()` Function Creates and Loads the Asteroid Bitmap, the Starry Background, and the Asteroid Sprites

```
 1: void GameStart(HWND hWindow)
 2: {
 3:   // Seed the random number generator
 4:   srand(GetTickCount());
 5:
 6:   // Create the offscreen device context and bitmap
 7:   _hOffscreenDC = CreateCompatibleDC(GetDC(hWindow));
 8:   _hOffscreenBitmap = CreateCompatibleBitmap(GetDC(hWindow),
 9:     _pGame->GetWidth(), _pGame->GetHeight());
10:   SelectObject(_hOffscreenDC, _hOffscreenBitmap);
11:
12:   // Create and load the asteroid bitmap
13:   HDC hDC = GetDC(hWindow);
14:   _pAsteroidBitmap = new Bitmap(hDC, IDB_ASTEROID, _hInstance);
15:
16:   // Create the starry background
17:   _pBackground = new StarryBackground(500, 400);
18:
19:   // Create the asteroid sprites
20:   RECT    rcBounds = { 0, 0, 500, 400 };
21:   Sprite* pSprite;
22:   pSprite = new Sprite(_pAsteroidBitmap, rcBounds, BA_WRAP);
23:   pSprite->SetNumFrames(14);
24:   pSprite->SetFrameDelay(1);
25:   pSprite->SetPosition(250, 200);
26:   pSprite->SetVelocity(-3, 1);
27:   _pGame->AddSprite(pSprite);
28:   pSprite = new Sprite(_pAsteroidBitmap, rcBounds, BA_WRAP);
29:   pSprite->SetNumFrames(14);
30:   pSprite->SetFrameDelay(2);
31:   pSprite->SetPosition(250, 200);
32:   pSprite->SetVelocity(3, -2);
33:   _pGame->AddSprite(pSprite);
34:   pSprite = new Sprite(_pAsteroidBitmap, rcBounds, BA_WRAP);
35:   pSprite->SetNumFrames(14);
36:   pSprite->SetFrameDelay(3);
37:   pSprite->SetPosition(250, 200);
38:   pSprite->SetVelocity(-2, -4);
39:   _pGame->AddSprite(pSprite);
40: }
```

The first few sections of code in the `GameStart()` function should be familiar to you from other program examples, so I'll spare you a recap. Instead, let's jump straight to the line of code that creates the `StarryBackground` object (line 17). As you can see, the starry background is set to a size of 500 by 400, which is the same size of the game screen. Because no other arguments are provided to the new object, the default values of 100 for the number of stars and 50 for the twinkle delay are assumed.

The remainder of the GameStart() function focuses on the creation of the asteroid sprites. Notice that the number of frames for each of these sprites is set to 14 (lines 23, 39, and 35), which indicates that 14 frame images are stored in the image for the asteroid. Also, the frame delay of each sprite is set differently so that the asteroids appear to tumble at different speeds (lines 24, 30, and 36). Beyond those settings, nothing is tricky or otherwise noteworthy regarding the asteroid sprites.

The GamePaint()function is responsible for drawing the graphics in the Roids program, as shown in Listing 18.9.

LISTING 18.9 The GamePaint() Function Draws the Starry Background and the Asteroid Sprites

```
1: void GamePaint(HDC hDC)
2: {
3:   // Draw the background
4:   _pBackground->Draw(hDC);
5:
6:   // Draw the sprites
7:   _pGame->DrawSprites(hDC);
8: }
```

The important line of code worth paying attention to here is the line that calls the Draw() method on the StarryBackground object (line 4). As long as the background is drawn before the sprites, everything works great.

The final function on the Roids agenda is GameCycle(),which takes care of updating the animated graphics in the program. Because the background is animated, it too must be updated in GameCycle() function, as shown in Listing 18.10.

LISTING 18.10 The GameCycle() Function Updates the Starry Background and Asteroid Sprites, and then Repaints the Game Screen

```
1: void GameCycle()
2: {
3:   // Update the background
4:   _pBackground->Update();
5:
6:   // Update the sprites
7:   _pGame->UpdateSprites();
8:
9:   // Obtain a device context for repainting the game
```

LISTING 18.10   Continued

```
10:   HWND   hWindow = _pGame->GetWindow();
11:   HDC    hDC = GetDC(hWindow);
12:
13:   // Paint the game to the offscreen device context
14:   GamePaint(_hOffscreenDC);
15:
16:   // Blit the offscreen bitmap to the game screen
17:   BitBlt(hDC, 0, 0, _pGame->GetWidth(), _pGame->GetHeight(),
18:     _hOffscreenDC, 0, 0, SRCCOPY);
19:
20:   // Cleanup
21:   ReleaseDC(hWindow, hDC);
22: }
```

The background is the first thing updated in the GameCycle() function (line 4), and this simply involves a call to the Update() method on the StarryBackground class. This call is sufficient enough to cause the entire background to come alive with twinkling stars. If you don't believe me, try commenting out this line of code and see what happens to the background—no animation, and therefore not much excitement!

Testing the Finished Product

Granted, the Roids program example isn't quite up to par with the classic Asteroids game. In fact, Roids isn't a game at all. The reason for this is because I wanted to focus on the specific task of using an animated background without the distraction of trying to assemble a complete game. If you're dying to build another complete game, your wishes will be answered in the next hour. But for now, take a look at Figure 18.2 to see the Roids program in action.

FIGURE 18.2

The asteroid sprites in the Roids program tumble over an animated starry background thanks to the new background classes in the game engine.

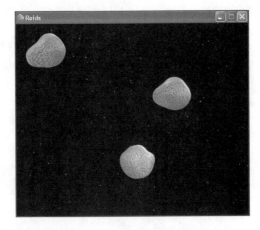

In addition to noticing how effective the twinkling stars are at presenting an interesting space background, hopefully you're now appreciating the power of animated sprites. This has to do with the fact that the animated asteroids in the Roids program are considerably smoother and more detailed than the animated guys in the Battle Office 2 game where you first learned about animated sprites. It's starting to become clear that you can get some surprisingly powerful visual effects out of the game engine when you combine an animated background with high quality sprite graphics.

Summary

Although you've certainly included backgrounds in several of the program examples and games that you've developed throughout the book thus far, this hour took a closer look at the role of backgrounds and why they are so important to games. You also found out about the main types of backgrounds, and what kinds of games demand each of them. The remainder of the hour focused on adding background support to the game engine in the form of two new classes, Background and StarryBackground. You now have a few classes you can reuse in your own games, as well as the knowledge to create custom animated backgrounds of your own.

The next hour accumulates much of what you've learned throughout the book in an example game called Meteor Defense. If you're familiar at all with the classic Missile Command game, you'll no doubt appreciate the Meteor Defense game.

18

Q&A

Q How does the twinkle delay in the Roids example cause the twinkling of the stars to take place at different speeds?

A The twinkle delay isn't a delay in a sense that it establishes a counter that counts down at a constant rate. Instead, the twinkle delay alters the probability that a star's color will be randomly changed. As an example, a twinkle rate of 1 means that a star's color will change every game cycle. Increasing the twinkle delay lessens the odds that a star's color will be changed. More specifically, a twinkle delay of 20 means that a star's color will only change an average of 1 in every 20 game cycles. Similarly, the default value of 50 for the twinkle delay in the StarryBackground class means that the color of a star is changed once in every 50 game cycles. However, because there are 100 stars in the Roids program, an average of two stars are being changed in every game cycle, which still results in a fair amount of twinkling when you consider that there are 30 game cycles per second.

Q How do I create my own custom animated backgrounds?

A The best way to create your own custom backgrounds is to model them after the StarryBackground class. Just copy the source code files for the StarryBackground class, and modify them to accommodate the needs of your specific background. Keep in mind that the Update() and Draw() methods are the two primary interfaces used to interact with the background from the perspective of a game. So, you'll want to make sure that all your animation code takes place in the Update() method and that the background is sufficiently painted in the Draw() method. Beyond that, it's pretty much anything goes when it comes to creating your own custom animated backgrounds!

Workshop

The Workshop is designed to help you anticipate possible questions, review what you've learned, and begin learning how to put your knowledge into practice. The answers to the quiz can be found in Appendix A, "Quiz Answers."

Quiz

1. What are the four main types of backgrounds used in games?

2. Why is the Update() method in the Background class empty?

3. How many stars is the StarryBackground class capable of showing?

Exercises

1. Change the number of stars in the Roids program example to see how they impact the appearance of the starry background.

2. Try a few different values for the twinkle delay in the Roids program example to see how they change the twinkling of the stars. You might decide that a different delay looks more realistic to you.

HOUR 19

Example Game: Meteor Defense

This hour guides you through the design and development of another complete game. You've spent the past couple of hours learning how to animate the appearance of sprites and spruce up the background of games, and it's now time to put this knowledge to work in an entirely new game. The game is called Meteor Defense, and it is loosely based on the classic Missile Command arcade game. Seeing as how there have been several news reports in the past few years about the potential of a significant meteor collision with the Earth, I thought it might make a neat premise for a game. It wouldn't necessarily be a bad idea to have a missile-based system for stopping incoming meteors, which is the premise behind the game Meteor Defense.

In this hour, you'll learn:

- About the conceptual overview of the Meteor Defense game
- How to design the Meteor Defense game
- How to add a few new sprite features to the game engine

- What it takes to build the Meteor Defense game
- How much fun it can be testing a new game

How Does the Game Play?

One of the classic arcade games that many people remember is Missile Command, which involves the defense of a group of cities against a nuclear attack. The nuclear attack involves missiles that travel down from the top of the screen toward the cities at the bottom. Your job is to fire upon the missiles and destroy them before they reach the cities. Although Missile Command made for an interesting game in the era of the hit movie *War Games*, the threat of nuclear attack is somewhat diminished these days, at least in terms of what most of us perceive as a realistic threat. However, there has been increasing talk in the past few years of the possibility of a meteor striking the Earth and causing major damage.

The premise of the game you develop in this hour is similar to Missile Command in that you're defending helpless cities against an incoming threat. In this case, however, the threat is giant meteors, not nuclear warheads. The Meteor Defense game employs a game play strategy similar to Missile Command in that you fire missiles at the incoming meteors to stop them from destroying the cities below. As you'll find out, the critical skill to becoming a good player at Meteor Defense (and Missile Command as well) is learning how to target a meteor and give a missile time to get there. In other words, you often have to lead a meteor by a certain distance to give the missile time to get there and make contact.

The object of Meteor Defense is to simply protect the cities against the incoming meteors for as long as possible. One interesting aspect of the game is that you lose points whenever you fire a missile, which makes it important to be efficient when you fire on the meteors. In other words, if you unleash missiles indiscriminately, you will no doubt protect the cities but your score will suffer. This is a subtle way to discourage sloppy game play. Small touches like this can often make a game much more appealing to serious game players.

Designing the Game

The design of the Meteor Defense game flows directly from the overview of the game that you just went through. The game is well suited for the starry background that you created and used in previous hours. It's also fairly obvious that the meteors should be represented by animated sprites similar to those found in the Roids program example from the previous hour. Because you must be able to detect a collision between a meteor and a city, the cities also need to be modeled as sprites even though they don't move. Representing cities as sprites also gives you the freedom to hide them whenever they are destroyed by a meteor.

In case you were wondering, the terms meteor, meteorite, and meteoroid are all closely related. A *meteoroid* is a chunk of rock in space that ranges in size from a speck of dust to 100 meters across. A *meteor* is the bright flash of light generated by a meteoroid when it travels through Earth's atmosphere. And finally, a *meteorite* is a meteor that has survived the transition through Earth's atmosphere and comes to rest on the Earth's surface.

The missiles in the game are ideal candidates for sprites because they move and collide with meteors. This is generally a good rule of thumb when it comes to deciding which graphical objects should be represented as sprites and which ones can simply be placed in the background: If the object needs to move, animate, or collide with other objects, it should be a sprite. A good application of this test is the guns used to fire missiles in the Meteor Defense game. The guns don't move, they don't animate, and it isn't important to detect a collision between them and anything else. Therefore, you can simply include the guns in the background image for the game.

Wait a minute, I just mentioned using a background image, but I already said that the background is the starry background from earlier in the book. The Meteor Defense game actually uses a hybrid background in that it displays an image of the ground over the starry background. This allows you to get the benefits of the animated starry sky while also showing the ground where the cities are located—not to mention the guns that fire the missiles. To help you get a feel for how the Meteor Defense game is laid out, take a look at Figure 19.1.

19

FIGURE 19.1

The Meteor Defense game consists of a starry background, a ground image with guns, several cities, incoming meteors, and missiles.

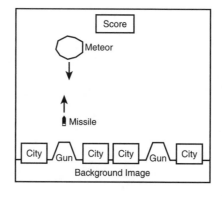

The figure reveals how the guns are part of the background image that appears along the bottom edge of the game screen. Keep in mind that a starry background still appears in the majority of the screen—the background image just shows the ground where the cities are located. The city sprites are laid on top of the edge of the ground so that they blend into the ground image. The missile and meteor sprites move around on top of the starry background, while the score is displayed centered near the top of the game screen. One last piece of the game not shown in the figure is the target sprite that you guide with the mouse, much like the target sprite you saw in the Battle Office game from earlier in the book.

Now that you understand the basics of the game and how it is laid out, it's time to examine what kinds of sprites need to be used. Following is a list of the sprites that go into the Meteor Defense game:

- City sprites
- Meteor sprites
- Missile sprites
- Explosion sprites
- Target sprite

The city sprites appear along the bottom of the screen, as shown in Figure 19.1. The meteor sprites are created at random, and fall from the top of the screen toward the cities at the bottom. The missile sprites are fired from the gun locations on the screen upward toward the meteors. I haven't mentioned the explosion sprites yet, and that's because there isn't a whole lot to them. An explosion sprite appears whenever a meteor is blown up or a city is destroyed and involves displaying an animation of a fiery explosion. Finally, the target sprite appears as a crosshair that you guide with the mouse to aim missiles that you launch via the left mouse button.

Beyond the sprites, the Meteor Defense game also requires several bitmaps. Following are the seven bitmap images required of the game:

- Background ground image
- City image
- Meteor image (animated)
- Missile image
- Explosion image (animated)
- Crosshair target image
- Game over image

These images should make sense based on the description of the game and the sprites that you've learned about.

With the graphical objects squared away, you need to turn your attention to the other information that must be maintained by the game. For example, the score needs to be maintained throughout the game, as well as the number of remaining cities; the game ends when all four of the cities are destroyed by meteors. This is a game in which it is important to increase the difficulty level as the game progresses. So, it's important to store the difficulty level of the game and gradually increase it as the player continues to keep his cities protected. The last critical piece of information to maintain is a Boolean variable to keep track of whether the game is over.

To recap, the design of the Meteor Defense game has led us to the following pieces of information that must be managed by the game:

- The number of cities remaining
- The score
- The difficulty level
- A Boolean game over variable

With this information in mind, you're now almost ready to take the big step of assembling the code for the Meteor Defense game. However, there is a modification you need to make to the game engine to support a critical feature of the game, and ultimately improve the game engine for future games.

Enhancing Sprites in the Game Engine

19

If you're a particularly inquisitive person, you might have wondered how exactly the explosion sprites will work in the game. The animation part is simple enough because the Sprite class in the game engine now allows you to flip through a series of animation images. However, an explosion sprite must cycle through its animation frames and then immediately go away, which sounds simple but presents a problem for the game engine. The problem is that there currently is no mechanism for a sprite to hide or kill itself automatically when it is no longer needed. Granted, you can kill a sprite from within the game code, but how would you keep track of when the frame animation for an explosion is finished?

The real problem I'm talking about here is that of allowing a sprite to animate through one cycle and then go away. The game engine doesn't currently support this feature, but it's not too difficult to add. Without this feature, there is no straightforward way to use a sprite such as an explosion that must cycle through its animation once and then exit the game. The key to adding this feature to the game engine is including a couple of new variables to the Sprite class:

```
BOOL m_bDying;
BOOL m_bOneCycle;
```

The m_bDying member variable determines whether a sprite has been flagged as dying. In other words, normal sprites have their m_bDying variable set to FALSE, whereas a sprite on the way out has it set to TRUE. The cool thing about this variable is that it allows you to kill a sprite at any time by simply setting the variable to TRUE. Of course, this requires some additional code in both the Sprite and GameEngine classes to make it actually work.

The second member variable, m_bOneCycle, indicates whether a sprite should animate once through its frames and then kill itself. Because this variable only makes sense within the context of a frame animated sprite, it is set when you call the SetNumFrames() method. You see how the SetNumFrames() method is modified to account for the m_bOneCycle variable in a moment.

For now, let's take a look at how the two new Sprite member variables are initialized in the Sprite() constructors:

```
m_bDying = FALSE;
m_bOneCycle = FALSE;
```

As you might expect, the default value of both variables is FALSE, which makes sprites behave normally.

The m_bDying member variable can be set to TRUE through the Kill() method, which is really just an accessor method because all it does is set the variable:

```
void Kill()   { m_bDying = TRUE; };
```

This method now gives you a clean and efficient means of killing any sprite—with the security of knowing that it will be properly removed from the sprite list maintained by the game engine. This is a crucial aspect of destroying a sprite because the sprite list in the game engine would go haywire if you were to simply delete a sprite from memory and not remove it from the list. The Kill() method provides a clean interface for carrying out this task.

Whereas the Kill() method provides an immediate way to kill a sprite that can be useful in some situations, the more elegant approach is to allow a sprite to kill itself when it finishes cycling through its frame animations. The UpdateFrame() method now supports this feature by examining the m_bOneCycle variable, and then setting the m_bDying variable accordingly. The original version of this method simply set the m_iCurFrame variable to 0 so that the animation starts over, which this method still does if the m_bOneCycle variable is FALSE. However, if the m_bOneCycle variable is TRUE, the m_bDying variable is set to TRUE, which starts the sprite on a path to destruction.

The m_bOneCycle variable is set in the SetNumFrames() method, which now looks like this:

```
void SetNumFrames(int iNumFrames, BOOL bOneCycle = FALSE);
```

As you can see, the SetNumFrames() method now includes a second argument for setting the m_bOneCycle member variable. To help make the transition to using the new version of the method easier, the bOneCycle argument is given a default value of FALSE. This allows you to use the method just as you've already grown accustomed. However, if you want to create a sprite that cycles through its animation once and then goes away, just pass TRUE as the second argument to SetNumFrames().

Getting back to the killing of a sprite via the m_bDying member variable, the place where the murder plot unfolds is in the Update() method, which is shown in Listing 19.1.

LISTING 19.1   The Sprite::Update() Method Kills a Sprite if It Is Flagged as Dying

```
 1: SPRITEACTION Sprite::Update()
 2: {
 3:   // See if the sprite needs to be killed
 4:   if (m_bDying)
 5:     return SA_KILL;
 6:
 7:   // Update the frame
 8:   UpdateFrame();
 9:
10:   ...
11: }
```

If you recall, the Sprite::Update() method is actually a large method, so I'm only showing you the beginning of it here because this is all that has changed. The method now checks the value of the m_bDying member variable (line 4), and then returns SA_KILL if it is set to TRUE (line 5). If you recall from earlier in the book, SA_KILL is a sprite action you created that notifies the game engine when a sprite needs to be killed. Prior to now, it was only used to kill a sprite when it encounters a boundary.

Simply killing a sprite isn't quite sufficient when it comes to improving the game engine for future games. You'll find out later in the hour that it can be incredibly useful to know when a sprite is being destroyed—regardless of why it is being destroyed. For example, when a meteor sprite is destroyed, you can create an explosion sprite to show the destruction of the meteor. The notification of a sprite being killed is made possible through the SpriteDying() function, which is called whenever a sprite is dying:

```
void SpriteDying(Sprite* pSprite);
```

Understand that the SpriteDying() function is a function that you must provide as part of a game. In other words, it is designed to house game-specific code that responds to particular types of sprites dying within a game.

The final change to the game engine to support the new sprite killing features appears within the GameEngine class in the UpdateSprites() method, which now includes a call to SpriteDying() that notifies a game of a sprite being destroyed and removed from the sprite list. This gives the game a chance to respond to the sprite's demise and carry out any appropriate actions.

Building the Game

You can breathe a sigh of relief because you're finished making changes to the game engine for a little while. However, the real challenge of putting together the Meteor Defense game now awaits you. Fortunately, the game isn't too difficult to understand because you've already worked through a reasonably detailed game design. The next few sections guide you through the development of the game's code and resources.

Writing the Game Code

The code for the Meteor Defense game begins in the MeteorDefense.h header file, which is responsible for declaring the global variables used throughout the game, as well as a couple of useful functions. Listing 19.2 contains the code for this file.

LISTING 19.2   The MeteorDefense.h Header File Declares Global Variables and Game-Specific Functions for the Meteor Defense Game

```
 1: #pragma once
 2:
 3: //---------------------------------------------------------------
 4: // Include Files
 5: //---------------------------------------------------------------
 6: #include <windows.h>
 7: #include "Resource.h"
 8: #include "GameEngine.h"
 9: #include "Bitmap.h"
10: #include "Sprite.h"
11: #include "Background.h"
12:
```

LISTING 19.2 Continued

```
13: //---------------------------------------------------------------
14: // Global Variables
15: //---------------------------------------------------------------
16: HINSTANCE          _hInstance;
17: GameEngine*        _pGame;
18: HDC                _hOffscreenDC;
19: HBITMAP            _hOffscreenBitmap;
20: Bitmap*            _pGroundBitmap;
21: Bitmap*            _pTargetBitmap;
22: Bitmap*            _pCityBitmap;
23: Bitmap*            _pMeteorBitmap;
24: Bitmap*            _pMissileBitmap;
25: Bitmap*            _pExplosionBitmap;
26: Bitmap*            _pGameOverBitmap;
27: StarryBackground*  _pBackground;
28: Sprite*            _pTargetSprite;
29: int                _iNumCities, _iScore, _iDifficulty;
30: BOOL               _bGameOver;
31:
32: //---------------------------------------------------------------
33: // Function Declarations
34: //---------------------------------------------------------------
35: void NewGame();
36: void AddMeteor();
```

As the listing reveals, the global variables for the Meteor Defense game largely consist of the different bitmaps that are used throughout the game. The starry background for the game is declared after the bitmaps (line 27), followed by the crosshair target sprite (line 28). Member variables storing the number of remaining cities, the score, and the difficulty level are then declared (line 29), along with the familiar game over Boolean variable (line 30).

The NewGame() function declared in the MeteorDefense.h file is important because it is used to set up and start a new game (line 35). Unlike the GameStart() function, which performs critical initialization tasks such as loading bitmaps, the NewGame() function deals with actually starting a new game once everything else is in place. The AddMeteor() function is a support function used to simplify the task of adding meteor sprites to the game (line 36). You find out more about how these functions work later in the hour.

The initialization of the game variables primarily takes place in the GameStart() function, which is shown in Listing 19.3.

19

LISTING 19.3 The `GameStart()` Function Initializes the Bitmaps and Background for the Game, and Calls the `NewGame()` Function

```
 1: void GameStart(HWND hWindow)
 2: {
 3:   // Seed the random number generator
 4:   srand(GetTickCount());
 5:
 6:   // Create the offscreen device context and bitmap
 7:   _hOffscreenDC = CreateCompatibleDC(GetDC(hWindow));
 8:   _hOffscreenBitmap = CreateCompatibleBitmap(GetDC(hWindow),
 9:     _pGame->GetWidth(), _pGame->GetHeight());
10:   SelectObject(_hOffscreenDC, _hOffscreenBitmap);
11:
12:   // Create and load the bitmaps
13:   HDC hDC = GetDC(hWindow);
14:   _pGroundBitmap = new Bitmap(hDC, IDB_GROUND, _hInstance);
15:   _pTargetBitmap = new Bitmap(hDC, IDB_TARGET, _hInstance);
16:   _pCityBitmap = new Bitmap(hDC, IDB_CITY, _hInstance);
17:   _pMeteorBitmap = new Bitmap(hDC, IDB_METEOR, _hInstance);
18:   _pMissileBitmap = new Bitmap(hDC, IDB_MISSILE, _hInstance);
19:   _pExplosionBitmap = new Bitmap(hDC, IDB_EXPLOSION, _hInstance);
20:   _pGameOverBitmap = new Bitmap(hDC, IDB_GAMEOVER, _hInstance);
21:
22:   // Create the starry background
23:   _pBackground = new StarryBackground(600, 450);
24:
25:   // Play the background music
26:   _pGame->PlayMIDISong(TEXT("Music.mid"));
27:
28:   // Start the game
29:   NewGame();
30: }
```

After loading the bitmaps for the game (lines 14–20) and creating the starry background (line 23), the `GameStart()` function starts playing the background music (line 26). The function then finishes by calling the `NewGame()` function to start a new game (line 29).

The `GameEnd()` function plays a complementary role to the `GameStart()` function and cleans up after the game. Listing 19.4 contains the code for the `GameEnd()` function.

LISTING 19.4 The `GameEnd()` Function Cleans Up After the Game

```
 1: void GameEnd()
 2: {
 3:   // Close the MIDI player for the background music
 4:   _pGame->CloseMIDIPlayer();
 5:
```

LISTING 19.4 Continued

```
 6:    // Cleanup the offscreen device context and bitmap
 7:    DeleteObject(_hOffscreenBitmap);
 8:    DeleteDC(_hOffscreenDC);
 9:
10:    // Cleanup the bitmaps
11:    delete _pGroundBitmap;
12:    delete _pTargetBitmap;
13:    delete _pCityBitmap;
14:    delete _pMeteorBitmap;
15:    delete _pMissileBitmap;
16:    delete _pExplosionBitmap;
17:    delete _pGameOverBitmap;
18:
19:    // Cleanup the background
20:    delete _pBackground;
21:
22:    // Cleanup the sprites
23:    _pGame->CleanupSprites();
24:
25:    // Cleanup the game engine
26:    delete _pGame;
27: }
```

The first step in the GameEnd() function is to close the MIDI player (line 4). The bitmaps and sprites are then wiped away (lines 7–20), as well as the background (line 20). Finally, the sprites are cleaned up (line 23) and the game engine is destroyed (line 26).

The game screen in the Meteor Defense game is painted by the GamePaint() function, which is shown in Listing 19.5.

19

LISTING 19.5 The GamePaint() Function Draws the Background, the Ground Bitmap, the Sprites, the Score, and the Game Over Message

```
 1: void GamePaint(HDC hDC)
 2: {
 3:    // Draw the background
 4:    _pBackground->Draw(hDC);
 5:
 6:    // Draw the ground bitmap
 7:    _pGroundBitmap->Draw(hDC, 0, 398, TRUE);
 8:
 9:    // Draw the sprites
10:    _pGame->DrawSprites(hDC);
11:
12:    // Draw the score
13:    TCHAR szText[64];
```

LISTING 19.5 Continued

```
14:    RECT  rect = { 275, 0, 325, 50 };
15:    wsprintf(szText, "%d", _iScore);
16:    SetBkMode(hDC, TRANSPARENT);
17:    SetTextColor(hDC, RGB(255, 255, 255));
18:    DrawText(hDC, szText, -1, &rect, DT_SINGLELINE | DT_CENTER | DT_VCENTER);
19:
20:    // Draw the game over message, if necessary
21:    if (_bGameOver)
22:      _pGameOverBitmap->Draw(hDC, 170, 150, TRUE);
23: }
```

This GamePaint() function is responsible for drawing all the graphics for the game. The
function begins by drawing the starry background (line 4), followed by the ground image
(line 7). The sprites are drawn next (line 10), followed by the score (lines 13–18). Notice
that the score text is set to white (line 17), whereas the background is set to transparent
for drawing the score so that the starry sky shows through the numbers in the score (line
16). The GamePaint() function finishes up by drawing the game over image, if necessary
(lines 21–22).

The GameCycle() function works closely with GamePaint() to update the game's sprites
and reflect the changes onscreen. Listing 19.6 shows the code for the
GameCycle()function.

LISTING 19.6 The GameCycle() Function Randomly Adds Meteors to the Game
Based on the Difficulty Level

```
1: void GameCycle()
2: {
3:   if (!_bGameOver)
4:   {
5:     // Randomly add meteors
6:     if ((rand() % _iDifficulty) == 0)
7:       AddMeteor();
8:
9:     // Update the background
10:    _pBackground->Update();
11:
12:    // Update the sprites
13:    _pGame->UpdateSprites();
14:
15:    // Obtain a device context for repainting the game
16:    HWND  hWindow = _pGame->GetWindow();
17:    HDC   hDC = GetDC(hWindow);
18:
```

LISTING 19.6 Continued

```
19:      // Paint the game to the offscreen device context
20:      GamePaint(_hOffscreenDC);
21:
22:      // Blit the offscreen bitmap to the game screen
23:      BitBlt(hDC, 0, 0, _pGame->GetWidth(), _pGame->GetHeight(),
24:        _hOffscreenDC, 0, 0, SRCCOPY);
25:
26:      // Cleanup
27:      ReleaseDC(hWindow, hDC);
28:    }
29: }
```

Aside from the standard GameCycle() code that you've grown accustomed to seeing, this function doesn't contain a whole lot of additional code. The new code involves randomly adding new meteors, which is accomplished by calling the AddMeteor() function after using the difficulty level to randomly determine if a meteor should be added (lines 6–7).

The MouseButtonDown() function is where most of the game logic for the Meteor Defense game is located, as shown in Listing 19.7.

LISTING 19.7 The MouseButtonDown() Function Launches a Missile Sprite Toward the Location of the Mouse Pointer

```
1: void MouseButtonDown(int x, int y, BOOL bLeft)
2: {
3:   if (!_bGameOver && bLeft)
4:   {
5:     // Create a new missile sprite and set its position
6:     RECT    rcBounds = { 0, 0, 600, 450 };
7:     int     iXPos = (x < 300) ? 144 : 449;
8:     Sprite* pSprite = new Sprite(_pMissileBitmap, rcBounds, BA_DIE);
9:     pSprite->SetPosition(iXPos, 365);
10:
11:     // Calculate the velocity so that it is aimed at the target
12:     int iXVel, iYVel = -6;
13:     y = min(y, 300);
14:     iXVel = (iYVel * ((iXPos + 8) - x)) / (365 - y);
15:     pSprite->SetVelocity(iXVel, iYVel);
16:
17:     // Add the missile sprite
18:     _pGame->AddSprite(pSprite);
19:
20:     // Play the fire sound
21:     PlaySound((LPCSTR)IDW_FIRE, _hInstance, SND_ASYNC |
22:       SND_RESOURCE | SND_NOSTOP);
23:
```

19

LISTING **19.7** Continued

```
24:    // Update the score
25:    _iScore = max(--_iScore, 0);
26:  }
27:  else if (_bGameOver && !bLeft)
28:    // Start a new game
29:    NewGame();
30: }
```

The `MouseButtonDown()` function handles firing a missile toward the target. The function first checks to make sure that the game isn't over and that the player clicked the left mouse button (line 3). If so, a missile sprite is created based on the position of the mouse (lines 6–9). The position is important first because it determines which gun is used to fire the missile—the left gun fires missiles toward targets on the left side of the game screen, whereas the right gun takes care of the right side of the screen. The target position is also important because it determines the trajectory and therefore the velocity of the missile (lines 12–15).

After the missile sprite is created, the `MouseButtonDown()` function adds it to the game engine (line 18). A sound effect is then played to indicate that the missile has been fired (lines 21 and 22). Earlier in the hour during the design of the game, I mentioned how the score would be decreased slightly with each missile firing, which discourages inaccuracy in firing missiles because you can only build up your score by destroying meteors with the missiles. The score is decreased upon firing a missile, as shown in line 25. The last code in the `MouseButtonDown()` function takes care of starting a new game via the right mouse button if the game is over (lines 27–29).

Another mouse-related function used in the Meteor Defense game is `MouseMove()`, which is used to move the crosshair target sprite so that it tracks the mouse pointer. This is necessary so that you are always in control of the target sprite with the mouse. Listing 19.8 shows the code for the `MouseMove()` function.

LISTING 19.8 The `MouseMove()` Function Tracks the Mouse Cursor with the Target Sprite

```
1: void MouseMove(int x, int y)
2: {
3:   // Track the mouse with the target sprite
4:   _pTargetSprite->SetPosition(x - (_pTargetSprite->GetWidth() / 2),
5:     y - (_pTargetSprite->GetHeight() / 2));
6: }
```

The target sprite is made to follow the mouse pointer by simply calling the
SetPosition() method on the sprite and passing in the mouse coordinates (lines 4 and
5). The position of the target sprite is calculated so that the target sprite always appears
centered on the mouse pointer.

The SpriteCollision() function is called in response to sprites colliding, and is
extremely important in the Meteor Defense game, as shown in Listing 19.9.

LISTING 19.9 The SpriteCollision() Function Detects and Responds to
Collisions Between Missiles, Meteors, and Cities

```
 1: BOOL SpriteCollision(Sprite* pSpriteHitter, Sprite* pSpriteHittee)
 2: {
 3:   // See if a missile and a meteor have collided
 4:   if ((pSpriteHitter->GetBitmap() == _pMissileBitmap &&
 5:     pSpriteHittee->GetBitmap() == _pMeteorBitmap) ||
 6:     (pSpriteHitter->GetBitmap() == _pMeteorBitmap &&
 7:     pSpriteHittee->GetBitmap() == _pMissileBitmap))
 8:   {
 9:     // Kill both sprites
10:     pSpriteHitter->Kill();
11:     pSpriteHittee->Kill();
12:
13:     // Update the score
14:     _iScore += 6;
15:     _iDifficulty = max(50 - (_iScore / 10), 5);
16:   }
17:
18:   // See if a meteor has collided with a city
19:   if (pSpriteHitter->GetBitmap() == _pMeteorBitmap &&
20:     pSpriteHittee->GetBitmap() == _pCityBitmap)
21:   {
22:     // Play the big explosion sound
23:     PlaySound((LPCSTR)IDW_BIGEXPLODE, _hInstance, SND_ASYNC |
24:       SND_RESOURCE);
25:
26:     // Kill both sprites
27:     pSpriteHitter->Kill();
28:     pSpriteHittee->Kill();
29:
30:     // See if the game is over
31:     if (--_iNumCities == 0)
32:       _bGameOver = TRUE;
33:   }
34:
35:   return FALSE;
36: }
```

19

The first collision detected in the SpriteCollision() function is the collision between a missile and a meteor (lines 4–7). You might be a little surprised by how the code is determining what kinds of sprites are colliding. In order to distinguish between sprites, you need a piece of information that uniquely identifies each type of sprite in the game. The bitmap pointer turns out being a handy and efficient way to identify and distinguish between sprites. Getting back to the collision between a missile and a meteor, the SpriteCollision() function kills both sprites (lines 10 and 11) and increases the score because a meteor has been successfully hit with a missile (line 14).

The difficulty level is also modified so that it gradually increases along with the score (line 15). It's worth pointing out that the game gets harder as the difficulty level decreases, with the maximum difficulty being reached at a value of 5 for the _iDifficulty global variable; the game is pretty much raining meteors at this level, which corresponds to reaching a score of 450. You can obviously tweak these values to suit your own tastes if you decide that the game gets difficult too fast or if you want to stretch out the time it takes for the difficulty level to increase.

The second collision detected in the SpriteCollision() function is between a meteor and a city (lines 19 and 20). If this collision takes place, a big explosion sound is played (lines 23 and 24), and both sprites are killed (lines 27 and 28). The number of cities is then checked to see if the game is over (lines 31 and 32) .

Earlier in the hour, you added a new SpriteDying()function to the game engine that allows you to respond to a sprite being destroyed. This function comes in quite handy in the Meteor Defense game because it allows you to conveniently create an explosion sprite any time a meteor sprite is destroyed. Listing 19.10 shows how this is made possible by the SpriteDying() function.

LISTING 19.10   The SpriteDying() Function Creates an Explosion Whenever a Meteor Sprite Is Destroyed

```
 1: void SpriteDying(Sprite* pSprite)
 2: {
 3:   // See if a meteor sprite is dying
 4:   if (pSprite->GetBitmap() == _pMeteorBitmap)
 5:   {
 6:     // Play the explosion sound
 7:     PlaySound((LPCSTR)IDW_EXPLODE, _hInstance, SND_ASYNC |
 8:       SND_RESOURCE | SND_NOSTOP);
 9:
10:     // Create an explosion sprite at the meteor's position
11:     RECT rcBounds = { 0, 0, 600, 450 };
12:     RECT rcPos = pSprite->GetPosition();
13:     Sprite* pSprite = new Sprite(_pExplosionBitmap, rcBounds);
```

LISTING **19.10**   Continued

```
14:      pSprite->SetNumFrames(12, TRUE);
15:      pSprite->SetPosition(rcPos.left, rcPos.top);
16:      _pGame->AddSprite(pSprite);
17:    }
18: }
```

The bitmap pointer of the sprite is used again to determine if the dying sprite is indeed a meteor sprite (line 4). If so, an explosion sound effect is played (lines 7 and 8), and an explosion sprite is created (lines 11–16). Notice that the SetNumFrames() method is called to set the number of animation frames for the explosion sprite, as well as to indicate that the sprite should be destroyed after finishing its animation cycle (line 14). If you recall, this is one of the other important sprite-related features you added to the game engine earlier in the hour.

The remaining two functions in the Meteor Defense game are support functions that are completely unique to the game. The first one is NewGame(), which performs the steps necessary to start a new game (Listing 19.11).

LISTING **19.11**   The NewGame() Function Gets Everything Ready for a New Game

```
 1: void NewGame()
 2: {
 3:   // Clear the sprites
 4:   _pGame->CleanupSprites();
 5:
 6:   // Create the target sprite
 7:   RECT rcBounds = { 0, 0, 600, 450 };
 8:   _pTargetSprite = new Sprite(_pTargetBitmap, rcBounds, BA_STOP);
 9:   _pTargetSprite->SetZOrder(10);
10:   _pGame->AddSprite(_pTargetSprite);
11:
12:   // Create the city sprites
13:   Sprite* pSprite = new Sprite(_pCityBitmap, rcBounds);
14:   pSprite->SetPosition(2, 370);
15:   _pGame->AddSprite(pSprite);
16:   pSprite = new Sprite(_pCityBitmap, rcBounds);
17:   pSprite->SetPosition(186, 370);
18:   _pGame->AddSprite(pSprite);
19:   pSprite = new Sprite(_pCityBitmap, rcBounds);
20:   pSprite->SetPosition(302, 370);
21:   _pGame->AddSprite(pSprite);
22:   pSprite = new Sprite(_pCityBitmap, rcBounds);
23:   pSprite->SetPosition(490, 370);
24:   _pGame->AddSprite(pSprite);
25:
```

19

LISTING 19.11   Continued

```
26:   // Initialize the game variables
27:   _iScore = 0;
28:   _iNumCities = 4;
29:   _iDifficulty = 50;
30:   _bGameOver = FALSE;
31:
32:   // Play the background music
33:   _pGame->PlayMIDISong();
34: }
```

The NewGame() function starts off by clearing the sprite list (line 4), which is important because you don't really know what might have been left over from the previous game. The crosshair target sprite is then created (lines 7–10), as well as the city sprites (lines 13–24). The global game variables are then set (lines 27–30), and the background music is started up (line 33).

The AddMeteor() function is shown in Listing 19.12, and its job is to add a new meteor to the game at a random position and aimed at a random city.

LISTING 19.12   The AddMeteor() Function Adds a New Meteor at a Random Position and Aimed at a Random City

```
 1: void AddMeteor()
 2: {
 3:   // Create a new meteor sprite and set its position
 4:   RECT    rcBounds = { 0, 0, 600, 390 };
 5:   int     iXPos = rand() % 600;
 6:   Sprite* pSprite = new Sprite(_pMeteorBitmap, rcBounds, BA_DIE);
 7:   pSprite->SetNumFrames(14);
 8:   pSprite->SetPosition(iXPos, 0);
 9:
10:   // Calculate the velocity so that it is aimed at one of the cities
11:   int iXVel, iYVel = (rand() % 4) + 3;
12:   switch(rand() % 4)
13:   {
14:   case 0:
15:     iXVel = (iYVel * (56 - (iXPos + 50))) / 400;
16:     break;
17:   case 1:
18:     iXVel = (iYVel * (240 - (iXPos + 50))) / 400;
19:     break;
20:   case 2:
21:     iXVel = (iYVel * (360 - (iXPos + 50))) / 400;
22:     break;
23:   case 3:
```

LISTING 19.12 Continued

```
24:     iXVel = (iYVel * (546 - (iXPos + 50))) / 400;
25:     break;
26:   }
27:   pSprite->SetVelocity(iXVel, iYVel);
28:
29:   // Add the meteor sprite
30:   _pGame->AddSprite(pSprite);
31: }
```

The AddMeteor() function adds a new meteor to the game, and its code is probably a little longer than you expected simply because it tries to add meteors so that they are aimed at cities, as opposed to just zinging around the game screen aimlessly. Granted, a real meteor wouldn't target a city; but this is a game, and the idea is to challenge the player by forcing them to save cities from incoming meteors. So, in the world of Meteor Defense, the meteors act more like incoming nuclear warheads in that they tend to target cities.

The function begins by creating a meteor sprite and setting it to a random position along the top edge of the game screen (lines 4–8). The big section of code in the middle of the function takes care of setting the meteor's velocity so that it targets one of the four cities positioned along the bottom of the screen (lines 11–27). I realize that this code looks a little tricky, but all that's going on is some basic trigonometry to figure out what velocity is required to get the meteor from point A to point B, where point A is the meteor's random position and point B is the position of the city. The AddMeteor() function ends by adding the new meteor sprite to the game engine (line 30).

That wraps up the code for the Meteor Defense game, which hopefully doesn't have your head spinning too much. Now you just need to put the resources together and you can start playing.

Testing the Game

It's safe to congratulate yourself at this point because you've now worked through the design and development of the Meteor Defense game, and you can now bask in the glory of playing the game. Granted, playing a game for the first time is certainly more of a test than it is a true playing experience, but in this case I can vouch that the game works pretty well. Figure 19.2 shows the game at the start, with a couple of meteors hurtling toward cities.

19

FIGURE **19.2**

The Meteor Defense game gets started with a couple of meteors hurtling at the cities.

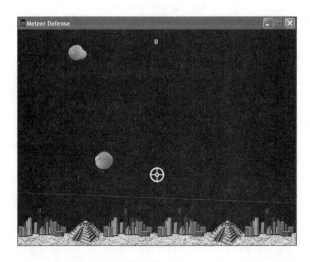

Saving the cities from the meteors involves targeting the meteors and blasting them with missiles. When you successfully blast a meteor, you'll see an explosion as the missile and meteor both are destroyed (see Figure 19.3)

FIGURE **19.3**

Successfully destroying a meteor results in an explosion being displayed.

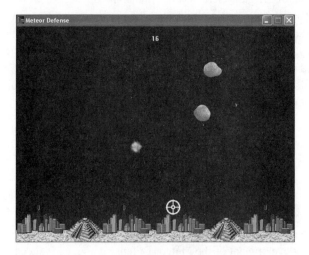

When the game progresses as more meteors fall, you'll eventually start losing cities to the meteors. Figure 19.4 shows an example of how the meteors can begin to overwhelm you late in the game.

When you finally lose all four cities to the meteors, the game ends. Figure 19.5 shows the end of the game, which involves displaying the game over image on the screen on top of the other game graphics.

FIGURE 19.4

As the game progresses, you tend to lose cities as the meteors start to overwhelm you.

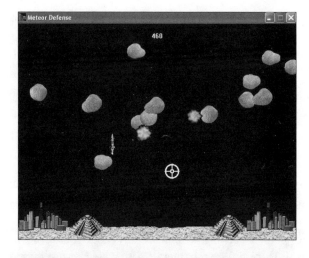

FIGURE 19.5

When all four cities are destroyed, the game ends and the game over image is displayed.

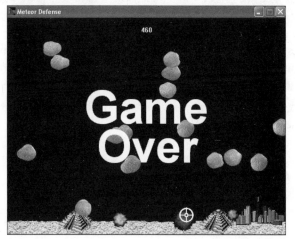

19

Although it's sad to think that you've ultimately failed to save the cities in the Meteor Defense game, you can sleep well knowing that you can always right-click the mouse to start over and take another stab at it.

Summary

This hour carried you through the design and construction of another complete game, Meteor Defense. The Meteor Defense game took advantage of the new game engine features you developed in the previous two hours, and also took a leap forward in terms of showing you how to create engaging action games. The game makes heavy use of sprites, including frame animation—not to mention a great deal of collision detection. Perhaps most important is the fact that the Meteor Defense game can serve as a great starting point for creating an action game of your own that takes full advantage of the game engine.

This hour concludes this part of the book. The next part of the book tackles artificial intelligence, or AI, which allows you to make your games more intelligent.

Q&A

Q Why was it necessary to add the `SpriteDying()` function to the game engine?

A The `SpriteDying()` function is important because it provides a means of carrying out a particular task in response to a sprite being destroyed. Keep in mind that the sprites in the game engine in many ways coexist in their own little world, and at times it can be difficult to interact with them because they are shielded from you. One of the limitations of the game engine prior to this hour was that there was no way to know when a sprite was being destroyed. The `SpriteDying()` function gives you a glimpse into the "sprite world" and lets you know whenever one of them is being killed. In the Meteor Defense game, this is important because it allows the game to create an explosion whenever a meteor is destroyed.

Q How does the `_iDifficulty` global variable control the difficulty level of the Meteor Defense game?

A The `_iDifficulty` global variable is used to determine how often new meteors are added. To make the game harder, you just add meteors more rapidly, which is carried out in the game by decreasing the value of the `_iDifficulty` variable in response to the score getting higher.

Workshop

The Workshop is designed to help you anticipate possible questions, review what you've learned, and begin learning how to put your knowledge into practice. The answers to the quiz can be found in Appendix A, "Quiz Answers."

Quiz

1. What's the difference between a meteor, a meteorite, and a meteoroid?
2. What is the purpose of the `m_bOneCycle` member variable in the `Sprite` class?
3. How do you destroy a sprite and have it removed from the sprite list in the game engine?

Exercises

1. Modify the calculation of the score and difficulty level so that the Meteor Defense game lasts a little longer and allows you to attain higher scores.

2. Modify the game so that you lose points and temporarily lose the ability to fire from one of the guns if the gun is hit by a meteor. You don't need to change the guns to sprites in order to add this feature—just use the position of the meteor when it is destroyed to determine if it hit one of the guns.

19

PART VI

Adding Brains to Your Games

Hours

Hour **20**

Teaching Games to Think

Creating truly engaging games is often a matter of effectively mimicking human thought within the confines of a computer. Because you no doubt want your games to be engaging, you need at least a basic understanding of how to give games some degree of brain power. This hour focuses on understanding the fundamental theories of artificial intelligence and how they can be applied to games. You will hopefully leave this hour with the fundamental knowledge required to begin implementing artificial intelligence strategies in your own games. You will definitely leave this hour with a practical example of how to incorporate simple AI into a program example.

In this hour, you'll learn:

- About the basics of artificial intelligence (AI)
- About the different types of AI used in games
- How to develop an AI strategy of your own
- How to put AI to work in a practical example program involving sprites that interact with each other "intelligently"

Understanding Artificial Intelligence

Artificial intelligence (*AI*) is defined as the techniques used to emulate the human thought process in a computer. This is a pretty general definition for AI, as it should be; AI is a very broad research area—with game-related AI being a relatively small subset of the whole of AI knowledge. The goal in this hour is not to explore every facet of AI because that would easily fill an entire book, but rather to explore the fundamental concepts behind AI as they apply to games.

As you might have already guessed, human thought is no simple process to emulate, which explains why AI is such a broad area of research. Even though there are many different approaches to AI, all of them basically boil down to attempting to make human decisions within the confines of a computer "brain." Most traditional AI systems use a variety of information-based algorithms to make decisions, just as people use a variety of previous experiences and mental rules to make a decision. In the past, the information-based AI algorithms were completely *deterministic*, which means that every decision could be traced back to a predictable flow of logic. Figure 20.1 shows an example of a purely logical human thought process. Obviously, human thinking doesn't work this way at all; if we were all this predictable, it would be quite a boring planet!

FIGURE 20.1

A completely logical human thought process involves nothing more than reason.

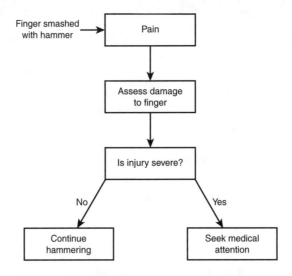

Eventually, AI researchers realized that the deterministic approach to AI wasn't sufficient to accurately model human thought. Their focus shifted from deterministic AI models to more realistic AI models that attempted to factor in the subtle complexities of human thought, such as best-guess decisions. In people, these types of decisions can result from a combination of past experience, personal bias, or the current state of emotion—in addition to the completely logical decision making process. Figure 20.2 shows an example of this type of thought process. The point is that people don't always make scientifically predictable decisions based on analyzing their surroundings and arriving at a logical conclusion. The world would probably be a better place if we did act like this, but again, it would be awfully boring!

FIGURE 20.2

A more realistic human thought process adds emotion and a dash of irrationality with reason.

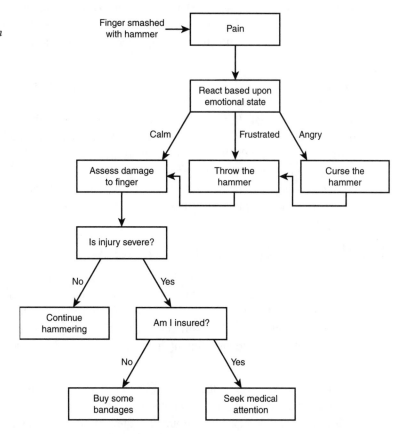

The logic flow in Figure 20.1 is an ideal scenario in which each decision is made based on a totally objective logical evaluation of the situation. Figure 20.2 shows a more realistic scenario, which factors in the emotional state of the person, as well as a financial angle (the question of whether the person has insurance). Examining the second scenario from a completely logical angle, it makes no sense for the person to throw the hammer because that only slows down the task at hand. However, this is a completely plausible

20

and fairly common human response to pain and frustration. For an AI carpentry system to effectively model this situation, there would definitely have to be some hammer throwing code in there somewhere!

This hypothetical thought example is meant to give you a tiny clue as to how many seemingly unrelated things go into forming a human thought. Likewise, it only makes sense that it should take an extremely complex AI system to effectively model human thought. Most of the time, this statement is true. However, the word "effectively" allows for a certain degree of interpretation, based on the context of the application requiring AI. For your purposes, effective AI simply means AI that makes computer game objects more realistic and engaging.

More recent AI research has been focused at tackling problems similar to the ones illustrated by the hypothetical carpentry example. One particularly interesting area is *fuzzy logic*, which attempts to make "best-guess" decisions rather than the concrete decisions of traditional AI systems. Another interesting AI research area in relation to games is *genetic algorithms*, which try to model evolved thought similarly to how scientists believe nature evolves through genetics. A game using genetic algorithms would theoretically have computer opponents that learn as the game progresses, providing the human player with a seemingly never ending series of challenges.

Exploring Types of Game AI

There are many different types of AI systems and even more specific algorithms that carry out those systems. Even when you limit AI to the world of games, there is still a wide range of information and options from which to choose when it comes to adding AI to a game of your own. Many different AI solutions are geared toward particular types of games—with a plethora of different possibilities that can be applied in different situations.

What I'm getting at is that there is no way to just present a bunch of AI algorithms and tell you which one goes with which particular type of game. Rather, it makes more sense to give you the theoretical background on a few of the most important types of AI, and then let you figure out how they might apply to your particular gaming needs. Having said all that, I've broken game-related AI down into three fundamental types:

- Roaming AI
- Behavioral AI
- Strategic AI

Please understand that these three types of AI are in no way meant to encompass all the AI approaches used in games; they are simply the most common types to recognize and use. Feel free to do your own research and expand on these if you find AI to be an interesting topic worthy of further study.

Roaming AI

Roaming AI refers to AI that models the movement of game objects—that is, the decisions game objects make that determine how they roam around a virtual game world. A good example of roaming AI is in shoot-em-up space games such as the classic arcade game Galaga, where aliens often tend to track and go after the player. Similarly, aliens that fly around in a predetermined pattern are also implemented using roaming AI. Basically, roaming AI is used whenever a computer-controlled object must make a decision to alter its current path—either to achieve a desired result in the game or simply to conform to a particular movement pattern. In the Galaga example, the desired result is following a pattern while also attempting to collide with and damage the player's ship.

Implementing roaming AI is usually fairly simple; it typically involves altering an object's velocity or position (the alien) based on the position of another object (the player's ship). The roaming movement of the object can also be influenced by random or predetermined patterns. Three different types of roaming AI exist: chasing, evading, and patterned. The next few sections explore these types of roaming AI in more detail.

Chasing

Chasing is a type of roaming AI in which a game object tracks and goes after another game object or objects. Chasing is the approach used in many shoot-em-up games, where an alien chases after the player's ship. It is implemented by altering the alien's velocity or position based on the current position of the player's ship. Following is an example of a simple chasing algorithm involving an alien and a ship:

```
if (iXAlien > iXShip)
  iXAlien--;
else if (iXAlien < iXShip)
  iXAlien++;
if (iYAlien > iYShip)
  iYAlien--;
else if (iYAlien < iYShip)
  iYAlien++;
```

As you can see, the XY position (`iXAlien` and `iYAlien`) of the alien is altered based on where the ship is located (`iXShip` and `iYShip`). The only potential problem with this code is that it could work too well; the alien will hone in on the player with no hesitation, basically giving the player no chance to dodge it. This might be what you want, but

20

more than likely, you want the alien to fly around a little while it chases the player. You probably also want the chasing to be a little imperfect, giving the player at least some chance of out-maneuvering the alien. In other words, you want the alien to have a *tendency* to chase the player without going in for an all-out blitz.

One method of smoothing out the chasing algorithm is to throw a little randomness into the equation, like this:

```
if ((rand() % 3) == 0) {
  if (iXAlien > iXShip)
    iXAlien--;
  else if (iXAlien < iXShip)
    iXAlien++;
}
if ((rand() % 3) == 0) {
  if (iYAlien > iYShip)
    iYAlien--;
  else if (iYAlien < iYShip)
    iYAlien++;
}
```

In this code, the alien has a one in three chance of tracking the player in each direction. Even with only a one in three chance, the alien will still tend to chase the player aggressively, while allowing the player a fighting chance at getting out of the way. You might think that a one in three chance doesn't sound all that effective, but keep in mind that the alien only alters its path to chase the player. A smart player will probably figure this out and change directions frequently.

If you aren't too fired up about the random approach to leveling off the chase, you probably need to look into patterned movement. But you're getting a little ahead of yourself; let's take a look at evading first.

Evading

Evading is the logical counterpart to chasing; it is another type of roaming AI in which a game object specifically tries to get away from another object or objects. Evading is implemented in a similar manner to chasing, as the following code shows:

```
if (iXAlien > iXShip)
  iXAlien++;
else if (iXAlien < iXShip)
  iXAlien--;
if (iYAlien > iYShip)
  iYAlien++;
else if (iYAlien < iYShip)
  iYAlien--;
```

This code basically does the opposite of the code used by the chasing algorithm—with the only differences being the unary operators (++, --) used to change the alien's position so that it runs away, as opposed to chasing. Similar to chasing, evading can be softened using randomness or patterned movement. A good example of evading is the ghosts in the classic arcade game Pac Man, who run away from the player when you eat a power pellet. Of course, the Pac-Man ghosts also take advantage of chasing when you don't have the ability to eat them.

Another good example of using the evading algorithm would be a computer-controlled version of the player's ship in a space game with a computer player. If you think about it, the player is using the evading algorithm to dodge the aliens; it's just implemented by hitting keys rather than in a piece of computer-controlled code. If you want to provide a demo mode in a game like this where the computer plays itself, you would use an evading algorithm to control the player's ship. Hour 23, "Showing Off Your Game with Demo Mode," shows you exactly how to create a demo mode for your games.

Patterned Roaming

Patterned movement refers to a type of roaming AI that uses a predefined set of movements for a game object. Good examples of patterned movement are the aliens in the classic Galaga arcade game, which perform all kinds of neat aerobatics on their way down the screen. Patterns can include circles, figure eights, zigzags, or even more complex movements. An even simpler example of patterned movement is the Space Invaders game, where a herd of aliens slowly and methodically inch across and down the screen.

 In truth, the aliens in Galaga use a combined approach of both patterned and chasing movement; although they certainly follow specific patterns, the aliens still make sure to come after the player whenever possible. Additionally, as the player moves into higher levels, the roaming AI starts favoring chasing over patterned movement in order to make the game harder. This is a really neat usage of combined roaming AI. This touches on the concept of behavioral AI, which you learn about in the next section.

20

Patterns are usually stored as an array of velocity or position offsets (or multipliers) that are applied to an object whenever patterned movement is required of it, like this:

```
int iZigZag[2][2] = { {3, 2}, {-3, 2} };
iXAlien += iZigZag[iPatternStep][0];
iYAlien += iZigZag[iPatternStep][1];
```

This code shows how to implement a very simple vertical zigzag pattern. The integer array iZigZag contains pairs of XY offsets used to apply the pattern to the alien. The `iPatternStep` variable is an integer representing the current step in the pattern. When this pattern is applied, the alien moves in a vertical direction at a speed of 2 pixels per game cycle, while zigzagging back and forth horizontally at a speed of 3 pixels per game cycle.

Behavioral AI

Although the types of roaming AI strategies are pretty neat in their own right, a practical gaming scenario often requires a mixture of all three. *Behavioral AI* is another fundamental type of gaming AI that often uses a mixture of roaming AI algorithms to give game objects specific behaviors. Using the trusted alien example again, what if you want the alien to chase some times, evade other times, follow a pattern still other times, and maybe even act totally randomly every once in a while? Another good reason for using behavioral AI is to alter the difficulty of a game. For example, you could favor a chasing algorithm more than random or patterned movement to make aliens more aggressive in higher levels of a space game.

To implement behavioral AI, you would need to establish a set of behaviors for the alien. Giving game objects behaviors isn't too difficult, and usually involves establishing a ranking system for each type of behavior present in the system, and then applying it to each object. For example, in the alien system, you would have the following behaviors: chase, evade, fly in a pattern, and fly randomly. For each different type of alien, you would assign different percentages to the different behaviors, thereby giving them each different personalities. For example, an aggressive alien might have the following behavioral breakdown: chase 50% of the time, evade 10% of the time, fly in a pattern 30% of the time, and fly randomly 10% of the time. On the other hand, a more passive alien might act like this: chase 10% of the time, evade 50% of the time, fly in a pattern 20% of the time, and fly randomly 20% of the time.

This behavioral approach works amazingly well and yields surprising results considering how simple it is to implement. A typical implementation simply involves a `switch` statement or nested `if-else` statements to select a particular behavior. A sample implementation for the behavioral aggressive alien would look like this:

```
int iBehavior = abs(rand() % 100);
if (iBehavior < 50)
  // chase
else if (iBehavior < 60)
  // evade
else if (iBehavior < 90)
  // fly in a pattern
else
  // fly randomly
```

As you can see, creating and assigning behaviors is open to a wide range of creativity. One of the best sources of ideas for creating game object behaviors is the primal responses common in the animal world (and unfortunately all too often in the human world, too). As a matter of fact, a simple fight or flight behavioral system can work wonders when applied intelligently to a variety of game objects. Basically, just use your imagination as a guide and create as many unique behaviors as you can dream up.

Strategic AI

The final fundamental type of game AI I want to mention is *strategic AI*, which is basically any AI designed to play a game with a fixed set of well-defined rules. For example, a computer-controlled chess player would use strategic AI to determine each move based on trying to improve the chances of winning the game. Strategic AI tends to vary more based on the nature of the game simply because it is so tightly linked to the rules of the game. Even so, there are established and successful approaches to applying strategic AI to many general types of games, such as games played on a rectangular board with pieces. Checkers and chess immediately come to mind as fitting into this group, and likewise have a rich history of AI research devoted to them.

Strategic AI, especially for board games, typically involves some form of *look-ahead* approach to determining the best move to make. The look-ahead is usually used in conjunction with a fixed table of predetermined moves. For a look-ahead to make sense, however, there must be a method of looking at the board at any state and calculating a score. This is known as *weighting*, and is often the most difficult part of implementing strategic AI in a board game. As an example of how difficult weighting can be, watch a game of chess or checkers and try to figure out who is winning after every single move. Then go a step further and think about trying to calculate a numeric score for each player at each point in the game. Obviously, near the end of the game it gets easier, but early on it is very difficult to tell who is winning simply because there are so many different things that can happen. Attempting to quantify the state of the game in a numeric score is even more difficult.

Nevertheless, there are ways to successfully calculate a weighted score for strategic games. Using a look-head approach with scoring, a strategic AI algorithm can test, for every possible move for each player, multiple moves into the future and determine which move is the best. This move is often referred to as the "least worst" move rather than the best because the goal typically is to make the move that helps the other player the least rather than the other way around. Of course, the end result is basically the same, but it is an interesting way to look at a game, nevertheless. Even though look-ahead approaches to implementing strategic AI are useful in many cases, they can require a fair amount of processing if very much depth is required (in other words, if the computer player needs to be very smart).

20

To better understand strategic AI, consider the case of a computer Backgammon player. The computer player has to choose two or four moves from possibly several dozen, as well as decide whether to double or resign. A practical Backgammon program might assign weights to different combinations of positions and calculate the value of each position reachable from the current position and dice roll. A scoring system would then be used to evaluate the worth of each potential position, which gets back to the often difficult proposition of scoring, even in a game such as Backgammon, with simple rules. Now apply this scenario to a hundred-unit war game—with every unit having unique characteristics, and the terrain and random factors complicating the issue still further. The optimal system of scoring simply cannot be determined in a reasonable amount of time, especially with the limited computing power of a workstation or PC.

The solution in these cases is to settle for a "good enough" move, rather than the "best" move. One of the best ways to develop the algorithm for finding the "good enough" move is to set up the computer to play both sides in a game, using a lot of variation between the algorithms and weights playing each side. Then sit back and let the two computer players battle it out and see which one wins the most. This approach typically involves a lot of tinkering and trial-and-error with the AI code, but it can result in very good computer players.

Developing an AI Strategy

Now that you understand the basic concepts behind AI in games, you can start thinking about an AI strategy for your own specific games. When deciding how to implement AI in a game, you need to do some preliminary work to assess exactly what type and level of AI you think is warranted. You need to determine what level of computer response suits your needs, abilities, resources, and project time frame.

If your main concern is developing a game that keeps human players entertained and challenged, go with the simplest AI possible. Actually, try to go with the simplest AI regardless of your goals because you can always enhance it in phases. If you think your game needs a type of AI that doesn't quite fit into any I've described, do some research and see whether something out there is closer to what you need. Most importantly, budget plenty of time for implementing AI because 90% of the time, it will take longer than you ever anticipated to get it all working at a level you are happy with.

What is the best way to get started? Start in small steps, of course. Many programmers like to write code as they design, and although that approach might work in some cases, I recommend at least some degree of preliminary design on paper. Furthermore, try to keep this design limited to a subset of the game's AI, such as a single computer opponent. Start with a small, simple map or grid and simple movement rules. Write the code to get a single opponent from point A to point B. Then add complications piece by piece, building onto a complete algorithm at each step. If you are careful to make each piece of the AI general and open enough to connect to other pieces, your final algorithms should be general enough to handle any conditions your game might encounter.

Getting back to more basic terms, a good way to build AI experience is to write a computer opponent for a simple board game, such as tic-tac-toe or checkers. Detailed AI solutions exist for many popular games, so you should be able to find them if you search around a little on the Web. Another good way to get some experience with AI is to modify an existing game in an attempt to make its computer-controlled characters a little smarter. For example, you could modify the Henway game so that the cars speed up and slow down deliberately to make it tougher on the chicken. You could also change the speed of the moving guys in the Battle Office game so that they speed up when you get close to shooting them.

Building the Roids 2 Program Example

Rather than modify an existing game to demonstrate AI programming, I decided that it would be better to demonstrate AI within the context of a program example that doesn't involve an objective. In other words, I wanted to create a program that you could tinker with without worrying about messing up the outcome of a game. The program I'm talking about is called Roids 2, and it's a revamped version of the Roids program from Hour 18. If you recall, the original Roids program displayed an animated asteroid field. You're now going to add a flying saucer to the program that is intelligent enough to dodge the asteroids, or at least do its best to dodge the asteroids.

The Roids 2 program example is very similar to the original Roids program, except for the addition of the flying saucer sprite. The remainder of the hour focuses on the development of this program, and how AI influences the flying saucer sprite.

Writing the Program Code

20

The Roids 2 program begins with the Roids.h header file, which declares global variables that are important to the program. More specifically, a flying saucer bitmap has been declared, along with sprites for the asteroids and the flying saucer:

```
Bitmap*        _pSaucerBitmap;
Sprite*        _pAsteroids[3];
Sprite*        _pSaucer;
```

The _pSaucerBitmap is a bitmap for the flying saucer image. The _pAsteroids and _pSaucer variables both store sprite pointers. These pointers are necessary so that you can compare the positions of the saucer and asteroids and alter the saucer's velocity; this is how you add "intelligence" to the flying saucer.

The Roids 2 program also includes a new helper function named UpdateSaucer(), which is responsible for updating the saucer sprite. Of course, the saucer sprite is already being updated in terms of its position and velocity in the game engine. However, in this case an additional update is taking place that alters the saucer's velocity based on its proximity to nearby asteroids. You learn exactly how this facet of the program works a little later in the hour.

The GameStart() function is similar to the previous version, except that it now contains code to initialize the flying saucer. Listing 20.1 shows the code for this function.

LISTING 20.1   The GameStart() Function Initializes the Flying Saucer Bitmap and Sprite

```
 1: void GameStart(HWND hWindow)
 2: {
 3:    // Seed the random number generator
 4:    srand(GetTickCount());
 5:
 6:    // Create the offscreen device context and bitmap
 7:    _hOffscreenDC = CreateCompatibleDC(GetDC(hWindow));
 8:    _hOffscreenBitmap = CreateCompatibleBitmap(GetDC(hWindow),
 9:      _pGame->GetWidth(), _pGame->GetHeight());
10:    SelectObject(_hOffscreenDC, _hOffscreenBitmap);
11:
12:    // Create and load the asteroid and saucer bitmaps
13:    HDC hDC = GetDC(hWindow);
14:    _pAsteroidBitmap = new Bitmap(hDC, IDB_ASTEROID, _hInstance);
15:    _pSaucerBitmap = new Bitmap(hDC, IDB_SAUCER, _hInstance);
16:
17:    // Create the starry background
18:    _pBackground = new StarryBackground(500, 400);
19:
20:    // Create the asteroid sprites
21:    RECT    rcBounds = { 0, 0, 500, 400 };
22:    _pAsteroids[0] = new Sprite(_pAsteroidBitmap, rcBounds, BA_WRAP);
23:    _pAsteroids[0]->SetNumFrames(14);
24:    _pAsteroids[0]->SetFrameDelay(1);
25:    _pAsteroids[0]->SetPosition(250, 200);
26:    _pAsteroids[0]->SetVelocity(-3, 1);
27:    _pGame->AddSprite(_pAsteroids[0]);
28:    _pAsteroids[1] = new Sprite(_pAsteroidBitmap, rcBounds, BA_WRAP);
29:    _pAsteroids[1]->SetNumFrames(14);
30:    _pAsteroids[1]->SetFrameDelay(2);
31:    _pAsteroids[1]->SetPosition(250, 200);
32:    _pAsteroids[1]->SetVelocity(3, -2);
```

LISTING 20.1 Continued

```
33:    _pGame->AddSprite(_pAsteroids[1]);
34:    _pAsteroids[2] = new Sprite(_pAsteroidBitmap, rcBounds, BA_WRAP);
35:    _pAsteroids[2]->SetNumFrames(14);
36:    _pAsteroids[2]->SetFrameDelay(3);
37:    _pAsteroids[2]->SetPosition(250, 200);
38:    _pAsteroids[2]->SetVelocity(-2, -4);
39:    _pGame->AddSprite(_pAsteroids[2]);
40:
41:    // Create the saucer sprite
42:    _pSaucer = new Sprite(_pSaucerBitmap, rcBounds, BA_WRAP);
43:    _pSaucer->SetPosition(0, 0);
44:    _pSaucer->SetVelocity(3, 1);
45:    _pGame->AddSprite(_pSaucer);
46: }
```

The changes to the GameStart() function primarily involve the addition of the flying saucer sprite. The saucer bitmap is first loaded (line 15), and then the saucer sprite is created and added to the game engine (lines 42–45). It's also worth pointing out that the asteroid sprite pointers are now being stored in the _pAsteroids array (lines 22, 28, and 34) because you need to reference them later when helping the saucer avoid hitting the asteroids.

The GameCycle() function in Roids 2 requires a slight modification to ensure that the flying saucer sprite is updated properly. This change involves the addition of a call to the UpdateSaucer() function, which is responsible for updating the velocity of the flying saucer sprite to help it dodge the asteroids.

Speaking of the UpdateSaucer() function, its code is shown in Listing 20.2.

LISTING 20.2 The UpdateSaucer() Function Updates the Flying Saucer's Velocity to Help It Dodge Asteroids

```
1: void UpdateSaucer()
2: {
3:   // Obtain the saucer's position
4:   RECT rcSaucer, rcRoid;
5:   rcSaucer = _pSaucer->GetPosition();
6:
7:   // Find out which asteroid is closest to the saucer
8:   int iXCollision = 500, iYCollision = 400, iXYCollision = 900;
9:   for (int i = 0; i < 3; i++)
10:  {
11:    // Get the asteroid position
12:    rcRoid = _pAsteroids[i]->GetPosition();
13:
```

20

LISTING 20.2 Continued

```
14:     // Calculate the minimum XY collision distance
15:     int iXCollisionDist = (rcSaucer.left +
16:       (rcSaucer.right - rcSaucer.left) / 2) -
17:       (rcRoid.left +
18:       (rcRoid.right - rcRoid.left) / 2);
19:     int iYCollisionDist = (rcSaucer.top +
20:       (rcSaucer.bottom - rcSaucer.top) / 2) -
21:       (rcRoid.top +
22:       (rcRoid.bottom - rcRoid.top) / 2);
23:     if ((abs(iXCollisionDist) < abs(iXCollision)) ||
24:       (abs(iYCollisionDist) < abs(iYCollision)))
25:       if ((abs(iXCollisionDist) + abs(iYCollisionDist)) < iXYCollision)
26:       {
27:         iXYCollision = abs(iXCollision) + abs(iYCollision);
28:         iXCollision = iXCollisionDist;
29:         iYCollision = iYCollisionDist;
30:       }
31:   }
32:
33:   // Move to dodge the asteroids, if necessary
34:   POINT ptVelocity;
35:   ptVelocity = _pSaucer->GetVelocity();
36:   if (abs(iXCollision) < 60)
37:   {
38:     // Adjust the X velocity
39:     if (iXCollision < 0)
40:       ptVelocity.x = max(ptVelocity.x - 1, -8);
41:     else
42:       ptVelocity.x = min(ptVelocity.x + 1, 8);
43:   }
44:   if (abs(iYCollision) < 60)
45:   {
46:     // Adjust the Y velocity
47:     if (iYCollision < 0)
48:       ptVelocity.y = max(ptVelocity.y - 1, -8);
49:     else
50:       ptVelocity.y = min(ptVelocity.y + 1, 8);
51:   }
52:
53:   // Update the saucer to the new position
54:   _pSaucer->SetVelocity(ptVelocity);
55: }
```

I realize that this function contains a lot of code, but if you take it a section at a time, it's really not too complex. First of all, let's understand how the UpdateSaucer() function is helping the flying saucer to dodge the asteroids. The idea is to check for the closest asteroid in relation to the saucer, and then alter the saucer's velocity so that it has a tendency to move in the opposite direction of the asteroid. I say "tendency" because you don't want the saucer to jerk and immediately start moving away from the asteroid. Instead, you gradually alter its velocity so that it appears to steer away from the asteroid. This is a subtle difference, but the effect is dramatic because it looks as if the saucer is truly steering through the asteroid field.

The first step in the UpdateSaucer() function is to obtain the position of the flying saucer (line 5). You can then loop through the asteroids and find out the minimum X and Y collision distance (lines 8 and 9), which is the closest distance between an asteroid and the saucer. Inside the loop, the asteroid position is first obtained (line 12), which is critical for determining the collision distance. The minimum XY collision distance is then calculated (lines 15–22) and used as the basis for determining if this asteroid is currently the closest one to the saucer. This is where the function gets a little tricky because you must add the X and Y components of the collision distance to see which asteroid is closer to the saucer (lines 23–30). This technique isn't flawless, but it helps to eliminate "false alarm" situations in which an asteroid is close to the saucer horizontally but far away vertically.

When the asteroid loop is exited, you have two pieces of important information to work with: the X collision distance and the Y collision distance. It's now possible to check and see if these distances are below a certain minimum distance that is required in order for the saucer to be in danger of colliding with an asteroid. My own trial-and-error testing led to a value of 60, but you might decide on a slightly different value in your own testing. In order to steer the saucer to safety horizontally, the X collision distance is checked to see if it is below the minimum distance of 60; in which case, the saucer's velocity is adjusted (lines 36–43). The same process is then repeated for the saucer's Y collision distance (lines 44–51). Finally, the new velocity of the saucer is set by calling the SetVelocity() method on the saucer sprite (line 54) .

Testing the Finished Product

The premise behind the Roids 2 program is to show how a certain degree of AI can be injected into a sprite object so that it can avoid other sprite objects. In this context, the evading sprite object is a flying saucer that is desperately trying to keep from colliding with asteroids in an asteroid field. Although you have to actually run the program yourself to see the flying saucer evade the asteroids, Figure 20.3 shows the saucer in the process of steering away from a close call.

20

FIGURE 20.3

FIGURE 20.3

The flying saucer in the Roids 2 program does its best to dodge the asteroids that are floating around the game screen.

This is one of those rare program examples that is actually fun to just sit back and watch because the program appears to have a mind of its own. In other words, you've created the logic for the flying saucer, and now you get to see how it responds in different situations. This is the part of the process of developing AI in games that is often frustrating because objects can do strange things that are quite unexpected at times. Even so, the flying saucer does a pretty good job of avoiding asteroids in the Roids 2 program.

Summary

If you find artificial intelligence to be a fascinating area of computer research, you hopefully enjoyed this hour. You learned about the three fundamental types of game AI (roaming, behavioral, and strategic), along with how they are used in typical gaming scenarios. As a game programmer with at least a passing interest in AI, your AI knowledge will likely grow a great deal as you encounter situations in which you can apply AI techniques. After you get comfortable with implementing the basics, you can move on to more advanced AI solutions based upon prior experience and research on the Web. I hope this hour at least provided you with a roadmap to begin your journey into the world of the computer mind.

The next hour applies your newfound AI knowledge to the most ambitious game in the book. The game is called Space Out, and it's a space shoot-em-up with a quirky cast of characters.

Q&A

Q **Everyone acts like computers are so smart, but you've made it sound like they're dumb. What gives?**

A Computers, in fact, are very "dumb" when it comes to what we humans refer to as thought. However, computers are very "smart" when it comes to mathematical calculations and algorithms. The trick with AI is to model the subtleties of human thought in such a way that the computer can do what it's good at, executing mathematical calculations and algorithms. The point is that thoughts we take for granted are often very difficult for computers simply because human thought takes into account an incredibly large number of subtle variables when arriving at even the simplest decision.

Q **If my game is designed to have only human players, do I even need to worry with AI?**

A Even though games with all human players might appear to not require any AI at first, it is often useful to control many of the background aspects of the game using simple AI. For example, consider a two player head-to-head space battle game. Even though you might not have any plans for computer ships, consider adding some AI to determine how the environment responds to the players' actions. For example, add a black hole near the more aggressive player from time to time, providing that player with more hassles than the other player. Although the intelligence required of a black hole is pretty weak by most AI standards, it could still use a simple chase algorithm to follow the player around.

Workshop

The Workshop is designed to help you anticipate possible questions, review what you've learned, and begin learning how to put your knowledge into practice. The answers to the quiz can be found in Appendix A, "Quiz Answers."

20

Quiz

1. What are the three types of roaming AI?
2. How does behavioral AI work?
3. In regard to strategic AI, what do the terms *look-ahead* and *weighting* mean?

Exercises

1. Play some video games with computer opponents and see whether you can tell which type of AI approach is being used.

2. Tinker with the AI code in the Roids 2 program example to see how changes to the minimum collision distance affect the movement of the flying saucer.

HOUR 21

Example Game: Space Out

This hour embarks yet again on the development of another complete game. The game is called Space Out, and it represents a culmination of everything you've learned about game programming throughout the book. Although this isn't the last hour of the book, this is the last complete game you'll be creating. The remaining hours focus on improving the Space Out game with some interesting features. This hour, however, explores the design and development of the basic Space Out game, which is a vertical space shoot-em-up. The closest arcade comparison I can make to Space Out is Galaga, but the aliens in Space Out don't move with as intricate of patterns as those in Galaga. Nevertheless, I think you'll find Space Out to be a fun and entertaining game, both from a programming and a playability perspective.

In this hour, you'll learn:

- About the basic premise behind the Space Out game
- How to design the Space Out game
- About the nuts and bolts of programming the Space Out game
- Why testing is still the most fun part of testing a new game

How Does the Game Play?

One of the most classic genres of video games has always been the vertical space shoot-em-up. Space Invaders started it all back in 1978, but many games followed and added their own unique contributions to the genre. One of the most enduring vertical space shooters is Galaga, which you learned about back in the introduction to Hour 9, "A Crash Course in Game Animation." In Galaga, a relentless sequence of invading aliens fly down from the top of the game screen and attack your ship, which is free to move horizontally across the bottom of the screen. The Space Out game that you develop in this hour is similar in some ways to Galaga, although the theme for the game is a little more whimsical.

In Space Out, you are the driver of a small green car on a trek across the desert. Whether you believe in UFOs, it's hard to argue that quite a few sightings seem to have occurred in remote desert places such as Roswell, New Mexico. For this reason, your traveler in the game can't seem to get away from a constant onslaught of alien visitors from above. Unfortunately, the aliens in Space Out are bent on putting an end to our traveler's trip. The cast of alien characters in the Space Out game are somewhat comical, and add a degree of whimsy to the game. Following are the three kinds of aliens that appear throughout the game:

- Blobbo the Galactic Ooze
- Jellybiafra (Jelly for short)
- Timmy the Space Worm

Granted, these probably aren't very realistic aliens when it comes to what you might imagine truly encountering in an extra-terrestrial sighting, but this game isn't about reality. Each of the aliens has its own style of attack, and they each fire different missiles. The idea here isn't to simulate a realistic alien invasion, but to have some fun with outlandish characters in the context of a vertical shoot-em-up.

 The characters and concept for the Space Out game were created by Rebecca Rose, a computer artist and game designer who has collaborated with me in the past on other game projects.

Designing the Game

Now that you understand the basic idea behind the game, let's focus on a few details regarding the design of the game. The player's car can move horizontally across the game screen, which means that its position is confined to the x axis. The player can shoot up vertically—with his Twinkie missiles terminating at the top of the screen, similar to the missiles in the Meteor Defense game from Hour 19, "Example Game: Meteor Defense."

The aliens in Space Out can move around in any direction and at different velocities. The Blobbo and Jelly aliens bounce off of the edges of the screen, while Timmy is allowed to wrap around and appear on the other side. This is because Timmy has a tendency to fly horizontally across the screen, whereas the others move around a little more randomly. All the aliens fire missiles down toward the player's car—with the missiles terminating when they strike the car or the ground. The aliens are immune from their own missiles, so they can't hit each other. This is a good thing for the aliens because they aren't very careful in terms of how they aim.

Space Out has no discrete levels and no real goal other than surviving. However, the difficulty level of the game does gradually increase as the player progresses through the game. The difficulty of the game increases by adding new aliens at a faster pace. Eventually the player will have his hands full trying to contend with a never-ending army of aliens. That's the whole fun of shoot-em-ups!

To help you get a feel for how the Space Out game is laid out, take a look at Figure 21.1.

FIGURE 21.1

The Space Out game consists of a starry background, a ground desert image, a car, aliens, and missiles that are fired between the car and aliens.

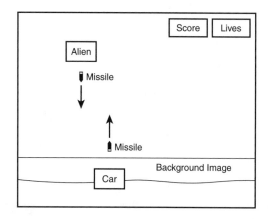

The figure shows the background image of the desert, which serves as a backdrop for the car to drive around on. The starry background still appears in the majority of the screen, whereas the background image shows the desert where the car drives around. The background image actually includes a horizontal band of sky that helps blend the desert landscape into the starry background. The car sprite moves around on top of the desert background image. The aliens appear in the sky and move around trying to hit the car by

21

firing various missiles. Of course, the car also fires missiles back at the aliens. The score for the game is displayed in the upper right corner of the game screen, along with the number of remaining lives (cars).

Now that you understand the basics of the game, it's important to examine the sprites that it requires. Following is a list of the sprites that go into the Space Out game:

- Car sprite
- Alien sprites
- Missile sprites (from the aliens and the car)
- Explosion sprites

The only type of sprite in this list that I haven't mentioned is the explosion sprite, which is used to show an alien being destroyed by a missile, as well as the car being destroyed by an alien missile. Two different sizes of explosions are actually used in the Space Out game. The larger explosion is used to show an alien or the car being destroyed, whereas the smaller explosion is used to show a missile exploding. This distinction is important because it shows how missiles cause a smaller explosion when they simply crash into the desert, as opposed to hitting the car.

In addition to the sprites, the Space Out game requires several bitmaps. Following are the bitmap images required of the game:

- Background desert image
- Car image
- Missile image (fired by car)
- Alien images (Blobbo, Jelly, and Timmy; animated)
- Missile images (fired by each of the three aliens)
- Explosion images (animated; small and large)
- Small car image
- Game over image

These images flow directly from the design of the game that you've covered thus far, so there hopefully shouldn't be any big surprises here. Perhaps the main thing to point out is that the aliens all rely on animated images to provide them with a more interesting appearance as they move around on the game screen. The only other animated images in the game are the explosion images, which go with the explosion sprites.

The score needs to be maintained throughout the game, as well as the number of remaining lives (cars); the game ends when all three of your cars have been destroyed. The difficulty level of the game is stored away in a global variable, and gradually increases as the player racks up points and progresses through the game. Another important piece of information is the familiar Boolean variable that keeps track of whether the game is over.

The last global game variable required of Space Out is an input delay variable that helps add some restraint to the player's ability to fire missiles rapidly. Without this input delay variable, it would be too easy to wipe out the aliens by holding down the fire key (Spacebar) and raining missiles on the aliens with little effort. By slowing down the number of missiles that can be fired, the player is forced to be more accurate and evade aliens when they miss. Establishing the appropriate delay is somewhat of a trial-and-error process, and you might decide that the game is more fun with a slightly different value than I used.

To recap, the design of the Space Out game has led us to the following pieces of information that must be managed by the game:

- The number of lives (cars) remaining
- The score
- The difficulty level
- A Boolean game over variable
- A delay variable for firing input

Before diving into the code for the Space Out game, you need to add a new feature to the game engine. Although the game engine is a flexible piece of software, you will likely find yourself adding new features in the future to accommodate the special needs of new games. This is a good thing because you get to reuse those features in any game that you create from then on.

Adding One Last Sprite Feature to the Game Engine

The missing feature in the game engine critical to the Space Out game is the capability for a sprite to automatically create another sprite. This might seem like a strange requirement, but think about an alien that is firing a missile at the car in the Space Out game. The missile must be created so that it appears to come from the alien, which means that the missile must know about the alien's position. Not only that, but the missile must be unique to the alien that fired it because each alien fires a different kind of missile. This presents a significant challenge to the current design of the game engine because there isn't a good way to automatically create a new sprite based on the properties of another sprite.

21

A good solution to this problem involves allowing a sprite to create another sprite whenever it needs to. For example, you can allow the alien sprites to create missile sprites
themselves, which makes it very easy to position the missile based on the alien's position—not to mention creating the appropriate missile for each different type of alien. The
problem with this approach is that it is impossible to add this functionality to the Sprite
class in a generic fashion. In other words, the specifics regarding what kind of sprite
needs to be created are unique to each game, and therefore can't be carried out in the
Sprite class. However, the Sprite class can establish the interface that makes it
possible.

An important part of this new "add sprite" feature is a new sprite action called
SA_ADDSPRITE. The following code shows how the SA_ADDSPRITE sprite action has been
added to the existing sprite actions:

```
typedef WORD        SPRITEACTION;
const SPRITEACTION  SA_NONE      = 0x0000L,
                    SA_KILL      = 0x0001L,
                    SA_ADDSPRITE = 0x0002L;
```

If you recall, sprite actions are used to signal to the game engine that some particular
action must be taken in regard to a sprite. The SA_ADDSPRITE sprite action simply results
in a special method being called on the Sprite object to which the action applies. This
method is called AddSprite(), and looks like this:

```
virtual Sprite* AddSprite();
```

The idea behind the AddSprite() method is that it gets called to allow a sprite to add a
new sprite to the game engine. The specifics of the new sprite are entirely dependent on
each individual game. In fact, the version of the AddSprite() method in the Sprite class
doesn't do anything, as the following code reveals:

```
Sprite* Sprite::AddSprite()
{
  return NULL;
}
```

This code shows how the base Sprite::AddSprite() method doesn't do anything other
than return a NULL sprite pointer, which reveals that the task of adding a sprite via the
AddSprite() method is left up to derived sprite classes. So, in order to take advantage of
this method, you must derive a sprite class for a particular kind of sprite, and then override the AddSprite() method with a version that actually creates a sprite.

The SA_ADDSPRITE action and AddSprite() method enter the picture in the game engine
in the GameEngine::UpdateSprites() method, which must check for the presence of the
SA_ADDSPRITE sprite action, and then call the AddSprite() method on the sprite if the

action is set. The return value of the sprite's AddSprite() method is passed along to the game engine's AddSprite() function, which handles inserting the sprite into the sprite list. This is all that is required of the game engine to support adding a sprite from within another sprite.

Building the Game

The construction of the Space Out game is similar to that of the other games you've developed throughout the book. However, Space Out is slightly more involved simply because it is a more complete game. The next few sections guide you through the development of the game's code and resources.

Writing the Game Code

Although the development of all the previous games in the book began with the header file for the game, Space Out is a little different in that it relies on a custom sprite class. For this reason, the code for the Space Out game begins with the header for this custom sprite class, AlienSprite, which is shown in Listing 21.1.

LISTING 21.1   The AlienSprite.h Header File Declares the AlienSprite Class, Which Is Derived from Sprite

```
 1: #pragma once
 2:
 3: //----------------------------------------------------------------
 4: // Include Files
 5: //----------------------------------------------------------------
 6: #include <windows.h>
 7: #include "Sprite.h"
 8:
 9: //----------------------------------------------------------------
10: // AlienSprite Class
11: //----------------------------------------------------------------
12: class AlienSprite : public Sprite
13: {
14: public:
15:   // Constructor(s)/Destructor
16:         AlienSprite(Bitmap* pBitmap, RECT& rcBounds,
17:           BOUNDSACTION baBoundsAction = BA_STOP);
18:   virtual ~AlienSprite();
19:
20:   // General Methods
21:   virtual SPRITEACTION  Update();
22:   virtual Sprite*       AddSprite();
23: };
```

21

The AlienSprite class is not very complex at all, as the listing hopefully reveals. It's important to notice that AlienSprite derives from Sprite (line 12), and declares a constructor and destructor (lines 16–18). More importantly, however, are the two methods in the Sprite class that AlienSprite overrides, Update() and AddSprite() (lines 21 and 22). These two methods are critical to providing the AlienSprite class with its own unique functionality separate from the Sprite class. In case you're wondering exactly what this functionality is, let me explain.

If you recall from earlier in the hour, one of the problems in the game engine was that it didn't allow a sprite to create another sprite on its own. You added code to the game engine, including a method called AddSprite() in the Sprite class, to allow for this task to be carried out by sprites. However, the version of the AddSprite() method in the Sprite class doesn't do anything—it's up to derived Sprite classes to create their own sprites. The AlienSprite class is an example of one of these derived classes that overrides the AddSprite() method to do something useful.

Before you get to the AlienSprite::AddSprite() method, however, let's take a quick look at some external global variables that are required of the AlienSprite class:

```
extern Bitmap*  _pBlobboBitmap;
extern Bitmap*  _pBMissileBitmap;
extern Bitmap*  _pJellyBitmap;
extern Bitmap*  _pJMissileBitmap;
extern Bitmap*  _pTimmyBitmap;
extern Bitmap*  _pTMissileBitmap;
extern int      _iDifficulty;
```

These global variables are part of the main Space Out game code, and are included in the file SpaceOut.h, which you see in a moment. They must be declared externally in the AlienSprite code because the code references the global variables. Listing 21.2 contains the code for the AlienSprite::AddSprite() method, which makes use of the external global variables to determine what kind of missile sprite to add.

LISTING 21.2   The AlienSprite::AddSprite() Method Adds a Missile Sprite Based on the Alien That Is Firing It

```
1: Sprite* AlienSprite::AddSprite()
2: {
3:    // Create a new missile sprite
4:    RECT    rcBounds = { 0, 0, 640, 410 };
5:    RECT    rcPos = GetPosition();
6:    Sprite* pSprite = NULL;
7:    if (GetBitmap() == _pBlobboBitmap)
8:    {
9:      // Blobbo missile
```

LISTING 21.2   Continued

```
10:        pSprite = new Sprite(_pBMissileBitmap, rcBounds, BA_DIE);
11:        pSprite->SetVelocity(0, 7);
12:      }
13:      else if (GetBitmap() == _pJellyBitmap)
14:      {
15:        // Jelly missile
16:        pSprite = new Sprite(_pJMissileBitmap, rcBounds, BA_DIE);
17:        pSprite->SetVelocity(0, 5);
18:      }
19:      else
20:      {
21:        // Timmy missile
22:        pSprite = new Sprite(_pTMissileBitmap, rcBounds, BA_DIE);
23:        pSprite->SetVelocity(0, 3);
24:      }
25:
26:      // Set the missile sprite's position and return it
27:      pSprite->SetPosition(rcPos.left + (GetWidth() / 2), rcPos.bottom);
28:      return pSprite;
29: }
```

The purpose of this `AddSprite()` method is to allow an alien sprite to create a missile
sprite. The important thing to notice in the `AddSprite()` method is that it fires a different
kind of missile for each different kind of alien. To determine what kind of alien is firing
the missile, the method checks the bitmap image for the sprite (lines 7, 13, and 19). A
missile sprite is then created based on which alien is firing the missile (lines 10, 11, 16,
17, 22, and 23). Finally, the new missile sprite's position is set so that it appears just
below the alien (line 27), and the sprite is returned from the method so that it can be
added to the sprite list in the game engine (line 28).

You might have noticed earlier in the `AlienSprite` class that the `Update()` method is
also overridden. Listing 21.3 contains the code for the `AlienSprite::Update()` method,
which handles randomly setting the `SA_ADDSPRITE` sprite action for the aliens.

LISTING 21.3   The `AlienSprite::Update()`Method Randomly Sets the
`SA_SPRITEACTION` Sprite Action so That the Aliens Fire Missiles

```
1: SPRITEACTION AlienSprite::Update()
2: {
3:    // Call the base sprite Update() method
4:    SPRITEACTION saSpriteAction;
5:    saSpriteAction = Sprite::Update();
6:
7:    // See if the alien should fire a missile
```

21

LISTING 21.3   Continued

```
 8:   if ((rand() % (_iDifficulty / 2)) == 0)
 9:     saSpriteAction |= SA_ADDSPRITE;
10:
11:   return saSpriteAction;
12: }
```

The most important line of code in this method is line 5, which calls the base class
Update() method so that the sprite is properly updated. The method then uses the
_iDifficulty global variable as the basis for randomly setting the SA_SPRITEACTION
sprite action (lines 8 and 9), which results in the alien firing a missile. This works
because the SA_SPRITEACTION sprite action causes the AlienSprite::AddSprite()
method to get called, which creates a new missile sprite and adds it to the game engine.

That wraps up the code for the AlienSprite class, which is a crucial component of the
Space Out game. The core of the Space Out game is laid out in the SpaceOut.h header
file, which is responsible for declaring the global variables used throughout the game
(Listing 21.4) .

LISTING 21.4   The SpaceOut.h Header File Declares Global Variables That Are
Used to Manage the Game

```
 1: #pragma once
 2:
 3: //------------------------------------------------------------
 4: // Include Files
 5: //------------------------------------------------------------
 6: #include <windows.h>
 7: #include "Resource.h"
 8: #include "GameEngine.h"
 9: #include "Bitmap.h"
10: #include "Sprite.h"
11: #include "Background.h"
12: #include "AlienSprite.h"
13:
14: //------------------------------------------------------------
15: // Global Variables
16: //------------------------------------------------------------
17: HINSTANCE         _hInstance;
18: GameEngine*       _pGame;
19: HDC               _hOffscreenDC;
20: HBITMAP           _hOffscreenBitmap;
21: Bitmap*           _pDesertBitmap;
22: Bitmap*           _pCarBitmap;
```

LISTING 21.2   Continued

```
23: Bitmap*              _pSmCarBitmap;
24: Bitmap*              _pMissileBitmap;
25: Bitmap*              _pBlobboBitmap;
26: Bitmap*              _pBMissileBitmap;
27: Bitmap*              _pJellyBitmap;
28: Bitmap*              _pJMissileBitmap;
29: Bitmap*              _pTimmyBitmap;
30: Bitmap*              _pTMissileBitmap;
31: Bitmap*              _pSmExplosionBitmap;
32: Bitmap*              _pLgExplosionBitmap;
33: Bitmap*              _pGameOverBitmap;
34: StarryBackground*    _pBackground;
35: Sprite*             _pCarSprite;
36: int                 _iFireInputDelay;
37: int                 _iNumLives, _iScore, _iDifficulty;
38: BOOL                _bGameOver;
39:
40: //-----------------------------------------------------------
41: // Function Declarations
42: //-----------------------------------------------------------
43: void NewGame();
44: void AddAlien();
```

The listing shows that the global variables for the Space Out game largely consist of the different bitmaps used throughout the game. The starry background for the game is declared after the bitmaps (line 34), followed by the car sprite that represents the player (line 35). Member variables storing the number of remaining lives, the score, and the difficulty level are then declared (line 37), followed by the familiar game over Boolean variable (line 38).

Similar to the Meteor Defense game in Hour 19, the Space Out game also relies on a couple of support functions. The first of these, NewGame(), is important because it is used to set up and start a new game (line 43). Unlike the GameStart() function, which performs initialization tasks such as loading bitmaps, the NewGame() function handles starting a new game once everything else is in place. The AddAlien() function is used to simplify the task of adding alien sprites to the game (line 44). You find out more about how these functions work a little later in the hour.

The primary setup code for the game takes place in the familiar GameStart() function, which is shown in Listing 21.5.

21

LISTING 21.5   The `GameStart()` Function Initializes the Bitmaps and Background for the Game, and Calls the `NewGame()` Function

```
 1: void GameStart(HWND hWindow)
 2: {
 3:   // Seed the random number generator
 4:   srand(GetTickCount());
 5:
 6:   // Create the offscreen device context and bitmap
 7:   _hOffscreenDC = CreateCompatibleDC(GetDC(hWindow));
 8:   _hOffscreenBitmap = CreateCompatibleBitmap(GetDC(hWindow),
 9:     _pGame->GetWidth(), _pGame->GetHeight());
10:   SelectObject(_hOffscreenDC, _hOffscreenBitmap);
11:
12:   // Create and load the bitmaps
13:   HDC hDC = GetDC(hWindow);
14:   _pDesertBitmap = new Bitmap(hDC, IDB_DESERT, _hInstance);
15:   _pCarBitmap = new Bitmap(hDC, IDB_CAR, _hInstance);
16:   _pSmCarBitmap = new Bitmap(hDC, IDB_SMCAR, _hInstance);
17:   _pMissileBitmap = new Bitmap(hDC, IDB_MISSILE, _hInstance);
18:   _pBlobboBitmap = new Bitmap(hDC, IDB_BLOBBO, _hInstance);
19:   _pBMissileBitmap = new Bitmap(hDC, IDB_BMISSILE, _hInstance);
20:   _pJellyBitmap = new Bitmap(hDC, IDB_JELLY, _hInstance);
21:   _pJMissileBitmap = new Bitmap(hDC, IDB_JMISSILE, _hInstance);
22:   _pTimmyBitmap = new Bitmap(hDC, IDB_TIMMY, _hInstance);
23:   _pTMissileBitmap = new Bitmap(hDC, IDB_TMISSILE, _hInstance);
24:   _pSmExplosionBitmap = new Bitmap(hDC, IDB_SMEXPLOSION, _hInstance);
25:   _pLgExplosionBitmap = new Bitmap(hDC, IDB_LGEXPLOSION, _hInstance);
26:   _pGameOverBitmap = new Bitmap(hDC, IDB_GAMEOVER, _hInstance);
27:
28:   // Create the starry background
29:   _pBackground = new StarryBackground(600, 450);
30:
31:   // Play the background music
32:   _pGame->PlayMIDISong(TEXT("Music.mid"));
33:
34:   // Start the game
35:   NewGame();
36: }
```

After the `GameStart()` function finishes loading the bitmaps for the game (lines 14–26) and creating the starry background (line 29), it starts playing the background music (line 32). The function then finishes up by calling the `NewGame()` function to start a new game (line 35). The `GameEnd()` function cleans up after the `GameStart()` function, and is called whenever the user exits the game. Since you've seen cleanup code for several games already, let's skip the details of how this `GameEnd()` function works.

The game screen in the Space Out game is painted by the GamePaint() function, which is shown in Listing 21.6.

LISTING 21.6 The GamePaint() Function Draws the Background, the Desert Ground Bitmap, the Sprites, the Score, and the Game Over Message

```
 1: void GamePaint(HDC hDC)
 2: {
 3:   // Draw the background
 4:   _pBackground->Draw(hDC);
 5:
 6:   // Draw the desert bitmap
 7:   _pDesertBitmap->Draw(hDC, 0, 371);
 8:
 9:   // Draw the sprites
10:   _pGame->DrawSprites(hDC);
11:
12:   // Draw the score
13:   TCHAR szText[64];
14:   RECT  rect = { 460, 0, 510, 30 };
15:   wsprintf(szText, "%d", _iScore);
16:   SetBkMode(hDC, TRANSPARENT);
17:   SetTextColor(hDC, RGB(255, 255, 255));
18:   DrawText(hDC, szText, -1, &rect, DT_SINGLELINE | DT_RIGHT | DT_VCENTER);
19:
20:   // Draw the number of remaining lives (cars)
21:   for (int i = 0; i < _iNumLives; i++)
22:     _pSmCarBitmap->Draw(hDC, 520 + (_pSmCarBitmap->GetWidth() * i),
23:       10, TRUE);
24:
25:   // Draw the game over message, if necessary
26:   if (_bGameOver)
27:     _pGameOverBitmap->Draw(hDC, 190, 149, TRUE);
28: }
```

The GamePaint() function takes care of drawing all graphics for the Space Out game. The function begins by drawing the starry background (line 4), followed by the desert ground image (line 7). The sprites are then drawn (line 10), followed by the score (lines 13–18). The number of remaining lives, which are represented by small car images, are drawn in the upper-right corner of the screen just right of the score (lines 21–23). Finally, the function finishes up by drawing the game over image, if necessary (lines 21–27).

The GameCycle() function works hand-in-hand with the GamePaint() function to update the game's sprites and reflect the changes onscreen. Listing 21.7 shows the code for the GameCycle() function.

21

LISTING 21.7   The `GameCycle()` Function Randomly Adds New Aliens to the Game

```
 1: void GameCycle()
 2: {
 3:   if (!_bGameOver)
 4:   {
 5:     // Randomly add aliens
 6:     if ((rand() % _iDifficulty) == 0)
 7:       AddAlien();
 8:
 9:     // Update the background
10:     _pBackground->Update();
11:
12:     // Update the sprites
13:     _pGame->UpdateSprites();
14:
15:     // Obtain a device context for repainting the game
16:     HWND  hWindow = _pGame->GetWindow();
17:     HDC   hDC = GetDC(hWindow);
18:
19:     // Paint the game to the offscreen device context
20:     GamePaint(_hOffscreenDC);
21:
22:     // Blit the offscreen bitmap to the game screen
23:     BitBlt(hDC, 0, 0, _pGame->GetWidth(), _pGame->GetHeight(),
24:       _hOffscreenDC, 0, 0, SRCCOPY);
25:
26:     // Cleanup
27:     ReleaseDC(hWindow, hDC);
28:   }
29: }
```

Aside from the standard `GameCycle()` code that you're already accustomed to seeing, this function doesn't add much additional code. The new code involves randomly adding new aliens, which is accomplished by calling the `AddAlien()` function after using the difficulty level to randomly determine if an alien should be added (lines 6–7).

With the alien sprites squared away, you still have to contend with how the user is going to control the car sprite. This is accomplished via a keyboard interface using the `HandleKeys()` function, which is shown in Listing 21.8.

LISTING 21.8   The `HandleKeys()` Function Allows the User to Control the Car Sprite Using Keys on the Keyboard

```
 1: void HandleKeys()
 2: {
 3:   if (!_bGameOver)
```

LISTING 21.8   Continued

```
 4:  {
 5:      // Move the car based upon left/right key presses
 6:      POINT ptVelocity = _pCarSprite->GetVelocity();
 7:      if (GetAsyncKeyState(VK_LEFT) < 0)
 8:      {
 9:        // Move left
10:        ptVelocity.x = max(ptVelocity.x - 1, -4);
11:        _pCarSprite->SetVelocity(ptVelocity);
12:      }
13:      else if (GetAsyncKeyState(VK_RIGHT) < 0)
14:      {
15:        // Move right
16:        ptVelocity.x = min(ptVelocity.x + 2, 6);
17:        _pCarSprite->SetVelocity(ptVelocity);
18:      }
19:
20:      // Fire missiles based upon spacebar presses
21:      if ((++_iFireInputDelay > 6) && GetAsyncKeyState(VK_SPACE) < 0)
22:      {
23:        // Create a new missile sprite
24:        RECT  rcBounds = { 0, 0, 600, 450 };
25:        RECT  rcPos = _pCarSprite->GetPosition();
26:        Sprite* pSprite = new Sprite(_pMissileBitmap, rcBounds, BA_DIE);
27:        pSprite->SetPosition(rcPos.left + 15, 400);
28:        pSprite->SetVelocity(0, -7);
29:        _pGame->AddSprite(pSprite);
30:
31:        // Play the missile (fire) sound
32:        PlaySound((LPCSTR)IDW_MISSILE, _hInstance, SND_ASYNC |
33:          SND_RESOURCE | SND_NOSTOP);
34:
35:        // Reset the input delay
36:        _iFireInputDelay = 0;
37:      }
38:    }
39:
40:    // Start a new game based upon an Enter (Return) key press
41:    if (_bGameOver && (GetAsyncKeyState(VK_RETURN) < 0))
42:      // Start a new game
43:      NewGame();
44: }
```

The HandleKeys() function looks to see if any of four keys are being pressed. Following are the meanings of these keys in the context of the Space Out game:

- Left arrow—Move the car left
- Right arrow—Move the car right

21

- Space—Fire a missile
- Enter (Return)—Start a new game (if the game is over)

By knowing the meanings of these keys, the code in the HandleKeys() function hopefully makes a bit more sense. The function begins by making sure that the game isn't over (line 3), and then proceeds to check on the status of each of the three keys that have relevance to the game play; the fourth key (Enter) only applies to a game that is over. If the left arrow key is pressed, the HandleKeys() function alters the car sprite's velocity so that it moves more to the left (lines 10 and 11). On the other hand, if the right arrow key is pressed, the car sprite's velocity is set so that it moves more to the right (lines 16 and 17). One interesting thing to note about this code is that the car is capable of moving faster to the right than it is to the left, which is because the car is aiming to the right. In other words, it can't go as fast in reverse as it can moving forward, which adds a little realism to the game.

Firing missiles is initiated by the user pressing the Space key (Spacebar), but it only takes place if the fire input delay has been triggered (line 21). The net effect of the fire input delay is to slow down the firing of missiles so that the player can't go crazy with a barrage of missiles; the game would be too easy if you could fire at that rate. To actually fire a missile, a missile sprite is created and set to a position just above the car sprite, which makes the missile appear to originate from the car (lines 24–29). A sound effect is also played to indicate that the missile was fired (lines 32 and 33).

The last section of code in the HandleKeys() function starts a new game in response to the user pressing the Enter (Return) key. The _bGameOver variable is checked to make sure that the game is over (line 41), and the NewGame() function is called to start the new game (line 43).

Another important function in the Space Out game is the SpriteCollision() function, which is called in response to sprites colliding (Listing 21.9).

LISTING 21.9 The SpriteCollision() Function Responds to Collisions Between Missiles, Aliens, and the Car Sprite

```
1: BOOL SpriteCollision(Sprite* pSpriteHitter, Sprite* pSpriteHittee)
2: {
3:   // See if a player missile and an alien have collided
4:   Bitmap* pHitter = pSpriteHitter->GetBitmap();
5:   Bitmap* pHittee = pSpriteHittee->GetBitmap();
6:   if ((pHitter == _pMissileBitmap && (pHittee == _pBlobboBitmap ||
7:     pHittee == _pJellyBitmap || pHittee == _pTimmyBitmap)) ||
8:     (pHittee == _pMissileBitmap && (pHitter == _pBlobboBitmap ||
9:     pHitter == _pJellyBitmap || pHitter == _pTimmyBitmap)))
```

LISTING 21.9 Continued

```
10:    {
11:      // Play the small explosion sound
12:      PlaySound((LPCSTR)IDW_LGEXPLODE, _hInstance, SND_ASYNC |
13:        SND_RESOURCE);
14:
15:      // Kill both sprites
16:      pSpriteHitter->Kill();
17:      pSpriteHittee->Kill();
18:
19:      // Create a large explosion sprite at the alien's position
20:      RECT rcBounds = { 0, 0, 600, 450 };
21:      RECT rcPos;
22:      if (pHitter == _pMissileBitmap)
23:        rcPos = pSpriteHittee->GetPosition();
24:      else
25:        rcPos = pSpriteHitter->GetPosition();
26:      Sprite* pSprite = new Sprite(_pLgExplosionBitmap, rcBounds);
27:      pSprite->SetNumFrames(8, TRUE);
28:      pSprite->SetPosition(rcPos.left, rcPos.top);
29:      _pGame->AddSprite(pSprite);
30:
31:      // Update the score
32:      _iScore += 25;
33:      _iDifficulty = max(80 - (_iScore / 20), 20);
34:    }
35:
36:    // See if an alien missile has collided with the car
37:    if ((pHitter == _pCarBitmap && (pHittee == _pBMissileBitmap ||
38:      pHittee == _pJMissileBitmap || pHittee == _pTMissileBitmap)) ||
39:      (pHittee == _pCarBitmap && (pHitter == _pBMissileBitmap ||
40:      pHitter == _pJMissileBitmap || pHitter == _pTMissileBitmap)))
41:    {
42:      // Play the large explosion sound
43:      PlaySound((LPCSTR)IDW_LGEXPLODE, _hInstance, SND_ASYNC |
44:        SND_RESOURCE);
45:
46:      // Kill the missile sprite
47:      if (pHitter == _pCarBitmap)
48:        pSpriteHittee->Kill();
49:      else
50:        pSpriteHitter->Kill();
51:
52:      // Create a large explosion sprite at the car's position
53:      RECT rcBounds = { 0, 0, 600, 480 };
54:      RECT rcPos;
55:      if (pHitter == _pCarBitmap)
56:        rcPos = pSpriteHitter->GetPosition();
57:      else
58:        rcPos = pSpriteHittee->GetPosition();
```

21

LISTING 21.9 Continued

```
59:        Sprite* pSprite = new Sprite(_pLgExplosionBitmap, rcBounds);
60:        pSprite->SetNumFrames(8, TRUE);
61:        pSprite->SetPosition(rcPos.left, rcPos.top);
62:        _pGame->AddSprite(pSprite);
63:
64:        // Move the car back to the start
65:        _pCarSprite->SetPosition(300, 405);
66:
67:        // See if the game is over
68:        if (--_iNumLives == 0)
69:        {
70:          // Play the game over sound
71:          PlaySound((LPCSTR)IDW_GAMEOVER, _hInstance, SND_ASYNC |
72:            SND_RESOURCE);
73:          _bGameOver = TRUE;
74:        }
75:    }
76:
77:    return FALSE;
78: }
```

The `SpriteCollision()` function is undoubtedly the heftiest function in the Space Out game, and for good reason: The collisions between the sprites in the game completely control the play of the game. The function begins by checking for a collision between a player missile and an alien (lines 6–9). If the collision occurred, the `SpriteCollision()` function plays a small explosion sound (lines 12 and 13), kills both sprites (lines 16 and 17), and creates a large explosion sprite at the alien's position (lines 20–29). The score is also increased to reward the player for taking out an alien (line 32). Of course, this also means that the difficulty level is recalculated to factor in the new score (line 33).

The other collision detected in the `SpriteCollision()` function is between an alien missile and the car sprite (lines 37–40). If this collision takes place, a large explosion sound is played (lines 43 and 44) and the missile sprite is killed (lines 47–50). A large explosion sprite is then created at the car's position (lines 53–62). The car sprite is then moved back to its starting position (line 65).

The last section of the `SpriteCollision()` function checks the number of lives to see if the game is over (line 68). If so, a game over sound is played and the `_bGameOver` variable is set to `TRUE` (lines 71–73).

Another important sprite-related function in the Space Out game is the `SpriteDying()` function, which is called whenever a sprite is being destroyed. In the case of Space Out, this function is used to create a small explosion sprite any time an alien missile sprite is destroyed. Listing 21.10 shows how this function works.

LISTING 21.10   The `SpriteDying()` Function Creates a Small Explosion Whenever an Alien Missile Sprite Is Destroyed

```
 1: void SpriteDying(Sprite* pSprite)
 2: {
 3:   // See if an alien missile sprite is dying
 4:   if (pSprite->GetBitmap() == _pBMissileBitmap ||
 5:     pSprite->GetBitmap() == _pJMissileBitmap ||
 6:     pSprite->GetBitmap() == _pTMissileBitmap)
 7:   {
 8:     // Play the small explosion sound
 9:     PlaySound((LPCSTR)IDW_SMEXPLODE, _hInstance, SND_ASYNC |
10:       SND_RESOURCE | SND_NOSTOP);
11:
12:     // Create a small explosion sprite at the missile's position
13:     RECT rcBounds = { 0, 0, 600, 450 };
14:     RECT rcPos = pSprite->GetPosition();
15:     Sprite* pSprite = new Sprite(_pSmExplosionBitmap, rcBounds);
16:     pSprite->SetNumFrames(8, TRUE);
17:     pSprite->SetPosition(rcPos.left, rcPos.top);
18:     _pGame->AddSprite(pSprite);
19:   }
20: }
```

The function begins by checking to see if the dying sprite is an alien missile (lines 4–6). If so, a small explosion sound is played (lines 9 and 10), and a small explosion sprite is created (lines 13–18).

The last two functions in the Space Out game are support functions that are completely unique to the game. The first one is `NewGame()`, which performs the steps necessary to start a new game (Listing 21.11).

LISTING 21.11   The `NewGame()` Function Gets Everything Ready for a New Game

```
 1: void NewGame()
 2: {
 3:   // Clear the sprites
 4:   _pGame->CleanupSprites();
 5:
 6:   // Create the car sprite
 7:   RECT rcBounds = { 0, 0, 600, 450 };
 8:   _pCarSprite = new Sprite(_pCarBitmap, rcBounds, BA_WRAP);
 9:   _pCarSprite->SetPosition(300, 405);
10:   _pGame->AddSprite(_pCarSprite);
11:
12:   // Initialize the game variables
13:   _iFireInputDelay = 0;
```

21

LISTING 21.11 Continued

```
14:    _iScore = 0;
15:    _iNumLives = 3;
16:    _iDifficulty = 80;
17:    _bGameOver = FALSE;
18:
19:    // Play the background music
20:    _pGame->PlayMIDISong();
21: }
```

The NewGame() function begins by clearing the sprite list (line 4), which is necessary because you aren't certain what sprites have been left over from the previous game. The car sprite is then created (lines 7–10), and the global game variables are set (lines 13–17). The function then finishes by starting the background music (line 20) .

The AddAlien() function is shown in Listing 21.12, and its job is to add a new alien to the game at a random location.

LISTING 21.12 The AddAlien() Function Adds a New Alien at a Random Position

```
 1: void AddAlien()
 2: {
 3:    // Create a new random alien sprite
 4:    RECT        rcBounds = { 0, 0, 600, 410 };
 5:    AlienSprite* pSprite;
 6:    switch(rand() % 3)
 7:    {
 8:    case 0:
 9:      // Blobbo
10:      pSprite = new AlienSprite(_pBlobboBitmap, rcBounds, BA_BOUNCE);
11:      pSprite->SetNumFrames(8);
12:      pSprite->SetPosition(((rand() % 2) == 0) ? 0 : 600, rand() % 370);
13:      pSprite->SetVelocity((rand() % 7) - 2, (rand() % 7) - 2);
14:      break;
15:    case 1:
16:      // Jelly
17:      pSprite = new AlienSprite(_pJellyBitmap, rcBounds, BA_BOUNCE);
18:      pSprite->SetNumFrames(8);
19:      pSprite->SetPosition(rand() % 600, rand() % 370);
20:      pSprite->SetVelocity((rand() % 5) - 2, (rand() % 5) + 3);
21:      break;
22:    case 2:
23:      // Timmy
24:      pSprite = new AlienSprite(_pTimmyBitmap, rcBounds, BA_WRAP);
25:      pSprite->SetNumFrames(8);
26:      pSprite->SetPosition(rand() % 600, rand() % 370);
27:      pSprite->SetVelocity((rand() % 7) + 3, 0);
```

LISTING 21.12   Continued

```
28:      break;
29:    }
30:
31:    // Add the alien sprite
32:    _pGame->AddSprite(pSprite);
33: }
```

The AddAlien() function adds a new alien to the game, which can be one of three types: Blobbo, Jelly, or Timmy. The code for the creation of each type of alien is similar, but each alien has slightly different characteristics. For example, Blobbo is capable of moving around fairly rapidly in any direction, but he bounces off the edges of the game screen (lines 12 and 13). Jelly also bounces off the screen edges (line 17), but his velocity is set differently so that he tends to move much more vertically than Blobbo (line 20). Finally, Timmy moves entirely horizontally (line 27), and is allowed to wrap off the screen from right to left (line 24). The AddAlien() function ends by adding the new alien sprite to the game engine (line 32).

You're probably relieved to find out that this wraps up the code for the Space Out game, which means that you're ready to put the resources together and take the game for a test spin.

Testing the Game

I've already said it numerous times that testing a game is the most fun part, and yet again you've arrived at the testing phase of a completely new game. Similar to the Meteor Defense game, the Space Out game requires a fair amount of testing simply because a lot of different interactions are taking place among the different sprites in the game. The great thing is that you test a game simply by playing it. Figure 21.2 shows the Space Out game at the beginning, with a single alien firing a few missiles at the car below.

You can move the car left and right using the arrow keys, and then fire back at the alien using the Space key (Spacebar). Shooting an alien results in a small explosion appearing, as shown in Figure 21.3.

Eventually, you'll venture into dangerous territory and get shot by an alien, which results in a large explosion appearing, as shown in Figure 21.4.

21

FIGURE 21.2

The Space Out game gets started with an alien firing a few missiles at the car below.

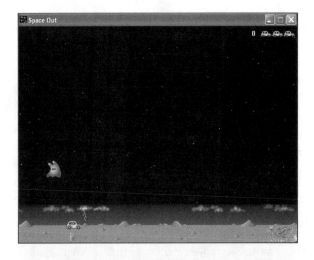

FIGURE 21.3

A small explosion appears when you successfully shoot an alien.

You only have three cars to lose, and the number of remaining cars is shown in the upper-right corner of the game screen next to the score. When you lose all three cars, the game ends, as shown in Figure 21.5.

The good news about the game ending in Space Out is that you can immediately start a new one by simply pressing the Enter (Return) key.

FIGURE 21.4

A large explosion appears when the car gets shot by an alien.

FIGURE 21.5

When you lose all three cars, the game ends and the game over image is displayed.

Summary

Regardless of whether you are a fan of shoot-em-up space games, I hope you realized the significance of the Space Out game that you designed and built in this hour. In addition to adding yet another complete game to your accomplishments, the Space Out game is important because it represents the most complete game in the book. In other words, it makes the most complete usage of the features you've worked so hard adding to the game engine. Not only that, but the Space Out game is a great game for experimenting with your own ideas, simply because it is the kind of game that can be expanded upon in

21

so many different ways. Before you get too crazy modifying the Space Out game, however, sit tight because I have a few modifications of my own to throw at you before I turn you loose in the wild world of game programming.

This hour concludes this part of the book, which was admittedly quite short. The next part of the book picks up right where you left off by showing you some sure-fire techniques to add pizzazz to your games. More specifically, you find out how to add interesting features to the Space Out game such as a splash screen, a demo mode, and a high score list.

Q&A

Q Why does the `HandleKeys()` function change the velocity of the car sprite in response to the arrow keys, instead of directly changing its position?

A The `HandleKeys()` function could certainly change the position of the car sprite to get a similar result, but by changing the velocity you get a smoother sense of control in the game. More specifically, the movement of the car isn't choppy because when it changes direction, it actually decelerates and then accelerates again. This is a minor detail, but one that helps to add a touch of realism to the game.

Q Why doesn't the Space Out game include a unique derived `Sprite` class for each kind of alien?

A The game could have been designed to utilize three derived `Sprite` classes such as `BlobboSprite`, `JellySprite`, and `TimmySprite`, but in reality it just wasn't necessary to break out the code that much. If the different aliens had required radically different functionality within them, this approach might have made more sense. And if you're a stickler for adhering to object-oriented design, you could still go back and redesign the game around three alien classes instead of one. However, I usually err on the side of simplicity, and in this case one class does the trick just fine.

Workshop

The Workshop is designed to help you anticipate possible questions, review what you've learned, and begin learning how to put your knowledge into practice. The answers to the quiz can be found in Appendix A, "Quiz Answers."

Quiz

1. What is the purpose of the SA_ADDSPRITE sprite action?

2. Why is it necessary to derive a class from the Sprite class in order for it to take advantage of the SA_ADDSPRITE sprite action?

3. What role does the AlienSprite class play in the Space Out game?

Exercises

1. Modify the Update() method in the AlienSprite class so that the aliens fly around in different flight patterns.

2. Create an entirely new alien and add it to the Space Out game. This involves creating an animated bitmap image for the alien, as well as adding appropriate code throughout the Space Out game code, including the AlienSprite class.

21

PART VII
Spicing up Your Games

Hours

HOUR **22**

Adding Pizzazz to Your Game with a Splash Screen

One of the problems with the games you've developed throughout the book thus far is that they don't adequately identify themselves when they first run. Sure, the title bar of the window has the name of the game, but it's important to clearly identify your game when it first starts up. In this way, a game is a lot like a movie in that it should present a title at the beginning. Unlike movies, however, titles in games are referred to as splash screens, and they can contain useful information such as a copyright notice and directions on how to play the game. This hour shows you how to spruce up the Space Out game by adding a splash screen.

In this hour, you'll learn:

- Why splash screens are an important part of just about any game
- What it takes to incorporate a splash screen into a game
- How to add a splash screen to the Space Out game

The Importance of a Splash Screen

Generally speaking, I get annoyed with opening credits in movies because I'm ready for the movie to get started. However, there are a few rare movies whose opening credits are creative and interesting enough to make them an enjoyable introduction to the movie. A big part of the opening credits for movies is the movie title, which is akin to splash screens used in video games. Similar to movie titles, a splash screen in a video game should convey the theme of the game and possibly provide a sneak preview of what's to come in the game. Of course, it's also possible to deliberately show very little in the splash screen for a game, with the idea being that you want to shroud the game in mystery until the game play actually starts.

Regardless of how much or how little you give away in the splash screen for a game, it's important to at least communicate the title of the game and any other pertinent information, such as the copyright for the game. If a certain action is required to start the game, it's also a good idea to mention it on the splash screen as well. No one likes a game that immediately throws you in the action without any warning when the game is launched, so at a bare minimum the splash screen should give you a chance to initiate the game starting.

A splash screen is also a good place to include abbreviated instructions for a game, as well as tips and hints about how to play. In the 1980s when arcade games were the rage, you could often read the splash screen for a game to quickly learn how to play the game. This isn't as critical of a feature in computer games, but it never hurts to provide information that allows people to get started playing a game quickly. One final piece of information to consider for a splash screen is a high score list. This list contains the top scores people have achieved in the game, and is popular in classic arcade games. Hour 24, "Keeping Track of High Scores," shows you how to create a high score list that saves high scores for the Space Out game to a file.

Many commercial games these days go far beyond a splash screen by including an introductory animation or video sequence. This "splash animation" is a lot flashier than a simple splash screen, but it often requires a considerable amount of effort to create, especially if it's an actual video. For example, many popular sports games include video clips of the actual sports being played. On the other hand, some games just display animation sequences directly from the game, which serves as kind of a demo for the game. You find out how to turn a splash screen into a demo mode for the Space Out game in the next hour. For now, let's continue to dig deeper into splash screens and how they work.

Looking Behind a Splash Screen

22

Although you could certainly dream up a complex approach to creating a splash screen, the simplest way to carry out the task is to simply create a bitmap image for the screen and then display it on the game screen before the game begins. The image for a splash screen can be large enough to fill the entire game screen or it can be smaller and displayed on top of the existing background for the game. The size of the splash screen for your own games is entirely up to you. However, for the Space Out game, I opted to create a splash screen that is smaller than the game screen. Figure 22.1 shows how the splash screen image is designed to overlay on top of the game background in the Space Out game.

FIGURE 22.1

The splash screen image in the Space Out game is designed to be displayed over the background for the game.

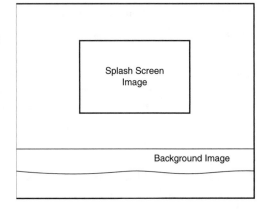

As you can see in the figure, there really isn't anything magical about displaying a splash screen, especially in the Space Out game. The only slightly tricky aspect of adding a splash screen to a game is establishing a separate mode of the game for the splash screen. For example, all the games you've created in the book are always in one of two modes, "game over" or "game not over." These two modes are directly controlled by the _bGameOver global variable, which has one of two Boolean values, TRUE or FALSE. Although you could associate the splash screen with a game being over, it is more accurate to give it a mode of its own.

Giving a splash screen a mode of its own basically means adding a global variable that indicates whether the splash screen should be displayed. This makes sense because you probably don't want to display the splash screen once a game has started and ended. In other words, the splash screen is only shown when the game first starts, and then it never appears again. You could create a splash screen that is shown in between games, but that's a role better suited to demo mode, which you learn about in the next hour.

Building the Space Out 2 Game

You now know enough about splash screens to take a stab at adding one to the Space Out game. In doing so, you'll be making it more of a complete game with a professional touch. The new version of the Space Out game with a splash screen is called Space Out 2, and it is the focus of the remainder of this hour. Space Out 2 is very similar to the original Space Out program. In fact, the play of the game doesn't change a bit; all that you're doing is adding a splash screen to spruce up the game a bit.

Writing the Game Code

The first step in adding a splash screen to the Space Out 2 game is to add a couple of global variables to the game that store the bitmap for the splash screen, as well as the mode for the splash screen. Following are these variables:

```
Bitmap* _pSplashBitmap;
BOOL    _bSplash;
```

The first variable, _pSplashBitmap, is pretty straightforward in that it represents the bitmap image for the splash screen. The other global variable, _bSplash, is a Boolean variable that indicates whether the game is in splash screen mode. More specifically, if the _bSplash variable is TRUE, the game is in splash screen mode and the splash screen is displayed; you can't play the game while the splash screen is being displayed. If the _bSplash variable is FALSE, the game plays as normal as if there were no splash screen. So, the idea is to set the _bSplash variable to TRUE at the beginning of the game, and then return it to FALSE after the user starts the game by pressing the Enter key.

As with any global variables, it's important to initialize the splash screen variables. This takes place in the GameStart() function, which is very similar to the previous version. The first change to the GameStart() function is the creation of the splash screen bitmap:

```
_pSplashBitmap = new Bitmap(hDC, IDB_SPLASH, _hInstance);
```

The only other change is the initialization of the _bSplash global variable, which must be set to TRUE in order to display the splash screen when the game starts:

```
_bSplash = TRUE;
```

A big part of making the splash screen work properly is disabling parts of the game when the game is in splash screen mode. Listing 22.1 contains the code for the GameActivate() and GameDeactivate() functions, which check the value of the _bSplash variable before resuming or pausing the MIDI background music.

LISTING 22.1   The `GameActivate()` and `GameDeactivate()` Functions Check the Value of the `_bSplash` Variable Before Resuming or Pausing the MIDI Background Music

```
 1: void GameActivate(HWND hWindow)
 2: {
 3:   if (!_bSplash)
 4:     // Resume the background music
 5:     _pGame->PlayMIDISong(TEXT(""), FALSE);
 6: }
 7:
 8: void GameDeactivate(HWND hWindow)
 9: {
10:   if (!_bSplash)
11:     // Pause the background music
12:     _pGame->PauseMIDISong();
13: }
```

There isn't too much explanation required for these functions because they simply check the `_bSplash` variable to see if the game is in splash screen mode before resuming or pausing the MIDI background music (lines 3 and 10).

The most important code in the Space Out 2 program in relation to the splash screen is contained in the `GamePaint()` function, which is where the splash screen is actually drawn. Listing 22.2 contains the code for the `GamePaint()` function.

LISTING 22.2   The `GamePaint()` Function Draws the Splash Screen Bitmap When the Game Is in Splash Screen Mode

```
 1: void GamePaint(HDC hDC)
 2: {
 3:   // Draw the background
 4:   _pBackground->Draw(hDC);
 5:
 6:   // Draw the desert bitmap
 7:   _pDesertBitmap->Draw(hDC, 0, 371);
 8:
 9:   if (_bSplash)
10:   {
11:     // Draw the splash screen image
12:     _pSplashBitmap->Draw(hDC, 142, 100, TRUE);
13:   }
14:   else
15:   {
16:     // Draw the sprites
17:     _pGame->DrawSprites(hDC);
18:
```

LISTING 22.2   Continued

```
19:        // Draw the score
20:        TCHAR szText[64];
21:        RECT  rect = { 460, 0, 510, 30 };
22:        wsprintf(szText, "%d", _iScore);
23:        SetBkMode(hDC, TRANSPARENT);
24:        SetTextColor(hDC, RGB(255, 255, 255));
25:        DrawText(hDC, szText, -1, &rect, DT_SINGLELINE | DT_RIGHT |
26:          DT_VCENTER);
27:
28:        // Draw the number of remaining lives (cars)
29:        for (int i = 0; i < _iNumLives; i++)
30:          _pSmCarBitmap->Draw(hDC, 520 + (_pSmCarBitmap->GetWidth() * i),
31:            10, TRUE);
32:
33:        // Draw the game over message, if necessary
34:        if (_bGameOver)
35:          _pGameOverBitmap->Draw(hDC, 170, 100, TRUE);
36:      }
37: }
```

The change to the GamePaint() function involves drawing the splash screen image if the _bSplash variable is TRUE (lines 9–13). If the _bSplash variable is FALSE, the GamePaint() function draws the sprites, score, and remaining lives, which are only pertinent to a game being played (lines 15–36). It's important to notice that the starry background and desert bitmap are both drawn regardless of the value of the _bSplash variable (lines 3–7). This results in the background and desert image being drawn even when the splash screen image is drawn, which is necessary because the splash screen doesn't fill up the entire game screen.

The last coding change in the Space Out 2 game involves the HandleKeys() function, which you know processes key presses for the game. If you recall, the Enter key is used to start a new game if the current game is over. Because the same key is used to leave the splash screen and start a game, it is necessary to change the value of the _bSplash variable when the user presses the Enter key. Listing 22.3 shows the new version of the HandleKeys() function with this change in place.

LISTING 22.3   The HandleKeys() Function Changes the Value of the _bSplash Variable if the Game Is Exiting the Splash Screen to Start a New Game

```
1: void HandleKeys()
2: {
3:   if (!_bGameOver)
4:   {
5:     // Move the car based upon left/right key presses
```

LISTING 22.3 Continued

```
 6:      POINT ptVelocity = _pCarSprite->GetVelocity();
 7:      if (GetAsyncKeyState(VK_LEFT) < 0)
 8:      {
 9:        // Move left
10:        ptVelocity.x = max(ptVelocity.x - 1, -4);
11:        _pCarSprite->SetVelocity(ptVelocity);
12:      }
13:      else if (GetAsyncKeyState(VK_RIGHT) < 0)
14:      {
15:        // Move right
16:        ptVelocity.x = min(ptVelocity.x + 2, 6);
17:        _pCarSprite->SetVelocity(ptVelocity);
18:      }
19:
20:      // Fire missiles based upon spacebar presses
21:      if ((++_iFireInputDelay > 6) && GetAsyncKeyState(VK_SPACE) < 0)
22:      {
23:        // Create a new missile sprite
24:        RECT   rcBounds = { 0, 0, 600, 450 };
25:        RECT   rcPos = _pCarSprite->GetPosition();
26:        Sprite* pSprite = new Sprite(_pMissileBitmap, rcBounds, BA_DIE);
27:        pSprite->SetPosition(rcPos.left + 15, 400);
28:        pSprite->SetVelocity(0, -7);
29:        _pGame->AddSprite(pSprite);
30:
31:        // Play the missile (fire) sound
32:        PlaySound((LPCSTR)IDW_MISSILE, _hInstance, SND_ASYNC |
33:          SND_RESOURCE | SND_NOSTOP);
34:
35:        // Reset the input delay
36:        _iFireInputDelay = 0;
37:      }
38:    }
39:
40:    // Start a new game based upon an Enter (Return) key press
41:    if (GetAsyncKeyState(VK_RETURN) < 0)
42:      if (_bSplash)
43:      {
44:        // Start a new game without the splash screen
45:        _bSplash = FALSE;
46:        NewGame();
47:      }
48:      else if (_bGameOver)
49:      {
50:        // Start a new game
51:        NewGame();
52:      }
53: }
```

Within the code that responds to the Enter (Return) key, you'll find the code that checks to see if the game is leaving splash screen mode. This code first checks to see if the game is in splash screen mode (line 42), and then clears the _bSplash variable and starts a new game if so (lines 45 and 46). If the game is not in splash screen mode, the function checks to see if the game is over (line 48). If the game is over, a new game is started (line 51), which is similar to how the HandleKeys() function worked prior to adding the splash screen code.

Testing the Finished Product

The Space Out 2 game represents one of the easiest tests you'll ever perform on a game. All you really have to do is run the game and make sure that the splash screen appears properly. Of course, you also need to make sure that the splash screen goes away when you press the Enter key to start a new game, but you get the idea. Figure 22.2 shows the splash screen displayed in the Space Out 2 game when the game first starts.

FIGURE 22.2
The splash screen in the Space Out 2 game presents the game title, copyright information, and information about how to start the game.

Keep in mind that you are free to get as fancy as you want with the splash screen image for your own games. I chose to keep the Space Out 2 splash screen relatively simple, but you might want to jazz it up to suit your own tastes. The important thing to note about this example is that the splash screen is properly displayed when the game starts.

Summary

This hour introduced you to an important feature of most games—the splash screen. Not only is the splash screen important in terms of conveying useful information about a game, such as a copyright notice, but it also serves as the player's first glimpse at what your game looks like. You can take advantage of a splash screen to dramatize the theme of your game and even exaggerate the game graphics. For example, it was common for arcade games to include a fully illustrated splash screen—even though the graphics in the actual games were simpler. This is an engaging way to grab the player's attention and get him interested in the game.

The next hour builds on what you learned about splash screens and shows you how to include a demo mode in your games. A demo mode is similar to a splash screen, but its goal is to provide a glimpse at how a game actually plays.

Q&A

Q Is it necessary for a splash screen bitmap to use a transparent color and be drawn with transparency?

A No. Although the splash screen bitmap in the Space Out 2 game does use a transparent color, this isn't necessary in all splash screen bitmaps. In fact, if you're creating a splash screen bitmap that fills the entire game screen, you probably wouldn't want to draw it with transparency. In Space Out 2, transparency makes sense because it allows the starry background to shine through between the letters, which is a nice effect.

Q Is it possible to create a splash screen that consists of more than one image?

A Yes, in fact this was done quite a lot in classic arcade games that not only needed to display a title for a game, but also provide instructions in a relatively small amount of screen space. The idea is to present the images as a simplified slide show, where they are displayed in succession after pausing a few seconds on each one. This is carried out programmatically by adding additional splash screen modes to a game so that you know which splash screen image should be displayed. In practice, this could be accomplished by using the existing _bSplash variable to determine whether any splash screen image is displayed, and then use an integer variable to keep track of which splash screen bitmap is displayed from an array of bitmaps. You would have to add some timing code to the GameCycle() function to flip between splash screen images after a brief delay, or allow the user to press a key to move between each.

Workshop

The Workshop is designed to help you anticipate possible questions, review what you've learned, and begin learning how to put your knowledge into practice. The answers to the quiz can be found in Appendix A, "Quiz Answers."

Quiz

1. In addition to the title of the game, what kind of information is good to place on the splash screen for a game?

2. What is the purpose of the _bSplash global variable in the Space Out 2 game?

3. Why are the background and the desert bitmaps drawn in the Space Out 2 game regardless of whether the game is in splash screen mode?

Exercises

1. Create your own splash screen bitmap image for the Space Out 2 game and incorporate it into the game.

2. Modify the splash screen for the Space Out 2 game so that it consists of two splash screen modes that display two images in succession for the splash screen. In other words, create one splash screen image for the game's title and another that describes how to play the game and what keys to use.

HOUR 23

Showing Off Your Game with Demo Mode

In the previous hour, you learned how important it is to display a splash screen that serves as a title for your games. This hour continues in the theme of making a game more complete by demonstrating the importance of demo mode. Demo mode is an animated sequence displayed when you're not playing the game that demonstrates how the game is played. Demo mode can be as simple as showing some of the game creatures moving around, or as complex as showing an entire simulated game being played. Demo mode is important because it gives a player a glimpse at how a game actually plays, which is a considerable step beyond the role of a splash screen.

In this hour, you'll learn:

- Why demo mode is useful in showing people how a game works
- What is involved in adding a demo mode to a game
- How to add a demo mode to the Space Out game

What Is Demo Mode?

If you've ever been hesitant to buy a product, you might have been offered an opportunity to "try before you buy," which allows you to try out a product before you spend any money on it. This sales technique is particularly useful in the automotive industry, where it is virtually impossible to justify purchasing a car without taking it for a test drive. In the early days of video games, it was important to convince game players that a game was worthy of spending a quarter for a play, so demo mode was invented. Demo mode is sort of like "try before you buy" applied to video games—you get to see how a game plays before you invest any time or money playing it. In regard to computer games, "try before you buy" now typically involves downloading a limited version of the game that you really can play. However, demo mode is still a useful and worthwhile feature to consider adding to your games.

The main idea behind demo mode is that it goes beyond a splash screen by showing more than just a title or stationary game graphics. Demo mode attempts to show the game actually being played, or at least show some of the main characters in the game going through the motions as you'll see them in the game. Demo mode can be as simple or as complex as you choose, but the idea is to provide a hook to convince someone to play the game. In other words, you're attempting to sell the game so that it looks fun and inviting. Demo mode can also be informative, similar to a splash screen. In fact, it's not a bad idea to design demo mode so that it serves as a more interesting splash screen.

Unlike a splash screen, demo mode is not something that appears at the beginning of the game, never to be seen again once the game starts. Instead, demo mode is displayed in between every game, and helps fill the space between games with interesting animations from the game. So, when a game ends, there should be a brief pause while the player is able to take in that the game is actually over, and then the game should return to demo mode. Of course, the game also starts in demo mode. In this way, demo mode replaces the splash screen for a game, and also goes a few steps beyond the role of a splash screen.

The Nuts and Bolts of Demo Mode

Similar to a splash screen, demo mode is a distinct mode that a game enters when a game is not underway. This mode is different from "game over" and "game not over" modes, and is entered when the game program first starts, as well as in between games. A single Boolean global variable is sufficient to keep track of when a game is in demo mode. This sounds very much like how the splash screen was managed in the previous hour. Demo mode differs from a splash screen in that it involves demonstrating the game, which means that sprites must be allowed to move around. If you recall, the splash screen for the Space Out 2 game deliberately disallowed sprites to be drawn.

The key to making demo mode work in a game is to simulate a game being played without actually involving a human player. One way to do this is to start up a new game as normal, and simulate key strokes using code that is somehow timed. Of course, this also involves disabling the real keys used in the game so that the player can't suddenly jump into a demo mode game. Although this approach can work very well, and is ultimately the ideal approach to creating a demo mode because it shows how the player interacts with other characters in a game, it is more difficult to create. The coding to replace a human player with a computer player can get tricky, and usually involves some degree of artificial intelligence programming. One work-around for this approach is to "record" the keystrokes made by a player during a real game, and store them in a file. You can then "play" the keystrokes back to recreate the demo game. This technique obviously requires some extra work, but will most likely be a lot simpler than trying to establish realistic AI for the computer player.

A simpler approach to creating a demo mode for a game is to simply show how the characters in the game move around without attempting to simulate the human player in the game. In other words, you aren't actually trying to make it look as if a human player is guiding his character through the game or otherwise interacting with the game. Instead, you're just demonstrating how the computer-controlled characters within the game move around and interact with one another. This approach simplifies things considerably because you aren't in a situation in which you have to try and control an otherwise human player using computer logic. Keep in mind that the whole premise of demo mode is to show off a game and make it look appealing. In many cases, it is sufficient to just show a few characters within the game to achieve this goal.

Creating a demo mode that shows a few characters and doesn't actually simulate play is still somewhat of a challenge because you have to create and use sprites just as if you were starting a real game. However, in this case, the idea is to disable any interaction from a human player other than initiating a new game. If you think about it, creating a demo mode for a game such as Space Out involves several changes throughout the game to allow it to appear somewhat as if the game is being played even though there is no user interaction. The remainder of the hour focuses on how to add a demo mode to this game.

Building the Space Out 3 Game

You've already learned that in some ways demo mode is similar to a splash screen because it appears in a game when the game is not actually being played. Unlike a splash screen, however, demo mode is responsible for displaying sprites and enabling them to interact to some degree. Adding a demo mode to the Space Out game represents a programming challenge, but one that isn't too terribly difficult to solve. The next few sections lead you through the modifications required in the game to add a demo mode. The new version of the game you'll be creating is called Space Out 3.

Writing the Game Code

The best place to start with the code for the Space Out 3 game is the SpaceOut.h header file, which includes a couple of new global variables. Demo mode for the game requires two new global variables; one of which replaces the _bSplash global variable that you added in the last hour for the splash screen. Following are the new global variables necessary to support demo mode in the Space Out 3 game:

```
BOOL _bDemo;
int  _iGameOverDelay;
```

The first variable, _bDemo, is very similar to the _bSplash variable in the Space Out 2 game from the previous hour. In fact, it serves virtually the same purpose in this game, except that demo mode impacts more code than the splash screen. The _iGameOverDelay global variable is used to provide a delay between when a game ends and when the game enters demo mode. This allows the player to take a moment and realize that the game is over before it cuts back to demo mode.

The first function of particular interest in the Space Out 3 game is the GameStart() function, which shouldn't come as too much of a surprise. The only change to the GameStart() function is the initialization of the _bDemo variable.

The GamePaint() function is where the code for the Space Out 3 game starts to diverge more significantly from the Space Out 2 game. However, the change is still somewhat subtle in that all the same code is here, it's just organized a little differently. Take a look at Listing 23.1 to see what I mean.

LISTING 23.1   The GamePaint() Function Draws the Game Graphics While Taking into Consideration Demo Mode

```
1: void GamePaint(HDC hDC)
2: {
3:    // Draw the background
4:    _pBackground->Draw(hDC);
5:
6:    // Draw the desert bitmap
7:    _pDesertBitmap->Draw(hDC, 0, 371);
8:
```

LISTING 23.1   Continued

```
 9:   // Draw the sprites
10:   _pGame->DrawSprites(hDC);
11:
12:   if (_bDemo)
13:   {
14:     // Draw the splash screen image
15:     _pSplashBitmap->Draw(hDC, 142, 100, TRUE);
16:   }
17:   else
18:   {
19:     // Draw the score
20:     TCHAR szText[64];
21:     RECT  rect = { 460, 0, 510, 30 };
22:     wsprintf(szText, "%d", _iScore);
23:     SetBkMode(hDC, TRANSPARENT);
24:     SetTextColor(hDC, RGB(255, 255, 255));
25:     DrawText(hDC, szText, -1, &rect, DT_SINGLELINE | DT_RIGHT |
26:       DT_VCENTER);
27:
28:     // Draw the number of remaining lives (cars)
29:     for (int i = 0; i < _iNumLives; i++)
30:       _pSmCarBitmap->Draw(hDC, 520 + (_pSmCarBitmap->GetWidth() * i),
31:         10, TRUE);
32:
33:     // Draw the game over message, if necessary
34:     if (_bGameOver)
35:       _pGameOverBitmap->Draw(hDC, 170, 100, TRUE);
36:   }
37: }
```

The GameCycle() function in Space Out 3 looks a lot like its predecessor, but there is a significant change you should pay close attention to. The change I'm talking about involves the fact that the sprites are drawn regardless of whether the game is in demo mode (line 10). In fact, all that is *not* drawn in demo mode is the score (lines 20–26), the number of remaining lives (lines 29–31), and the game over message (lines 34 and 35). Also notice that the same splash screen image is displayed when the game is in demo mode (lines 12–16), which means that the game is combining demo mode with the splash screen. This isn't a problem, but it does mean that the game is being demonstrated behind the splash screen image.

The GameCycle() function must be modified to accommodate demo mode as well. In fact, the GameCycle() function is where the timing delay is established that displays the game over screen for a period of time before reverting back to demo mode when a game ends. Listing 23.2 shows the code for the new version of the GameCycle() function.

LISTING 23.2   The GameCycle() Function Establishes a Timing Delay Before Moving to Demo Mode from the Game Over Screen

```
 1: void GameCycle()
 2: {
 3:   if (!_bGameOver)
 4:   {
 5:     if (!_bDemo)
 6:     {
 7:       // Randomly add aliens
 8:       if ((rand() % _iDifficulty) == 0)
 9:         AddAlien();
10:     }
11:
12:     // Update the background
13:     _pBackground->Update();
14:
15:     // Update the sprites
16:     _pGame->UpdateSprites();
17:
18:     // Obtain a device context for repainting the game
19:     HWND  hWindow = _pGame->GetWindow();
20:     HDC   hDC = GetDC(hWindow);
21:
22:     // Paint the game to the offscreen device context
23:     GamePaint(_hOffscreenDC);
24:
25:     // Blit the offscreen bitmap to the game screen
26:     BitBlt(hDC, 0, 0, _pGame->GetWidth(), _pGame->GetHeight(),
27:       _hOffscreenDC, 0, 0, SRCCOPY);
28:
29:     // Cleanup
30:     ReleaseDC(hWindow, hDC);
31:   }
32:   else
33:     if (--_iGameOverDelay == 0)
34:     {
35:       // Stop the music and switch to demo mode
36:       _pGame->PauseMIDISong();
37:       _bDemo = TRUE;
38:       NewGame();
39:     }
40: }
```

In addition to changing the _bSplash variable to _bDemo (line 5), the GameCycle() function establishes a timing delay for the game over screen (lines 33–39). When this delay
finishes counting down, it means that the game over message has been displayed long
enough and it's okay to go ahead and put the game in demo mode. This is accomplished

by setting the _bDemo variable to TRUE (line 37), and then calling the NewGame() function to add a few alien sprites to demo mode (line 38). Notice that the MIDI music isn't actually stopped until the game switches to demo mode (line 36), which makes sense when you consider that the game over screen is still a reflection on the last game played.

Demo mode also impacts the HandleKeys() function in the Space Out 3 game, as you can see in Listing 23.3.

LISTING 23.3 The HandleKeys() Function Supports Demo Mode by Changing the Value of the _bDemo Variable if the Game Is Exiting Demo Mode to Start a New Game

```
 1: void HandleKeys()
 2: {
 3:   if (!_bGameOver && !_bDemo)
 4:   {
 5:     // Move the car based upon left/right key presses
 6:     POINT ptVelocity = _pCarSprite->GetVelocity();
 7:     if (GetAsyncKeyState(VK_LEFT) < 0)
 8:     {
 9:       // Move left
10:       ptVelocity.x = max(ptVelocity.x - 1, -4);
11:       _pCarSprite->SetVelocity(ptVelocity);
12:     }
13:     else if (GetAsyncKeyState(VK_RIGHT) < 0)
14:     {
15:       // Move right
16:       ptVelocity.x = min(ptVelocity.x + 2, 6);
17:       _pCarSprite->SetVelocity(ptVelocity);
18:     }
19:
20:     // Fire missiles based upon spacebar presses
21:     if ((++_iFireInputDelay > 6) && GetAsyncKeyState(VK_SPACE) < 0)
22:     {
23:       // Create a new missile sprite
24:       RECT  rcBounds = { 0, 0, 600, 450 };
25:       RECT  rcPos = _pCarSprite->GetPosition();
26:       Sprite* pSprite = new Sprite(_pMissileBitmap, rcBounds, BA_DIE);
27:       pSprite->SetPosition(rcPos.left + 15, 400);
28:       pSprite->SetVelocity(0, -7);
29:       _pGame->AddSprite(pSprite);
30:
31:       // Play the missile (fire) sound
32:       PlaySound((LPCSTR)IDW_MISSILE, _hInstance, SND_ASYNC |
33:         SND_RESOURCE | SND_NOSTOP);
34:
35:       // Reset the input delay
36:       _iFireInputDelay = 0;
```

LISTING 23.3 Continued

```
37:     }
38:  }
39:
40:  // Start a new game based upon an Enter (Return) key press
41:  if (GetAsyncKeyState(VK_RETURN) < 0)
42:    if (_bDemo)
43:    {
44:      // Switch out of demo mode to start a new game
45:      _bDemo = FALSE;
46:      NewGame();
47:    }
48:    else if (_bGameOver)
49:    {
50:      // Start a new game
51:      NewGame();
52:    }
53: }
```

The only changes in this function involve renaming the _bSplash variable to _bDemo
(lines 3, 42, and 45).

The new code in the SpriteCollision() function involves the timing delay for the game
over screen. More specifically, the _iGameOverDelay variable is set to 150, which means
that the game screen will be displayed for 150 cycles before the game returns to demo
mode:

```
if (--_iNumLives == 0)
{
  // Play the game over sound
  PlaySound((LPCSTR)IDW_GAMEOVER, _hInstance, SND_ASYNC |
    SND_RESOURCE);
  _bGameOver = TRUE;
  _iGameOverDelay = 150;
}
```

Any idea how much time 150 cycles is? You know that the frame rate for the game is set
at 30 frames per second, which is the same thing as saying that the game goes through
30 cycles per second. Knowing this, you can divide 150 by 30 to arrive at a delay of 5
seconds for the game over screen. Pretty neat, right?

The SpriteDying() function involves an interesting change related to demo mode that
you might not have thought about. Analyze Listing 23.4 and see if you can figure out
why the change is necessary.

LISTING 23.4 The `SpriteDying()` Function Makes Sure Not to Play the Sound of Exploding Alien Missiles When the Game Is in Demo Mode

```
 1: void SpriteDying(Sprite* pSprite)
 2: {
 3:   // See if an alien missile sprite is dying
 4:   if (pSprite->GetBitmap() == _pBMissileBitmap ||
 5:     pSprite->GetBitmap() == _pJMissileBitmap ||
 6:     pSprite->GetBitmap() == _pTMissileBitmap)
 7:   {
 8:     // Play the small explosion sound
 9:     if (!_bDemo)
10:       PlaySound((LPCSTR)IDW_SMEXPLODE, _hInstance, SND_ASYNC |
11:         SND_RESOURCE | SND_NOSTOP);
12:
13:     // Create a small explosion sprite at the missile's position
14:     RECT rcBounds = { 0, 0, 600, 450 };
15:     RECT rcPos = pSprite->GetPosition();
16:     Sprite* pSprite = new Sprite(_pSmExplosionBitmap, rcBounds);
17:     pSprite->SetNumFrames(8, TRUE);
18:     pSprite->SetPosition(rcPos.left, rcPos.top);
19:     _pGame->AddSprite(pSprite);
20:   }
21: }
```

23

When you think about it, demo mode for a computer game shouldn't be something that annoys you, which means that it's probably best for it to not make a bunch of noise. Because the aliens in demo mode will be firing missiles that explode when they hit the ground, it's necessary to quiet the missiles in the `SpriteDying()` function so that they don't make noise in demo mode (lines 9–11).

The `NewGame()` function is the last of the functions impacted by the switch to demo mode in the Space Out 3 game, and it's also the most interesting. Listing 23.5 shows the code for the `NewGame()` function.

LISTING 23.5 The `NewGame()` Function Adds a Few Aliens to the Game When It Is in Demo Mode

```
 1: void NewGame()
 2: {
 3:   // Clear the sprites
 4:   _pGame->CleanupSprites();
 5:
 6:   // Initialize the game variables
 7:   _iFireInputDelay = 0;
 8:   _iScore = 0;
 9:   _iNumLives = 3;
```

LISTING 23.6   Continued

```
10:    _iDifficulty = 80;
11:    _bGameOver = FALSE;
12:
13:    if (_bDemo)
14:    {
15:      // Add a few aliens to the demo
16:      for (int i = 0; i < 6; i++)
17:        AddAlien();
18:    }
19:    else
20:    {
21:      // Create the car sprite
22:      RECT rcBounds = { 0, 0, 600, 450 };
23:      _pCarSprite = new Sprite(_pCarBitmap, rcBounds, BA_WRAP);
24:      _pCarSprite->SetPosition(300, 405);
25:      _pGame->AddSprite(_pCarSprite);
26:
27:      // Play the background music
28:      _pGame->PlayMIDISong(TEXT("Music.mid"));
29:    }
30: }
```

Although you might think of the NewGame() function as only being used to start a new
game that you're going to play, it is also used to start a new demo game. A demo game is
a "game" that includes a few aliens and nothing else. In other words, there is no car,
which eliminates the difficulty of trying to simulate a human player in code. Fortunately,
the aliens in the Space Out game are interesting enough that they do a pretty good job of
conveying the premise of the game without having to throw in the car.

The NewGame() function actually adds six alien sprites to the game engine when the
game is in demo mode (lines 13–18). One neat thing about this code is that the
AddAlien() function is designed to add a random alien, which means that demo mode is
different each time the game goes into it; the six aliens added are always different.
Granted, this demo mode could have been made more interesting by adding the car sprite
and having it fight back with the aliens, but for the sake of simplicity, you can't help but
like the approach of just adding a few aliens and letting them cruise around the game
screen firing missiles on their own.

Testing the Finished Product

Testing demo mode in the Space Out 3 game is a little like testing the splash screen in
Space Out 2—just launch the game and watch it go! Figure 23.1 shows the Space Out 3
demo mode with the aliens flying around having a good time.

FIGURE 23.1

Demo mode in the Space Out 3 game involves several aliens flying around the game screen behind the splash screen image.

As you can see, the aliens in demo mode help to demonstrate how the game is played even though they aren't interacting directly with a simulated player through the car sprite. Like I said earlier, the car sprite would be a very nice improvement for demo mode, but the idea here is to keep things simple. Any time you can achieve a desired effect with less code, and therefore less complexity, it is a good thing.

Figure 23.2 shows a game that has just ended in Space Out 3. In this figure, the game over screen is shown while the time delay is ticking away.

FIGURE 23.2

When a game finishes in Space Out 3, the game over screen is displayed for a few seconds.

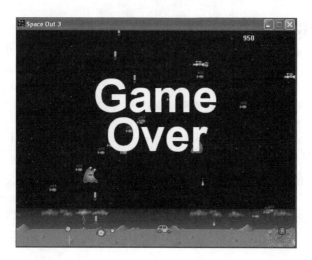

The game over screen in Space Out 3 is displayed for a few seconds before the game goes back to demo mode, as shown in Figure 23.3.

FIGURE 23.3

After the game over screen has been shown for a few seconds, the Space Out 3 game reverts back to demo mode, although each demo mode is a little different.

I'm showing a shot of demo mode one more time just to demonstrate how it varies each time the game goes into it. If you compare this figure with Figure 23.1, you'll notice that the aliens are distributed a little differently. This is a subtle detail of demo mode that helps to make the game a little more interesting.

Summary

This hour demonstrated an interesting feature of many commercial games that you now know how to add to your own games. I'm referring to demo mode, which allows a game to present to the game player a glimpse of how the game plays. Demo mode was a critical feature in arcade games, where a game needed to sell itself in order to convince someone to spend a quarter on a play. Computer games don't rely as heavily on demo mode because they don't live on quarters, but it's nonetheless an important touch on a game that might otherwise do nothing in between plays.

The next hour wraps up the book by showing you one last game feature that we've all grown to love: the high score list. The high score list is an important part of most classic video games because it provided a means of measuring your skill at a game and saving it for others to see.

Q&A

Q Why does the Space Out 3 game combine demo mode with the splash screen image?

A Displaying the splash screen image as part of demo mode in the Space Out 3 game has more to do with efficiency than anything else. The game is fairly simple, and it just doesn't seem necessary to complicate things with a bunch of different screens. The aliens moving around behind the splash screen image are sufficient to demonstrate how the game plays, which is the ultimate goal of creating demo mode. I view the solution as killing two birds with one stone!

Q Does it make sense to create a multi-screen demo mode?

A Yes. If a game is interesting enough to warrant more than one screen of demo mode, it's a great idea. For example, a game with multiple levels that have different backgrounds and characters would benefit greatly from several different screens in demo mode. You could accomplish this by starting a new game as you move between each demo mode screen. You aren't really starting a new game, but you're placing the code in the NewGame() function and using it to clear the sprite list and add new sprites for each different screen. You'll learn quickly that demo mode can be as simple or as complex as you choose to make it.

Workshop

The Workshop is designed to help you anticipate possible questions, review what you've learned, and begin learning how to put your knowledge into practice. The answers to the quiz can be found in Appendix A, "Quiz Answers."

Quiz

1. What's the difference between demo mode and a splash screen?

2. What's the purpose of the _iGameOverDelay global variable in the Space Out 3 game?

3. If the _iGameOverDelay global variable is set to 300, how much time does it end up causing for the delay?

Exercises

1. Experiment with adding more or less aliens to demo mode in the Space Out 3 game to get a different effect. You might also consider changing the AddAlien() function so that the aliens behave a little differently when in demo mode.

2. Add the car sprite to demo mode in the Space Out 3 game, and just have it move randomly back and forth on the screen to simulate a human player who isn't too smart.

Hour **24**

Keeping Track of High Scores

Unless you grew up during the heyday of arcade games in the 1980s, you might not have an appreciation for the sense of nerd accomplishment associated with a top spot on a game's high score list. The high score list in arcade games serves as a public acknowledgement of who has the time, skills, and quarters to be the best of the best. If you think I'm dramatizing this a bit, keep in mind that a major plot device within a *Seinfeld* episode involved the character George Castanza attempting to move a Frogger game across a busy street while connecting it to a temporary battery supply to keep his high score from being lost. Even if you don't have a large nerd ego, it can be rewarding to know that you placed within the upper ranks of those who have played a game before you. This hour shows you how to develop a high score list for the Space Out game that is saved to disk so that the scores are retained between games.

In this hour, you'll learn:

- Why it's important to keep track of high scores
- How to represent high score data in a game
- How to store and retrieve high score data using a file
- How to add a high score list to the Space Out game

The Significance of Keeping Score

When you think of video games, the word "achievement" might not be the first thing that comes to mind. You might not approach video games with the idea that you could be the best player of a particular game, but people are out there who do. In fact, the concept of a professional "cyber athlete" is already alive and real—companies are paying the best of the best video game players to test and promote their games. If you aspire to such a unique career, I have to warn you that thousands of hours of game play await you.

I brought up the issue of "cyber athletes" because it has a lot to do with the topic of this hour, high scores. Nowadays, the best video game players are determined in national tournaments where people get together and compete head-to-head. However, in years past, the best players were known only by their three initials that appeared in the high score lists of arcade games. The high score list in a classic arcade game was quite important to many early gamers because it was their only way to show off their gaming achievements.

It's kind of sad really that high score lists aren't as popular as they once were, but we can't lament advances in technology. On the other hand, it doesn't mean that high scores are entirely a thing of the past. For example, many popular games, such as Tony Hawk Pro Skater, still rely on a score to indicate how well a player performed. So, the idea of using a numeric score to measure your video game playing prowess is still valid. What has changed is that the shift away from arcade games has made it less of an issue to keep track of high scores. However, I still like the idea of a high score list—even if it's only shared between friends.

This hour focuses on adding a high score list to the Space Out game that you've worked on in previous hours. A high score list presents a new challenge to you as a game programmer because you must store away the scores so that they can be retrieved even when a game program is closed. This requires storing the scores to disk and then reading them back later, which is a unique discipline in game programming. The first step is to figure out how to model the high score data, which means that you need to determine what you're going to keep up with, and how.

Modeling High Score Data

I would love to tell you that I'm going to show you how to create a classic arcade game high score feature in which you get to enter your name or initials, and then see them displayed for all to see. Unfortunately, the seemingly simple task of allowing a player to enter his name or initials is fairly complex from a game programming perspective. Or more accurately, it requires a significant enough sidestep from the topic at hand that I don't want to burden you with the details. So, you're instead going to focus on a high score list that simply keeps up with the top five scores for a game, without any personalization associated with the scores. Although this approach to keeping track of a high score list doesn't give credit for each score, it's still a useful means of keeping up with the top five scores for a game.

Because you aren't going to worry with storing the name of the person for each score, you only have to contend with storing away five numbers. At this point, you have to consider how many digits you need to represent the maximum possible score for a game. In the case of the Space Out game, it's virtually impossible to score beyond four digits, which means that you can safely make a five-digit score the maximum. This also means that each score in the high score list is capable of having five digits. Of course, the number of digits in an integer in the game isn't really a critical factor; the number of digits enters the picture when it comes time to store the scores to disk, and then read them back.

The maximum number of digits in a high score is important because you're going to store that many digits for a score even if it doesn't need that many. This makes the scores much easier to read after you've written them to disk. So, as an example, if the highest score is 1250, you obviously only need four digits to represent the score. However, the score needs to be stored on disk as 01250 to make it fit within a five-digit storage space. Each of the numbers in the high score list is stored this way.

Getting back to the Space Out game itself, after the high scores are read from disk, they are treated as normal integers. In fact, a simple array of integers is sufficient to represent the high score list. So, the process of reading and writing the high score list involves initializing and then storing away an array of integers. The next section gets into more detail about how exactly you use the Win32 API to read and write data using files.

Storing and Retrieving High Score Data

Before you learn about the specific Win32 API functions used to read and write files, let's go over exactly what happens to the array of high score integers when they are read from and written to a file. You've already learned that each number in the array of integers gets converted to five digits. However, I didn't mention that these digits aren't actually numbers, but instead are text characters. In other words, the number 1250 gets converted to "01250" before being written to a file. This process is known as *streaming* the high score data to a file because you are converting the numeric data into a stream of characters. Figure 24.1 shows what the streaming process looks like.

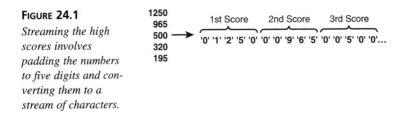

FIGURE 24.1

Streaming the high scores involves padding the numbers to five digits and converting them to a stream of characters.

As the figure reveals, the five high scores are converted to a stream of five-digit characters during the streaming process. Along with making it very straightforward to store the numbers to a file, streaming the numbers also makes it much easier to read them back in. More specifically, you just read five digits of characters at a time, and then convert the character string into an integer number.

I've talked about how to read and write files in general terms, but I haven't given you any specifics. All file input and output in Windows involves a small set of Win32 API functions. The most important of these functions is CreateFile(), which looks like this:

```
HANDLE CreateFile(
    LPCTSTR szFileName,
    DWORD dwDesiredAccess,
    DWORD dwShareMode,
    LPSECURITY_ATTRIBUTES pSecurityAttributes,
    DWORD dwCreationDisposition,
    DWORD dwFlagsAndAttributes,
    HANDLE hTemplateFile);
```

The CreateFile() function is important because it is used to both open and close files. Although it takes quite a few arguments, not all of them apply to basic reading and writing; you don't need to worry about some of the arguments unless you're performing more advanced file input and output. Knowing this, I want to point out the arguments that are relevant to reading and writing high scores. The first argument, szFileName, is used to provide the name of the file to be created or opened. The second argument, dwDesiredAccess, determines what you want to do with the file, such as read from or write to it. The fifth argument, dwCreationDisposition, determines whether you want to open an existing file or create a new file. And finally, the sixth argument, dwFlagsAndAttributes, allows you to control various other aspects of opening or creating a file, such as whether you want to limit access to read only.

Rather than have you memorize the arguments to the CreateFile() function, I'd rather just show you how to use it to open and create files. Following is an example of using the CreateFile() function to create a new file ready for writing:

```
HANDLE hFile = CreateFile(TEXT("HiScores.dat"), GENERIC_WRITE, 0, NULL,
  CREATE_ALWAYS, FILE_ATTRIBUTE_NORMAL, NULL);
```

In this example, the new file is called HiScores.dat, and it is created and ready to be written to using the file handle returned from the CreateFile() function. The hFile handle is what you'll use with a write function later to actually write data to the file. For now, let's take a quick look at how you open a file for reading:

```
HANDLE hFile = CreateFile(TEXT("HiScores.dat"), GENERIC_READ, 0, NULL,
  OPEN_EXISTING, FILE_ATTRIBUTE_READONLY, NULL);
```

As you can see, the CreateFile() function is called in a similar manner as it is called for writing, with a few small changes. The second argument indicates that this is a read operation, whereas the fifth argument indicates that an existing file should be opened, as opposed to creating a new one. Finally, the sixth argument specifies that the file is read-only, which prevents you from writing to it using the provided file handle even if you wanted to.

Now that you have a file handle that can be used for reading or writing, depending on how you called the CreateFile()function, you're ready to find out how to write data to a file and then read it back. The Win32 API function used to write data to a file is called WriteFile(), and looks like this:

```
BOOL WriteFile(
  HANDLE hFile,
  LPCVOID pBuffer,
  DWORD dwNumberOfBytesToWrite,
  LPDWORD pNumberOfBytesWritten,
  LPOVERLAPPED pOverlapped);
```

As with the CreateFile() function, not every argument to WriteFile() is critical for our purposes. You obviously need to provide the file handle in the first argument, as well as a data buffer from which the data is written. It's also important to specify the number of bytes to write, as well as a pointer to a DWORD that is to receive the number of bytes actually written. The last argument is the one that you don't need to worry about. To show you how easy it is to use the WriteFile() function, following is code to write a five-digit high score to a file:

```
DWORD dwBytesWritten;
WriteFile(hFile, &cData, 5, &dwBytesWritten, NULL);
```

This code assumes that the high score has already been converted from an integer into a five-character string that is stored in the cData variable. Notice that the number of bytes to write is specified as 5, which makes sense considering that the score consists of five digits.

Reading from a file is similar to writing to a file, except that it involves the ReadFile() function instead of WriteFile(). Following is the ReadFile() function as it is defined in the Win32 API:

```
BOOL ReadFile(
   HANDLE hFile,
   LPVOID pBuffer,
   DWORD dwNumberOfBytesToRead,
   LPDWORD pNumberOfBytesRead,
   LPOVERLAPPED pOverlapped);
```

As you can see, the ReadFile() function actually takes the same arguments as the WriteFile() function. However, it uses the arguments a little differently because data is being read into the buffer instead of being written from it. Following is an example of reading an individual high score from a file using the ReadFile() function:

```
char  cData[6];
DWORD dwBytesRead;
ReadFile(hFile, &cData, 5, &dwBytesRead, NULL);
```

It's important for the array of characters that holds each score to be null-terminated, which is why the cData variable is declared as being six characters long, instead of just five. In this code, the ReadFile() function reads five characters from the file and stores them in the cData variable.

When you're finished reading from or writing to a file, it's important to close the file. This is accomplished with the CloseHandle() Win32 function, which is called like this:

```
CloseHandle(hFile);
```

You now have the fundamental knowledge required to store and retrieve high score data to and from a file on disk, which is what you need to add a high score feature to the Space Out game.

Building the Space Out 4 Game

The final version of the Space Out game that you create in this book is called Space Out 4, and it completes the game by including a high score list that is stored to a file on disk. You've learned enough about high scores and file I/O in this hour to handle the task of adding a high score list to the game. So, let's get started!

Writing the Game Code

The Space Out 4 game requires only one new global variable, which is the array of integers that stores the high score list. Following is the _iHiScores variable as it appears in the SpaceOut.h header file:

```
int _iHiScores[5];
```

This variable is pretty straightforward in that it stores away five integers that represent the top five scores for the game. The scores are arranged in order of most to least.

Several new functions are required to successfully update, read, and write the high score list in the Space Out 4 game:

```
void UpdateHiScores();
BOOL ReadHiScores();
BOOL WriteHiScores();
```

The UpdateHiScores() function is used to determine if a new score has made it into the high score list. If so, the function makes sure to insert the score in the correct position and slide the lower scores down a notch to make room for the new score. The ReadHiScores() and WriteHiScores() functions use the _iHiScores array as the basis for reading and writing the high score list from and to the HiScores.dat file. You learn how each of these functions work a little later in the hour, but for now it's important to see how they are used in the context of the game.

The GameStart() function is responsible for initializing the game, which now includes reading the high score list. The only change to this function is the new call to the ReadHiScores() function:

```
ReadHiScores();
```

This call makes sure that the high score list is properly initialized before the game attempts to draw the scores later in the GamePaint() function.

The GameEnd() function cleans up resources used by the game, and serves as a great place to write the high score list to a file. A simple addition to this function is all that is required to write the high score list:

```
WriteHiScores();
```

Of course, the high score list wouldn't be of much use if the game didn't display it for all to see. This takes place in the GamePaint() function, which is shown in Listing 24.1.

LISTING 24.1   The `GamePaint()` Function Draws the High Score List if the Game Is in Demo Mode

```
 1: void GamePaint(HDC hDC)
 2: {
 3:   // Draw the background
 4:   _pBackground->Draw(hDC);
 5:
 6:   // Draw the desert bitmap
 7:   _pDesertBitmap->Draw(hDC, 0, 371);
 8:
 9:   // Draw the sprites
10:   _pGame->DrawSprites(hDC);
11:
12:   if (_bDemo)
13:   {
14:     // Draw the splash screen image
15:     _pSplashBitmap->Draw(hDC, 142, 20, TRUE);
16:
17:     // Draw the hi scores
18:     TCHAR szText[64];
19:     RECT  rect = { 275, 230, 325, 250};
20:     SetBkMode(hDC, TRANSPARENT);
21:     SetTextColor(hDC, RGB(255, 255, 255));
22:     for (int i = 0; i < 5; i++)
23:     {
24:       wsprintf(szText, "%d", _iHiScores[i]);
25:       DrawText(hDC, szText, -1, &rect, DT_SINGLELINE | DT_CENTER |
26:         DT_VCENTER);
27:       rect.top += 20;
28:       rect.bottom += 20;
29:     }
30:   }
31:   else
32:   {
33:     // Draw the score
34:     TCHAR szText[64];
35:     RECT  rect = { 460, 0, 510, 30 };
36:     wsprintf(szText, "%d", _iScore);
37:     SetBkMode(hDC, TRANSPARENT);
38:     SetTextColor(hDC, RGB(255, 255, 255));
39:     DrawText(hDC, szText, -1, &rect, DT_SINGLELINE | DT_RIGHT |
40:       DT_VCENTER);
41:
42:     // Draw the number of remaining lives (cars)
43:     for (int i = 0; i < _iNumLives; i++)
44:       _pSmCarBitmap->Draw(hDC, 520 + (_pSmCarBitmap->GetWidth() * i),
45:         10, TRUE);
46:
47:     // Draw the game over message, if necessary
```

LISTING 24.1 Continued

```
48:     if (_bGameOver)
49:       _pGameOverBitmap->Draw(hDC, 170, 100, TRUE);
50:   }
51: }
```

The high score list is drawn just after the splash screen image by looping through each score and drawing it a little below the previous score (lines 17–29). Notice that the high score list is only drawn if the game is in demo mode (line 12), which makes sense when you consider that the high score list is something you want to see in between games.

The last game function impacted by the high score list is the `SpriteCollision()` function, which is important because it detects when a game ends. Listing 24.2 contains the code for the `SpriteCollision()` function.

LISTING 24.2 The `SpriteCollision()` Function Updates the High Score List Whenever a Game Ends

```
 1: BOOL SpriteCollision(Sprite* pSpriteHitter, Sprite* pSpriteHittee)
 2: {
 3:   // See if a player missile and an alien have collided
 4:   Bitmap* pHitter = pSpriteHitter->GetBitmap();
 5:   Bitmap* pHittee = pSpriteHittee->GetBitmap();
 6:   if ((pHitter == _pMissileBitmap && (pHittee == _pBlobboBitmap ||
 7:     pHittee == _pJellyBitmap || pHittee == _pTimmyBitmap)) ||
 8:     (pHittee == _pMissileBitmap && (pHitter == _pBlobboBitmap ||
 9:     pHitter == _pJellyBitmap || pHitter == _pTimmyBitmap)))
10:   {
11:     // Play the small explosion sound
12:     PlaySound((LPCSTR)IDW_LGEXPLODE, _hInstance, SND_ASYNC |
13:       SND_RESOURCE);
14:
15:     // Kill both sprites
16:     pSpriteHitter->Kill();
17:     pSpriteHittee->Kill();
18:
19:     // Create a large explosion sprite at the alien's position
20:     RECT rcBounds = { 0, 0, 600, 450 };
21:     RECT rcPos;
22:     if (pHitter == _pMissileBitmap)
23:       rcPos = pSpriteHittee->GetPosition();
24:     else
25:       rcPos = pSpriteHitter->GetPosition();
26:     Sprite* pSprite = new Sprite(_pLgExplosionBitmap, rcBounds);
27:     pSprite->SetNumFrames(8, TRUE);
28:     pSprite->SetPosition(rcPos.left, rcPos.top);
```

LISTING 24.2   Continued

```
29:        _pGame->AddSprite(pSprite);
30:
31:      // Update the score
32:      _iScore += 25;
33:      _iDifficulty = max(80 - (_iScore / 20), 20);
34:    }
35:
36:    // See if an alien missile has collided with the car
37:    if ((pHitter == _pCarBitmap && (pHittee == _pBMissileBitmap ||
38:      pHittee == _pJMissileBitmap || pHittee == _pTMissileBitmap)) ||
39:      (pHittee == _pCarBitmap && (pHitter == _pBMissileBitmap ||
40:      pHitter == _pJMissileBitmap || pHitter == _pTMissileBitmap)))
41:    {
42:      // Play the large explosion sound
43:      PlaySound((LPCSTR)IDW_LGEXPLODE, _hInstance, SND_ASYNC |
44:        SND_RESOURCE);
45:
46:      // Kill the missile sprite
47:      if (pHitter == _pCarBitmap)
48:        pSpriteHittee->Kill();
49:      else
50:        pSpriteHitter->Kill();
51:
52:      // Create a large explosion sprite at the car's position
53:      RECT rcBounds = { 0, 0, 600, 480 };
54:      RECT rcPos;
55:      if (pHitter == _pCarBitmap)
56:        rcPos = pSpriteHitter->GetPosition();
57:      else
58:        rcPos = pSpriteHittee->GetPosition();
59:      Sprite* pSprite = new Sprite(_pLgExplosionBitmap, rcBounds);
60:      pSprite->SetNumFrames(8, TRUE);
61:      pSprite->SetPosition(rcPos.left, rcPos.top);
62:      _pGame->AddSprite(pSprite);
63:
64:      // Move the car back to the start
65:      _pCarSprite->SetPosition(300, 405);
66:
67:      // See if the game is over
68:      if (--_iNumLives == 0)
69:      {
70:        // Play the game over sound
71:        PlaySound((LPCSTR)IDW_GAMEOVER, _hInstance, SND_ASYNC |
72:          SND_RESOURCE);
73:        _bGameOver = TRUE;
74:        _bGameOverDelay = 150;
75:
76:        // Update the hi scores
```

LISTING 24.2 Continued

```
77:        UpdateHiScores();
78:      }
79:    }
80:
81:    return FALSE;
82: }
```

When a game ends, the SpriteCollision() function plays a game over sound and sets the game over delay, which you already know about (lines 71–74). However, what you don't already know about is the line of code that calls the UpdateHiScores() function to give the game a chance to insert the new score in the high score list (line 77). You don't have to worry about whether the score is high enough to make the high score list because this is determined by the UpdateHiScores() function, which is shown in Listing 24.3.

LISTING 24.3 The UpdateHiScores() Function Checks to See if a High Score Should Be Added to the High Score List, and Adds It if Necessary

```
 1: void UpdateHiScores()
 2: {
 3:   // See if the current score made the hi score list
 4:   int i;
 5:   for (i = 0; i < 5; i++)
 6:   {
 7:     if (_iScore > _iHiScores[i])
 8:       break;
 9:   }
10:
11:   // Insert the current score into the hi score list
12:   if (i < 5)
13:   {
14:     for (int j = 4; j > i; j--)
15:     {
16:       _iHiScores[j] = _iHiScores[j - 1];
17:     }
18:     _iHiScores[i] = _iScore;
19:   }
20: }
```

Although the code for the UpdateHiScores() function looks a little tricky at first, it really isn't too bad. The first loop checks to see if the score is higher than any of the existing high scores (lines 5–9). If so, the second loop is entered, which handles the task of inserting the score in the correct position in the list, as well as sliding down the lower scores in the list (lines 12–19). You might notice that the list is looped through in reverse, which allows it to easily move scores down the list to make room for the new score (lines 14–17). After a space has been made, the new score is placed in the high score list (line 18).

The high scores are written to a data file in the WriteHiScores() function, which is shown in Listing 24.4.

LISTING 24.4 The WriteHiScores() Function Writes the High Score List to the File HiScores.dat

```
 1: BOOL WriteHiScores()
 2: {
 3:   // Create the hi score file (HiScores.dat) for writing
 4:   HANDLE hFile = CreateFile(TEXT("HiScores.dat"), GENERIC_WRITE, 0, NULL,
 5:     CREATE_ALWAYS, FILE_ATTRIBUTE_NORMAL, NULL);
 6:   if (hFile == INVALID_HANDLE_VALUE)
 7:     // The hi score file couldn't be created, so bail
 8:     return FALSE;
 9:
10:   // Write the scores
11:   for (int i = 0; i < 5; i++)
12:   {
13:     // Format each score for writing
14:     CHAR cData[6];
15:     wsprintf(cData, "%05d", _iHiScores[i]);
16:
17:     // Write the score
18:     DWORD dwBytesWritten;
19:     if (!WriteFile(hFile, &cData, 5, &dwBytesWritten, NULL))
20:     {
21:       // Something went wrong, so close the file handle
22:       CloseHandle(hFile);
23:       return FALSE;
24:     }
25:   }
26:
27:   // Close the file
28:   return CloseHandle(hFile);
29: }
```

Most of this code should look familiar to you because it is very similar to the code you saw earlier in the hour when discussing how to create a new file and write a score using the CreateFile() and WriteFile() functions. A new HiScores.dat file is first created with a call to the CreateFile() function (lines 4–8); even if the file already exists, a new one is created to replace it. After the file is created, the function prepares to write to the file by looping through the high scores (line 11). Each score must be formatted into a five-digit character string before it can be written (lines 14 and 15). The score is then written to the file with a call to the WriteFile() function (line 19). If an error occurs during the write, the file handle is closed with a call to CloseHandle() (line 22). If all goes well and the data is successfully written, the function finishes by closing the file with a call to CloseHandle() (line 28).

Not surprisingly, the ReadHiScores() function works similarly to WriteHiScores(), except everything happens in the reverse. Listing 24.5 contains the code for the ReadHiScores() function.

LISTING 24.5 The ReadHiScores() Function Reads the High Score List from the File HiScores.dat

```
 1: BOOL ReadHiScores()
 2: {
 3:   // Open the hi score file (HiScores.dat)
 4:   HANDLE hFile = CreateFile(TEXT("HiScores.dat"), GENERIC_READ, 0, NULL,
 5:     OPEN_EXISTING, FILE_ATTRIBUTE_READONLY, NULL);
 6:   if (hFile == INVALID_HANDLE_VALUE)
 7:   {
 8:     // The hi score file doesn't exist, so initialize the scores to 0
 9:     for (int i = 0; i < 5; i++)
10:       _iHiScores[i] = 0;
11:     return FALSE;
12:   }
13:
14:   // Read the scores
15:   for (int i = 0; i < 5; i++)
16:   {
17:     // Read the score
18:     char  cData[6];
19:     DWORD dwBytesRead;
20:     if (!ReadFile(hFile, &cData, 5, &dwBytesRead, NULL))
21:     {
22:       // Something went wrong, so close the file handle
23:       CloseHandle(hFile);
24:       return FALSE;
25:     }
26:
27:     // Extract each integer score from the score data
28:     _iHiScores[i] = atoi(cData);
29:   }
30:
31:   // Close the file
32:   return CloseHandle(hFile);
33: }
```

24

The ReadHiScores() function reads the high score list from the HiScores.dat file. The CreateFile() function is again used to obtain a file handle, but this time an existing file is opened, as opposed to creating a new file (lines 4 and 5). If there is an error reading the file, such as if the file doesn't exist, the high score array is simply filled with scores of 0 (lines 9 and 10). This code is very important because the first time you play the game, there won't be a high score file.

If the file is opened okay, the function starts a loop to read each score from the file (line 15). Each score is then read by calling the ReadFile() function (line 20). Simply reading the scores from the file isn't sufficient to place the score in the high score list because the scores are read as five-digit character strings. Each score must be converted to an integer number before you can add it to the high score array (line 28). After reading and converting all the scores, the ReadFile() function finishes by calling the CloseHandle() function to close the file (line 32) .

Testing the Finished Product

Similar to a few of its predecessors, the Space Out 4 game is quite simple to test. In fact, it's also a fun test to perform because you need to play the game a few times and build up some scores on the high score list. Figure 24.2 shows the high score list in the game upon playing the game for the first time, which means that the list is filled with scores of 0.

FIGURE 24.2

Prior to playing the Space Out 4 game for the first time, the high score list is full of zero scores.

Keep in mind that in this figure the game still tried to read the high scores from a file, but the file didn't exist, so the scores were zeroed out. After you play a few games, the list will start looking better as it fills out with new high scores. Whenever you exit the game, the high score list gets stored to a file. Upon restarting the game, the high score list is restored by reading the scores from the same file. Figure 24.3 shows a high score list that has just been restored from a file.

FIGURE 24.3

The high score list was read from a file, which causes it to persist between games.

The high score list really is a neat enhancement to the Space Out game because it allows you to keep track of the best games you've played, potentially over a long period of time. Keep in mind that you can easily clear out the high score list by simply deleting the HiScores.dat file.

Summary

This hour explored a facet of games that you might have overlooked, the high score list. Granted, high score lists aren't as popular these days because arcades aren't as important as they were in the early days of video games, but it doesn't necessarily mean that players don't like to know what their highest gaming achievements are. High score lists are a great way to remember the best games you've played, and also serve as a way for competitive gamers to share a high score with friends. Although a high score list isn't necessary in all games, you should consider adding it to games where it makes sense. The Space Out game is a good example of a game that benefits from keeping track of high scores.

This hour is the last hour in the book, and therefore serves as your send-off into the expansive world of game programming. Hopefully you've had fun learning the ins and outs of game construction, and are excited to embark on some game development projects of your own. Have fun!

Q&A

Q What is the purpose of a file handle?

A Similar to other handles in Windows, such as window handles and bitmap handles, a file handle is a reference to a location in memory that stores information about a file. More importantly, a file handle serves as your interface to a file, and is required in all file operations. You can think of a file handle as working a lot like a key for a locker in an airport terminal. When you open the file, you receive the handle (key) that you must then use in order to read from or write to the file. When you're finished with the file, you close the file, which returns the handle to Windows.

Q Why exactly can't I read and write the scores as integers in the Space Out 4 game?

A The reason for having to convert the integer scores to characters has to do with the fact that characters are a little easier to manipulate when it comes to reading and writing files. Because the number of digits in a score actually varies, it becomes difficult to parse a number from a data file if it is stored as a raw integer. Therefore, it's easier to convert the integers into readable text that can be read from and written to files a character at a time. A side benefit of this approach is that you can open the HiScores.dat file and see the scores. Of course, this could also be perceived as a drawback because technically people could cheat and change the scores in the data file, but only you know this secret!

Workshop

The Workshop is designed to help you anticipate possible questions, review what you've learned, and begin learning how to put your knowledge into practice. The answers to the quiz can be found in Appendix A, "Quiz Answers."

Quiz

1. What is the name of the Win32 function used to open and create files?

2. How do you read and write data using files in Windows?

3. How do you clear the high score list in the Space Out 4 game?

Exercises

1. Try opening the HiScores.dat file in a text editor and modifying the high score list by hand. Although this isn't a very honest way to register a high score, you might have some fun tweaking a high score to play a trick on a friend.

2. Modify the Space Out 4 game so that it includes more than the top five scores in the high score list. You'll need to modify the splash screen image to make room for the new scores, as well as modify the storage of the scores, and how they are read from and written to a file.

24

PART VIII

Appendixes

Hours

APPENDIX A

Quiz Answers

This appendix lists the answers to the quiz questions in the Workshop sections at the end of each hour.

Hour 1, "Learning the Basics of Game Creation"

1. The different types of video games are arcade games, console games, and computer games.

2. The main priority to consider when designing a game is making the game fun. No amount of fancy graphics or sound will fix a game that just isn't fun to play.

3. A storyboard tells a story scene by scene using rough sketches of each scene.

4. The highest quality sound you can use in a game is CD-quality sound, which is the same quality found on audio CDs.

Hour 2, "A Windows Game Programming Primer"

1. A handle is a number that refers to a Windows object; handles are used a great deal in Windows programming.

2. Hungarian notation attempts to solve the problem of variable names not reflecting the data types of variables. Although Hungarian variable names are possibly more cryptic than normal variable names, they convey more information about variables.

3. The `WinMain()` function plays a role in Windows programs that is similar to the `main()` function in traditional C/C++ programs.

4. The windows.h header file is required as an import into all Windows programs because it defines important data types, constants, and Win32 API functions.

Hour 3, "Creating an Engine for Games"

1. A game cycle is one slice of time, which usually corresponds to a snapshot of the game's graphics and data.

2. Except for some rare situations, the minimum speed you should shoot for in games is 12 cycles per second. This is the minimum speed required to trick your eyes into thinking that it is seeing movement instead of a series of changing images.

3. "Putting a game to sleep" simply means that the game engine stops sending cycle messages. Because no cycle messages are being sent, the game is effectively paused.

Hour 4, "Learning to Draw Basic Graphics"

1. The Windows coordinate system has an origin that is located in the upper-left corner of the window, with positive X values increasing to the right and positive Y values increasing down.

2. The three colors that form the components of a color in Windows are red, green, and blue; hence the term RGB color.

3. The `GetDC()` function must be paired with `ReleaseDC()` in order to release the device context.

4. The drawing position for the `TextOut()` function is based on the upper left corner of the first string character of the text.

Hour 5, "Drawing Graphical Images"

1. Storing bitmaps as resources in an executable program, as opposed to using them straight from files, is helpful from an organizational perspective because it bundles the bitmaps into the main program file, and therefore eliminates the need to distribute separate image files with the program.

2. The color table in a bitmap is used to store the palette of colors that are used by the bitmap. This applies to 8-bit bitmaps, which have color tables consisting of 256 different colors. The color of each pixel in an 8-bit bitmap is determined by a reference to the color in this color table.

3. The Bitmap class created in this lesson supports 8-bit (256 color) uncompressed bitmaps; any other bitmaps will not work.

Hour 6, "Controlling Games with the Keyboard and Mouse"

1. Choosing between supporting the keyboard or the mouse is ultimately a decision that is determined by the specific needs of each game. However, assuming that both input devices are equally viable, the keyboard is a safer bet because there is less variance between keyboards across different computers.

2. Trackballs are considered the same as mice, and therefore you don't have to do anything special to support them other than support the mouse.

3. It's important to extract information from the lParam argument when responding to a mouse message because lParam contains the XY position of the mouse cursor in its low (X) and high (Y) words.

Hour 7, "Improving Input with Joysticks"

1. A joystick in Windows is allowed to have up to six axes, but that's a great deal of input by just about any game standard. Traditional joysticks support only two axes, x and y.

2. Calibrating joysticks is important because a joystick can wear mechanically and lose its alignment. Joystick calibration is kind of like having your car aligned; when a joystick isn't properly calibrated, it has a tendency to pull to one side.

3. The Win32 joyGetDevCaps() function allows you to determine the ranges of joystick axes, among other things. This function fills a JOYCAPS structure with more information about a joystick than you'll probably ever want to know.

A

Hour 8, "Example Game: Brainiac"

1. The Brainiac game doesn't support the keyboard or joystick because they aren't nearly as intuitive to use with the game as the mouse. Although it certainly doesn't hurt to support multiple user input devices, in this case the mouse is by far the superior approach to user input.

2. The Brainiac game can't keep track of its state with a single 4x4 array because there is simply too much information to retain. More specifically, the game needs to know which bitmap image is associated with each tile position, as well as whether the tile has been matched yet. Without creating a new tile state data type that combines a bitmap with a Boolean, there is no way to store both of these pieces of information in a single array.

3. It's necessary to keep up with the number of matches in the Brainiac game because there is no other good way to tell when the game is over. By keeping up with the matches, you can quickly tell if eight matches have occurred; in which case, you know the game is over.

Hour 9, "A Crash Course in Game Animation"

1. Animation is the illusion of movement, and it is created by displaying a rapid succession of images with slight changes in their appearance.

2. 2D animation involves objects moving or being manipulated within two dimensions, while 3D animation involves placing and manipulating objects in a three-dimensional virtual world. Whereas a 2D object is modeled by an image, a 3D object is defined by a 3D mathematical model.

3. The two main techniques used for 2D animation are frame-based animation and cast-based animation; cast-based animation is also known as sprite animation.

Hour 10, "Making Things Move with Sprites"

1. The bounding rectangle of a sprite is important because it establishes an area in which a sprite is allowed to move; the sprite cannot venture beyond the bounding rectangle.

2. A bounds action determines how a sprite responds when it encounters a boundary. The Sprite class currently supports three bounds actions: Wrap, Bounce, and Stop. However, a fourth bounds action, Die, is also defined in the Sprite class, and will be supported in the next hour.

3. The Sprite class contains a pointer to a Bitmap object because the sprite's appearance is represented by a bitmap.

Hour 11, "Managing a World of Sprites"

1. The STL `vector` class allows you to store away and manage a list of objects of any type, and then easily manipulate them using a set of methods. It's much better than a normal array because it can grow as necessary to accommodate more objects.

2. The `SA_KILL` sprite action is used to destroy a sprite from the sprite list. This action is necessary because a sprite isn't exactly capable of killing itself and removing itself from the list. You'll realize the importance of the `SA_KILL` sprite action as you begin developing real games that take advantage of the sprite engine.

3. Double buffering involves performing all of your erasing and drawing for game graphics on an offscreen drawing surface that isn't visible to the user. Once all the drawing is finished, the end result is painted straight to the game screen in one pass. This eliminates the common flicker problem associated with traditional single-buffer animation.

Hour 12, "Example Game: Henway"

1. The `_pChickenSprite` member variable is used to store the chicken sprite pointer, and it is necessary to keep around so that you can change the chicken's position in response to user input events.

2. The `SpriteCollision()` function is used to detect when the chicken is hit by a car. If the chicken gets hit, the `SpriteCollision()` function moves the chicken back to the start, decreases the chicken lives, and checks to see if the game is over.

3. The `MoveChicken()` function is used to move the chicken, and serves as a good place to check for the chicken making it across the highway. If the chicken's horizontal position crosses a certain spot on the screen, then you know the chicken made it across. When this happens, the chicken's position is set back to the Start Area and the score is increased.

Hour 13, "Getting Acquainted with Digital Sound and Music"

1. A decibel (dB) is a unit of measure used to indicate the amplitude of a sound wave. The threshold of human hearing is 0dB, whereas the threshold of pain is 120dB, which is the amplitude level at which humans experience physical pain.

2. A CD-quality sound is a 44kHz 16-bit stereo sound; this is the highest sound quality supported on most computers.

A

3. MIDI stands for Musical Instrument Digital Interface, and serves as a technology to interface musical instruments with each other.

Hour 14, "Playing Wave Sounds"

1. Because the Win32 `PlaySound()` function doesn't support wave mixing, you can't use the function to play more than one wave sound at a time. This is a problem because games often involve multiple sounds playing at the same time.

2. Synchronous wave playback involves a program waiting to do anything else until a wave finishes playing, whereas asynchronous playback involves a wave being played while a program continues to do other things.

3. To stop a wave from playing once it has started, you call the `PlaySound()` function and use the `SND_PURGE` flag in the final argument. If you want to stop any wave from playing without regard to what it is, you can pass `NULL` as the first two arguments to `PlaySound()`, along with `SND_PURGE` as the final argument.

Hour 15, "Playing MIDI Music"

1. A command message allows you to have a conversation with a multimedia device by sending it a message that tells it what to do. In the case of MIDI music, a command message can be used to play or pause a MIDI song, as well as open and close the MIDI player.

2. The device used to play MIDI music is called the MIDI synthesizer, and its job is to take notes of music and play them aloud.

3. It's important to pause a MIDI song in a game whenever the main game window is deactivated. This keeps the song from playing when another program is currently active.

Hour 16, "Example Game: Battle Office"

1. It is necessary to hide the target sprite before checking to see if the player clicked the mouse on a guy sprite because the target sprite has a higher Z-order than the guy sprites. This would cause the target sprite to always register a mouse hit, which wouldn't allow you to determine if a guy was clicked.

2. The purpose of the `MouseMove()` function is to force the target sprite to follow the mouse pointer. This has the effect of allowing you to guide the target with the mouse.

3. It isn't necessary to respond to sprite collisions because no part of the game logic is dependent on sprites colliding with each other. Your only real concern is determining when a guy sprite has been clicked with the mouse, and this really has nothing to do with sprite collision.

Hour 17, "Animating the Appearance of Sprites"

1. The main Pac-Man character relies on frame animation to show his mouth opening and closing, which makes it look like he's eating the dots on the game board. Without frame animation, Pac-Man would either be a solid ball or a wide-open mouth that never closed.

2. Frame images in a frame-animated sprite are stored together in a single bitmap image; they are arranged horizontally across the image next to each other.

3. A frame delay is used to control the speed at which a frame-animated sprite cycles through its frame images. Without a frame delay, an animated sprite would rapidly cycle through its frames at maximum speed without any control.

Hour 18, "Creating Backgrounds for Your Sprites"

1. The four main types of backgrounds used in games are solid backgrounds, image backgrounds, animated backgrounds, and scrolling backgrounds.

2. The Update() method in the Background class is empty because the Background class doesn't directly support animation. The Update() method is there for derived background classes, which place their animation code there.

3. The StarryBackground class is capable of showing 100 stars.

Hour 19, "Example Game: Meteor Defense"

1. A *meteoroid* is a chunk of rock in space that ranges in size from a speck of dust to 100 meters across. A *meteor* is the bright flash of light generated by a meteoroid when it travels through Earth's atmosphere. And finally, a *meteorite* is a meteor that has survived the transition through Earth's atmosphere and comes to rest on Earth's surface.

A

2. The m_bOneCycle member variable in the Sprite class is used to create a sprite that automatically kills itself after finishing its animation sequence. A good example of where this kind of sprite comes in handy is explosions, which must animate and then go away.

3. To destroy a sprite and have it removed from the sprite list in the game engine, you just call the Kill() method on the sprite object.

Hour 20, "Teaching Games to Think"

1. The three types of roaming AI are chasing, evading, and patterned, although you are free to use any combination of these types in your own games.

2. Behavioral AI works by assigning probabilities to behaviors for an object, and then selecting a behavior based on these probabilities. Each behavior represents a particular type of action such as fighting or fleeing.

3. *Look-ahead* refers to any technique that attempts to determine the best move to make in a game by looking ahead a few turns. For a look-ahead to make sense, there must be a method of looking at the game at any state and calculating a score; this is known as *weighting*.

Hour 21, "Example Game: Space Out"

1. The purpose of the SA_ADDSPRITE sprite action is to let the game engine know that a sprite needs to add a sprite. For example, an alien in the Space Out game fires a missile by adding the missile sprite via the SA_ADDSPRITE sprite action.

2. It is necessary to derive a class from the Sprite class in order for it to take advantage of the SA_ADDSPRITE sprite action because the default Sprite::AddSprite() method does nothing. Classes derived from the Sprite class should override this method with a version that actually creates a new sprite to be added.

3. The AlienSprite class is derived from the Sprite class, and overrides the AddSprite() and Update() methods to provide a means for aliens to fire missiles. All three of the aliens in the Space Out game are created from the AlienSprite class.

Hour 22, "Adding Pizzazz to Your Game with a Splash Screen"

1. Beyond the title of the game, information good to place on the splash screen for a game includes the copyright for the game, how to start playing the game, and brief directions of how the game is played.

2. The _bSplash global variable in the Space Out 2 game is used to represent splash screen mode, which is the state of the game when the splash screen is displayed. More specifically, the game is in splash screen mode when it first begins, before the first game is started.

3. The background and the desert bitmap are drawn in the Space Out 2 game regardless of whether the game is in splash screen mode because the splash screen bitmap is smaller than the game screen, and therefore looks much better with game graphics surrounding it.

Hour 23, "Showing Off Your Game with Demo Mode"

1. The difference between demo mode and a splash screen is that demo mode shows more than just a title or stationary game graphics. Demo mode attempts to show the game actually being played, or at least show some of the main characters in the game going through the motions.

2. The _iGameOverDelay global variable in the Space Out 3 game is used to provide a delay between when a game ends and when the game enters demo mode.

3. Setting the _iGameOverDelay global variable to 300 results in a delay of 10 seconds.

Hour 24, "Keeping Track of High Scores"

1. The name of the Win32 function used to open and create files is CreateFile().

2. To read and write data using files in Windows, you must use the ReadFile() and WriteFile() Win32 API functions, which require a file handle that you must obtain with the CreateFile() function.

3. You can clear the high score list in the Space Out 4 game by deleting the HiScores.dat file. This causes the game to clear out the scores when it doesn't find the file.

A

APPENDIX B

Selecting a Game Development Tool

The programming techniques described in this book rely on the C++ programming language in a Windows environment. This means that you use C++ code to develop programs that run on the Windows operating system. In order to compile C++ code into an executable Windows program, you need a C++ compiler that targets the Windows operating system. Fortunately, there are several C++ development tools available that support Windows.

You might think that you can use any C++ compiler to build games for Windows, but in order to support Windows a compiler must include the Windows *API (Application Programming Interface)*. From a programming perspective, the Windows API is a set of unique functions and data structures that allow you to create programs for Windows. From the perspective of a development tool, the Windows API is a set of header and library files that are essential in allowing you to build Windows programs. So, you must use a compiler that is capable of creating Windows programs using the Windows API.

The next few sections introduce you to a few of the popular C++ development tools available for creating Windows games. All of the code examples throughout the book are targeted for Microsoft Visual C++, which simply means that I've included project files to make it easier to build the programs in Visual C++. I chose Visual C++ simply because it is the most widely used C++ development tool for Windows. However, if you choose to use one of the other tools, you shouldn't have any problem creating new projects within the tool and building the examples.

Project files are used to inform a compiler of the source code files that need to be compiled, along with library files that should be linked into the executable program, as well as other compiler and linker settings.

Microsoft Visual C++

It's safe to say that Microsoft Visual C++ is the industry standard for C++ program development in Windows. It is technically part of the Visual Studio development suite, but you can also purchase it as a standalone tool. Although it's not the cheapest option for game development, you aren't likely to find a better solution when it comes to a professional grade C++ development environment for Windows. The program examples and games created throughout the book were developed using Visual C++, and I've provided Visual C++ project files with the source code that is also available for download online (http://www.michaelmorrison.com/cbooks.html). For the record, this isn't an endorsement for Microsoft; it's just that Visual C++ has long been the industry standard for serious Windows application development.

The latest version of Visual C++ is actually called Visual C++ .NET, which has to do with Microsoft's .NET framework for creating Web applications. None of the games developed in this book have anything to do with .NET or features of Visual C++ related to .NET.

To find out more about Microsoft Visual C++, visit its Web site at http://msdn.microsoft.com/visualc/.

Borland C++Builder

A close rival to Visual C++ is Borland C++Builder, which is also a very popular professional grade C++ development tool. There was a time when an earlier version of this tool
was pretty much the only C++ development environment for Windows, but Microsoft
quickly geared up and challenged Borland with Visual C++. Nevertheless, Borland
C++Builder is a very capable development tool for game construction. There is a version
of C++Builder called C++Builder Personal that is geared toward individual developers,
and it is priced accordingly. I highly encourage you to check it out.

To learn more about C++Builder and download a trial version to take for a test drive,
visit http://www.borland.com/cbuilder/.

Bloodshed Dev-C++

If you think that the cost of this book is about as much as you're willing to invest in
game programming, you'll probably want to steer clear of Visual C++ and C++Builder.
Fortunately, there is a high-quality C++ development environment available that is completely free. I'm referring to Dev-C++ by Bloodshed Software, which relies on an open
source C++ compiler to power its graphical development interface. Although Dev-C++
doesn't have all the bells and whistles of Visual C++ or C++Builder, it can definitely get
the job done.

> Open source software is software that is created by a community for the
> purpose of being freely accessible to anyone. Open source software is typi-
> cally free, with any voluntary costs usually consisting of a donation to help
> support open source initiatives.

B

To find out more about Dev-C++ and download it free online, visit the Bloodshed
Software Web site at http://www.bloodshed.net/.

DJGPP

Another option in the realm of open source C++ development tools is DJGPP, which is a
command-line tool that is designed to work on several different platforms, including
Windows. Because it is a command-line tool, DJGPP is a little trickier to install and use
than a graphical environment, but it comes with straightforward directions that really

aren't too tough to follow. The biggest challenge to using DJGPP is setting up projects for your programs so that they compile in a single step. Again, the documentation for DJGPP will help you along in this task.

For more information on DJGPP, including a free online download, visit `http://www.delorie.com/djgpp/`.

INDEX

C

Other Related Titles

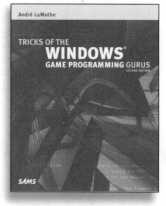

Tall Tales

The Game of Myths, Legends, and Creative One-Upmanship

Tall Tales is the exciting new social/trivia game from the author of *Teach Yourself Game Programming in 24 Hours*. Ask for Tall Tales at your local toy store, bookstore, or coffee shop. Or purchase the game online at **www.talltalesgame.com**.

Topper

We all have a friend who can't resist the urge to top any story you share. Tall Tales allows you to become the "topper" by one-upping your friends and family with a humdinger. If you've ever narrowly escaped the jaws of a man-eating lion or spent a weekend aboard a flying saucer as a UFO abductee, then this is your chance to tell all!

Tall Tale

Is there really a prehistoric sea serpent living in the depths of Britain's Loch Ness, and is Walt Disney really frozen and stored beneath the Pirates of the Caribbean exhibition at Disneyland? Tall Tales gives you a chance to answer these questions and find out where the truth really lies.

Fact or Fiction

Maybe you've heard that red M&M's cause cancer and hair grows back faster when cut. Tall Tales separates truth from myth by challenging you to identify popular misconceptions and interesting phenomena as being fact or fiction.

Tall Tale

The Burbank Bigfoot was a hoax involving an artificial Bigfoot carcass made by Hollywood makeup artist John Chambers that was thought to be used in a traveling sideshow. What real person served as the body cast for the artificial Bigfoot?

A: Kareem Abdul-Jabbar, the star basketball player for the Los Angeles Lakers

B: actor Richard Kiel, who played the villain Jaws in several James Bond movies

C: actor Lee Majors, who played Colonel Steve Austin in "The Six Million Dollar Man" television show

Topper

The most interesting thing you've run over with lawn equipment

Fact or F

Q: In 1492 Christo Columbus beca person to repor events while sa an area of ocean later become kn Bermuda Triangl

ct. Columbus did inde nts while sailing throu gle in 1492, but they ght to be attributed to nable events such as repancy between rth and magnetic s well as a meteor shower.

What's on the CD-ROM

The companion CD-ROM contains all of the source code for the games developed in the book, Borland's C++ 5.5 Compiler and an evaluation version of C++Builder 6.

Windows Installation Instructions

1. Insert the disc into your CD-ROM drive.

2. From the Windows desktop, double-click the My Computer icon.

3. Double-click the icon representing your CD-ROM drive.

4. Double-click on start.exe. Follow the on-screen prompts to access the CD-ROM information.

> If you have the AutoPlay feature enabled, start.exe will be launched automatically whenever you insert the disc into your CD-ROM drive.

This CD-ROM uses long and mixed-case filenames requiring the use of a protected-mode CD-ROM Driver.